ARGENTINA SINCE INDEPENDENCE

edited by

LESLIE BETHELL

Professor of Latin American History
University of London

CAMBRIDGE
UNIVERSITY PRESS

Published by the Press Syndicate of the University of Cambridge
The Pitt Building, Trumpington Street, Cambridge CB2 1RP
40 West 20th Street, New York, NY 10011–4211, USA
10 Stamford Road, Oakleigh, Victoria 3166, Australia

The contents of this book were previously published as parts of volumes III,
V, and VIII of The Cambridge History of Latin America, © Cambridge University
Press, 1985, 1986 and 1991.

© Cambridge University Press 1993

First published 1993

Library of Congress Cataloging-in-Publication Data
Argentina since independence / edited by Leslie Bethell.
p.   cm.
"Previously published as parts of volumes III, V, and VIII of the
Cambridge history of Latin America, Cambridge University Press,
1985, 1986, and 1991" – CIP t.p. verso.
Includes bibliographical references and index.
ISBN 0–521–43376–2 (hard). – ISBN 0–521–43988–4 (pbk.)
1. Argentina – History – 1810–   I. Bethell, Leslie.   II. Cambridge
history of Latin America.
F2843.A67   1993
982'.04–dc20   92–26994
CIP

A catalog record for this book is available from the British Library.

ISBN 0–521–43376–2 hardback
ISBN 0–521–43988–4 paperback

Transferred to digital printing 2002

CONTENTS

MAPS

PREFACE

The Cambridge History of Latin America is a large scale, collaborative, multi-volume history of Latin America during the five centuries from the first contacts between Europeans and the native peoples of the Americas in the late fifteenth and early sixteenth centuries to the present.

Argentina since Independence brings together chapters from Volumes III, V and VIII of *The Cambridge History* to provide in a single volume an economic, social, and political history of Argentina since independence. This, it is hoped, will be useful for both teachers and students of Latin American history and of contemporary Latin America. Each chapter is accompanied by a bibliographical essay.

1

FROM INDEPENDENCE TO NATIONAL
ORGANIZATION

Argentina became independent in the second decade of the nineteenth century with few of the assets considered essential in a Latin American state. It had minerals but no mines, land but little labour, commerce but few commodities. The economy of Buenos Aires emerged from its colonial past not as a primary producer but as a pure entrepôt. The merchants of Buenos Aires made their profits not by exporting the products of the country but by importing consumer goods for a market stretching from the Atlantic to the Andes, in exchange for precious metals which had been produced or earned in Potosí. The city's rural hinterland was little developed. At the time of independence pastoral products accounted for only 20 per cent of the total exports of Buenos Aires; the other 80 per cent was silver. Until about 1815 20 land exploitation continued to be a secondary activity, and cattle estates were few in number and small in size. As for agriculture, it was confined to a few farms on the outskirts of towns, producing barely enough for the urban market.

Independence altered this primitive economy. First, the merchants of Buenos Aires were squeezed out by foreigners. With their superior resources, their capital, shipping and contacts in Europe, the British took over the entrepreneurial role previously filled by Spaniards. Unable to compete with the newcomers, local businessmen sought outlets in land and cattle. Then the province of Buenos Aires, hitherto a poor neighbour of richer cattle areas, profited from the misfortunes of its rivals. In the years after 1813 Santa Fe, Entre Ríos and Corrientes were devastated by wars of secession, while the other rich pastoral zone, the Banda Oriental, was ruined by revolution, counter-revolution and the Portuguese invasion of 1816. Buenos Aries took advantage of this opportunity, and those with capital found good returns in cattle ranching. Pasture began to expand at the expense of arable farming, the province increased its export of cattle products, and soon it came to rely upon imported grain. Finally, the trade of Buenos Aires with the interior diminished. This had always depended upon the interior's ability to earn silver from the sale of its products in the mining economies. But the competition of British imports depressed the rural and artisan industries of the interior at a time when war and secession were removing established markets in Chile and Upper Peru.

The conjuncture of British competition, the ravages of war and the decline of the interior rendered the traditional economy of Buenos Aires incapable of sustaining the ruling groups. They began, therefore, to diversify their interests, to acquire *estancias*, to establish a rural base. Land was plentiful, the soil was rich and deep, and there was normally a good supply of surface water on the pampas. The greatest danger lay on the frontier, and the frontier was uncomfortably close. The Pampa Indians, immediately to the south and west of the Río Salado, were the fiercest of all the Indians of the plains. Irredeemably savage, they lived and fought on horseback, a mobile and elusive enemy, handling the lance and the *bola* with supreme skill in their swift raids against settlements, *estancias*, personnel and property. The expansion of the *estancias* from 1815 was a disaster for the Indians. Settlers began to occupy their hunting grounds to the south of the Salado, and they retaliated by increasing their raids and enlarging their plunder. They were often joined by vagrant gauchos, deserters from the army, delinquents fleeing the justices of the peace, refugees from social or political conflicts; and their alliance was sometimes invoked in the civil wars of the time by one side or another. The new *estancieros* wanted law and order in the pampas and peace on the frontier. They also sought security of tenure.

From 1822 Bernardino Rivadavia, the modernizing minister in the provincial government of Martín Rodríguez, introduced the system of emphyteusis. Authority was given to rent public land (the sale of which was prohibited) to individuals and corporations for twenty years at fixed and extremely low rentals; the applicant simply had to measure and claim a chosen area. This simultaneously put land to productive use, especially the immense reserves of land on the expanding southern frontier, and satisfied the land hunger of prosperous families. The system favoured latifundism and land concentration. There was no limit to the area which the landowner might rent; he was then free to sell his rights and to sublet; and the commissions which determined land values and administered distribution were dominated by *estancieros*. From 1824 to 1827 a number of enormous grants were made, some individuals receiving over 10 square leagues each (66,710 acres). By 1828 almost 1,000 square leagues (over 6½ million acres) had been granted to 112 people and companies, of whom ten received more than 130,000 acres each. By the 1830s some 21 million acres of public land had been transferred to 500 individuals, many of them wealthy recruits from urban society, like the Anchorena, Santa Coloma, Alzaga and Sáenz Valiente families, the founders of Argentina's landed oligarchy.

As the pastoral economy entered a period of growth, expansion was extensive rather than intensive, for it was land, not capital, which was abundant, and there was as yet no technical innovation, no attempt to improve stock or modernize production. The number of cattle and the size of estates were all that counted. But there came a time when the pressure on grazing land and the shortage of further emphyteusis land brought the livestock sector to the limits of profitable expansion. Ranchers were pushing south once more into Indian territory in search of cheap and empty land. Government action was needed to occupy new territory and to protect it. While Rivadavia had been active in allocating land, he had done little for rural order or frontier security. Juan Manuel de Rosas, a pioneer on the southern frontier, owner of vast estates, lord of numerous peons, a militia commander who could parley with the Indians and frighten the politicians, and governor of Buenos Aires from 1829, stood for a policy of expansion and settlement and took a number of positive steps to improve the security of landholding. He organized and led the Desert Expedition of 1833 to the Río Colorado and the Río Negro, with the object of containing Indian aggression, expanding the frontier and imposing an enduring peace. His policy included diplomacy as well as force, presents as well as punishment. And it succeeded, adding to the province of Buenos Aires thousands of square miles, not desert, but land watered by great rivers. Rewards were instantaneous. The provincial government transferred large tracts of the new land to private hands in the years following 1833, especially to the senior officers of the expeditionary force itself. And as the settlers pushed southwards, they encroached once more on Indian hunting grounds. But now, in the 1840s, they were viewed by the Indians with more respect, partly because of the military reputation of Rosas, partly because of the policy of pacification by subsidy.

Rosas also introduced important and permanent modifications to the legal structure of landholding. There were three methods of land acquisition – rent, purchase and grant. Emphyteusis had now outlived its usefulness. It had facilitated land exploitation (and land concentration), but the state had profited hardly at all, for the rent was minimal. Rosas therefore decided to sell public land outright and to receive a specific revenue when he needed it. Laws of land sale in 1836–8 placed vast tracts of land on the open market. Most of it obviously went to the wealthy, the powerful, the favoured; and the names of the large purchasers were almost identical with those of the large tenants under emphyteusis, the Anchorena, Díaz Vélez, Alzaga and Arana. By 1840 3,436 square leagues (20,616,000 acres) of the province were in the possession of 293 people. Yet there was not a rush to buy land, and many would-be purchasers were deterred, either by economic recession, as during the French blockade of 1838–40, or by political insecurity. As an alternative to selling land, therefore, Rosas gave it away. Generous land grants were made to supporters of the regime, to the military who fought its wars or crushed its rebels, to bureaucrats and to favourites. Land became almost a currency and sometimes a wages and pensions fund. It was the ultimate source of patronage and, when confiscated, a terrible punishment.

By the 1840s the great plains of Buenos Aires were divided into well-stocked *estancias* and supported some 3 million head of cattle, the prime wealth of the province and the source of an export economy. They were animals of inferior grade, raised in the open range under the care of a few herdsmen; but they yielded hides and salt meat, and that was what the market demanded.

The *estancia* had to sell its products in Buenos Aires and beyond, but the infrastructure of the province was even more primitive than the estates which it served. This was a country without roads or bridges, and with tracks only on the main routes. Almost everything was done and supplied from horseback, and horses were as important a product of the *estancia* as cattle. Horses carried gauchos across the plains and armies into battle. Fishermen fished in the river on horseback; beggars even begged on horseback. But the chief method of freight transport were bullock carts, made in the workshops of Tucumán and led by hard-bitten drivers operating chiefly along the two high roads which traversed Argentina, one from Buenos Aires through San Luis and Mendoza to Chile, the other from Buenos Aires via Córdoba, Santiago, Tucumán, Salta and Jujuy to Bolivia. They travelled in trains of some fourteen carts, each drawn by six oxen with three spare, moving slowly across pampas and

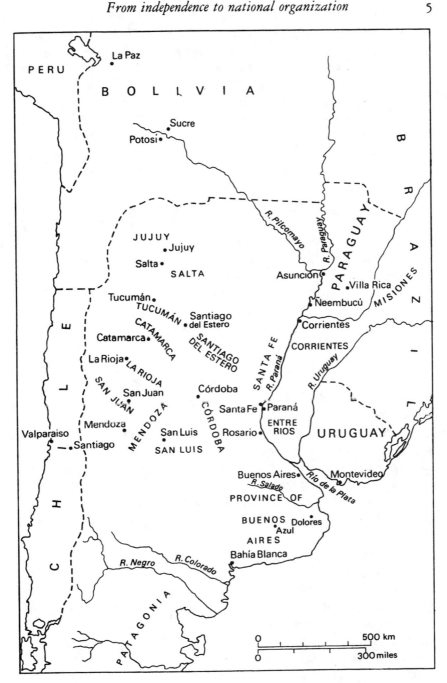

PERU

La Paz

B O L I V I A

Sucre
Potosí

JUJUY
Jujuy
Salta
SALTA

R. Pilcomayo

R. Paraguay

Asunción
Villa Rica
PARAGUAY

Tucumán
TUCUMÁN
Santiago
del Estero
CATAMARCA
Catamarca
SANTIAGO
DEL ESTERO
La Rioja
LA RIOJA
SAN JUAN
San Juan
Córdoba
MENDOZA
CÓRDOBA
Mendoza
Valparaiso
Santiago
San Luis
SAN LUIS
Rosario

Neembucú
Corrientes
CORRIENTES

SANTA FE
R. Paraná
Santa Fe
Paraná
ENTRE
RIOS

R. Uruguay

URUGUAY

MISIONES

B R A Z I L

C H I L E

Buenos Aires
R. Salado
PROVINCE OF
BUENOS
AIRES
Azul
Dolores

Río de la Plata
Montevideo

Bahía Blanca

R. Negro
R. Colorado

P A T A G O N I A

0   500 km
0   300 miles

Argentina, 1820–70

hills in journeys of weeks and months. Freight charges were high, £20 a ton including provincial duties, and transport alone accounted for 40 or even 50 per cent of first cost. Cattle were much easier to move than goods, being driven rapidly by expert herdsmen from ranch to port.

The principal outlet of the *estancia* was the *saladero*. These were large establishments, where cattle were slaughtered, tallow extracted, flesh salted and dried and hides prepared for export. They opened in Buenos Aires in 1810, were closed in 1817 as the alleged cause of an urban meat shortage, but began to operate again from 1819 and to proliferate at the southern approaches to the city. By the mid-1820s there were about twenty *saladeros*; they now consumed more animals than the urban slaughter-houses, exporting their hides to Europe and their jerked beef to Brazil and Cuba. The *saladero* represented the only technical improvement in the livestock economy. By the 1840s, while the number of plants operating in and around Buenos Aires was still only twenty, their output had grown enormously and each slaughtered some 200 to 400 animals a day during the season. The *saladero* constituted a sizeable investment in plant, steaming apparatus and other equipment; most belonged to associations rather than to individuals, and many foreigners had capital in the industry. They were an integral part of the *estancia* system, managed by experts, supplied by ranchers, favoured by the government. The export of jerked beef rose from 113,404 quintals in 1835, to 198,046 in 1841, to 431,873 in 1851.

The state favoured cattle-breeders at the expense of small farmers, and the country depended ultimately on imported grain. In an age of capital scarcity, inferior technology and labour shortage, it was realistic to concentrate on pastoral farming, to realize the country's natural assets and to promote its most successful exports, even if it meant diverting resources from worthy though less profitable enterprises. The economic policy of Rivadavia was to subsidize immigration and rely on a fertile soil and market forces. But the agricultural colonization schemes of the 1820s failed through lack of capital, organization and security, in contrast to the great *estancia* expansion with its own internal dynamism. In any case agriculture was subject to particular obstacles and required special treatment. Labour was scarce and expensive, methods were primitive, and yield was low. The high cost of transport forced farmers to move nearer to cities where land prices were higher; and there was always competition from foreign grain. So agriculture needed capital and protection: at this point governments hesitated, fearful of causing dearer food and losing popular support. From independence to 1825 a low-tariff policy prevailed, in favour of consumer and export interests, and in spite of farmers' complaints. But farmers were not the only critics of free trade.

The littoral provinces and those of the interior differed from Buenos Aires in a number of ways. In the first place they were less prosperous. The wars of independence and the subsequent civil wars damaged the economies of the littoral provinces – Santa Fe, Entre Ríos and Corrientes – and retarded their development. When at last they began to recover, they found Buenos Aires dominant, resolved to monoplize trade and navigation – and the customs revenue therefrom – and to dictate a policy of free trade. The negotiations for a federal pact between the provinces, therefore, were marked by bitter debates over economic policy. In the course of 1830 Pedro Ferré, representative of Corrientes and leader of the protectionist movement in the littoral, demanded not only nationalization of the customs revenue and free navigation of the rivers, but also a revision of the tariff policies of Buenos Aires. José María Rojas y Patrón, the Buenos Aires delegate, argued in reply that protection hurt the consumer without really helping the producer; if domestic industries were not competitive, nor capable of suppling the nation's needs, no amount of protection could save them. The pastoral economy depended upon cheap land, cheap money and a constant demand for hides in foreign markets. Protection would raise prices, raise costs and damage the export trade; then the mass of the people would suffer, for the sake of a small minority outside the cattle economy. Ferré rejected these arguments, denounced free competition, demanded protection for native industries against more cheaply produced foreign goods and called also for the opening of other ports than Buenos Aires to direct foreign trade, thus cutting distances and transport costs for the provinces. Only in this way would the littoral and the interior develop their economies, save existing investments and reduce unemployment. Buenos Aires refused to yield and the Pact of the Littoral (1831) was concluded without Corrientes, though it subsequently adhered to it. The fact that Corrientes took the lead in demanding protection was not a coincidence. In addition to cattle ranches it had a vital agricultural sector producing cotton, tobacco and other subtropical products, the expansion of which needed protection against Paraguayan and still more Brazilian competition. But during the first government of Rosas (1829–32) fiscal policy was designed primarily to serve the cattle industry of Buenos Aires. The changes proposed in 1831 – reduced tax on salt and on transport of cattle to the city – were only meant to protect the *saladero* industry, which claimed that it was suffering from competition from Montevideo and Rio Grande do Sul. In 1833 duties on the export of hides were reduced, and the tax on salt carried in national vessels from southern provinces was abolished. But *porteño* farming, the products of the littoral and the industries of the interior, these did not receive special treatment.

The economy of the interior – the mid-west and the west – was isolated to some degree from the direct impact of independence and suffered less than the littoral from civil wars and devastation. For a few years, it is true, the north-west frontier was a war zone, and the traditional links with the markets of Upper Peru and Chile were temporarily broken. But from 1817 the Chilean economy began to function again, stimulated now by a more active overseas trade. The Argentine west was re-incorporated into the trans-Andean market, exporting mules to the mining zone, cattle to the *saladeros* and the consumers of the towns, together with other Andean products such as fruits and wines. These outlets were opportune, for after independence the competition of European wines virtually closed the east-coast market to those of Mendoza. Salta was little more than a subsistence economy, though it still fattened mules for export outside the province. Tucumán continued to produce rice and tobacco, and to manufacture sugar, aguardiente and tanned leather. But the province was a high-cost producer and situated too far from its markets to compete, for example, with Brazilian sugar. The Andean mines, too, were outside the economy. La Rioja's gold, silver, copper and iron, San Juan's gold, silver and lead, Mendoza's gold, all were dormant assets. Rivadavia's dream of mining development through British capital was never realized. Their utter remoteness, great scarcity of labour, deficient technology and almost complete lack of transport to the coast made Argentine mines too high in cost and low in yield to warrant investment. The 'industries of the interior', therefore, consisted of little more than textiles, wine and grain, none of which, in the opinion of Buenos Aires, were worth protecting.

Yet there was a protectionist interest in Buenos Aires, sometimes voiced in the assembly, sometimes expressed in public debate, which demanded measures to safeguard national industry as well as agriculture. These opinions reflected variously the anxiety of certain manufacturing enterprises, a latent but powerful resentment of foreigners, and a kind of grass-roots federalism; but representing as they did diverse minorities and interest groups rather than a broad united front, they hardly amounted to economic nationalism. Buenos Aires had a small industrial sector consisting of textile manufacturers, silversmiths, harness-makers and blacksmiths. They supplied local and lower-class needs, and sometimes the demands of the state; indeed war kept many of them in business, for it brought orders for uniforms, equipment and hardware. In 1831 Buenos Aires contained 94 leather workshops, 83 carpenters' workshops, 47 forges and iron-works and 42 silversmiths. These were mainly artisan industries but the beginnings of a factory system could be seen, some manufacturers employing a number of workers in one place, with specialization and use of machinery; this applied to textiles, hat-making, furniture and a few other activities. Few of these enterprises could compete in price and quality with foreign imports, and they constantly pressed for state intervention in their favour. In January 1836, for example, the shoe-makers of Buenos Aires petitioned the government to prohibit the import of foreign shoes, on the grounds that they could not compete with foreign manufacturers, whose low production costs, cheaper raw materials, abundant labour and modern machinery gave them an overwhelming advantage. The *estancieros*, on the other hand, including Rosas and the Anchorena, preferred free trade to protection on grounds of economic interest and in favour of the export-orientated livestock sector. They were supported by those who opposed state intervention on principle and argued that industry would only flourish when it was qualified to do so, that national manufactures which could not compete in price and quality with foreign imports were not worth protecting. The historian and journalist, Pedro de Angelis, one of the more enlightened spokesmen for the Rosas regime, strongly attacked the idea of giving protection to the provincial wine industry and the *porteño* shoe industry, on the grounds that protection would raise prices for the mass of consumers, and divert to industry labourers who would be better employed in the agrarian sector.

Nevertheless, concern for the adverse balance of payments was sufficient to keep the protectionist lobby alive, and in due course Rosas heeded the case for intervention. In the Customs Law of December 1835 he introduced higher import duties. From a basic import duty of 17 per cent, the tariff moved upwards, giving greater protection to more vulnerable products, until it reached a point of prohibiting the import of a large number of articles such as textiles, hardware and, depending on the domestic price, wheat. Rosas thus sought to give positive assistance to arable agriculture and the manufacturing industries.

Why did he do it? Did he really believe that Argentina could become more self-sufficient in industry? Was he convinced that his regime could decrease its dependence on foreign imports, resist foreign competition, and tolerate the higher living costs? Or did he act under political constraint, a need to widen the social base of his regime? There appeared to be no reason why, in 1835–6, Rosas required the support of popular or middle groups. The regime was based firmly on the *estancieros*, who remained the dominant interest in the province and the closest allies of the government. The objectives of Rosas seem to have been to sustain the existing economic structure, while protecting those minority groups who suffered most from it. The tariff of 1835, therefore, was designed to relieve distress in the industrial and farming sectors, without subverting the livestock export economy. At the same time the law had a strong inter-provincial content; it was intended to make the federalist policy credible by giving protection to the provinces as well as to Buenos Aires.

In the event national industries, *porteño* as well as provincial, failed to respond to the protection given by the customs law and the French blockade. Even under the most favourable conditions, when they could take advantage of rising scarcity prices, local manufactures proved unable to satisfy the needs of the country. If existing industries failed to expand, there was little incentive to risk scarce capital in new enterprises. The government could not afford to continue placing undue burdens on consumers, and Rosas began to have second thoughts about protection. In 1838 import duties were reduced by one-third to minimize the effects of the French blockade (see below). Then, claiming the need to procure new revenues and pointing to the shortage of certain articles, Rosas decided (31 December 1841) to allow the entry of a large list of goods previously prohibited. The argument for free trade had been proved correct: national production had not been able to take advantage of protection, the tariff had merely caused shortages and high prices, and the principal victims were the consumers and the treasury. Rosas himself appears to have lost faith in protection, which meant in effect giving artificial respiration to the weakest sector of the economy, while strangling the stronger. Very few people would have thanked him for that. Industry therefore remained on the margin of economic life confined to workshops and artisans. When the Englishman Charles Mansfield visited the River Plate in 1852–3, he travelled like a walking advertisement for British goods: his white cotton poncho, bought in Corrientes, was made in Manchester; his electro-plated spurs, bought in Buenos Aires, were made in Birmingham. The bias towards an agropecuarian economy reflected the social structure as well as economic conditions. The upper groups preferred imported manufactures, while the rest of the population did not form a consumer market for a national industry. There were few freedoms in Buenos Aires under Rosas, but free trade was one of them.

Buenos Aires lived by foreign trade, and its expanding *estancias* depended on foreign markets. In the early years after independence there was a sizeable trade gap, as exports of precious metals fell and imports of consumer goods rose, and it took two decades for livestock exports to redress the balance. In 1829 and 1832 there was still a large excess of imports over exports, and the difference had to be met by exporting specie. The result was a shortage of currency at home and its replacement by ever larger issues of paper money. The medium of international trade was letters of credit drawn on the London exchange, and British merchants came to dominate the financial market of Buenos Aires. The essential link was the trade in textiles from Britain against hides from Argentina, a trade which underwent steady if unspectacular growth, except during the years of blockade, in 1838–9 and 1845–6, when it suffered a sharp drop. From 1822 to 1837 exports from Buenos Aires rose in value from about £700,000 to £1 million; from 1837 to 1851 they doubled in value to £2 million a year. Hides formed the bulk of these exports. There was an average annual export of 798,564 cattle hides from Buenos Aires in the 1830s; 2,303,910 in the 1840s. In 1836 hides amounted to 68.4 per cent of the total value of exports from Buenos Aires; in 1851 they amounted to 64.9 per cent. If jerked beef and other cattle products are added to hides, then the livestock industry contributed 82.8 per cent of total exports in 1836, 78 per cent in 1851. The basic cause of export growth was the incorporation of more land into the economy, especially the expansion of the southern frontier after the Desert Campaign of 1833; the province of Buenos Aires now produced about two-thirds of all hides exported from the littoral provinces. A secondary cause was the blockade of Buenos Aires by foreign powers, which helped to increase the cattle stock by temporarily stopping shipment of hides, thus leaving the cattle to multiply in the pampas.

Meanwhile imports into Buenos Aires rose from a total of £1.5 million in 1825 to £2.1 million in 1850, an increase which was probably even greater in quantity than in value, owing to the falling price of manufactured goods in Europe. There was very little saving or capital accumulation. Imports of luxury and consumer goods used up any surplus capital which might otherwise have been invested. Pianos, clocks, jewelry and precious stones comprised 10 per cent of imports. Consumer goods of a luxury kind – furniture and hardware, clothes and shoes – for the quality market amounted to 32 per cent. Thus almost half of the imports were manufactured goods for the upper end of the market. Industrial raw materials such as coal, iron and other metals accounted for only 3 per cent of imports, an indication of the small degree of industrialization, the absence of technology and the low level of artisan employment.

Argentina was already developing close economic ties with Britain. In the early years of the republic British shippers carried 60 per cent of the trade in and out of Buenos Aires; by mid-century, with competition growing, British shipping in Buenos Aires was 25 per cent of the total. Most of the trade went to Britain (322 vessels and 22.8 per cent of tonnage in 1849–51) and the United States (253 vessels and 21.6 per cent), though this still left a substantial portion of trade (33 per cent) to less developed countries, Cuba, Brazil, Italy and Spain. The value of British trade to Argentina did not rise spectacularly in the first half of the nineteenth century. The average annual exports in the period 1822–5 were between £700,000 and £800,000 sterling. In 1850 the value of British exports to Argentina was still about £900,000. Yet in spite of the growing competition, the value of British trade to the River Plate up to 1837 exceeded that of all foreign countries put together; and even in 1850 it was not far short of this. Argentina relied upon British manufactures, British shipping, British markets, but it did not yet need – could not yet use – British capital and technology, it made its own economic decisions, and its independence was never in doubt. And by mid-century it was already moving towards a better balance of trade as the British market consumed more of its raw materials.

The structure of society was simple and its scale was small. Argentina, a land full of cattle, was empty of people, and its one million square miles of territory contained in 1820 a population about one-third that of contemporary London. Yet Argentina underwent steady demographic growth in the half-century after independence, from 507,951 inhabitants in 1816, to 570,000 in 1825, 1,180,000 in 1857 and 1,736,923 in 1869. In the thirty-two years from 1825 to 1857 the population roughly doubled itself. Growth was due essentially to a fall in the mortality rate: at a time when economic conditions were improving, there was no major epidemic, and the great outbreaks of cholera and yellow fever were yet to come. There was only moderate immigration in this period, though a number of Basques, French, Canarians, Italians and British entered Buenos Aires in the 1840s, once the blockades were over. The greatest population upswing was registered in the littoral provinces, which increased their share of the total from 36 per cent in 1800 to 48.8 per cent in 1869. Buenos Aires and Córdoba had over one-third of the total. Buenos Aires was an insanitary and pestilential city, without amenities, without drainage, without even a pure water supply. But it grew in numbers from 55,416 in 1822 to 177,787 in 1869, while the total of city and province combined grew from 118,646 to 495,107 in the same period.

Society was rooted in land. It was the large *estancia* which conferred status and imposed subordination. *Estancieros* or their clients dominated the administration, the house of representatives, local government and the militia. The polarization of society was absolute. There was an upper class of landowners and their associates, and a lower class comprising the rest of the population. Some social margins, it is true, were blurred. Commerce was economically important and socially respectable, and it provided the original fortunes of some of the leading families of Argentina such as the Anchorena, the Alzaga and the Santa Coloma. But the urban elite of the early nineteenth century did not acquire a separate identity or become an independent middle class. Faced with insistent British competition in the years after independence, local businessmen began to divert their capital into land and without abandoning their urban occupations to become *estancieros* and identify themselves with a new aristocracy. Meanwhile there were no others to fill the middle ranks. The entrepreneurial function came to be exercised by foreigners: British businessmen soon dominated commercial activities, while European immigrants went into artisan occupations, supplementing the roles of local craftsmen. But whereas socially the creole merchants moved upwards into the landed aristocracy, the artisans and manufacturers merged unmistakably into the lower sectors, branded by their manual occupations which were often filled by coloured people.

If there was little prospect of a native middle sector in the towns, there was even less likelihood of finding one in the countryside, where a great gulf separated the landed proprietor from the landless peon. The homogeneity of the landed class was not absolute. While some *estancieros* were owners of truly immense properties, others possessed relatively modest estates. The former were often capitalists of urban origin with some education and aspirations to higher standards of living. The latter were more likely to come from generations of country dwellers and were little removed in culture from the gauchos around them, illiterate, indifferent to material comforts and investing nothing in improvement. Yet, in spite of differences of income, culture and social style, the *estancieros* were as one compared with the peons on their estates and the gauchos of the pampas. There was strong group cohesion and solidarity among the landed class. Rosas himself was the centre of a vast kinship group based on land. He was surrounded by a closely-knit economic and political network, linking deputies, law officers, officials and military, who were also landowners and related among themselves or with their leader. Rosas used his extensive patronage to bind this small oligarchy ever closer. The Anchorena in particular were able to extend their urban and rural properties with his direct assistance, making a profit from their alleged services to the state.

At the end of the colonial period the pampas were inhabited by wild cattle, indomitable Indians and untamed gauchos. The gaucho was a product of race mixture; the components have been disputed, but there is no doubt that there were three races in the littoral, Indians, whites and blacks. By simple definition the gaucho was a free man on horseback. But the term was used by contemporaries and by later historians in a wide sense to mean rural people in general. Greater precision would distinguish between the sedentary rural dwellers working on the land for themselves or for a *patrón* and the pure gaucho, who was nomadic and independent, tied to no estate. And further refinement of terms would identify the *gaucho malo*, who lived by violence and near-delinquency and whom the state regarded as a criminal. Whether good or bad, the classical gaucho asserted his freedom from all formal institutions; he was indifferent to government and its agents, indifferent to religion and the Church. He did not seek land; he lived by hunting, gambling and fighting. The nomadism of the gaucho had many social implications. It prevented settled work or occupation. Property, industry, habitation, these were alien concepts. So too was the gaucho family. The upper sector enjoyed great family stability and drew strength from the ties of kinship. The lower sector was much weaker institutionally. This was partly an urban-rural division between two cultures; it was also a feature of the social structure. Among the gauchos and peons unions were temporary and the resulting families were only loosely joined together. Marriage was the exception, and it was the unmarried mother who formed the nucleus of the rural family, for she was the only permanent parent. Even if the father was not prone to gaucho nomadism, he had to sell his labour where he could, or else he was recruited into armies or *montoneros*.

The ruling groups in the countryside had traditionally imposed a system of coercion upon people whom they regarded as *mozos vagos y mal entretenidos*, vagrants without employer or occupation, idlers who sat in groups singing to a guitar, drinking *mate* or liquor, gambling, but apparently not working. This class was seen as a potential labour force and it was subject to many constraints by the landed proprietors – punitive expeditions, imprisonment, conscription to the Indian frontier, corporal punishment and other penalties. Legislation sought to brand *vagos y mal entretenidos* as a criminal class by definition and vagrancy itself as a crime. Applied stringently by the justices of the peace, anti-vagrancy laws were designed to impose order and discipline in the countryside, to provide a labour pool for *hacendados* and to produce conscripts for the army. The militia became in effect an open prison, into which the most miserable part of the rural population was forcibly herded. For the gaucho the years after independence were even harsher than before. Property concentration prevented the mass of the people from acquiring land, while *estancia* expansion raised the demand for labour. During the colonial period the existence of common usages in the pampas gave the gaucho access to wild cattle on the open range. But these traditional practices came to an end when *estancias* were implanted and endowed, private property spread across the plains, and cattle was appropriated by landowners. Republican laws, those of Rivadavia as well as of Rosas, attacked vagrancy and mobilized the rural population. People were forced to carry identity cards and certificates of employment; a peon caught out of his *estancia* without permission would be conscripted into the army or assigned to public works. Thus, the gaucho was forcibly converted from a free nomad into a hired ranch-hand, a *peón de estancia*.

This primitive society was not qualified for constitutional government or political participation. The *estancia* dominated economic and social life and became the model of government. *Estancieros* ruled their domains by personal authority and demanded unqualified obedience. They were a powerful and cohesive class, unrivalled by any other. Argentina did not yet possess a middle sector of commerce or industry, and there was no great concentration of peasants. The popular classes, superior in numbers, were heterogeneous in composition and divided into disparate groups, peons on *estancias*, wage labourers, small farmers or tenants, marginal gauchos and delinquents. The subordinate condition of the lower sectors, their poor expectations and their isolation in the immense plains, combined to prevent the formation of an autonomous political movement from below. On the other hand they were ideal material for military mobilization and they were easily transformed into *montoneros*, the guerrilla forces of the plains. The causes for which they fought were not class conflicts: they were sectional struggles within the upper groups, disputes between landed proprietors or among leading families, attacks upon the existing government, or clashes with neighbouring provinces. In a situation of equilibrium between factions, leaders would call on their dependants and round up their reserves of manpower the better to tip the balance against their enemies. The use of popular forces, however, did not imply popular objectives. The *estancia* could mobilize its peons either for work or for war, and a regional chieftain in turn could call upon his client *estancieros*. These struggles within the oligarchy, moreover, occurred in peculiar demographic conditions, where a relatively small population was spread thinly across the plains. While ties of kinship at the top of society were close, communications between members of the popular classes, especially in the countryside, were meagre, partly because of the great distances separating rural communities, partly because peons were tied to their estates and immobilized by the rules of the *estancia*. The masses, therefore, were ordered, recruited, manipulated, but not politicized. How was it done?

The relation of patron and client, this was the essential link. The landowner wanted labour, loyalty and service in peace and war. The peon wanted subsistence and security. The *estanciero*, therefore, was a protector, possessor of sufficient power to defend his dependants against marauding Indians, recruiting sergeants and rival hordes. He was also a provider, who developed and defended local resources and could give employment, food and shelter. By supplying what was needed and exploiting what was offered, a *hacendado* recruited a *peonada*. This primitive political structure, founded on individual power, raised upon personal loyalties, cemented by the authority of the patron and the dependence of the peon, was finally built into the state and became the model of *caudillismo*. For individual alliances were magnified into a social pyramid, as patrons in turn became clients to more powerful men, until the peak of power was reached and they all became clients of a super-patron. Thus, from his rural base a local caudillo, supported by his client *estancieros* and their dependents, might conquer the state, for himself, his family, his region. Then, as representative of a group, or a class, or a province, he would reproduce the personalism and patronage in which he had been nurtured and by which he had been raised. *Caudillismo* was the image of society, and the caudillos were its creatures.

The caudillo was first a warrior, a man qualified to lead and defend; during wars of liberation, civil wars, national wars, the caudillo was the strong man who could recruit troops, command resources, protect his people. The union of military power and personal authority was inherent in the caudillo. He responded, however, not only to military needs but also to civilian pressures. He was often the agent of an extended family, who constituted in effect a ruling dynasty; he was sometimes the representative of regional economic interests, which needed a defender against other regions or against the centre; and he was occasionally the man who succeeded in making a particular interest – the export-oriented *estancia*, for example – into a national one. With the resources of the state at his disposal, the caudillo then emerged as a distributor of patronage, allocating spoils to his clientage and earning yet further service from them; for in granting office and land, the caudillo, the super-patron, redeemed his promises to his followers and kept them in a state of political peonage.

The origins and the careers of the Argentine caudillos conformed to these prototypes. They came, in the majority of cases, from families which had been wealthy and powerful since colonial times, most of them owners of landed property, and many of them holders of military appointments. The caudillos themselves preserved this inheritance. Among the eighteen caudillos who ruled in the various provinces of Argentina between 1810 and 1870, thirteen were great landowers, one had landed property of medium size, one was the owner of a shipyard. They all held military appointments, either in the army or in the militia; and of the twelve who had been old enough to fight in the wars of independence, nine had done so. Wealth was an intrinsic qualification. Fifteen of the group were extremely wealthy, two were of medium wealth. Virtually all had some level of education. Political expectations were not good; nine died violently, three in exile. There was little evidence of social mobility in these careers. No doubt the revolution for independence allowed the creoles greater access to politics, the bureaucracy and commerce; but social structure based upon land, wealth, prestige and education remained essentially unchanged. According to the criterion of wealth, only two of the eighteen caudillos (Estanislao

López and Félix Aldao) showed any signs of moving upwards, from medium to great wealth. The rest followed the traditions of their family in wealth and prestige, and simply added to their patrimony. The occupational route they followed had familiar signposts, from *estanciero*, via the military, to caudillo.

The year 1820 was a year of anarchy. Independence from Spain had culminated not in national unity but in universal dismemberment. After a decade of conflict between Buenos Aires and the provinces, between central government and regional interests, between unitarians and federalists, the framework of political organization in the Río de la Plata collapsed. Independent republics proliferated throughout the interior, and when Buenos Aires sought to subdue them they fought back. Provincial caudillos – Estanislao López of Santa Fe, Francisco Ramírez of Entre Ríos – led their irregular gaucho hordes, the fearsome *montoneros*, against the capital. On 1 February 1820 they defeated the forces of Buenos Aires at the battle of Cepeda and proceeded to destroy all trace of central authority. Only the provincial government of Buenos Aires survived, and this too was harassed into anarchy, while persons and property lay at the mercy of petty caudillos, gauchos and Indians. Buenos Aires looked for protection to the countryside. While two of its leaders, Martín Rodríguez and Manuel Dorrego, desperately stemmed the tide, the *estancieros* of the south were asked to come to the rescue with their rural militias. They responded promptly, not least Rosas, appreciating the danger to their own interests from the seeping anarchy of the times. It was with the backing of the *estancieros* that Rodríguez was elected governor in September 1820 and made a negotiated peace with the caudillos.

The inspiration behind the Rodríguez administration was its chief minister, Bernardino Rivadavia, educated, liberal and bureaucratic. Rivadavia wanted to modernize Argentina. He sought economic growth through free trade, foreign investment and immigration. He applied the system of emphyteusis, the renting out of state land, to put the natural resources of Argentina to productive use. He had a vision of liberal institutions and a new infrastructure, in which the framework of modernization would be enlarged to comprise a great and unified Argentina, undivided by political and economic particularism. This was Rivadavia's plan, enlightened, developmental and unitarian. In truth it was more of a dream than a plan: some of its ideas were impractical, others were ahead of their time. But the entire model was rejected as irrelevant by Rosas and his associates, who represented a more primitive economy – cattle production for export of hides and salt meat – but one which brought immediate returns and was in harmony with the country's traditions. They were alarmed by the innovations of the new regime. On 7 February 1826 Rivadavia was appointed president of the United Provinces of the Río de la Plata; he had a unitary constitution and innumerable ideas. In March the city of Buenos Aires was declared capital of the nation and federalized. On 12 September Rivadavia sent to congress his proposal to divide the non-federalized part of the province of Buenos Aires into two, the Provincia del Paraná in the north and the Provincia del Salado in the south. These measures went to the heart of *estanciero* interests. The federalization of the city of Buenos Aires and its environs amputated the best part of the province and a large section of its population. It also involved nationalizing the revenues of the port, which amounted to 75 per cent of the provincial government's income, arousing the fear that the next step would be to raise alternative revenue by an income or land tax. To the world of the landowners, for whom Buenos Aires and its hinterland, port and province were one, these measures threatened division and disaster.

The policy of Rivadavia struck at too many interest groups to succeed. His immediate political opponents, the federalists, rejected unitary policy as undemocratic and, influenced by United States federalism, sought a federal solution to the problem of national organization. The *estancieros* saw Rivadavia as a danger to their economic and fiscal assets, an intellectual who neglected rural security and, while promoting urban progress of a European kind, allowed the savage Indians to roam the plains. Immigration they opposed as expensive, unnecessary and probably subversive, bringing competition for land and labour and raising the cost of both. The anti-clerical policy of the regime, designed primarily to curtail the temporal power of the Church, to extend religious freedom, and to bring Argentina into conformity with foreign expectations, was anathema not only to the clergy but to all those with conservative values, and served to unite federalists, *estancieros* and priests under the banner of *religión o muerte*. Rosas and the Anchorena took the lead in organizing resistance to Rivadavia's plans. Until now Rosas had not belonged to the federal party or associated with its leader Manuel Dorrego. But in the latter half of 1826, at the head of a network of friends, relations and clients, he allied himself to the party which he was eventually to absorb and destroy. He joined the federalists not for reasons of political ideology, which he did not possess, but because unitary policy threatened his plans of hegemony in the countryside.

Rivadavia yielded to the combined forces of his opponents and resigned from the presidency on 27 June 1827. In the ultimate analysis he did not have a constituency: he represented intellectuals, bureaucrats and professional politicians, groups which did not form an identifiable social sector. Rosas on the other hand had a specific power base, the *estancieros*, who possessed the principal resources of the country and considerable paramilitary force. But Rosas did not rule. It was the real federalists who came to power and Manuel Dorrego was elected governor on 12 August 1827. Dorrego's popularity, his independence and his refusal to take advice alerted Rosas and his friends: previous experience showed the danger of divergence between those who ruled in the *estancias* and those who governed in Buenos Aires. In the event Dorrego was overthrown, on 1 December 1828, not by his enemies within but by the unitarians from without, when General Juan Lavalle led a coalition of military returned from the war with Brazil, professional politicians, merchants and intellectuals. The December revolution was made in the name of liberal principles, against rural conservatism, caudillism and provincialism, and it was an attempt to restore the system of Rivadavia. But Lavalle gave a bonus to his enemies when he ordered the execution of Dorrego, a man of peace and moderation. This savage sentence caused revulsion in all sectors, especially among the populace. It branded the unitarians as political assassins and aggravated the anarchy of the times. It also left the way open for Rosas to lead the federal party. Backed by his *estanciero* allies and his rural hordes, Rosas reconquered power from Lavalle and the unitarians and was elected governor by a grateful assembly on 6 December 1829. It was no ordinary election, for the new governor was given dictatorial powers and a mandate to restore order.

The hegemony of Rosas, how can it be explained? He was in part a creature of circumstances. He represented the rise to power of a new economic interest, the *estancieros*. The classic elite of the revolution of 1810 were the merchants and bureaucrats. The struggle for independence created a group of career revolutionaries – professional politicians, state officials, a new military, men who lived by service to and income from the state. The merchants of Buenos Aires, emerging from the colony as the leading economic interest, were at first powerful allies of the new elite. From about 1820, however, many merchant families began to seek other outlets and to invest in land, cattle and meat-salting plants. These were the dominant social group of the future, a landowning oligarchy with roots in commerce and recruited from urban society. For the moment, however, they did not possess the executive power in the state, and the fact remained that those with economic power did not rule and those who ruled lacked an economic base. Inevitably the landowners began to seek direct political control. In defeating Rivadavia and Lavalle in 1827–9, they overthrew not only the unitarians but the existing ruling class, the career politicians, and took possession of the government through Rosas.

Conditions, therefore, created Rosas. He was the individual synthesis of the society and economy of the countryside, and when the interests of this sector coincided with those of the urban federalists, Rosas was at once the representative and the executive of the alliance. But he also had specific qualifications: his origins, career and control over events all made him a power in the land before he was even elected governor and narrowed the choice open to the *estancieros*. His personal career was unique and did not conform exactly to the model of merchant turned landowner which characterized so many of his supporters. He began on the *estancia*, learned the business from the working end, accumulated capital in the rural sector itself and advanced from there. He was a pioneer in the expansion of landowning and cattle-raising, starting some years before the big push southwards from 1820. He was a working, not an absentee, landlord, operating at every stage of cattle raising. Thus, he came into direct contact with the gauchos, delinquents, Indians and other denizens of the pampas, partly to hire them for his estates, partly to mobilize them for his militia. For Rosas was militia commander as well as *estanciero*, and he had more military experience than any of his peers. In the recruitment of troops, the training and control of militia, and the deployment of units not only on the frontier but in urban operations, he had no equal. It was the military dimension of Rosas's early career which gave him the edge over his rivals. This culminated in his role during the guerrilla war of 1829, when he raised, controlled and led anarchic popular forces in the irregular army which defeated Lavalle's professionals. Rosas, then, was a self-made caudillo.

Rosas divided society into those who commanded and those who obeyed. Order obsessed him, and the virtue which he most admired in a people was subordination. If there was anything more abhorrent to

Rosas than democracy, it was liberalism. The reason why he detested unitarians was not that they wanted a united Argentina but that they were liberals who believed in secular values of humanism and progress. He identified them with freemasons and intellectuals, subversives who undermined order and tradition and whom he held ultimately responsible for the political assassinations which brutalized Argentine public life from 1828 to 1835. The constitutional doctrines of the two parties did not interest him, and he was never a true federalist. He thought and ruled as a centralist, and he stood for the hegemony of Buenos Aires. Rosas destroyed the traditional division between federalists and unitarians and made these categories virtually meaningless. He substituted *rosismo* and anti-*rosismo*.

What was *rosismo*? Its power base was the *estancia*, a focus of economic resources and a system of social control. The domination of the economy by the *estancia* was continued and completed under Rosas. At the beginning of his regime much of the territory which eventually constituted the province of Buenos Aires was still controlled by Indians. And even within the frontier, north of the Salado, there were large areas unoccupied by whites. Rosas stood for a policy of territorial settlement and expansion. The Desert Campaign of 1833 added thousands of square miles south of the Río Negro to the province of Buenos Aires, together with new resources, new security and the confidence born of a great victory over the Indians. The land to the south, and the unoccupied or emphyteusis land in the north, gave the state a vast reserve of property which it could sell or give away. Rosas himself was one of the principal beneficiaries of this prodigious distribution. The law of 6 June 1834 granted him the freehold of the island of Choele-Choel in recognition of his leadership in the Desert Campaign. He was allowed to exchange this for sixty square leagues of public land wherever he chose. His followers were also rewarded. The law of 30 September 1834 made land grants up to a maximum of 50 square leagues altogether to officers who had participated in the Desert Campaign; while a law of 25 April 1835 granted land up to 16 square leagues for allocation to soldiers of the Andes Division in the same campaign. The military who took part in crushing the rebellion of the south in 1839 were rewarded by a land grant of 9 November 1839; generals received 6 square leagues, colonels 5, non-commissioned officers half a league, and privates a quarter of a league. Civilians too were recompensed for their loyalty.

The *boletos de premios en tierras*, or land certificates as rewards for military service, were one of the principal instruments of land distribution; 8,500 were issued by the government of Rosas, though not all were used by the recipients. No doubt this was a means by which an impecunious government paid salaries, grants and pensions to its servants. But there was also a political element present, for land was the richest source of patronage available, a weapon for Rosas, a welfare system for his supporters. Rosas was the great *patrón* and the *estancieros* were his *clientela*. In this sense *rosismo* was less an ideology than an interest group and a fairly exclusive one. For there was no sector outside the *estancieros* equipped to use these grants. Certificates of less than one league were virtually useless in the hands of soldiers or minor bureaucrats, when the existing agrarian structure averaged eight leagues per estate. But in the hands of those who already possessed estates or had the capital to buy them up cheaply, they were a powerful instrument for land concentration. More than 90 per cent of land certificates granted to soldiers and civilians ended up in the hands of landowners or those who were buying their way into land.

The trend of the Rosas regime, therefore, was towards greater concentration of property in the hands of a small group. In 1830 980 landowners held the 5,516 square leagues of occupied land in Buenos Aires province; of these, 60 proprietors monopolized almost 4,000 square leagues, or 76 per cent. In the period 1830–52 occupied land grew to 6,100 square leagues, with 782 proprietors. Of these 382 proprietors held 82 per cent of holdings above one square league, while 200 proprietors, or 28 per cent, held 60 per cent of holdings above ten square leagues. There were 74 holdings of over 15 square leagues (90,000 acres), and 42 holdings of over 20 square leagues (120,000 acres). Meanwhile small holdings accounted for only one per cent of the land in use. Among the eighty or so people who were members of the House of Representatives between 1835 and 1852, 60 per cent were landowners or had occupations connected with land. This was the assembly which voted Rosas into power and continued to vote for him. To some degree they could control policy making. They consistently denied Rosas permission to increase the *contribución directa*, a tax on capital and property, and they always prevented him from raising any revenue at the expense of the *estancieros*. In 1850, when total revenues reached 62 million pesos, chiefly from customs, the *contribución directa* provided only 3 per cent of the total, and most of this portion was paid by commerce rather than land. The administration too was dominated by landowners. Juan N. Terrero, economic adviser of Rosas, had 42 square leagues and left a fortune of 53 million pesos. Angel Pacheco, Rosas's principal general, had 75 square leagues. Felipe Arana, minister of foreign affairs, possessed 42 square leagues. Even Vicente López, poet, deputy and president of the high court, owned 12 square leagues. But the greatest landowners of the province were the Anchorena, cousins of Rosas and his closest political advisers; their various possessions totalled 306 square leagues (1,856,000 acres). As for Rosas himself, in 1830 in the group of about seventeen landowners with property over 50 square leagues (300,000 acres), he occupied tenth place with 70 square leagues (420,000 acres). By 1852, according to the official estimate of his property, he had accumulated 136 square leagues (816,000 acres).

The *estancia* gave Rosas the sinews of war, the alliance of fellow *estancieros* and the means of recruiting an army of peons, gauchos and vagrants. He had an instinct for manipulating the discontents of the masses and turning them against his enemies in such a way that they did not damage the basic structure of society. While Rosas identified cultur-ally with the gauchos, he did not unite with them socially, or represent them politically. The core of his forces were his own peons and depen-dants, who were his servants rather than his supporters, his clients rather than his allies. When Rosas needed to make a critical push, in 1829, 1833 or 1835, he enlisted the gauchos in the countryside and the mob in the city. They were the only manpower available, and for the moment they had a value outside of the *estancia*. But the normal agrarian regime was very different: employment was obligatory, the *estancia* was a prison and conscription to the Indian frontier was an imminent alternative. And the gaucho forces lasted only as long as Rosas needed them. Once he had the apparatus of the state in his possession, from 1835, once he controlled the bureaucracy, the police and, above all, the regular army, he did not need or want the popular forces of the countryside. Rosas quickly recruited, equipped, armed and purged an army of the line, detachments of which were used against the countryside to round up conscripts. With the ultimate means of coercion in his hand, he ceased to rely on the irregular rural forces. The gaucho militias, moreover, were 'popular' forces only in the sense that they were composed of the peons of the countryside. They were not always volunteers for a cause, nor were they politicized. The fact of belonging to a military organization did not give the peons power or representation, for the rigid structure of the *estancia* was built into the militia, where the *estancieros* were the commanders, their over-

seers the officers and their peons the troops. These troops did not enter
into direct relationship with Rosas; they were mobilized by their own
particular patron, which meant that Rosas received his support not from
free gaucho hordes but from *estancieros* leading their peon conscripts, a
service for which the *estancieros* were paid by the state. The province was
ruled by an informal alliance of *estancieros*, militia commanders and
justices of the peace.

The severity of the rural regime reflected the emptiness of the pampas,
the great population scarcity and the ruthless search for labour in a
period of *estancia* expansion. The survival of slavery in Argentina was
another indication of labour shortage. Rosas himself owned slaves and
he did not question their place in the social structure. In spite of the May
Revolution, the declarations of 1810 and the subsequent hope of social as
well as political emancipation, slavery survived in Argentina, fed by an
illegal slave trade which, until the late 1830s, the government openly
tolerated. At the end of the colonial period the Río de la Plata contained
over 30,000 slaves out of a population of 400,000. The incidence of
slavery was greatest in the towns, especially Buenos Aires. In 1810 there
were 11,837 blacks and mulattos in Buenos Aires, or 29.3 per cent, in a
total population of 40,398, and most of the blacks were slaves. Slave
numbers were depleted during the wars of independence, when emancipation was offered in return for military service, and military service
often led to death. In 1822, of the 55,416 inhabitants of the city of Buenos
Aires, 13,685, or 24.7 per cent, were blacks and mulattos; of these 6,611,
or 48.3 per cent, were slaves. In 1838 non whites constituted 14,928 out
of 62,957, or 23.71 per cent. Mortality rates were higher among non
whites than among whites, and much higher among mulattos and free
blacks than among slaves. Yet from 1822 to 1838 the number of non
whites remained stationary, as their ranks were replenished from abroad.
Rosas was responsible for a revival of the slave trade. His decree of 15
October 1831 allowed the sale of slaves imported as servants by foreigners; and an illegal slave trade from Brazil, Uruguay and Africa survived in
the 1830s. It was not until 1839, when Rosas needed British support
against the French, that a comprehensive anti-slave trade treaty was
signed. By 1843, according to a British estimate, there were no more than
300 slaves in the Argentine provinces; and slaves who joined the
federalist army, especially if they belonged to unitarian owners, gained
freedom in return for military service. When, in the Constitution of 1853,
slavery was finally abolished in the whole of Argentina, there were few

slaves left. Meanwhile, Rosas had many blacks in his employment and many more in his political service. He seems to have been free of race prejudice, though he did not raise the non whites socially. They occupied the lowest situations: they were porters, carters, carriers, drivers and washerwomen, as well as domestic servants. They gave Rosas useful support in the streets and were part of his 'popular' following. They were deployed in a military role in Buenos Aires and the provinces where they formed a militia unit, the *negrada federal*, black troops in red shirts, many of them former slaves. But in the final analysis the demagogy of Rosas among the blacks and mulattos did nothing to alter their position in the society around them.

The hegemony of the landowners, the abasement of the gauchos, the dependence of the peons, all this was the heritage of Rosas. Argentina bore the imprint of extreme social stratification for many generations to come. Society became set in a rigid mould, to which economic modernization and political change had later to adapt. The Rosas state was the *estancia* writ large. Society itself was built upon the patron-peon relationship. It seemed the only alternative to anarchy.

Rosas ruled from 1829 to 1832 with absolute powers. After an interregnum during which instability in Buenos Aires and insubordination in the provinces threatened to restore anarchy, he returned to office on his own terms in March 1835 and ruled for the next seventeen years with total and unlimited power. The House of Representatives remained a creature of the governor, whom it formally 'elected'. It consisted of 44 deputies, half of whom were annually renewed by election. But only a small minority of the electorate participated, and it was the duty of the justices of the peace to deliver these votes to the regime. The assembly, lacking legislative function and financial control, was largely an exercise in public relations for the benefit of foreign and domestic audiences, and it normally responded sycophantically to the initiatives of the governor. While he controlled the legislature, Rosas also dominated the judicial power. He not only made law, he interpreted it, changed it and applied it. The machinery of justice no doubt continued to function: the justices of the peace, the judges for civil and criminal cases, the appeal judge and the supreme court, all gave institutional legitimacy to the regime. But the law did not rule. Arbitrary intervention by the executive undermined the independence of the judiciary. Rosas took many cases to himself, read the evidence, examined the police reports and, as he sat alone at his desk, gave judgement, writing on the files 'shoot him', 'fine him', 'imprison him', 'to the army'. Rosas also controlled the bureaucracy. One of his first and most uncompromising measures was to purge the old administration; this was the simplest way of removing political enemies and rewarding followers, and it was inherent in the patron-client organization of society. The new administration was not extravagantly large, and some of the early vacancies were left unfilled as part of the expenditure cuts which the government was obliged to make. But appointments of all kinds were reserved for political clients and federalists; other qualifications counted for little.

Propaganda was an essential ingredient of *rosismo*: a few simple and violent slogans took the place of ideology and these permeated the administration and were thrust relentlessly at the public. People were obliged to wear a kind of uniform and to use the federal colour, red. The symbolism was a form of coercion and conformity. To adopt the federal look and the federal language took the place of orthodoxy tests and oaths of allegiance. Federal uniformity was a measure of quasi-totalitarian pressure, by which people were forced to abandon a passive or apolitical role and to accept a specific commitment, to show their true colours. The Church was a willing ally, except for the Jesuits, who were re-admitted and re-expelled. Portraits of Rosas were carried in triumph through the streets and placed upon the altars of the principal churches. Sermons glorified the dictator and extolled the federal cause. The clergy became essential auxiliaries of the regime and preached that to resist Rosas was a sin. Political orthodoxy was conveyed by word as well as by deed, and the printing presses of Buenos Aires were kept fully employed turning out newspapers in Spanish and other languages containing official news and propaganda, for circulation at home and abroad. But the ultimate sanction was force, controlled by Rosas, applied by the military and the police.

The regime was not strictly speaking a military dictatorship: it was a civilian regime which employed a compliant military. The military establishment, consisting of the regular army and the militia, existed, however, not only to defend the country but to occupy it, not only to protect the population but to control it. Conscripted from peons, vagrants and delinquents, officered by professional soldiers, kept alive by booty and exactions from the *estancias*, the army of Rosas was a heavy burden on the rest of the population. If it was not an efficient military, it was a numerous one – perhaps 20,000 strong – and an active one, constantly engaged in foreign wars, interprovincial conflicts and internal security. But war and the economic demands of war, while they meant misery for the many, made fortunes for the few. Defence spending provided a secure market for certain industries and employment for their workers: the fairly constant demand for uniforms, arms and equipment helped to sustain a number of small workshops and artisan manufactures in an otherwise depressed industrial sector. Above all, the military market favoured several large landowners. Proprietors such as the Anchorena had long had valuable contracts for the supply of cattle to frontier forts; now the armies on other fronts became voracious consumers and regular customers. The army and its liabilities, however, increased at a time when revenue was contracting, and something had to be sacrificed. When the French blockade began to bite, from April 1838, not only were people thrown out of work and hit by rapid inflation but the regime saw its revenue from customs – its basic income – fall dramatically. Faced with heavy budget deficits, it immediately imposed severe expenditure cuts. Most of these fell on education, the social services and welfare in general. The University of Buenos Aires was virtually closed. When priorities were tested, Rosas did not even make a pretence of governing 'popularly'.

The contrast between military and social spending reflected circumstances as well as values. The enemy within, conflict with other provinces and with foreign powers, and the obligation to succour his allies in the interior, all caused Rosas to maintain a heavy defence budget. Some of these choices were forced upon him, others were preferred policy, yet others reflected a universal indifference towards welfare. In any case the consequences were socially retarding. In the 1840s the ministry of government, or home affairs, received on average between 6 and 7 per cent of the total budget, and most of this was allocated to police and political expenditure, not to social services. Defence, on the other hand, received absolute priority. The military budget varied from 4 million pesos, or 27 per cent of the total, in 1836, to 23.8 million, 49 per cent, during the French blockade in 1840, to 29.6 million, 71.11 per cent, in 1841. For the rest of the regime it never fell below 15 million, or 49 per cent.

This was the system of total government which sustained Rosas in power for over two decades. The majority of people obeyed, some with enthusiasm, others from inertia, many out of fear. But it was more than tyranny arbitrarily imposed. The government of Rosas responded to conditions inherent in Argentine society, where men had lived for too long without a common power to keep them all in awe. Rosas superseded a state of nature, in which life could be brutish and short. He offered an escape from insecurity and a promise of peace, on condition that he were granted total power, the sole antidote to total anarchy. To exercise his sovereignty Rosas used the bureaucracy, the military and the police. Even so there was some opposition. Internally there was an ideological opposition, partly from unitarians and partly from younger reformists; this came to a head in an abortive conspiracy in 1839 and continued to operate throughout the regime from its base in Montevideo. A second focus of internal opposition was formed by the landowners of the south of the province, whose resentment derived not from ideology but from economic interest. Already harassed by demands upon their manpower and resources for the Indian frontier, they were particularly hit by the French blockade, which cut off their export outlets and for which they blamed Rosas. But their rebellion of 1839 did not synchronize with the political conspiracy and they too were crushed. Finally, there was an external opposition to the regime, partly from other provinces and partly from foreign powers. If this could link with internal dissidents, Rosas would be in real danger. He therefore held in reserve another constraint, terror.

Rosas used terror as an instrument of government, to eliminate enemies, to discipline dissidents, to warn waverers and, ultimately, to control his own supporters. Terror was not simply a series of exceptional episodes, though it was regulated according to circumstances. It was an intrinsic part of the Rosas system, the distinctive style of the regime, its ultimate sanction. Rosas himself was the author of terror, ordering executions without trial by virtue of the extraordinary powers vested in him. But the special agent of terrorism was the *Sociedad Popular Restaurador*, a political club and a para-police organization. The Society had an armed wing, commonly called the *mazorca*. These were the true terrorists, recruited from the police, the militia, from professional cut-throats and delinquents, forming armed squads who went out on various missions, killing, looting and menacing. While the *mazorca* was a creature of Rosas, it was more terrorist than its creator: like many such death squads it acquired in action a semi-autonomy which its author believed he had to allow as a necessary means of government. Cruelty had its chronology. The incidence of terrorism varied according to the pressures on the regime, rising to a peak in 1839–42, when French intervention, internal rebellion, and unitarian invasion threatened to destroy the

Rosas state and inevitably produced violent counter-measures. Rosas never practised mass killing; selective assassination was enough to instil terror. And the peak of 1839–42 was not typical of the whole regime but rather an extraordinary manifestation of a general rule, namely, that terrorism existed to enforce submission to government policy in times of national emergency.

The system gave Rosas hegemony in Buenos Aires for over twenty years. But he could not apply the same strategy in the whole of Argentina. In the first place he did not govern 'Argentina'. The thirteen provinces governed themselves independently, though they were grouped in one general Confederation of the United Provinces of the Río de la Plata. Rosas accepted this and preferred inter-provincial relations to be governed by informal power rather than a written constitution. He refused to prepare an Argentine constitution, arguing that before the time was opportune for national organization the provinces must first organize themselves, that the progress of the parts must precede the ordering of the whole, and that the first task was to defeat the unitarians. Even without formal union, however, the provinces were forced to delegate certain common interests to the government of Buenos Aires, mainly defence and foreign policy, and also an element of legal jurisdiction, which enabled Rosas occasionally to reach out and arraign his enemies as federal criminals. Rosas, therefore, exercised some *de facto* control over the provinces; this he regarded as necessary, partly to prevent subversion and anarchy from seeping into Buenos Aires, partly to secure a broad base for economic and foreign policy and partly to acquire a national dimension for his regime. To impose his will he had to use some force, for the provinces did not accept him voluntarily. In the littoral and in the interior Rosas was seen as a caudillo who served the local interests of Buenos Aires; in these parts the loyalty of the *hacendados* and the service of their peons were not so easily procured. In many of the provinces of the interior the federal party had weaker economic roots and a narrower social base than in Buenos Aires; and in the remoter parts of the confederation Rosas could not instantly apply autocratic domination or regulate the use of terror. The unification of Argentina, therefore, meant the conquest of Argentina by Buenos Aires. Federalism gave way to *rosismo*, an informal system of control from the centre which Rosas achieved by patience and exercised with persistence.

The Federal Pact of 4 January 1831 between the littoral provinces, Buenos Aires, Entre Ríos, Santa Fe and later Corrientes, inaugurated a decade of relative stability in the east, though this could not disguise the hegemony of Buenos Aires, its control of customs revenue and river navigation, and its indifference to the economic interests of the other provinces. Rosas began to expand his power in the littoral in the years 1835–40. First, the governor of Entre Ríos, Pascual de Echagüe, moved away from the influence of the powerful Estanislao López and submitted himself unconditionally to Rosas. Then Corrientes, resentful of its economic subordination, declared war on its new metropolis; but the defeat and death of Governor Berón de Astrada at Pago Largo (31 March 1839) brought Corrientes too under the domination of Buenos Aires. Now there was only Santa Fe. Its governor, Estanislao López, was the most powerful of the provincial caudillos, experienced in the politics of the confederation and possessing a reputation equal to that of Rosas. But Rosas waited, and in 1838 López died. The subsequent election of Domingo Cullen, independent and anti-*rosista*, provoked a minor crisis, which was resolved by the triumph of Juan Pablo López, a protégé and now a satellite of Rosas. In each of the eastern provinces, therefore, Rosas succeeded gradually in imposing allied, dependent or weak governors. In Uruguay, an independent state since 1828, success did not come so easily, however. His ally, President Manuel Oribe, was overthrown in June 1838 by the rival caudillo, Fructuoso Rivera, backed by General Lavalle and acclaimed by the émigré unitarians. This was a serious challenge.

Rosas could not allow these local fires to remain unquenched, for there was danger of their being sucked into international conflagrations. The French government knew little about Rosas, but what it saw it did not like. Anxious to extend its trade and power in the Río de la Plata, and irritated by a dispute with Rosas over the status of its nationals under his jurisdiction, France authorized its naval forces to institute a blockade on Buenos Aires; this began on 28 March 1838 and was followed by an alliance between the French forces and Rosas's enemies in Uruguay. The French blockade, which lasted until 29 October 1840, harmed the regime in a number of ways. It caused the economy to stagnate and deprived the government of vital customs revenue; it de-stabilized the federal system and gave heart to dissidents in the littoral and the interior; and it led Rosas to rule with yet greater autocracy. But it had too little military muscle to be decisive. General Lavalle, assisted by the French and by other units from Montevideo, was expected to disembark at the port of Buenos Aires in support of the two rebel fronts within, the conspirators of the capital and the landowners of the south. In fact the various movements failed to synchronize. Lavalle led his forces not to Buenos Aires but to Entre Ríos, promising to free the Confederation from the tyrant and to give the provinces self-rule. But his association with the French, whom many considered aggressors against the Confederation, deprived him of support in Entre Ríos. He then turned aside to Corrientes, where Governor Pedro Ferré accepted him and declared against Rosas. But Corrientes was a long way from Buenos Aires, and by the time Lavalle's army reached striking distance it lacked money, arms and perhaps conviction. The French gave him naval support and arms, but could not supply military thrust. Lavalle entered the province of Buenos Aires on 5 August 1840 and finally appeared poised to attack Rosas. At this point his judgement, or his nerve, failed him. He paused to await French reinforcements, which did not come, and he lost the advantage of surprise. On 5 September, to the dismay of his associates and the bewilderment of historians, he withdrew towards Santa Fe, and his army, already demoralized by failure and desertion, began its long retreat towards the north.

The liberating expedition, humiliated in Buenos Aires, achieved a degree of success elsewhere. Its mere existence served to arouse Rosas's enemies in the interior. From April 1840 the Coalition of the North organized by Marco Avellaneda, governor of Tucumán, and including Salta, La Rioja, Catamarca and Jujuy, took the field under the command of General Aráoz de La Madrid in alliance with Lavalle, and threatened Rosas anew from the interior. Altogether, 1840 was a dangerous year for Rosas. Yet he survived, and at the beginning of 1841 the tide began to turn. The federal caudillos dominated Cuyo in the far west and began to strike back. Ex-president Oribe of Uruguay also fought bloodily for Rosas. On 28 November 1840 he defeated Lavalle's liberating army at Quebracho Herrado and completed the conquest of Córdoba. In the following year he destroyed the remnants of the Coalition of the North, first the spent forces of Lavalle at Famaillá (19 September 1841), then those of La Madrid at Rodeo del Medio (24 September 1841). These were cruel wars, and Rosas's generals wore down the enemy as much by terror as by battle. Lavalle himself was killed at Jujuy on 8 October 1841 on his way to Bolivia. The destruction of the unitarian forces in the interior, however, provoked rather than paralysed the littoral provinces. Their rebellion was eventually frustrated as much by their own disunity as by the energy of Oribe, who forced them to desist and disarm in December

1841. By February 1843 Oribe dominated the littoral. Rivera and the émigrés were enclosed within Montevideo, while Oribe and the *rosistas* were stationed at the Cerrito on the outskirts. And in the river the Buenos Aires fleet, completing the encirclement of the unitarians, destroyed the naval forces of Montevideo, imposed a blockade, and waited for victory. Yet the siege of Montevideo lasted for nine years.

British intervention was now the complicating factor. In the course of 1843 British naval forces broke the blockade of Montevideo and allowed supplies and recruits to reach the defenders. The action was crucial in saving the city, prolonging the war and pinning down Rosas to a long and painful siege. In addition to defending the independence of Uruguay, Britain also sought to open the rivers to free navigation: Rosas was branded as a threat to the first and an obstacle to the second. Anglo-French naval forces imposed a blockade on Buenos Aires from September 1845, and in November a joint expedition forced its way up the River Paraná convoying a merchant fleet to inaugurate direct trade to the interior. But the expedition encountered neither welcoming allies nor promising markets, only high customs duties, local suspicion, sluggish sales and the problem of returning down river. The blockade was no more effective than the expedition. This was a slow and clumsy weapon which hit trade rather than the enemy. Argentina's primitive economy made it virtually invulnerable to outside pressure. It could always revert to a subsistence economy and sit it out, waiting for pent-up trade to reopen while its cattle resources accumulated. As for the British, they simply blockaded their own trade. Rosas meanwhile gained great credit from the intervention of 1843–46. His defiance, determination and ultimate success placed him high in the pantheon of Argentine patriots. Argentina rallied round Rosas, and when the emergency was over and the British returned to seek peace and trade, they found the regime stronger than ever, the economy improving and a golden age beginning. But appearances were deceptive.

Rosas tamed the interior by relentless diplomacy and military force, establishing for himself an informal but enduring sovereignty. But he could not apply the same methods to the littoral provinces, where economic grievances coincided with powerful foreign interests. These provinces wanted trading rights for the river ports of the Paraná and the Uruguay, they wanted a share in customs revenue, and they wanted local autonomy. With outside assistance they could become the Achilles' heel of Rosas. The British had negotiated with the caudillos of Entre Ríos,

Corrientes and Paraguay for a coalition against Buenos Aires, but the governor of Entre Ríos, Justo José de Urquiza, was too careful to risk his future without the guarantee of powerful land forces. If the British could not supply these, Brazil could.

Brazil had its own account to settle with Rosas. Determined to prevent satellites of Buenos Aires becoming entrenched in Uruguay and the littoral, and anxious to secure free navigation of the river complex from Matto Grosso to the sea, Brazil was ready to move in opposition to the 'imperialism' of Rosas, or impelled by an imperialism of its own. An ally was at hand in Entre Ríos. Urquiza, like Rosas, was a rural caudillo, the owner of vast estates, the ruler of a personal fiefdom several hundred square miles in extent, with tens of thousands of cattle and sheep, and four *saladeros*. He made a fortune in the 1840s as a supplier to besieged Montevideo, an importer of manufactured goods and an exporter of gold to Europe. His private ambitions combined easily with provincial interests, and as a politician he was willing to supplant Rosas and initiate a constitutional reorganization of Argentina. He displayed, moreover, greater deference to education, culture and freedom than his rival and he had a superior reputation with the émigré intellectuals in Montevideo. In the person of Urquiza, therefore, the various strands of opposition came together, and he placed himself at the head of provincial interests, liberal exiles and Uruguayan patriots in an alliance which was backed by sufficient Brazilian money and naval forces to tip the balance against Rosas. The dictator was thus confronted not from within but from without, by the Triple Alliance of Entre Ríos, Brazil and Montevideo, which went into action from May 1851.

Buenos Aires was the privileged beneficiary of *rosismo*, but here too enthusiasm waned. Rosas was expected to guarantee peace and security; this was the justification of the regime. But in the wake of so many conflicts and so much waste he was still ready to wage war, even after 1850, relentlessly pursuing his objectives in Uruguay and Paraguay, always looking for one more victory. His army was now weak and disorganized, his military commanders were not to be trusted. By his terrorist methods and his de-politicization of Buenos Aires he had destroyed whatever existed of 'popular' support. And when, in early 1852, the invading army of the Triple Alliance advanced, his troops fled and the people in town and country did not rise in his support. On 3 February, at Monte Caseros, he was defeated: he rode alone from the field of battle, took refuge in the house of the British consul, boarded a British vessel, and sailed for England and exile.

Rosas was destroyed by military defeat. But the economic structure and the international links on which his system rested were already beginning to shift. Cattle-raising was the preferred policy of the Rosas regime. It required relatively low investments in land and technology, and, if practised on an extensive scale in large units capable of dealing with fluctuating export markets, it yielded very high profits. Investments had to be concentrated in cattle; therefore abundant, cheap and secure land was required. But cattle-raising gave a limited range of exports, mainly hides and jerked beef, for which international demand was not likely to grow. The market for hides was far from dynamic, even when continental Europe began to supplement Great Britain; and the demand for salt beef, limited to the slave economies of Brazil and Cuba, was more likely to contract than expand. The Rosas economy therefore faced present stagnation and future decline. Meanwhile, by the mid-1840s, other areas of South America were entering into competition. The *saladeros* of Rio Grande do Sul began to undercut Buenos Aires. And within the confederation the balance was no longer so overwhelmingly in Buenos Aires's favour. From 1843 the littoral provinces made the most of the peace which they enjoyed while Rosas concentrated his fighting forces on Uruguay. Cattle resources multiplied: Entre Ríos, with six million cattle, two million sheep and seventeen *saladeros*, was a new economic power. Competition was not yet critical; exports of jerked beef from Entre Ríos were still only 10 per cent of those of Buenos Aires. But there were political implications. The *estancieros* of Entre Ríos and Corrientes, profiting to some degree from the blockade of Buenos Aires, were not prepared to endure for ever the stranglehold exercised by their metropolis. Why should they sustain the commercial monopoly of Buenos Aires? Should they not by-pass its customs house and gain direct access to outside markets? To respond to these challenges the economy of Buenos Aires needed diversification and improvement. These came in the form of an alternative activity. Sheep farming had already begun to threaten the dominance of the cattle *estancia*. It was through the export of wool that Argentina would first develop its link with the world market, its internal productive capacity and its capital accumulation. Rosas thus became an anachronism, a legacy from another age.

The 'merinization' of Buenos Aires, the rise of a large sheep and wool economy, began in the 1840s and soon led to a scramble for new land. The external stimulus was the expansion of the European textile industry, which provided a secure export market. Internal conditions were also favourable, consisting of good soil and a local stock capable of improvement. In 1810 the province had a stock of 2–3 million sheep, but these were of poor quality and occupied marginal lands. By 1852 the number had grown to 15 million head, and in 1865 40 million. Wool exports increased from 333.7 tons in 1829, to 1,609.6 tons in 1840, to 7,681 tons in 1850; they then accelerated to 17,316.9 tons in 1860, 65,704.2 tons in 1870. In 1822 wool represented 0.94 per cent of the total value of exports from Buenos Aires, cattle hides 64.86 per cent; in 1836, 7.6 per cent and 68.4 per cent respectively; in 1851, 10.3 per cent and 64.9 per cent; in 1861, 35.9 per cent and 33.5 per cent; in 1865, 46.2 per cent and 27.2 per cent.

In the early years of independence *estancieros* showed little interest in improving breeds of sheep. It was left to a few Englishmen, John Harratt and Peter Sheridan in particular, to show the way: from the 1820s they began to purchase Spanish merinos, to preserve and refine the improved breeds and to export to Liverpool, encouraged by the almost total abolition of import duties on wool in England. The growing interest in sheep breeding was reflected in further imports of merinos from Europe and the United States in 1836–8, while the pampa sheep were also crossed with Saxony breeds. To improve the quality of sheep required not only the import of European breeds but also new forms of production – improvement of the grasses of the pampa, fencing of fields, building of sheds for shearing and storing wool, opening of wells. All this in turn raised the demand for labour. The gaucho was gradually replaced by the shepherd. Immigrant settlers arrived, either as hired labourers or as partners in profit-sharing schemes or as tenant farmers. Irish immigrants were particularly welcome as shepherds, but Basques and Galicians also came; and while this was not a massive immigration, it brought needed labour, skills and output. The new arrivals were often given a stake in the flocks of a sheep farmer through five-yearly contracts in which they became partners, receiving one-third of the increase and one-third of the wool in return for caring for the flock and paying expenses. An immigrant could earn enough in a few years to purchase an interest in half a flock and at the end of this time he had enough sheep and money to set up on his own. On the pampas between Buenos Aires and the River Salado sheep were beginning to drive cattle from the land; from the 1840s *estancia* after *estancia* passed into the hands of the sheep farmers. Cattle *estancias* survived, of course, either as mixed farms or on low and marshy lands whose reedy grasses were unsuitable for sheep. In general the lands which had been longest occupied, in the northern parts of the province, were the best adapted for sheep, while the new lands in the south were more suited to the breeding of cattle. Rosas himself had always encouraged sheep rearing, if not improvement, on his own *estancias*.

The large purchases of land by foreigners, the multiplication of sheep, the appearance of more sophisticated consumer trends, all were signs of a new Argentina. The city of Buenos Aires was growing and improving, as paved streets, horse-drawn public transport and gas supplies enhanced the environment. Near the towns the enclosure of lands for agriculture and horticulture proceeded, so that within ten years after Rosas all lands over a radius of 15–20 miles around the city of Buenos Aires were subdivided and enclosed as farms or market gardens, cultivated by Italians, Basques, French, British and German immigrants, and supplying an ever-growing urban market. Railways began to connect the interior of the province with the capital, and a fleet of steam vessels placed the various river ports in daily communication with the great entrepôt. Ocean steamers arrived and departed every two or three days. Between 1860 and 1880 the total value of imports from Europe doubled, comprising mainly textiles, hardware and machinery from Britain, and luxury goods from the continent. Meanwhile foreign trade was dominated by the customary commodities, by wool, hides and salt meat, which constituted more than 90 per cent of the total value of exports.

Economic performance differed, of course, between the three major regions. Buenos Aires maintained its dominance in spite of the obstacles to growth presented by civil and foreign wars, the exactions of the state and the raids of frontier Indians. The littoral lagged some way behind, its growth uneven but its prospects promising. Santa Fe, unlike Buenos Aires, had empty lands to fill; schemes of agricultural colonization were begun, offering a harsh life for the immigrants but a profitable one for those entrepreneurs who bought up land to re-sell to the colonists. Rosario was now an active river port, poised for further development. Entre Ríos, where Urquiza himself was the greatest proprietor, had a more established prosperity, with rich cattle *estancias* and sheep farms, and trading links with Brazil and Uruguay. Foreigners now penetrated the up-river markets more frequently. Even Corrientes, part *estancia*, part tobacco plantation, where English bottled beer was drunk on all social occasions, was emerging at last from a subsistence economy. The interior, on the other hand, was the underdeveloped region of Argentina, its production damaged by distance from the east coast and by cheap competition from Europe, its only compensating outlet being the Chilean mining market. Economic poverty and the concentration of usable land in large estates drove the poor off the soil into the hands of caudillos, who, while Buenos Aires and the littoral were moving into another age, still looked towards the past.

The defeat of Rosas did not destroy existing structures. The hegemony of the landed oligarchy survived. The dominance of Buenos Aires continued. And inter-provincial conflict simply entered another stage. The provinces conferred upon Urquiza, the victor of Caseros, the title Provisional Director of the Argentine Confederation and gave him a national role; he in turn decreed the nationalization of the customs and free navigation of the rivers Paraña and Uruguay. But Buenos Aires broke away, refused to place itself at the mercy of other provinces, some of them little more than deserts, and remained aloof from the constituent congress which Urquiza convened. The constitution, approved on 1 May 1853, reflected a number of influences – previous Argentine constitutions, the example of the United States and the bitter lessons of past conflict. But perhaps the most powerful influence was the political thought of Juan Bautista Alberdi, who advised a just balance between central power and provincial rights, and a programme of immigration, education and modernization. The constitution provided for a federal republic and incorporated the classical freedoms and civil rights. It divided power between the executive, the legislative and the judiciary. The legislature consisted of two houses, a senate to which each provincial legislature elected two members, and a chamber of deputies elected by male suffrage in public voting. While assuring local self-government to the provinces, the constitution gave countervailing authority to the federal government. The president, who was chosen by an electoral college for six years, was given strong executive powers: he could introduce his own bills, appoint and dismiss his ministers without reference to congress. The president was also empowered to intervene in any province in order to preserve republican government against internal disorder or foreign attack; to this effect he could remove local administrations and impose federal officials. The economic provisions of the constitution also addressed federal problems. Inter-provincial tariffs were abolished. The income from Buenos Aires customs house was to be nationalized and not to remain the exclusive property of the province of

Buenos Aires, which was another reason for *porteño* resistance. Urquiza was elected president for six years. But he did not preside over a nation state. A sense of national identity did not exist, or else it was not strong enough to overcome provincial and personal loyalties. While the provinces accepted the Constitution of 1853, they continued to be ruled by caudillos, even if they were called governors, and the confederation was essentially a network of personal loyalties to its president.

Argentina was now split into two states, on the one hand the city and province of Buenos Aires, ruled by its governor (from 1860 Bartolomé Mitre) and a liberal party, on the other the Argentine confederation, consisting of thirteen provinces under Urquiza and a federal party. Whereas in the past the provinces had refused to accept the domination of Buenos Aires, now Buenos Aires refused to co-operate with the provinces, or to obey a constitution which it considered a facade for *caudillismo*. And Buenos Aires could not be forced into a confederation against its wishes: it was powerful, it was rich, and its customs house was still the chief source of revenue in Argentina, the focus of foreign trade, and the property of one province. The confederation therefore established its capital at Paraná, in Entre Ríos, where Urquiza, whatever his constitutional sentiments, ruled as an old-style caudillo, though with the added role of leader of the littoral and the interior. As first president, Urquiza signed commercial treaties with Britain, France and the United States, and opened the rivers Paraná and Uruguay to free navigation for foreign trade. In normal times almost 70 per cent of imports into Buenos Aires were destined for the provinces. Now it was the policy of the confederation to free itself from Buenos Aires, trade directly with the outside world and make Rosario a new entrepôt. Urquiza was personally involved in commercial enterprises with Europe, in schemes for the establishment of import-export houses in Rosario and in the search for outside capital. But foreign shipping did not respond to the new opportunities and continued to unload at Buenos Aires: the fact remained that Rosario was not yet a sufficient market or entrepôt to justify an extra five-day journey. Further stimulus was provided in 1857 when a differential tariff was issued in the hope of tempting European trade into by-passing Buenos Aires: but even this, which only lasted until 1859, could not overcome the facts of economic life. Commercial war therefore gave way to military conflict.

By 1859 both sides were ready for a new trial by battle. Urquiza's army defeated that of Mitre at the battle of Cepeda, but Buenos Aires accepted incorporation into the confederation with great reluctance. It still had reserves of money and manpower, and in 1861 it fought back once more. The two sides met at the battle of Pavón, an encounter which was interpreted if not as a victory for Mitre at least as a defeat for the confederation, demonstrably incapable of imposing its will on the recalcitrant province. Urquiza withdrew from the battlefield, apparently convinced that if the confederation could not win quickly it would not win at all. He took his forces to Entre Ríos to guard at least his provincial interests, and left the confederation weakened and disorientated. Mitre meanwhile advanced on various fronts. He sent his military columns in support of liberal regimes in the provinces of the littoral and the interior. He negotiated with Urquiza from a position of strength and persuaded him voluntarily to dismantle the confederation. And he pressed the politicians of his own province of Buenos Aires to accept his programme of national reorganization and to proceed by negotiation rather than force.

The resultant settlement was a compromise between unitarism and federalism. Mitre accepted the constitution of 1853, with its bias towards centralism and presidential power, and was then declared national as well as provincial leader. Thus, in 1861, the idea of a federation, with Buenos Aires its centre and the interior represented there, was accepted. And Mitre, a *porteño*, a hero of the siege of Montevideo, was elected first constitutional president for the whole nation in October 1862. Now, the union of the provinces was achieved and for the first time Argentina was called Argentina and not by a clumsy circumlocution.

The opportunity for national reorganization after 1862 could have been lost had not power been held by two distinguished presidents, Bartolomé Mitre (1862–8) and Domingo F. Sarmiento (1868–74), intellectuals and men of letters as well as politicians and statesmen. Both had given many years of service towards the ideal of a greater Argentina; both now stood for three objectives, national unity, liberal institutions and modernization. In combating the confederation Mitre had fought not simply for one particular province but against fragmentation and *caudillismo*. He sought to place and keep Buenos Aires at the head of a united Argentina, and he fought on after 1862. For the caudillos did not die without a struggle. In 1863 and again in 1866–8 Mitre had to suppress rebellions in the interior. The political occasion of these insurrections was caudillo resistance to the new order. But the deeper causes were the depressed economies of the interior, the impoverishment of the provinces and their inability to sustain their populations in occupation or subsistence. Lack of work and food drove the rural peoples to the life of *montoneros*, to live in effect by banditry and booty. Forces of this kind sustained Angel Vicente Peñaloza, 'El Chacho', caudillo of wild and remote La Rioja, where one school sufficed for the entire province but where the caudillo provided personally for the welfare of his followers. When El Chacho revolted in 1863, Mitre permitted Sarmiento, governor of San Juan and a federal pro-consul in the interior, to wage a war to the death against the rebels, and the forces of Sarmiento, defending civilization with barbarism, killed their prisoners and displayed the head of El Chacho on a pole. In 1866–7 Felipe Varela, former officer of El Chacho, invaded western Argentina from Chile and raised another *montonera*, but he too was defeated and his followers mercilessly crushed by the national army. The end of the *montonera* was in sight, though it evinced further paroxysms before it was extinguished. Urquiza, reconciled now to the central state, held aloof from the provincial movements which he was supposed to patronize but now disavowed, and played his own role in supporting the new Argentina. But in the end he fell a victim to the system which he had once represented; he was assassinated in his own *estancia*, by order of a rival caudillo and former protégé, in April 1870. His killer, Ricardo López Jordán, kept alive in Entre Ríos the spirit of rebellion and the cult of *caudillismo*, until 1876. In the meantime, as president, Sarmiento, who declared that he was a *porteño* in the provinces and a provincial in Buenos Aires, had continued the work of Mitre, had defended national unity with the sword and the pen and had been even more ruthless with rebels.

In spite of provincial traditions and caudillo resistance, central power and national organization survived and took root. They were assisted by the growth of institutions with an Argentine dimension, the press, the postal service, the National Bank, the railway system. But two particular agencies promoted national identity and unity – federal justice and the national army. By law of 1862 a national judicial power was established, and in 1865–8 the Argentine Civil Code was drawn up. The supreme court and the various lower courts completed the structure of the modern state. The supreme court had power to declare unconstitutional any laws or decrees, national or provincial, in conflict with the supreme law, and thus became the interpreter of the constitution, though it was not competent to decide conflicts between the powers. The executive had the right of intervention in the provinces, a right which became more effective once it was backed by a national army. By decree of 26 January 1864 the government created a permanent army of 6,000 men distributed between artillery, infantry and cavalry. A Military Academy was established in 1869 and the formation of a professional officer corps was begun. The law of recruitment of 21 September 1872 anticipated national conscription. This was the institutional framework for the new army. But a more effective impetus was given by its operations during the rebellions of the caudillos and the War of Paraguay, when it increased its numbers and added to its experience. The army gave the president real power and enabled him to extend the executive's reach into the furthest corners of Argentina. Gradually the local oligarchies became compliant, and in return for collaboration they were offered a place in a national ruling class.

The political principles animating the presidencies of Mitre and Sarmiento were those of classical liberalism. Mitre led an identifiable Liberal Party, and after Pavón his strategy of national reorganization rested not only on the extension of federal power but also on the proliferation of liberal governments throughout the provinces, instruments of union by voluntary choice. Liberalism represented an intellectual aristocracy, survivors and heirs of the generation of 1837, now free to apply their ideas, to promote political and material progress, the rule of law, primary and secondary education, to dispel the barbarism which Sarmiento abhorred and to make the poor gaucho into a useful man. But the liberal elite held out little for the popular masses: for the gauchos and peons, who were beyond the political pale, their status to serve, their function to labour. They were represented by nothing but an epic poem, *Martín Fierro*, lamenting the departure of a noble past. The only opposition recognized by the Liberal Party was that of the federalists, who followed Urquiza and tradition and who clearly belonged to the political nation. The Liberals split into two groups during Mitre's presidency, the autonomists, who came to incorporate those federalists left leaderless by the death of Urquiza, and the nationalists, who continued to preserve pure *mitrista* principles. Meanwhile in the provinces liberalism, like federalism, was often simply another name for *caudillismo*, and political party bosses soon became known as 'caudillos'.

Modernization meant growth through exports from the rural sector, investment in a new infrastructure and immigration. Some local capital was employed in the primary sector, in cattle *estancias*, sheep farms and sugar estates. But investment depended essentially upon the import of foreign capital, mainly from Britain. Up to the early 1870s British trade to Argentina was predominantly a trade in textiles, and British investment was confined to commerce and private *estancias*. But from 1860 new trends appeared. First, several joint-stock enterprises were organized in 1861–5. These were established by British entrepreneurs with British capital and were applied to railways and banks. On 1 January 1863 the first branch of the London and River Plate Bank was opened in Buenos Aires, and in 1866 the Rosario branch went into operation. From this time iron and steel, metal manufactures and coal became more important among British exports to Argentina. The second stage comprised investment in development, encouraged by Argentina and promoted by the British who wanted to improve the market for their goods. In 1860 a loan of £2.5 million was marketed in London by Barings on behalf of the Argentine government. This was the beginning of a steady flow of capital from Britain to Argentina, much of it applied to the infrastructure, either as direct investment or as loans to the state. More substantial foreign investment had to await the period after 1870, when banks, factories and public utilities became major recipients. But one area of investment was already established, the railways, and these were essential to economic growth, bringing out agricultural exports from the vast hinterland of Buenos Aires and carrying in imported goods.

The first track was opened in 1857; this ran six miles west from Buenos Aires and was built with private local capital. During the 1860s the Northern and Southern Railways began to fan out from Buenos Aires; and in 1870 the Central Argentine Railway linked Rosario and Córdoba, and opened up the great central plains. For this line the government contracted with British capital, guaranteeing a minimum return and granting adjacent lands, necessary concessions to attract capital to an empty territory, whose value lay in future prospects rather than present performance. In twenty years 1,250 miles of track was laid in Argentina. Meanwhile communications with the outside world were improving, as steam replaced sail. The Royal Mail Company began regular service to the River Plate in 1853; Lamport and Holt in 1863; the Pacific Steam Navigation Company in 1868. The journey from England to the River Plate was cut to 22 days in a fast ship. Steamships also joined the river ports, and by 1860 a number of services were in operation. Improved docks and harbours became an urgent need, as did cable and telegraph links with Europe, and all these would soon be provided by foreign capital and technology.

The new Argentina also needed people. The growth of federal power and the hegemony of Buenos Aires in the period 1852–70 was not simply a constitutional or military process. It also represented demographic and economic forces. Argentina's population grew more rapidly after 1852, from 935,000 to 1,736,923 in 1869. The balance in favour of the coast became more pronounced. The province of Buenos Aires contained 28 per cent of the whole population in 1869; the littoral 48.8 per cent. The city of Buenos Aires increased its inhabitants from 90,076 in 1854 to 177,787 in 1869, of whom 89,661 were Argentines, 88,126 foreigners. Immigration now significantly fed population growth. After 1852 the confederation made a special effort to attract immigrants from Europe. The Constitution of 1853 gave foreigners virtually all the rights of Argentines without the obligations. In the years 1856–70 European families were brought in by the provincial government of Santa Fe to form agricultural colonies, pioneers of the 'cerealization' of the pampas. After 1862 immigration became a national policy and offices were set up in Europe, though the government did not finance the process, leaving passage and settlement to the free play of economic forces. From the late 1850s about 15,000 immigrants a year entered Argentina.

Sarmiento and others, influenced by the American model of frontier expansion, preached the virtues of agriculture and small farms, the importance of settling the immigrants in rural areas, the need to provide land for colonization and to discourage speculation and latifundism. But the actual result was different. The government viewed land as a valuable resource which could be sold or leased for fiscal purposes. Cattle and sheep raising were the basic activities of the country. The *estancieros* formed a powerful interest group, linked to the commercial leaders of the city; they regarded access to land as a vital factor for stock raising. And land speculation, either by the purchase of public land to be sold later at a profit or by subdivision and subletting of holdings, was too lucrative a business to stop. By the 1880s, therefore, most of the public land of the province of Buenos Aires, by a series of laws, had been transferred as private property to latifundists and speculators: and the pattern was repeated in other provinces. No doubt in the decades after 1850 the trend was towards smaller holdings, as the pampas became effectively occupied, land became scarce and expensive, sheep farming brought subdivision of property and new owners bought their way in and displaced the old. But this was a trend from superlatifundism to mere latifundism.

National organization delimited as well as defined Argentina. The vice-royalty was a thing of the past; Uruguay and Paraguay were left intact, although not in peace. To complete the victory of union and liberalism, the Argentine government thought it necessary to destroy the power of Paraguay, an enduring and perhaps contagious example of the centrifugal and conservative forces which appealed to federal caudillos. Argentina also wanted a stable, friendly and preferably liberal Uruguay. When Venancio Flores, caudillo of the *colorado* party, invaded Uruguay from Argentina in April 1863 and began his ascent to power, he enjoyed the support of President Mitre, assistance from the Argentine navy and funds from sympathizers in Buenos Aires. Flores was also aided by Brazil, which sought his alliance in its own confrontation with Paraguay, a dispute over territory and navigation. Thus, in the course of 1864, Argentina moved towards a triple alliance with Brazil and Uruguay against Paraguay.

A war against Paraguay was by no means a popular cause in Argentina. It was regarded by many as an illiberal expedient, whose results would be to magnify the power of the state, aggrandize the national army, and, while enabling some to profit from supplying the armed forces, to lay intolerable burdens on the community. Brazil, moreover, was regarded as an obnoxious ally: the shedding of Argentine blood and expenditure of Argentine money to support a slave state in its imperialist ambitions was condemned by many as contrary to Argentine interests. The war was therefore divisive. It also gave the provincial caudillos a chance to revert to a more primitive Argentina in opposition to Buenos Aires and in support of regional interests. In the event, the ruler of Paraguay, Francisco Solano López, did not have the skill to exploit these divisions within Argentina, or between Argentina and Brazil, and he recklessly wasted his assets. When, in January 1865, Solano López requested permission from Argentina to cross Misiones to reach Brazil, he was rebuffed, and in March he declared war on Argentina and invaded Corrientes. This enabled Mitre to carry through the Brazilian alliance without political disaster at home. He thus declared war on Paraguay, joining Brazil and the government of Flores in Uruguay. As for Argentina's own dissidents, they were now leaderless, for Urquiza committed himself to the war and became one of the army's principal suppliers.

The overt object of the triple alliance was merely to secure free navigation of the rivers and to crush the Paraguayan dictator; the war was presented as a crusade on behalf of civilization and liberty. This was propaganda. The treaty of alliance contained secret clauses providing for the annexation of disputed territory in northern Paraguay by Brazil and regions in the east and west of Paraguay by Argentina; and the war would not cease until the total destruction of the Paraguayan government. Basically the allies were determined to remove the focus of attraction which a strong Paraguay exercised on their peripheral regions. After a long and harrowing war (1865–70), Argentina prised from a prostrate Paraguay territory in Misiones between the Paraná and the Uruguay and other land further west.

The Paraguayan war coincided for Argentina with monetary instability and a crisis in Europe to throw the Argentine economy out of gear. The markets for cattle products and for wool exports contracted and production declined; even sheep farming suffered depression. The internal causes of the crisis lay in the land and derived from an excessive expansion of the flocks in the relatively restricted areas of soft grasses suitable for sheep-raising. Overstocking coincided with a severe drought, which was a further setback to owners of cattle and sheep. The policy of the state did not help. The law of November 1864 decreeing the sale of all public lands available within the frontier set prices which were too high and aggravated the rural crisis. So a period of expansion and land hunger was followed by a slump.

Recovery was rapid, but the experience caused a re-appraisal of Argentina's problems and prospects. Worried *estancieros* began to discuss the need for diversification of agrarian production, modernization of methods and greater capital investment. There was talk, too, of combining agriculture and livestock, investing urban capital in the rural sector, incorporating new land, establishing model farms. Innovatory ideas of this kind were characteristic of the group of *estancieros* who, in 1866, founded the Argentine Rural Society as a medium of debate and development. A mood of protectionism grew. One of the most notable, though abortive, projects of the Society was to establish the first textile factory in the country, in the hope that a national textile industry might develop, using Argentina's own raw materials and freeing her from dependence on foreign markets and foreign imports. Rural labour, its plight and its supply, became a matter of increasing concern. The insecurity, impoverishment and low status of the peon had often been attributed to Rosas and his military exactions, but there were few signs of improvement after 1852, and the demands of the Paraguayan War became a new scourge of the pampas. The need for more people was urgent and accepted. And mass immigration, which began as a drive to fill the desert, ended by swelling the towns. Argentina had come to the end of one age and the beginning of another.

2

THE GROWTH OF THE ARGENTINE
ECONOMY, c. 1870–1914

A traveller arriving in the Río de la Plata region in the 1870s would have been struck first by the width of the estuary and then, on entering the port of Buenos Aires, by the lowness and simplicity of the buildings. Travelling inland, he would have been stunned by the vast expanses of flat, treeless land, the pampas, stretching away as far as the eye could see, where the overwhelming sense of solitude was only interrupted by the sight of a herd of cattle, or by the sudden appearance of an ostrich or some other example of the local fauna. At that time, the most important commercial activity was carried on in a coastal strip along the estuary of the Río de la Plata and the Paraná, and along the southern course of the river Uruguay in its navigable reaches. The shortage of wood, in addition to the huge distances, was an obstacle to the establishment of permanent settlements inland: prospective settlers were obliged to transport building materials from distant ports or urban areas. Apart from the Paraná, a section of the Uruguay, and the Río Negro, which was in territory still occupied by the Indians, the rivers of Argentina were not navigable, and railways were only just beginning to be built. Moreover, Indians still occupied what was called the 'desert', not far beyond the populated areas of Buenos Aires and Santa Fe provinces, and Indian raids were common. Apart from the provincial capitals, administrative centres which dated from colonial times, there was no extensive network of towns in the interior, and the rural population was sparse. Nevertheless, although there was much to discourage settlement and the putting of land to productive use, the temperate climate was favourable, and conditions, though harsh, were less harsh than in some parts of Europe.

* Translated from the Spanish by Dr David Brookshaw; translation revised by the Editor. The Editor wishes to thank Dr Colin Lewis for his help in the final preparation of this chapter.

During the first half of the nineteenth century, in the area of effective settlement, the north-west and the riverine and coastal corridor which joined it to Buenos Aires, the main economic activity had been cattle ranching which required little labour and capital. Hides and jerked beef were produced for export, and meat for internal consumption. It was not that there was no agriculture, but the high cost of transport limited agricultural activity to the areas near urban centres where the markets were located. The cost of overland transport meant that until the 1870s it was more convenient to import wheat and flour.

Whereas during the colonial period the centre of economic life lay in upper Peru, with the mining camps of Potosí joined to Buenos Aires by a trade route that went through Salta, Tucumán, and Córdoba, the first half of the nineteenth century had witnessed the formation of another economic axis, based initially in the so-called Mesopotamian provinces (Entre Ríos and Corrientes) and later in the province of Buenos Aires, where cattle ranching activities developed, using the river system as an outlet for their products. Later, new circumstances required the expansion of the frontiers in the search for new territories, to the west and south, in Buenos Aires, in Córdoba and Santa Fe, and also in what is now the province of La Pampa.

For it should not be assumed that there were no changes prior to 1870. Leather found a market in the industrialized countries, and there was a significant increase in trade, despite the fluctuations caused, among other things, by blockades and wars. To exports of hides and jerked beef were added fats and tallows by the 1840s. Moreover, sheep rearing had also begun in the 1820s, and exports of unwashed wool became important during the 1840s. In 1822, Argentine exports reached five million silver pesos and stayed at this level until the 1840s, despite considerable annual variations. They then increased, and towards the end of the period reached seven million. Another jump in exports occurred in the period after 1860, when they reached 14 million, and a decade later, in 1870, they had increased still more, to 30 million silver pesos.[1] The increase in the value of Argentina's exports resulted, on the one hand, from the recovery of international prices, which had been declining from the 1820s until the late 1840s, and, on the other hand, from the increasing importance of fats, tallow, and above all wool. Wool represented 10.8 per cent of

[1] Francisco Latzina, *El comercio exterior argentino* (Buenos Aires, 1916).

exports in 1837, rose to 12.5 per cent in 1848, and reached 33.7 per cent in 1859.[2]

The expansion of wool production and exports came in response to growing demand from the countries of continental Europe, in particular France, and from the United States. Wool production required a more intensive use of land, labour and capital. In order to provide better care for the sheep, it was necessary to move manpower to the rural areas and thus to improve both transport facilities and internal security. Furthermore the overall growth of the stock of animals, especially sheep – the number of sheep rose from 23 million in 1846 to 70 million in 1884, cattle from 10 million to 23 million – led to an additional demand for new land. Nevertheless, in the 1870s, the country, with a basically pastoral economy, still had vast tracts of land, much of which was not utilized, lying beyond the 'frontier'. Population was sparse, the railway network was rudimentary, port facilities were inadequate and capital was scarce.

FACTORS OF PRODUCTION

Land

Extraordinary economic growth in Argentina between 1870 and 1914, sustained at an annual rate of approximately 5 per cent[3] was, according to many authors, the result of important changes in international trade, changes which brought the New Worlds of America and Oceania into the mainstream of world commerce. It has also been stressed that the decisive factor in the establishment of new trade routes was the reduction in costs of maritime transport. No less important than the increase in world trade and a certain international division of labour was the movement of factors of production, such as capital and labour, between continents which made such changes possible. Nevertheless, this outline, while correct in general terms, does not reflect all the complexity and richness of an historical process which had other less obvious facets. Numerous obstacles and difficulties had to be faced; and various adjustments were needed so that, on the supply side, an adequate

[2] Jonathan C. Brown, A socio-economic history of Argentina, 1776–1860 (Cambridge, 1979). See also Tulio Halperín Donghi, 'La expansión ganadera en la campaña de Buenos Aires', Desarrollo Económico, 3 (April–September 1963). And on Argentina before 1870 in general, see Lynch, this volume, ch. 1.
[3] Carlos Díaz Alejandro, Essays on the economic history of the Argentine Republic (New Haven, 1970), 3.

response might be made to real or potential increases in world demand. Studies of the period have concentrated on aspects related to the growth of demand in the principal centres of consumption of primary products; supply adjustments in the main primary producing economies have still not been studied in depth.

Producers needed to reorganize production so as to increase the output of those commodities (cereals, and later meat in the case of Argentina), where the degree of comparative advantage was greatest. To achieve this, hitherto unused productive resources had to be exploited. In Argentina there was land in abundance, but the vast expanses of territory where Indian tribes still roamed freely had not been settled. In addition, colonization of the land presupposed adequate means of transport in order to take settlers to isolated areas and bring products from those areas to market. How and when did this process come about? Although the complexity of the process defies the construction of a facile chronology, the incorporation of vast tracts of land is the most important starting point.

During the 1870s, it became more and more obvious that the frontier needed to be extended in order to accommodate the growing flocks of sheep and to facilitate the relocation of *criollo* cattle away from prime lands now given over to sheep. The increase in stock led to over-grazing and soil erosion in the land in longest use, which was curious for a new country. At that time, there was no surplus population in search of unoccupied land, at least until the 1870s and 1880s. Rather, there was a need to seek new pastures for an ever larger stock of cattle. However, curiously enough, during the 1870s this expansion in cattle was not due to any significant increase in international demand transmitted by the price mechanism; rather it was due to a different phenomenon. The prices of agricultural exports (hides, wool, etc.) declined after the mid 1870s. This led to a fall in the profitability of livestock raising, which could only be compensated for by an increase in the volume of production, provided that this increase in output could be achieved at lower costs in order to ensure profit. The only way of doing this was through the incorporation of new lands at low or even zero cost, so as to make it possible to increase stocks (capital goods) at minimal additional cost to increase output (wool or hides), thereby increasing earnings. A characteristic of livestock raising is that it produces both consumer goods and capital. The greater availability of grazing land means that more animals may be kept as breeding stock, thus increasing the capital goods. So the incorporation of new lands had the definite effect of increasing the herds and expanding production at minimal cost, thereby compensating for the fall in prices and maintaining the profitability of cattle raising. Thus expansion was not generated by a rise in prices but by the availability of new land and the need to reduce costs in order to maintain the economic viability of stock raising.

It is true that territorial expansion was made possible by an earlier upturn in economic activity, which also made possible the military occupation of the new territories. The fact that the old frontier could be reached more quickly thanks to the railway, and that the Indian campaign of 1879–80 led by General Julio A. Roca could be conducted from a considerable distance thanks to the telegraph, was an important element in the conquest of the desert, but did not mean that the rail network, settlers and arable farming were introduced into the new areas. On the contrary, by 1881 zones that had been settled beyond the Indian frontier of 1876 were almost totally given over to cattle. The proportion of settlers involved in arable agriculture was minimal. It was only later, in areas reached by the railways, that arable farming began to expand and the grain frontier advanced beyond the old cattle frontier. In the early 1880s the railways had not reached the areas which were incorporated after the 'conquest of the desert', and which amounted to 30 million hectares (about 8 million in the province of Buenos Aires, 5 million in Santa Fe, 2 million in Córdoba, and another 14 million in the whole territory of La Pampa).

In contrast, the expansion of agriculture in the late 1880s and 1890s, and especially the production of wheat, first in Santa Fe between 1888 and 1895, then in Buenos Aires after 1895, was directly linked to the growth of the rail network. It grew from 732 kilometres of track in 1870 and 1,313 kilometres in 1880 to 9,254 kilometres in 1890. The tonnage of goods transported increased from 275,000 tons in 1870 and 742,000 tons in 1880 to 5.42 million tons in 1890. In 1884, in the north of the province of Buenos Aires, the area of older settlement, some 7.1 per cent of the land was under cultivation; in the central and southern regions, which included extensive territories incorporated during the 1870s and early 1880s, 1.1 per cent and 0.3 per cent respectively was under cultivation. By 1896, 44.5 per cent of the north was under cultivation, 28.3 per cent of the centre, and 14.6 per cent of the south. And some 83.7 per cent of wheat, and 53.7 per cent of maize produced was transported by rail.[4]

Regional characteristics, but more especially proximity to markets (which was influenced by transport costs), determined the pattern of land use at different times and in different areas during this period. In isolated areas, where there were no navigable rivers and no railways, and where transport costs were therefore high, there was less likelihood of settlement and the development of arable farming. In such areas there was extensive livestock raising on holdings of considerable size worked by the landowners. There was also a system of tenancy and share-cropping, especially in sheep rearing, but it never became as widespread as it did in arable farming in later years. In regions where soil conditions and transport costs allowed, agriculture expanded. Between 1888 and 1895 the area under cultivation increased from 2.5 million to almost 5 million hectares. The most notable expansion occurred in the province of Santa Fe where the actual size of the holdings was smaller, and a great many were owner occupied. At the end of the nineteenth century and during the first two decades of the twentieth, a new wave of agricultural expansion occurred in lands which had already been either totally or partially given over to cattle raising. One of the features of this process is that it did not lead to arable farming replacing cattle raising; rather, the two complemented each other. The result was that on cattle ranches certain areas were set aside for grain production and let out to tenant farmers, whose number thus greatly increased during the period from 1885 to 1914.

The existence of such a large number of tenant farmers has been influential in shaping a common picture of Argentine historiography which has an honourable ancestry among authors of such importance as Miguel Angel Cárcano and Jacinto Oddone, not to mention more recent scholars like Sergio Bagú and James Scobie. Scobie has the following to say on the subject:

Those whose forebears had been able to acquire and keep enormous land grants or who now secured estates enjoyed a gilded existence. Lands whose only worth had been in their herds of wild cattle, lands which could be reached only by

---

[4] On the connection between railway expansion and the incorporation of new lands, see Colin M. Lewis, 'La consolidación de la frontera argentina a fines de la década del setenta. Los Indios, Roca y los ferrocarriles', in Gustavo Ferrari and Ezequiel Gallo (eds.), *La Argentina del ochenta al centenario* (Buenos Aires, 1980); Roberto Cortés Conde, 'Patrones de asentamiento y explotación agropecuaria en los nuevos territorios argentinos (1890–1910)', in Alvaro Jara (ed.), *Tierras nuevas* (Mexico, 1969).

horseback or oxcart, land occupied largely by hostile Indians underwent a total
transformation. British capital had built railroads. Pastoral techniques had been
improved and the resources of the pampas were being utilized more thoroughly.
Immigrants, newly arrived from European poverty, were available not only for
railroad and urban construction but also as sharecroppers, tenant farmers, or
peons to raise corn, wheat, flax, and alfalfa, to put up fences, and to tend cattle
and sheep. Under such conditions land provided an annual return of from 12 to
15 per cent to the owner and land values often rose 1000 per cent in a decade.
Those who already had land, power, or money monopolized the newly
developed wealth of the pampas. The man who tilled the soil or cared for the
herds eked out a meager existence. If he had left Europe because of poverty and
despair, at least he did not starve in Argentina, but few incentives were offered
him and, for the most part, title to the land was beyond his grasp.[5]

The opinions of those who have supported this thesis could be
summed up as follows: in order to increase earnings from the rent of land
the large landowners restricted the supply of land by keeping it off the
market; they then left the land they monopolized uncultivated. But in
fact the situation was far more complex; the purchase and sale of land was
far more fluid than supposed; and the size of estates, as well as the system
of tenancy, was linked to other circumstances related to the particular
pattern of agricultural and pastoral development in the region. In fact, it
happened that whereas towards the end of the century large amounts of
land were becoming available as the railways created new links to the
markets, there were still not enough farmers prepared to work it. There
was therefore no limited resource nor an unsatisfied demand for land. In
contrast, during the second decade of the twentieth century, with twenty
million hectares under cultivation, new farmers would compete with the
old for the best land in a situation where there was no possibility of
incorporating new land suitable for agriculture.

The system of tenancy did not hinder access to landownership. In
many cases, indeed, it constituted an intermediate step towards it. As a
tenant rather than an owner, the farmer's labour yielded better returns
because the scale was greater. Moreover, it provided full employment for
a family working group who had immigrated precisely because of the
availability of land. Finally, there was a fairly active market in medium-
and small-sized estates, while transactions in larger properties were
fewer. In addition, although land prices rose during the 1880s, they fell

[5] James Scobie, *Revolution on the pampas: a social history of Argentine wheat* (Austin, Texas, 1964), 5.

during the 1890s and the possibilities of acquiring land increased. In his annual report for 1893 the British consul commented:

The prices of lands were exceedingly low in gold in 1891 and 1892; now they are dearer, but are still fairly cheap. The fall in the value of land after the crisis of 1890 was extraordinary . . . The price of the land is soon paid off with good seasons, and the facilities of becoming landowners on a small scale are great. All lands in the Argentine Republic are freehold. The transfer and the registration of properties and the examination of titles is remarkably simple as compared with England.[6]

During the first decade of the twentieth century, the price of land again increased dramatically. This was, however, not a case of speculation, but reflected a significant increase in the profitability of land, especially land given over to livestock due to the shift to meat production and the introduction of British breeds.

Labour supply

The shortage of manpower in Argentina was a persistent problem throughout the nineteenth century and, from the time of the first proposals on the matter by Bernardino Rivadavia in the 1820s, had prompted the idea of pursuing a policy of immigration and colonization which before 1870 met with scant success. Apart from the little interest shown in the subject by landowners, and the complete absence of any interest on the part of political leaders such as Juan Manuel de Rosas, who supposedly did not encourage projects for colonization by foreigners, no consideration was given to the fact that the major difficulty in settling colonists in areas far inland lay in the high cost of transport, which hindered the marketing of products over long distances. From the first years of the Confederation, more successful attempts were made to encourage immigration and colonization. In 1869, the year of the First National Census, Argentina had a population of under 1.8 million inhabitants. By 1895, twenty-five years later, according to the Second National Census the population had grown to almost 4 million, and by the time of the third Census in 1914, it had reached almost 8 million (see table 1). This striking increase could scarcely have been achieved through natural growth alone. It was due in

---

[6] Great Britain, Foreign Office, Report for the year 1893 on the agricultural condition of the Argentine Republic (Annual Series, 1893, Diplomatic and Consular Reports on Trade and Finance, No. 1283), 1893.

Table 1. *Population and rates of growth*

Year	Population	Average annual increase per 1,000 inhabitants
1869	1,736,923[a]	28.5
1895	3,954,911	30.4
1914	7,885,237	34.8

Note: [a]Excluding the indigenous population, and Argentinians abroad or serving in the army in Paraguay.
Sources: **1869**: Argentina, *Primer censo de la República Argentina, 1869* (Buenos Aires, 1872); **1895**: Argentina, *Segundo censo de la República Argentina, 1895*, vol. II (Buenos Aires, 1898); **1914**: Argentina, *Tercer censo nacional, 1914*, vol. II (Buenos Aires, 1916); Zulma L. Recchini de Lattes and Alfredo E. Lattes, *Migraciones en la Argentina* (Buenos Aires, 1969).

large measure to foreign immigration. Between 1870 and 1914 almost 6 million immigrants, mostly Spanish and Italian, arrived in Argentina, although only a little over half of these settled permanently (for annual figures, see table 2). Foreigners represented 12.1 per cent of the total population in 1869, 25.4 per cent in 1895 and 29.9 per cent in 1914. It is important to note not only the effect which immigration had on the absolute size of the population, but also its influence on changes in the birth rate through its effect on the age structure. Between 1869 and 1895 the population as a whole grew at the rate of 30.4 per thousand annually with immigration accounting for 17.2 and natural growth for 13.2. Between 1895 and 1914, the annual growth rate of the population as a whole increased to 34.8 per thousand, immigration accounting for 17.2 and natural growth for 17.6.[7]

The influence of migration on the formation of the labour force was reflected in various ways: first, in its direct contribution to the growth of total population and the increase in the natural growth rate of the population; and secondly in its annual supply of manpower which went straight into the labour market. The vast majority of immigrants were young and male. In 1895, 47.4 per cent of foreigners fell into the 20–40 age range and 23.4 per cent of native-born Argentines. Figures for the

[7] Zulma L. Recchini de Lattes and Alfredo E. Lattes, *Migraciones en la Argentina* (Buenos Aires, 1969), 79, 86.

Table 2. *Immigration and emigration, 1870–1914*[a]

Year	Immigrants	Emigrants	Net gain or loss
1870	39,967	—	+ 39,967
1871	20,933	10,686	+ 10,247
1872	37,037	9,153	+ 27,884
1873	76,332	18,236	+ 58,096
1874	68,277	21,340	+ 46,937
1875	42,036	25,578	+ 16,458
1876	30,965	13,487	+ 17,478
1877	36,325	18,350	+ 17,975
1878	42,958	14,860	+ 28,098
1879	55,155	23,696	+ 31,459
1880	41,651	20,377	+ 21,274
1881	47,484	22,374	+ 25,110
1882	51,503	8,720	+ 42,783
1883	63,243	9,510	+ 53,733
1884	77,805	14,444	+ 63,361
1885	108,722	14,585	+ 94,137
1886	93,116	13,907	+ 79,209
1887	120,842	13,630	+107,212
1888	155,632	16,842	+138,790
1889	260,909	40,649	+220,060
1890	110,594	80,219	+ 30,375
1891	52,097	81,932	− 29,835
1892	73,294	43,853	+ 29,441
1893	84,420	48,794	+ 35,626
1894	80,671	41,399	+ 39,272
1895	80,989	36,820	+ 44,169
1896	135,205	45,921	+ 89,284
1897	105,143	57,457	+ 47,686
1898	95,190	53,536	+ 41,654
1899	111,083	62,241	+ 48,842
1900	105,902	55,417	+ 50,485
1901	125,951	80,251	+ 45,700
1902	96,080	79,427	+ 16,653
1903	112,671	74,776	+ 37,895
1904	161,078	66,597	+ 94,481
1905	221,622	82,772	+138,850
1906	302,249	103,852	+198,397
1907	257,924	138,063	+119,861
1908	303,112	127,032	+176,080
1909	278,148	137,508	+140,640
1910	345,275	136,405	+208,870
1911	281,622	172,041	+109,581
1912	379,117	172,996	+206,121
1913	364,271	191,643	+172,628
1914	182,659	221,008	− 38,349

Note: [a]Excluding first-class passengers.
Source: Extracto estadístico de la República Argentina, correspondiente al año 1915 (Buenos Aires, 1916).

Table 3. *Urban and rural population (percentages)*

Year	Total		Foreigners	
	Rural	Urban	Rural	Urban
1869	71	29	52	48
1895	63	37	41	59
1914	47	53	37	63

Source: First, Second and Third National Censuses, 1869, 1895, 1914.

o–20 age range were 21.8 per cent for foreigners, and 60 per cent for native-born.[8] In 1914, there were more foreign than native-born men in the 20–40 age range. This explains why the influence of immigrants in the labour force was greater than their influence in the population as a whole. Among foreigners, there was a ratio of men to women of 1.7 in both 1895 and 1914. In the native population, there were more women, with a man:woman ratio of 0.97 in 1895 and 0.98 in 1914. Immigration also affected regional distribution, as up until 1914 84 per cent of the immigrants settled in the pampa. Finally, foreigners were more prone than natives to settle in the urban areas (see table 3).

There are no studies showing the general levels of employment in Argentina at the end of the nineteenth century. Census figures on jobs, however, for all their imperfections, do provide information on the economically active. In 1869, they amounted to 857,164 out of a potentially active population aged fourteen and over of 1,014,075 (85 per cent). In 1895, the economically active accounted for 1,645,830 out of a potentially active population of 2,451,761 (67 per cent), and in 1914, 3,235,520 out of 5,026,914 (64 per cent).

For 1895 and 1914 respectively, those in regular employment were distributed as follows: 24 and 16 per cent in agriculture or cattle raising, 22 and 26 per cent in industry, and 29 and 33 per cent in service activities. Some 21 and 28 per cent were without fixed occupation – a category which consisted largely of day-labourers (*jornaleros*) and peons, basically a large mass of seasonal workers who were employed in the countryside

[8] Second National Census, 1895, II, xcix.

at harvest time and spent the rest of the year in the city. The most useful indicators for studying changes in employment patterns, not at their absolute level but rather in their variations, are, for urban employment, figures relating to investment in public works and private construction; for employment in the construction of infrastructure, the variations in the extent of the rail network; and for agricultural employment, variations in the area of cultivated land. These sectors, apart from industrial employment where variations were less marked, provided the greatest demand for labour. Annual immigration figures (see above, table 2) measure variations in the supply of labour. Another useful indicator is that of import figures (see below, table 5). Imports in some ways determine variations in industrial activity, public works and railway construction, all of which require imported inputs, but not variations in private construction and cultivated land, which did not require imported goods. It should be stressed that there is a fairly close correlation between variations in imports and net immigration figures.

In the period under consideration, there were sudden changes in the supply of and demand for labour. The increase in imports and in the economic activity that accompanied them produced a sustained increase in the demand for labour. With the crisis of 1890 and the sudden fall in imports, followed by a decline in public works and railway construction, not only did demand for labour fall, but there was also a noticeable reduction in supply, due to a drastic plunge in immigration. A report by the British consul on this subject is revealing:

In 1890 it will be noticed that not only had immigration decreased 60 per cent, as compared with the previous year, but that emigration had increased 107 per cent. The estimated figures for 1891 show that immigration is still decreasing at an alarming rate, and that emigration during the year has, in all probability, exceeded last year's departures. It should be noted that in 1888–89 the immigration direct from abroad alone, not including the arrivals via Monte Video, greatly exceed the 90,000 to 100,000 immigrants estimated by the Chief of the Immigration Department in his report as being the utmost number the country can properly absorb and employ in the course of a year, the number being 130,271 and 218,744 respectively. It is surprising that with a total influx (including via Monte Video) of over 548,000 persons during the last three years there is not even more distress in this country; and the more so as 871,000 immigrants have arrived in the Argentine Republic during the last six years, 1885–90, or 52 per cent, of the total immigration during the past 34 years. The estimated population of this country is 4,000,000 only, so that the number of immigrants landed here in the last six years forms 22 per cent of the total population of the country. Never has such a proportionally large immigration entered a country in so short a period before.[9]

Some of the manpower already in the country moved to the rural sector where the area under cultivation continued to expand during the crisis of the 1890s. This alleviated the problem of unemployment and prevented the crisis from becoming even more serious. Demand for labour increased again when economic activity revived, especially after 1900, and was immediately met by a larger increase in the inflow of immigrants. The labour market which was characterized by excess demand became after 1910, when the rate of growth in cultivated land began to slow down, one of an excess of supply.[10]

It is widely accepted that the notable growth in wealth in Argentina in the period from 1870 to the first world war did not benefit all sectors of the population equally. While the landowners made the greatest gains, the workers did not receive a proportionate share of the growth in the national income. It has even been argued that for various reasons wage levels dropped during most of the period under consideration. For example, Ricardo M. Ortiz maintained that

limited ownership of land . . . [increased] the rate of emigration, encouraged temporary migration, and made it more likely that new arrivals would take up occupations to which they were not accustomed and which in no way corresponded to their objectives. These people came to form an urban proletariat, a social sector which was both large and unstable. This sector consisted of immigrants who sold their labour at a low price, and put up with a life of poverty and extreme privation with their sights set on the time when they could return to their homeland having saved enough to secure their future.[11]

Low and declining wages during the 1880s have generally been attributed, first, to the effects of inflation and, secondly, to surplus labour in the urban sector caused by the lack of opportunities in the rural sector due to a system of landholding which did not favour poor immigrants. James Scobie also maintained that wages were low for most of the period under consideration, especially during the 1890s, although they did begin to climb after 1905. He held that a firm estimate of the fluctuations in wages could be arrived at by converting wages paid in

[9] Great Britain, Foreign Office, Consular Reports, Report on emigration to the Argentine Republic and demand of labour, 1891 (Miscellaneous Series, 1892, No. 216).

[10] See Alejandro E. Bunge, *La desocupación en la Argentina, actual crisis del trabajo* (Buenos Aires, 1917).

[11] Ricardo M. Ortiz, *Historia económica de la Argentina, 1850–1930* (2 vols., Buenos Aires, 1955), I, 209.

paper money to day labourers and skilled workers into a common gold unit. Daily wages paid in peso notes in 1871 had a value of 1.20 in gold pesos; in 1880 they were worth 0.75 gold pesos; in 1885, 1.00; in 1890, 0.60; in 1896, between 0.50 and 0.60; in 1901, 0.55 and in 1910, between 1.20 and 1.50.[12] The high cost of living, Scobie added, had an adverse effect on wage levels.

In fact in real terms (that is, in terms of their purchasing power), wages rose until 1886, then fell until the mid 1890s. However, between 1890–5 and the end of the century, there was a significant real increase caused by an increase in money wages which had lagged behind inflation in the later 1880s and early 1890s, but which had then gradually moved ahead as the cost of living fell after 1895. The increase after 1905 was less marked than Scobie believed because of the effect of the rise in food prices during this period. Some authors have confused stability in the exchange rate with stability of prices in this period. In real terms, the increase in wages was minimal between 1900 and 1910 because of the effect of increases in food prices.

Allowing for important fluctuations which occurred over the 30 years, real wages in Argentina increased during this period. Towards the end of the period, a worker could acquire a third more goods and services than his equivalent some three decades previously. The increase would have been greater for those who had actually begun to work 30 years before, due to the effect which their better training, seniority and great experience must have had on their wages. This does not mean to say that workers' lives were easy and that they were not affected by periods of high cost of living, unemployment and poverty, as their own evidence and that of their contemporaries makes clear.[13] And it is true that immigrants wanting to return home faced the problem that wages in gold pesos fell during the period between 1889 and 1895. Foreign consuls warned potential immigrants that they should not confuse wages paid in gold pesos with those paid in paper pesos.[14] Those who remained on a permanent basis, however, were not affected by this particular problem.

12 James Scobie, *Buenos Aires, plaza to suburb 1870–1910* (New York, 1974), 266.
13 For further discussion on real wages, see Roberto Cortés Conde, *El progreso argentino 1880–1914* (Buenos Aires, 1979).
14 See, for example, Great Britain, Foreign Office, Consular Reports, Report on emigration to the Argentine Republic and demand for labour, 1891 (Miscellaneous Series, 1892, No. 216), and consular reports on the years 1892, 1895, and 1899.

Table 4. *British direct and portfolio investments in Argentina, 1865–1913*
(million pounds sterling)

	1865	1875	1885	1895	1905	1913
Total investment	2.7	22.6	46.0	190.9	253.6	479.8
Direct investment	0.5	6.1	19.3	97.0	150.4	258.7
Portfolio investment	2.2	16.5	26.7	93.9	103.2	221.6
Government loans	2.2	16.5	26.7	90.6	101.0	184.6
Corporate securities	—	—	—	3.4	2.2	37.0

Source: Irving Stone, 'British direct and portfolio investment in Latin America before 1914', *Journal of Economic History*, 37 (1977), 706. Uncorrected figures.

Capital

In an economy as primitive as that of Argentina at the beginning of this period, capital was scarce. Native inhabitants owned fixed assets in the form of large tracts of land or urban housing, and moveable assets such as cattle; there were virtually no other outlets for their savings. Financial institutions were few. Yet the need for enormous investments in infrastructure was critical. In a new country of such vast distances as Argentina, with no settled population in the rural areas and with an economy geared towards the export of products to the other side of the Atlantic, cheap overland and maritime transport was absolutely indispensable. Ports and warehouses were equally important. There was considerable activity on the part of private groups both national and foreign, mainly British, with links to international banking, especially in the railway sector. But it was the state which provided the initial impetus. However, since the state was unable to provide all the necessary finance to fund social overhead investment because its revenue, based primarily on import duties, was insufficient, it had to obtain it by means of loans from Europe, mainly Britain. (On British direct and portfolio investment in Argentina in 1865–1913, see table 4.)

It has been said that Argentina lacked the institutions capable of channelling funds into profitable areas of investment. In reality the situation was somewhat different. The sectors of the economy which sought finance always looked to the government to provide money at lower than market interest rates through the public banks. Throughout a large part of the period under consideration, these institutions, in

the first instance the Banco de la Provincia de Buenos Aires founded in
1854 and then particularly from the 1880s the Banco Nacional, considerably expanded the supply of money, greatly increasing credit to the
private as well as the public sector and reducing their cash reserves to
such an extent that they were unable to meet the demands of their
depositors – which on two separate occasions, in 1873 and in 1885, albeit
under different circumstances, led to a declaration of inconvertibility and
in 1890, as we shall see, to their ultimate collapse.

The principal focus of private and foreign banking operations was
commerce, particularly overseas trade. This did not mean that the
commercial banks had any intrinsic preference for such activities; rather,
these were the safest and most profitable areas of operation. It should
also be remembered that the rural sector could count on other sources of
capital, the best-known of which were the mortgage facilities provided
by national and provincial mortgage banks. But credit was also provided
by commercial suppliers or their agents, both national and foreign, and
grain exporters would offer advances against the harvest. In this way,
fencing and agricultural machinery were imported, grazing lands were
fenced and millions of hectares sown. In addition, pedigree breeding
stock was imported, and the value of livestock and land, one of the main
components of national wealth, thereby increased enormously.

It cannot be said that all capital formation originated overseas. We
have seen that local capital played no small part in improvements to land
and cattle and in urban construction. Table 5 gives an indication of the
enormous growth in the capital stock which occurred in Argentina in the
period under consideration. Ports, railways, roads, housing, machinery
and cattle ranches were all part of a large volume of capital established
throughout the three decades from the period of national unification to
the eve of the first world war. Both the gold and constant currency series
in table 5 yield a rate of growth for the period as a whole of 7.5 per cent,
although the crisis of 1890, when the depreciation of the peso against
gold was greater than the loss in its domestic purchasing power, led
temporarily to a decline in the gold value of the nation's capital stock.

THE PHASES OF GROWTH

The economic history of Argentina from the 1870s to the first world war
can be divided into three periods: the first, which began with the end of
the 1873–6 crisis and reached its climax with the 1890 crash, was one of

Table 5. *Capital formation: growth of the capital stock, 1857–1914*

Year	Millions of pesos (gold)	Millions of pesos (paper)	Consumer Price[a] Index (1884 = 100)	In paper pesos deflated by Consumer Price Index
1857	368	—	—	—
1884	1.875	1.875	100	1.875
1892	1.407	3.264	159	2.052
1895	2.840	8.577	190	4.514
1914	14.955	33.989	206	16.499

Note: [a] Based on Consumer Price Index (Food Prices) in Roberto Cortés Conde, *El progreso argentino (1880–1914)* (Buenos Aires, 1979).
Sources: **1857, 1884 and 1892:** M. G. and E. T. Mullhall, *Handbook of the River Plate* (reprint, Buenos Aires and London, 1982); **1895:** The Second National Census; **1914:** Study by Alberto Martínez for the Third National Census.

rapid and dynamic growth; the next, which began in 1890 and ended in the second half of the decade, was one of depression; the last, from the late 1890s, was one of great expansion which, except for two short-lived recessions in 1899 and 1907, was sustained until the crisis of 1912.

The factor which determined whether there was expansion or recession in the short or medium term was the balance of payments, which was in turn determined by trade and the movement of capital (for the most part British). Variations in these figures affected money supply, levels of employment and the demand for labour (the latter through the effect which the importation of capital goods had on the level of economic activity). Other variables which had an important effect on the economy, such as the extent of land under cultivation and private construction, fluctuated independently of changes in the external sector.

The period from 1880 to 1890

During the first half of the 1880s, the most significant development was the increase in the number of head of cattle and the output of cattle-based products. Sheep production lagged behind in comparison to the previous decade, but arable farming began to gather momentum and reached considerable heights during the second half of the decade. However, contrary to what is generally thought, expansion in this decade was not fuelled chiefly by the arable and stock-raising export sectors, but by investment in transport, public works, and private building. Thanks to the great inflow of direct and indirect foreign investment, funds were obtained to import capital goods which were transformed into thousands of kilometres of rail track and into important public works. All this kept economic activity at a high pitch, and was the main factor in the expansion which occurred during the period.

Exports grew, but at a slower rate than imports. Moreover, while their volume increased considerably during the 1880s, they were offset by a fall in prices. There was a trade deficit for most of the period (see table 6), but the inflow of capital kept the balance of payments positive. This had an expansionary effect on the money in circulation, thus, like the incorporation of capital goods and the increase in fiscal revenue from rising imports, giving a further boost to economic activity.

1881 saw for the very first time the issue of a single currency for the whole country: the national gold peso (1 gold peso = 25 paper pesos (*corrientes*); 5 gold pesos = £1). Four banks, of which the Banco Nacional and the Banco de la Provincia de Buenos Aires were the most important, were used from 1883 to issue banknotes. With the aid of a foreign loan, the Banco Nacional increased its capital from 8 million to 20 million pesos, whereupon it considerably increased the issue of currency from 42 million in 1883 to 75 million in 1885. In 1885, however, as a result of the heavy demand for gold thanks to a deficit in the balance of payments and a policy of credit expansion, the Banco Nacional, faced with an exhaustion of its reserves, asked the government to suspend the convertibility of its banknotes. The government granted this request and soon extended the suspension to the other banks of issue. Thus Argentina returned to the inconvertible paper currency system. Under the terms of the Guaranteed Banks Law of 1887 banks multiplied in the interior, where the silver standard had up until then been dominant. They were a determining factor in the increase in circulation to 163 million pesos in 1889.

Unlike the United States' system on which it was based, the Argentine arrangement established by the Guaranteed Banks Law of 1887 did not imply government backing for all notes in circulation. The law required banks to buy national bonds in exchange for gold. Each bank would then receive from the government an issue of notes equivalent to their respective purchases of bonds. However, the principle of a national currency backed by gold was breached in two important respects: first, the government in effect exempted the Banco Nacional, the largest bank

Table 6. *Argentina's external trade, 1870–1914 (in millions of gold pesos)*

Year	Imports	Exports	Balance
1870	49.1	30.2	− 18.9
1871	45.6	27.0	− 18.6
1872	61.6	47.3	− 14.3
1873	73.4	47.4	− 26.0
1874	57.8	44.5	− 13.3
1875	57.6	52.0	− 5.6
1876	36.1	48.1	+ 12.0
1877	40.4	44.8	+ 4.3
1878	43.7	37.5	− 6.2
1879	46.4	49.4	+ 3.0
1880	45.5	58.4	+ 12.8
1881	55.7	58.0	+ 2.2
1882	61.2	60.4	− 0.9
1883	80.4	60.2	− 20.2
1884	94.0	68.0	− 26.0
1885	92.2	83.9	− 8.3
1886	95.4	69.8	− 25.6
1887	117.4	84.4	− 33.0
1888	128.4	100.1	− 28.3
1889	164.6	90.1	− 74.4
1890	142.2	100.8	− 41.4
1891	67.2	103.2	+ 36.0
1892	91.5	113.4	+ 22.0
1893	96.2	94.1	− 2.1
1894	92.8	101.7	+ 8.9
1895	95.1	120.1	+ 25.0
1896	112.2	116.8	+ 4.6
1897	98.3	101.2	+ 2.9
1898	107.4	133.8	+ 26.4
1899	116.9	184.9	+ 68.0
1900	113.5	154.6	+ 41.1
1901	113.9	167.7	+ 53.8
1902	103.0	179.5	+ 76.4
1903	131.2	221.0	+ 89.8
1904	187.3	264.2	+ 76.8
1905	205.2	322.8	+ 117.7
1906	270.0	292.3	+ 22.3
1907	286.0	296.2	+ 10.3
1908	273.0	366.0	+ 93.0
1909	302.8	397.4	+ 94.6
1910	351.8	372.6	+ 21.0
1911	366.8	324.7	− 42.1
1912	384.9	480.4	+ 95.5
1913	421.3	483.5	+ 62.2
1914	271.8	349.2	+ 77.4

Source: Extracto estadístico de la República Argentina correspondiente al año 1915 (Buenos Aires, 1916).

of issue, from the requirement to purchase national bonds; secondly, the government accepted *documentos a oro* (promissory notes in gold) in lieu of gold from other banks, including provincial banks. As a result, although approximately 150 million gold-backed peso notes were issued, actually gold reserves stood at 76 million. The new regulations caused an abrupt increase in issuance – up 95 per cent in three years – which prompted a 41 per cent depreciation in the currency. The sharp increase in prices that followed led to a shortage in money supply and while the public needed more money to finance its transactions, banks were unable to obtain gold with which to buy bonds and hence put new banknotes into circulation. The result was a reversion to a period of gold scarcity, exacerbated by the need to carry on remitting payments abroad. Various attempts were made to salvage the situation: including an unauthorized issue of 35 million pesos, one of the antecedents of the July 1890 revolution which brought down the government of Juárez Celman.[15] The new government of Carlos Pellegrini, however, had no alternative but to issue a further 60 million pesos. In London the Argentine representative, Victorino de la Plaza, attempted to obtain a moratorium from Baring Brothers, the country's principal creditors. In November 1890 the crisis came to a head with the news that Barings would not allow a postponement on payments nor would they continue the quarterly transfer of existing loans.

The enormous external debt incurred in this period – it rose from 100 million pesos in 1885 to 300 million in 1892 – was another determining factor in the crisis. Foreign loans had had far-reaching effects in expanding public spending, imports and money supply to a very high degree. The end of the flow of loans (with the issue of the last tranche of 25 million pesos for sanitation works in 1889) together with the continuing obligation to carry on sending remittances abroad, in payment of existing loans and services, reversed the balance of payments position (which in 1888, for example, had been in surplus by 150 million despite a 28 million trade deficit). In concrete terms, this had a contractual effect and exerted extreme pressure on the gold market.

Government expenditure had risen from 26.9 million pesos in 1880 to 107 million in 1889 and 95 million in 1890 (in gold pesos from 26.9 to 55.8 and 38.1 million). Revenue, on the other hand, though it also increased, did not increase as much, rising from 19.6 million in 1880 to 72.9 million in 1889 and 73.1 million in 1890 (in gold pesos from 19.6 to 38.2 and 29.1 million). The deficit had been covered mainly by foreign loans. Between 1890 and 1891, the government found it necessary to make very considerable payments with the treasury coffers empty, declining revenue and rising gold prices as a result of heavy demand in the market, in order to prop up the Banco Nacional whose metallic reserves were exhausted. Barings' refusal to grant a moratorium brought an end to the initial attempts to avert the crisis and an even more difficult period began. In April 1891, the Banco Nacional and the Banco de la Provincia de Buenos Aires were wound up, followed in June by various provincial banks. The government adopted severe fiscal measures, re-establishing export taxes and imposing a 2 per cent tax on bank deposits and taxes on tobacco and alcohol, and so on. In London, Victorino de la Plaza renewed negotiations with the Committee of the Bank of England. After intense deliberations, a Funding Loan of £15 million was granted to consolidate previous loans, and a capital and interest moratorium was declared. On 1 December 1891 the Banco de la Nación re-opened its doors and issued an additional 50 million pesos. In accordance with the agreements made with the creditors, there was to be no further issuance until the end of the century. (In fact the currency in circulation was reduced by several million pesos – from 306 million in 1893 to 295 million in 1898.) In 1893, a new agreement – the Romero Agreement – extended the time allowed for debt payment. Within a strict scheme of monetary discipline, and helped by a notable increase in the quantity and value of agricultural exports, Argentina's financial situation was reversed: the price of gold dropped, the peso revalued and the country managed to comply in advance with its external obligations.

The period from 1890 to 1900

In 1891 at the height of the financial crisis Allois Fliess made the following comments in a report to the minister of finance, Vicente López:

Agriculture and livestock production improved under the most favourable auspices. But what was of the greatest interest to the whole Republic, and filled all social classes with a sense of deep satisfaction, was the excellent wheat harvest . . . Superior in quality and of an extraordinarily high yield in Santa Fe, Entre Ríos, and certain districts of the other provinces, good to normal in practically the whole Republic, commanding fairly high prices in the great consumer centres of Western Europe, partly because of news of poor harvests in North America and Russia . . . Exports were handled with great speed and in the first four months about 220,000 tons had been exported, while all the wheat visible in the great deposits and elevators of Rosario and Buenos Aires had already been sold and was in the hands of the exporters.[16]

The export of wheat, which in 1888 amounted to 179,000 tons, rose to 1,608,000 tons in 1894. Production, which totalled 845,000 tons in 1891, increased to 2,138,000 tons in 1894.[17] In the urban sector, the situation was different. As a result of the decrease in imports, the construction of the rail network, which continued throughout 1890–2 because of work begun in the late eighties, came almost to a halt after 1893. Railway construction virtually stopped for most of the decade and began to recover only towards the end of the period. Nevertheless it expanded from 11,700 km of track in 1891 to 16,700 km in 1900; and goods carried increased from 4.6 million tons in 1891 to 12.6 million in 1901.

Whereas the private building sector which did not depend so much on imported inputs continued to expand despite the crisis, thus alleviating urban unemployment, public works, like to some extent the railway, slumped. Using 1885 as the base year (= 100), the index for private construction rose from 108 in 1891 to 171 in 1900, and for public works fell from 244 in 1891 to 58 in 1900. Industrial production, for which machinery and capital goods had been obtained during the preceding period, was given a boost because it was protected by the exchange rate, which raised the cost of imported articles. However, industrial growth did not stem from protectionist tariffs, but from the reduction in costs and the winning of new markets. It occurred mainly in products using local raw materials (food and drink), and was able to develop as markets widened, thanks to the railways. This was the case with sugar in Tucumán, wine in Mendoza, and the flour mills in Santa Fe and Córdoba.

Exports rose from 103 million gold pesos in 1891 (nominal values) to 154.6 million in 1900, largely because of exports of agricultural produce, especially wheat, while imports rose from 67.2 in 1891 to 113.5 in 1900 (see above, Table 6). In sharp contrast to the 1880s there was a favourable trade balance during almost the whole decade.

From 1893, the government imposed a restrictive policy as regards the money supply. Between 1893 and 1899, as we have seen, money in circulation fell. The ratio of notes and coins in circulation to exports (if

[16] Allois E. Fliess, *La producción agrícola-ganadera de la República Argentina en el año 1891* (Buenos Aires, 1892), 10.

[17] See Ministerio de Agricultura, *Estadísticas agrícolas* (Buenos Aires, 1912), and E. Tornquist, *Desarrollo económico en la República Argentina* (Buenos Aires, 1919).

these are taken as a proxy for the growth of economic activity), given that there are no data for gross domestic product, fell from 2.43 in 1890 to 1.59 in 1899, that is to say, a drop of 79 per cent. From 1895, the paper peso went through a process of revaluation. However, this situation had an adverse effect on exporters and agricultural producers who sought to halt the steady appreciation of the peso. This led in 1899 to a monetary reform and a return to the gold standard.

Government expenditure, meanwhile, which had fallen from 55.8 million gold pesos in 1889 to 33.6 million in 1891, remained below 50 million until 1895. Thereafter it began to rise again, reaching 69.6 million in 1900.

The period from 1900 to 1912

There are two central factors in this period. First, the production of cereals, which had been largely confined to Santa Fe where the acreage given over to wheat tripled between 1887 and 1897, spread throughout the province of Buenos Aires, though complementing rather than displacing cattle raising. Secondly, meat became as important as cereals in Argentina's export trade.

Numerous complaints had been made against the conservatism of the cattle producers of Buenos Aires because of the limited growth of cereal production in the province. Large estates, it was said, were an obstacle to farming, which required a system of exploitation based on small producers. But by the 1890s the situation was already beginning to change. Several factors were contributing to a shift towards grain production and mixed farming. The railway made settlement possible in outlying areas of the province, and, following the railway, wheat cultivation spread to the south and west of the province, and also to the north as far as the department of General López in Santa Fe. At the same time new techniques for freezing meat and refrigerated transport across the Atlantic transformed the meat industry. Meat production became more labour-intensive, but it now required the establishment of artificial year-round pastures on which cattle (of improved imported stock) might be fattened. This led to the cultivation of alfalfa, maize and other crops used as fodder being extended into the cattle-producing areas of Buenos Aires province and into areas of Córdoba and La Pampa hitherto given over exclusively to cattle. By the end of the period more of the pampas was given over to alfalfa than to wheat, and more sheep were driven off the pampas to Patagonia. All this was a function of the significant increase in frozen and chilled beef exports (mainly to Britain), which, along with the continued expansion of wheat and maize exports, raised total exports to almost 500 million gold pesos in both 1912 and 1913 (see above, table 6).

To produce prime meat for overseas markets required important measures of domestic adaptation. These included changes in the use of land, in the system of land tenure and in the size of cattle ranches. These changes were further reflected in a sizeable increase in productivity as measured in kilos of meat per hectare, and also in productivity per employee. All this had further consequences: new settlements of population in the rural areas, the creation of towns, and the establishment of transport routes and commercial networks. In cattle-raising areas, tenancy became common where previously the large cattle ranch had predominated. The number of large and small estates decreased, while medium-sized properties increased. This new wave of agricultural and pastoral activity was on a smaller scale than the cattle raising of old, but larger than the agricultural colonies of Santa Fe. A significant increase in the productivity and profitability of land led to the jump in prices after 1905.

The establishment of the rail network had different effects on the formation of markets. In the first place, old regional markets were re-established, but were now linked to the coast, thus forming one national market. Secondly, produce was transported first to the railway centres, which thus became primary markets, and then to the secondary markets on the coast. Produce was transported in waggons to the railheads, which were never more than 18 kilometres from the point of production. At the stations, primary markets were established where the crop was sold and despatched to secondary markets, or else stored when there were no freight cars available. More than 70 per cent of cereal production had to be transported between the months of December and May; hence sheds and rudimentary storehouses were built at many up-country stations. From the primary markets, cereals were transported directly either to the centres of consumption (if destined for domestic use), or to the ports for export. Some 30 per cent of total railway freight was destined for export and about 28 per cent was produce for domestic consumption.[18] Another 34 per cent of rail traffic corresponded to imported goods which were distributed throughout the domestic

---

[18] Emilio Lahitte, *Informes y estudios de la Dirección de Economía Rural y Estadística*, Ministerio de Agricultura (Buenos Aires, 1916).

market. In 1904, the railways transported almost 12.5 million tons, excluding the 1.4 million tons of stores carried for railway use. Attention should be drawn here not only to the size of the traffic between distant markets, but also to the importance of the transport of locally produced goods for domestic consumption, namely 28 per cent of total rail traffic, and the significance of imports shipped inland for local consumption.

A further characteristic of this trade was that the primary markets had a positive balance in relation to the secondary markets, in terms of the physical volume of goods transported. The secondary markets were concentrated in the coastal areas. According to the volume of goods exported, in 1906 the main markets were the centres of Buenos Aires, Rosario, Paraná and Santa Fe. In 1914, there was an important transfer of secondary markets away from the riverine areas towards the maritime coast. After Rosario and Buenos Aires, Bahía Blanca became the third port for the shipment of exports followed by San Nicolás, La Plata and Santa Fe. While secondary markets were at first established in a number of small ports, the railways gradually led to the concentration of the three main secondary markets at Rosario (on the Central Argentine Railway which transported cereals from Córdoba and Santa Fe), Buenos Aires for west and central Buenos Aires, and Bahía Blanca for southern Buenos Aires and La Pampa. However, of even greater importance was the growth of the primary markets, mainly in the new areas. Between 1885 and 1914 in the older coastal areas of the province of Buenos Aires the number of stations (primary markets) rose from 5 in 1885, to 22 in 1895, to 36 in 1914. In the south and west, the same years saw an increase in stations from 33 to 123. In southern Santa Fe, the number of stations increased from 111 in 1895 to 141 in 1914; in the central area, there was an increase from 68 to 80. In the pampas area of Córdoba, the number of stations rose from 55 in 1895 to 172 in 1914: in the northwestern zone of the province, they rose from 14 to 21. Not only should the vast increase in new markets be noted, but also some important differences. Between 1895 and 1914, growth was much greater in the pampas area of Córdoba than in the province of Santa Fe. This was due to the much earlier development of Santa Fe, which had already reached a significant size in 1895. The difference lies in the fact that more new primary markets appeared in the new areas of Córdoba, which were linked to the general region of the pampas, and not to the traditional northern area, where there was little if any development.

The technological character of arable farming had considerable effects on the economy. The fact that it was more labour intensive led to a more favourable distribution of income. It also led to the settlement of workers in rural areas, the establishment of diverse transport facilities, and the appearance of various activities providing goods and services for the rural population. This resulted in the formation of urban centres in country districts and the formation of a market in the rural sector which had not existed previously. Railways linked inland markets to the urban markets of the coast and thereby ultimately created a national market. When the census of 1914 was carried out, local production was already catering for a high percentage of domestic demand, some 91 per cent of food, 88 per cent of textiles, 80 per cent of construction, 70 per cent of furniture and 33 per cent of metallurgical products.[19] Local demand began to compete with foreign markets for domestically produced foodstuffs.

Growth was thus not only limited to the export sector. Domestic demand increased given the related processes of rural population growth, urbanization and improved means of internal communication. An increase in the number of wage earners and rising real incomes promoted domestic market growth and provided an expanding range of domestic investment opportunities. These were associated with transport and commerce, with construction, with food processing and with textile production.

Some of these activities, such as services and construction, could only be supplied locally. Others, in the first instance, were supplied by imports. However, when transport costs caused the price of imported goods to exceed those produced locally, there was a strong incentive for local production, which was still greater when cheap local raw materials were used. The location of industry was determined by various factors: (1) the site of raw materials (flour, wines, sugar); (2) the existence of a port of exit to overseas markets for frozen meat; (3) the existence of a port for the supply of fuel, raw materials or imported inputs; and (4) the existence of markets with a high density of population and greater capacity for consumption.

Some 30 per cent of all national industrial establishments and investment in manufacturing was concentrated in the Federal capital. Between 1895 and 1913 this preponderance tended to decrease, from 35.1 per cent in 1895 to 21.1 per cent in 1913, as regards the number of

---

[19] Third National Census, 1914, VII, 71.

establishments, and from 36 to 30 per cent as regards capital. Conversely, in the province of Buenos Aires, the number of establishments rose from 23.9 to 30.4 per cent and the amount of industrial capital from 21.6 to 26.3 per cent in the same period. Other provinces in which there was a growth of industry, listed in order of importance of capital invested in manufacturing, were, in 1895, Santa Fe, Tucumán, Entre Ríos and Mendoza, and in 1913 Santa Fe, Mendoza, Tucumán, Córdoba and Entre Ríos. Between 1895 and 1914 the number of industrial establishments increased from 22,204 to 48,779. Capital rose from 327 million pesos to 1,787 million and numbers employed in industry from 175,000 to 410,000.

The most important event during this period was the monetary reform of 1899, which effected the return to the gold standard after several years of continual revaluation of the currency. A strict monetary policy had been applied since 1893; the stock of money remained almost constant for the rest of the decade – in fact it declined slightly – and resulted in the appreciation of the external value of the paper peso during the years immediately prior to the return to gold. Currency appreciation was also facilitated by favourable trade balances, due not only to fewer imports and to the agreements reached for paying off the foreign debt, but also because of the significant increase in exports and the higher prices these fetched. Parity was fixed at 2.2727 paper pesos to each gold peso. This new parity, while taking into account the new purchasing power of Argentine currency and that of other export countries like the United States, nevertheless implied a certain undervaluation of the peso with respect to the dollar.

A Conversion Board was established to regulate the issue of paper money and build up a gold reserve. By 1903, a metallic reserve of 38.7 million gold pesos had been accumulated; this had risen to 55.5 million in 1904, 101.9 million in 1905 and reached 263.2 million in 1913. The issue of notes was then regulated automatically in accordance with the fluctuations in gold reserves, and these in turn were linked to the balance of payments. Because of the excellent results achieved by exports and rising prices there was a substantial increase in the circulation of notes, although not in the same proportion, given that the legal reserve rose from 23.1 per cent in 1903 and 30.9 per cent in 1904 to 72.7 per cent in 1913.

The notes stock, which had declined to 291.3 million pesos in 1899, rose to 380.2 million in 1903, climbing at an annual rate of 8.0 per cent to

823.3 million in 1913. The ratio of currency to exports was 1.72 in 1903 and 1.70 in 1913. In pesos at their 1903 value, the stock of currency rose from 324 million in 1900 to 615 million in 1912. In other words, in twelve years the stock of currency rose, at constant prices, by 90 per cent, at a rate of 5.5 per cent per year.

The boom in exports was reflected in commercial activity and also had repercussions on banking. The Banco de la Nación, founded in 1890, played a leading role and represented 24 per cent of the capital of all banks, 32 per cent of the loans and 37 per cent of the deposits. Foreign banks represented 11 per cent of the capital, 20 per cent of the loans and 20 per cent of the deposits, the remainder corresponding to other independent Argentine banks.[20] The Banco de la Nación established numerous branches in the interior of the country, which enabled credit to reach the most distant rural areas and to play an important role. In 1905, the charter of the Banco de la Nación was reformed. Among other things, this turned it into an exclusively official entity which was authorized to handle rediscounted documents from other banks. The Banco de la Nación, which held 41 per cent of the gold reserves of all banks, sought to lessen the sudden fluctuations in the supply of and demand for gold by withholding it when it was plentiful and selling it when it was in short supply. Other commercial banks soon followed suit.

The process of general expansion was followed by increased government expenditure, which rose from 69.6 million gold pesos in 1900 to 189.6 million in 1914 (158 million paper pesos in 1900 to 419 million in 1914). Revenues, however, did not increase to the same extent, rising from 148 million to 250 million in 1914. Comparing 1900 and 1912 on the basis of the peso at its 1903 level, it can be seen that revenue rose from 162.6 million in 1900 to 258.5 million in 1912 and expenditure increased from 173.6 million in 1900 to 380 million in 1912. This is to say that at constant prices revenue had increased by 59 per cent while expenditure rose by 118 per cent. The public debt, which had grown steadily from 47.5 million gold pesos in 1870 to 88.3 million in 1880, 355.7 million in 1890 and 447.1 million in 1900, rose by a further 28 per cent to 545 million by 1914.

CONCLUSION

The outstanding feature of the period 1880–1912, with the exception of the years 1890–5, was rapid economic growth. All the indicators point to

[20] Angel M. Quintero Ramos, *Historia monetaria y bancaria de Argentina (1500–1949)* (Mexico, 1970).

an average annual growth rate of more than 5 per cent over the three decades, which distinguishes this period from any other in Argentine history. However, it was not just a question of growth. Substantial changes occurred at the same time which modified the face of Argentina and changed the character of its economy.

On the eve of the first world war, Argentina, with a population of almost eight million, had been transformed from a relatively backward country into a modern one. The empty spaces of the pampas had been settled and 24 million hectares were under cultivation, compared to less than half a million 40 years earlier. A vast network of towns had been formed in the rural areas, and an extensive railway network had been constructed which had 34 thousand kilometres of track in 1914, which had permitted the movement of population towards the interior of the country and the development of a market of factors of production and goods at national level. In addition, ports had been constructed to facilitate the entry and exit of goods and people, and considerable impetus had been given to urban construction.

This growth which changed Argentina was based on the exploitation of staples: agricultural and cattle products which found an outlet in international markets. However, it was not limited to this. Because agriculture and meat production were more labour intensive, they had more linkages, especially backward linkages. On the one hand, transport, housing and clothes were required for the population of the new rural agricultural areas and the urban centres which grew up nearby, apart from the ports. These centres were the primary and secondary markets for agricultural production. Demand for these goods led to the appearance of domestic industries in residential construction, food and drink, and textile production, the location and comparative advantages of which depended on the proximity of markets, lower transport costs and, in the case of food, the lower cost of local raw material.

The more intensive use of labour also permitted a better distribution of income and an increase in demand. Equally, it provided an added incentive for investments in other activities within the domestic market.

Although the influence of the foreign sector was considerable, the situation was not such that other sectors remained undeveloped, especially in the domestic market. Indeed, these other sectors even found facilities, in a period of large surpluses, to import capital goods. On the other hand, exports became reasonably diversified and adjusted quite quickly to fluctuations in prices. During the period under consideration, a great effort was made to encourage capital formation.

Without any doubt, the crucial factor in the growth of the Argentine economy in this period was the existence of foreign demand, which was made possible by the reduction in ocean freight charges. However, apart from the demand for foodstuffs, the period witnessed greater fluidity in the international money market, made possible by the greater frequency and speed of communications. It should be added that during the long cycle of recession which began in the 1870s and continued until the end of the century, prices and interest rates fell in the most developed countries, which meant that capital began to seek larger profits outside the domestic markets. On the other hand, it should be pointed out that during a period of railway fever, there was a strong tendency to produce and export capital goods such as railway equipment.

As for the population, the same factors which affected the commercial and money markets made possible the displacement, on a massive scale, of labour across the Atlantic. The fall in freight costs, insurance, and especially the decrease in agricultural prices resulting from the supplies of American cereals, were all responsible for the displacement of Europe's rural population to America. Rural labour was used with greater efficiency in new, fertile lands. This led to better income and higher wages. Although not the main focus of this chapter, the legal and political aspect should be mentioned. The effective exercise of civil liberty and the legal security promised by the constitution, and which was put into practice with the final organization of the state – that is to say, with the organization of the supreme court of Justice and the Federal courts in the provinces – were important prerequisites for guaranteeing the free movements of labour and capital.

All these factors relate to the question of demand. There is also, however, the question of supply. As we have said, around the 1870s meat and grain were not being produced in great quantity for the domestic market, so that, when foreign demand transmitted by means of price mechanisms grew, meat and grain production could not be increased and geared to the export market. Domestic production was tiny in comparison to what was later to be exported, but, basically, there were no incentives for any increase in demand, given that prices were at a low as a result of the heavy demand for American cereals in Europe during the 1870s and 1880s. Argentina needed to make different adjustments in order to incorporate unused resources, such as land, and to obtain other resources such as capital and labour, and in this way reduce its production costs in order to compete in the world markets. This is precisely what it did when it began to make productive use of a vast area of fertile land, organizing agricultural production on a large scale in order to make it more competitive, and at the same time reducing transport and labour costs. Finally, Argentine exports arrived on the European markets when they could compete in terms of price and quality with produce from other new countries.

To put all this into effect in such a vast new country, investment in public goods such as ports and transport facilities was required over and above individual effort. This investment had to be provided within a short period, and on a hitherto unknown scale. However, basically, most of the effort came from the private sector which opened up new land, introduced improvements and agricultural machinery, created pastures, brought in breeding stock and improved the cattle markets, while at the same time carrying out urban construction and developing industries. It was changes taking place on the supply side which enabled Argentina to achieve high rates of economic growth, to compete in foreign markets and, eventually, to become one of the world's leading exporters of foodstuffs on the eve of the first world war.

3

SOCIETY AND POLITICS, 1880 – 1916

At the end of the 1870s, few Argentines would have imagined that they were on the verge of a prodigious process of social transformation. Little had happened in the 1870s to make anyone expect that the dreams of progress of the politicians active during the 'National Organization' period (1852–62) would be realized. On the contrary, during the presidencies of Domingo F. Sarmiento (1868–74) and Nicolás Avellaneda (1874–80) economic and social progress, though significant, had been slow and laborious. Of the factors which subsequently contributed to Argentina's rapid economic growth, some had not yet appeared and others were only beginning to emerge. Livestock was still of poor quality; the country imported wheat; only a small part of Argentine territory was covered by the transport network; banking services were still in the rudimentary state; and the influx of capital and immigrants was small. Even this hesitant progress had been interrupted by the severe economic crisis of 1874–7. It is not surprising, therefore, that some people had begun to doubt that the progress of the country could be based on the fertility of the pampas, as had always been imagined. Among clear indications of this incipient attitude were the various studies at the time directed towards determining the location of mineral resources, and the 'protectionist' ideology that emerged in the parliamentary debates of 1876.

The first national census of 1869 had provided clear evidence of widespread backwardness in Argentina. That vast area had a population of under 1.8 million, a density of 0.43 inhabitants per square kilometre. Poverty was reflected in the low quality of housing: 78.6 per cent of Argentines lived in miserable *ranchos* of mud and straw. Furthermore,

---

* Translated from the Spanish by Dr Richard Southern; translation revised by Mr Jeremy Butterfield and the author.

77.9 per cent of those over six years of age were unable to read or write. A large part of the territory was totally uninhabited, and what were later to become the fertile pastures of a large part of the provinces of Buenos Aires, Santa Fe and Córdoba were hardly exploited at all. The 'desert', that obsession of the Argentines, seemed untamable, not only on account of the distances that were economically impossible to bridge, but also because of the indomitable armed resistance of the Indian tribes that inhabited the area. Until well into the 1870s, Indian raids were a continuous nightmare for rural authorities and producers.

President Avellaneda was right to point out that 'the frontier question is the most important of all . . . it is the beginning and the end . . . to get rid of the Indians and the frontier means . . . populating the desert'.[1] It was during his tenure as president that the military campaign led by General Julio A. Roca in 1879 put an end to the long-standing problem. Until then, Indian incursions had occurred repeatedly. In 1872, for example, the Indians reached Cañada de Gómez, only a few minutes' journey from Rosario, the second most important city in the country. In 1875 and 1876 a series of invasions carried out by a confederation of Indian tribes led by their most battle-hardened chieftains devastated important districts, including Azul, Olavarría and Tres Arroyos, in Buenos Aires province. Colonel Manuel Pardo recalled these incursions as follows: 'The settlements burned, as though fire from Heaven had descended on them, the fields were shorn of their crops . . . along the trail of the invaded ranches . . . and meanwhile we heard the echoes . . . of men having their throats cut and women and children being carried off into captivity . . .'[2]

Nor was violence confined to the Indian frontier. Although 1870 marked the end of the long war with Paraguay, it did not mark the end of armed confrontation between different regions within the country. During the 1870s, two major rebellions led by López Jordan, the political leader of Entre Ríos, posed a serious threat to internal peace. And in 1880, as we shall see, the most formidable of all the provincial forces, the militias of Buenos Aires province led by Governor Tejedor, rose in arms against the national authorities. It is not possible to give a detailed description here of the many small-scale insurrections of various kinds which took place in the provinces during these years. Particularly noteworthy, however, was a rising led by General Mitre, a former

[1] Nicolás Avellaneda, in his prologue to Alvaro Barros, *Indios, fronteras y seguridad interior* (first published 1872–6; Buenos Aires, 1975), 137.
[2] Quoted in J. C. Walther, *La conquista del desierto* (Buenos Aires, 1973), 384.

president of the Republic and leader of the Nationalist party, in 1874 to prevent the president-elect Avellaneda from taking office.

The years before and after 1874 were marked by bitter disputes between the two Buenos Aires-based parties – the Nationalists and the Autonomists led by Dr Adolfo Alsina – which at that time dominated politics in Argentina. In 1877, President Avellaneda (who formed the National party) tried to solve the institutional crisis by means of the so-called policy of *conciliación*. Many Nationalist and Autonomist leaders accepted Avellaneda's invitation to participate in a national government. This peace, however, lasted only a short time, and on the occasion of the presidential elections of 1880 the Argentines were again divided into two irreconcilable factions: the supporters of General Roca and the supporters of Governor Tejedor of Buenos Aires. So much greater was the economic strength of the province of Buenos Aires that the representative of Baring Brothers, for example, prophesied a decisive victory for Governor Tejedor.

In the event Roca emerged triumphant. First, he was able to count on the support of most of the officers of the National Army. Secondly, the recently formed League of Governors guaranteed him the support of almost all the provinces. Furthermore, although public opinion in Buenos Aires mostly supported Tejedor, Roca succeeded in acquiring powerful allies in important sectors of the political and economic life of the province, including many Buenos Aires Autonomists and a few supporters of General Mitre. The great confrontation of 1880 was military as well as political, and it was no mere skirmish: about 20,000 men took part and approximately 2,500 were killed or wounded. The heaviest fighting was in the surroundings of the city of Buenos Aires, where many of the inhabitants fought on the losing side. It is in the scale and cohesiveness of the political and military coalition formed in the last years of the 1870s that the key to Roca's final success is to be found. At the same time, displaying great political intuition, Roca had put himself at the head of a growing body of opinion in favour of the strengthening of the central government as the only solution to Argentina's political problems. Even old liberals like Domingo Sarmiento began to emphasize the importance of order and peace: 'The synthesis of the modern republican is less sublime [than *"fraternity, equality* and *liberty"*]; . . . it is *peace, tranquillity* and *liberty*.'[3]

---

[3] Domingo F. Sarmiento, *Obras completas* (Buenos Aires, 1953), xxxix, 68.

'It is as though we were a people recently born to national life, for you have to legislate about everything that constitutes the attributes, resources and power of the nation.'[4] With these words, President Roca (1880–6) inaugurated the parliamentary session of 1881. The following years witnessed the approval of a series of laws that overwhelmingly transferred power to the central government. The city of Buenos Aires was federalized, which partially weakened the dominant position enjoyed by the province of Buenos Aires. The National Army was put on a sound footing, and the provincial militias were disbanded. For the first time a common unit of currency for the whole country was adopted. Primary education and the Civil Register (which until then had been in the hands of the Catholic church) were made subject to the jurisdiction of the national authorities. A series of laws reorganized the judiciary, the municipalities and other spheres of public administration.

Many supporters of Roca in the interior had believed that the defeat of Buenos Aires would strengthen their respective provinces. The consequences of Roca's victory, however, seemed to confirm the most gloomy predictions of those who had been defeated. Leandro N. Alem, the future leader of the Radical opposition party, was not very far from the truth when he asserted in 1880 that the future would see the creation of a central government so strong that it would absorb 'all the strength of the peoples and cities of the Republic'.[5] The legislation passed in the 1880s consolidated the authority of the central government and placed the reins of power firmly in the hands of the head of the National Executive. In a sense the presidentialism which followed was merely the consequence of putting into practice the ideas originally proclaimed by the framers of the constitution of 1853. Scarcity of resources, insuperable geographical barriers and strong local political traditions had prevented these ideas being implemented before 1880.

From 1880 Argentina enjoyed several decades of relative political unity and stability. This coincided with, itself facilitated and was underpinned by exceptional economic growth at an average rate of 5 per cent per annum up to the first world war, and beyond.[6] This in turn resulted in, and was to some extent a consequence of, fundamental

---

[4] For the message of Roca, see H. Mabragaña, *Los Mensajes. Historia del desenvolvimiento de la nación Argentina, redactada cronológicamente por sus gobernantes, 1810–1910* (6 vols., Buenos Aires, 1910), IV, 1.

[5] Quoted by H. Rivarola and C. García Belsunce, 'Presidencia de Roca', in R. Levillier (ed.), *Historia Argentina* (Buenos Aires, 1968), IV, 2489.

[6] See Cortés Conde, this volume, ch. 2.

changes in the demographic and social structure of the country. The pampas in particular were thoroughly transformed, as Walter Larden, who lived and worked on a farm in southern Santa Fe until 1888, discovered. When he returned in 1908, he found everything changed: 'Alas, for the change. Prosperity had come, and romance had gone for ever.'[7]

SOCIETY, 1880–1914

Argentina had 1,736,490 inhabitants in 1869, 3,956,060 in 1895, and 7,885,237 in 1914. The principal cause of this marked increase in population was the massive influx of immigrants. Between 1871 and 1914, 5,917,259 people entered the country; of these, 2,722,384 returned to their countries of origin and 3,194,875 settled in Argentina. The great majority of these immigrants came from Italy and Spain, but there were sizeable contingents from Central Europe, France, Germany, Great Britain and the Ottoman Empire. A very large number of those who settled did so in the provinces of the littoral (the federal capital and the provinces of Buenos Aires, Santa Fe, Córdoba and Entre Ríos), thus consolidating and strengthening a trend that had its origins in the last decades of the eighteenth century. At the same time internal migration, although smaller in quantity than migration from overseas, was by no means insignificant. Between 1869 and 1914 the littoral provinces increased their share of the total population from 48 to 72 per cent. Population growth in the individual provinces in this period ranged from a spectacular 909 per cent in Santa Fe to 216.8 per cent in Entre Ríos. There were also considerable increases in the new territories (especially La Pampa and the Chaco) which had been only sparsely inhabited in 1869. Except for Mendoza and Tucumán, whose populations grew by 324.5 and 205.6 per cent respectively, figures for the remaining provinces are much lower than those recorded for the littoral. In these other provinces, the demographic increase for the period between the censuses of 1869 and 1914 ranged from 118.2 per cent in San Luis to a mere 25.4 per cent in Catamarca.

The ratio of urban to rural population was also substantially modified. The percentage of inhabitants living in urban areas rose from 29 per cent in 1869 to 53 per cent in 1914. The increase recorded in the city of Buenos

---

[7] Walter Larden, *Argentine plains and Andean glaciers* (London, 1911), 49.

Aires was simply phenomenal: the population shot from 181,838 in 1869 to 1,575,814 in 1914. The population of the city of Rosario, in the province of Santa Fe, rose from 23,139 in 1869 to 224,592 in 1914. In the city of Córdoba, too, where growth was encouraged by the development of cereal-growing in the southern departments of the province, there was a significant increase, from 28,523 inhabitants in 1869 to 121,982 in 1914. The cities of Mendoza and Tucumán also expanded rapidly, as a consequence of the development of vineyards in the former and of the sugar industry in the latter. Mendoza grew from 8,124 inhabitants in 1869 to 58,790 in 1914, and Tucumán from 17,438 inhabitants to 92,824 during the same period. Other examples of this rapid increase in the urban population can be found in the districts which today constitute Greater Buenos Aires, but which had not at that stage been incorporated into the Federal Capital. Avellaneda, for example, which had only 5,645 inhabitants in 1869, grew to 139,527 in 1914, while La Plata, which had not even existed in 1869, had 137,413 inhabitants. Other urban centres in the province of Buenos Aires also showed great increases; for example, the southern port of Bahía Blanca grew from 1,057 inhabitants in 1869 to 62,191 in 1914.

In addition to the rapid growth of the cities, there was also a considerable growth in the number of small townships in the littoral. This was one of the factors which, together with the expansion of the railway network, helped to lessen the traditional isolation of the rural areas. The emergence of these centres of population was caused by the changes that occurred in the economic structure of the region. At first, the expansion of sheep raising led not only to a significant reduction in the scale of livestock raising, but also to an increased division of labour within this sector. Both these developments encouraged a greater settlement of people in the region and a notable diversification of the social and occupational structure. As a consequence of this process, which took place from around 1860 to around 1880, the first rural settlements of any importance appeared, especially in the provinces of Buenos Aires and Entre Ríos. Much more marked, however, was the impact in the period after 1880 of the expansion of cereal growing. This process originated in the centre and south of the province of Santa Fe, and spread to the south of Córdoba and the north-west of Buenos Aires province. The expansion of cereal growing led to a significant increase in the number of rural settlements of between 2,000 and 10,000 inhabitants in the pampas from a mere 20 in 1869 to 221 in 1914.

The massive influx of immigrants in this period upset Argentina's demographic and regional equilibrium. At the same time, there were significant changes in the social and occupational structure of the country. Between the censuses of 1869 and 1895, the expansion of the agricultural sector and of tertiary activities coincided with a market reduction in employment in the traditional craft industries and the obsolete transport system. Between the censuses of 1895 and 1914, the mechanization of agriculture caused a comparative reduction in the level of employment in the primary sector, the level of employment in the newly established industries of the littoral increased and the tertiary sector continued to grow; there was a notable expansion in the building industry, especially in the big cities of the littoral. The part played by immigrants in the occupational structure was all-important, and perhaps without parallel elsewhere in the world. In 1914, no fewer than 62.1 per cent of those employed in commerce, 44.3 per cent of those in industry, and 38.9 per cent of those in the agricultural and stock-raising sector were foreign-born. The figures were lower in the case of the public administration and the educational sector, where the proportions were 17.6 and 14 per cent respectively. There was a significant increase in all these proportions in the three areas where the influx of foreign immigrants had been greatest. In the city of Buenos Aires, immigrants employed in commerce and industry made up 72.5 and 68.8 per cent of the respective totals. In Buenos Aires province, the proportion of foreigners employed in the rural sector was 55.1 per cent, while in Santa Fe it was as high as 60.9 per cent. These figures do not include the children of immigrants who, according to existing legislation, were considered to be Argentine. If they are included, then the number of people of recent immigrant origin in the total economically active population is even greater. In cities like Buenos Aires and Rosario, and in cereal-growing areas such as Santa Fe, third generation Argentinians did not account for more than 20 per cent of the total population.

At the entrepreneurial level this phenomenon is even more striking. The majority of the proprietors of commercial establishments (68.4 per cent) and of factories (68.7 per cent), and a significant proportion of the owners of agricultural and stock-raising undertakings (31.9 per cent) had been born outside Argentina. In the three areas of the littoral already mentioned, the proportions were as follows: 78.3 per cent of the commercial entrepreneurs, 73.4 per cent of the industrialists and 56.9 per cent of the rural proprietors. Within the rural sector, there were appreciable differences between agriculturists and stock-raisers. In the first category, the proportion of foreigners in the country as a whole was 40.7 per cent, reaching 62.4 per cent in the province of Buenos Aires and Santa Fe. Of the stock-raisers, the foreigners constituted 22.2 per cent in the country as a whole, and 49.1 per cent in Buenos Aires and Santa Fe.

The disparity between the rural and urban sectors reflected the fact that commerce and industry were concentrated in the region (the littoral) where the great majority of immigrants had settled. In contrast, rural enterprises were distributed evenly throughout the country, and therefore covered regions where immigration had had a very marginal impact. As to the differences between agriculture and stock raising, two factors are worth mentioning. Firstly, stock raising had been the activity undergoing the greatest development even before the beginning of mass European immigration, whereas the expansion of agriculture coincided with the arrival of immigrants on a large scale. Secondly, given the scale of stock-raising enterprises, capital requirements were much higher than those needed to start agricultural activities.

All these figures point to a very marked process of upward mobility, which reached its greatest extent in the urban areas and the cereal-growing region. However, it was also significant in the stock-raising region where the figures would be even more startling if the offspring of immigrants were taken into consideration. The changes in people's relative social positions affected all strata of local society with equal intensity. At certain times and in certain places, this process was so violent that it bewildered even the most perceptive observers. In 1888, the manager of the Rosario branch of the Bank of London and the River Plate reported to London that 'The rapid progress of this province is making it difficult to keep you at all well posted as to the responsibilities of our clients, for it often happens that one year suffices to change a man's position so much for the better that we can no longer bind him to former limits.'[8]

One consequence of this rapid process of social mobility was the great expansion of the middle sectors of society. Estimates based on the census data are not very precise, but it may be roughly calculated that these groups grew from 12–15 per cent of the economically active population in 1869 to around 35–40 per cent in 1914. In the urban areas this expansion was linked to the growth of the tertiary sector and, to a lesser degree, to

---

[8] Rosario Manager to Buenos Aires (19 June 1888), Bank of London and South America Archives, University College London library.

industrial development. The growth of the administrative apparatus and the educational system was also important. In the rural areas, in contrast, the growth recorded for the middle sectors was closely related to the spread of cereal cultivation. The smaller size of agricultural undertakings made possible the expansion of a stratum of middling and small-scale proprietors who had existed only in limited numbers during the period when stock raising had predominated. At the same time, the greater complexity of cereal-growing undertakings led to the rise of a range of connected activities (commerce, industry and transport), which emerged in the settlements and towns established during those years. There thus arose a very extensive intermediate sector in the rural areas, and this became one of the distinctive characteristics of River Plate society as compared with the subcontinent as a whole.

Not everybody in the intermediate groups, of course, was in the same situation, as is demonstrated by the case of the tenant-farmers. Until the very end of the century it was comparatively easy for tenants to acquire the ownership of the properties which they worked.[9] Thereafter, a change in the scale of agricultural enterprises, the introduction of modern labour-saving machinery and an increase in the price of land due to the exhaustion of new frontier areas made such acquisition increasingly difficult. This phenomenon (which also occurred in countries such as Australia and the United States) led to a marked increase in the comparative numbers of tenants, who around 1914 constituted 60 per cent of all farmers.

The situation of the Argentine immigrant who became a tenant farmer was substantially different from that of his European counterpart. Working a plot of between 200 and 400 hectares, he was himself an employer of labour, especially at harvest time. However, even though he was in a much better position than was normal in his country of origin, he was not as favourably placed as those who had acquired ownership of land in Argentina. This difference was due to the insecurity of tenure, which was reflected in a standard of living (housing, for example) definitely inferior to that enjoyed by the owner-farmers.

Of the immigrants who settled permanently, not all reached highly placed or even intermediate positions in society. Many continued to carry on the same activities as they had when they arrived. The emerging industry of the littoral area employed, for the most part, labour of foreign

---

[9] On this point, cf. this volume, Cortés Conde, ch. 2, and Rock, ch. 4.

origin. In the city of Buenos Aires, for instance, 72 per cent of the workers and employees were immigrants. The living conditions of the urban working class varied according to circumstances. The wages received were, of course, very much higher than in the immigrants' native countries. During certain periods, Argentina experienced the curious phenomenon of foreign immigration of a seasonal character. The famous *golondrinas* ('swallows') immigrated from Italy for the three months of the harvest season: 'in search of perpetual harvest wages, like swallows in search of perpetual summer'.[10]

Within the country, conditions in general tended to improve markedly during the period from 1870 to 1914. In spite of the great increase in the number of inhabitants, there was a substantial reduction in illiteracy, which fell from 77.9 per cent in 1869 to 35 per cent in 1914. There was also a marked improvement in public health, and there were no longer epidemics of yellow fever and cholera in the big cities. In addition, progress was made in housing. Whereas, as we have seen, 79 per cent of the population lived in mud and straw *ranchos* in 1869, this figure had fallen to 50 per cent in 1895. For 1914 there are no data, but all the evidence indicates a continuation of the trend observable between the censuses of 1869 and 1895. The massive influx of immigrants did, however, lead to serious problems in housing. In the last twenty years of the period, especially in the big cities, there was an increase in the number of persons per dwelling, and this gave rise to a series of problems to which the literature of the period amply testifies. Progress in the sphere of labour legislation was hesitant and slow. Nevertheless, laws were passed about days of rest on Sundays and national holidays; there were regulations governing the labour of women and children, and also legislation on industrial accidents. During this period there was also a continuous reduction in the length of the working day, and by the first world war the eight-hour day was becoming the norm in the majority of urban enterprises.

Conditions in the littoral differed from those in the rest of the country. Although there was progress almost everywhere, the disparities between regions continued to be very significant. These disparities were due to various factors, many of which had obtained before the beginning of the period under discussion. The displacement of the centre of economic activity from Upper Peru to the Río de la Plata, which had begun in the

---

[10] 'Correspondence respecting emigration to the Argentine Republic', in *Parliamentary Papers. Commercial Reports*, vol. LXXVI (London, 1889).

late colonial period, led to the comparative stagnation of those regional economies that did not adapt themselves adequately to new conditions. This happened in the case of Santiago del Estero and most of the old provinces of the north-west. Although with less intensity, a similar process took place in the region of Cuyo, which was closely linked to the Chilean economy. Even in the littoral itself, the province of Corrientes, bordering on Paraguay, suffered a relative decline during the period 1870–1914.

Disparities can also be detected between regions which did experience rapid growth during this period. In Tucumán, for example, which became an area of seasonal migration from the neighbouring provinces, such as Santiago del Estero and Catamarca, and whose growth was based on the rapid development of the sugar industry, social conditions remained markedly inferior to those in the areas where cereal cultivation predominated. Indeed, among the provinces of the interior only Mendoza enjoyed living standards approximately similar to those common in the littoral.

Levels of education in the different provinces serve to illustrate the problem of regional disparity. In 1914, the national illiteracy rate was 35.2 per cent. In the littoral, however, it was only 26.9 per cent, whereas it rose to 57.6 per cent in the rest of the country. These differences become even more striking if one compares extremes, for instance the city of Buenos Aires (22.2 per cent) and the province of Jujuy (64.9 per cent). The 1914 census provides no data regarding the different types of housing, but the 1895 census figures, though indicating in comparison with 1869 a demonstrable recovery in absolute terms, still do not show significant changes in the relative positions of the provinces. The proportion of sub-standard dwellings (*ranchos*), which was around 50 per cent in the country as a whole, was only 35 per cent in the littoral, but rose as high as 78 per cent in the rest of the country.

Economic progress of this nature naturally produced its victims, to be found generally among the inhabitants of the areas of less rapid development. The most striking case is the people whose trades were severely affected by the modernization of the economy. These included the individual weavers of the interior, whose craft activities could not withstand the competition from imported products, and people employed in internal transport, who were swiftly displaced by the extremely rapid expansion of the railway network. In other cases, the impact of this expansion did not lead to a fall in incomes, but it did affect living

conditions in the regions concerned. The reorganization and modernization of stock-raising undertakings had a profound effect on the
established rhythm of labour and style of life. The disappearance of the
Indian frontier, the increasing commercialization of all stock-raising
products and the striking development of the fencing of pastures all
began to establish less erratic rhythms of labour and to limit the great
mobility that had characterized life in the stock-raising areas. In spite of
its picturesque and romantic distortions, contemporary literature
reflected some of these features in its nostalgic evocation of the past life
of the *gauchos* of the Río de la Plata region.

The different social sectors into which the population was divided
gradually became organized. As early as 1854, the Buenos Aires
Commercial Exchange had been founded, and during the period after
1870 several minor chambers of commerce were established, both in the
capital and in the principal cities of the rest of the country. In 1866, the
influential Argentine Rural Society had been founded; its members were
the stock raisers of the province of Buenos Aires. It became firmly
established, however, only after 1880, when similar organizations were
founded in other provinces. The Argentine Industrial Union, formed by
manufacturers from all over the country, was established in 1886. This
was also the period of the earliest workers' organizations, which grew to
very significant dimensions in Buenos Aires, Rosario and the chief
railway centres. Until the end of the nineteenth century the progress of
trade unionism was slow and erratic, but it expanded very rapidly during
the first decade of the twentieth century. In 1901 the FOA (Argentine
Workers' Federation) was established, but this soon yielded place to the
FORA (Argentine Regional Workers' Federation). In 1905 the FORA,
at its Fifth Congress, came under anarchist control. Even though
anarchist influence waned after 1910, FORA remained under anarchist
control until its Ninth Congress in 1915, when syndicalists gained control
of most of the labour movement. In 1907 the UGT (General Workers'
Union) had been founded; this was a minority organization consisting of
trade unions with socialist tendencies. The labour movement of that
period had two principal centres: first, the big ports, at that time true
emporia of labour, in which the most varied activities and occupations
were closely interconnected. Later, the network of transport and related
industries which grew up around the principal railway centres became
the second centre.

The massive influx of immigrants, their assimilation into society, the rise and decline of social groups and the speed of the process of social change naturally led to a series of conflicts and tensions. During the 1870s there were clashes between native Argentines and foreigners, and some of these, like the Tandil massacres in 1871, involved bloodshed. The areas most affected were the rural districts of Santa Fe and Buenos Aires, while the capital and Rosario also witnessed conflicts of a similar nature. Between 1890 and 1895 there were similar clashes, for which once again the agricultural colonies of Santa Fe province were the principal scene. In Buenos Aires city, the crisis of 1890 produced 'chauvinist' reactions which were not of a serious character. Thereafter, this sort of conflict declined, though they recurred occasionally during periods of strikes and terrorist activities, which some people attributed to the action of foreign agitators.

Of much greater importance were various conflicts between different sectors of the population. In Argentina, confrontations between agriculturalists and industrialists, or between national and foreign undertakings, were rare and of little importance. However, there were conflicts between employers and workers, and sometimes between trade unions and the national authorities. Between 1907 and 1916, a period for which we have reliable data, there were 1,290 strikes in the city of Buenos Aires. Of these, five were general strikes.

The sectors most affected by labour stoppages were the lumber industry, clothes manufacturing, building, foodstuffs, metallurgy and textiles. Over half the strikes were aimed at winning increases in wages or reductions in working hours. As might be supposed in this formative period for the trade unions, many of the strikes (35 per cent) had as their objective the consolidation of union organizations. Nearly 40 per cent of the strikes obtained total or partial satisfaction of the workers' demands; most of them, however, were in the end disadvantageous to the strikers.

The above figures are somewhat distorted owing to the occurrence of general strikes of a political nature which were always unsuccessful. The theory of the general strike, which was in vogue in certain European countries, was restricted to a few districts in the country. On most occasions, such strikes did not even affect all the factories situated in the big cities: they were usually confined to the dock areas of Buenos Aires and Rosario and the principal railway centres. One demand always made by the participants in these general strikes was the repeal of the so-called Residence Law of 1902, which enabled the Executive Power to deport foreigners whom it considered dangerous to internal security.

In the rural areas, labour unrest on the same scale as in the big cities did not occur. The most serious conflict took place in 1912. Based on southern Santa Fe province, with ramifications in Córdoba and Buenos Aires, it affected the tenant-farmers of the prosperous maize-growing region, who at that time were facing low prices and high rents. For two months, the tenant-farmers refused to harvest the crop, and did so only when some of their demands had been met by the proprietors. It was after this curious episode, which was a mixture of strike and lock-out, that the Argentine Agrarian Federation was founded by the tenant-farmers of the cereal-growing region. During this period, in contrast, the peons of the stock-raising areas and workers in the north only established organizations very erratically.

Massive immigration had a profound impact on the style of life prevailing in the Río de la Plata littoral. Nevertheless, despite tensions and conflicts, the process of assimilation was, generally speaking, both rapid and peaceful. The residential quarters of Buenos Aires and the agricultural colonies of Santa Fe, to cite two examples, soon developed into real cosmopolitan centres where people of different nationalities were blended together. All aspects of daily life, from eating habits to language, were affected by this rapid assimilation of the immigrants into local society.

Various factors contributed to the rapidity with which the process of assimilation took place. First, in many regions, as has been observed above, the immigrants never constituted an ethnic minority, being sometimes more numerous than the local inhabitants. Furthermore, the majority of immigrants came from countries such as Italy and Spain, which had similar cultural, linguistic and religious characteristics. Moreover, civil legislation and everyday practice were extremely liberal towards the new arrivals, to such an extent that some people complained that the native born suffered discrimination. Of fundamental importance was the part played by the primary educational system (in accordance with Law No. 1,420), which created state schools without ethnic or religious discrimination, and gave education a markedly integrative character. Finally, participation in many shared activities accelerated the process of integration. Around 1914, for example, Buenos Aires had 214 mutual-aid societies, with 255,000 members. The majority (51.4 per cent) of the members belonged to mixed-national societies, consisting of people of different origins. Second in importance were the societies whose members were immigrants of the same nationality; and at the bottom of the list were a small minority of societies formed by native Argentines.

Local usages and customs were transformed not only by immigration but also by the sudden prosperity resulting from the long economic boom. We have already observed how the introduction of cereals modified the physical and social character of the areas concerned. To a lesser extent, there were similar transformations in the stock-raising area. The long barbed-wire fences, the fields planted with alfalfa and the high-quality stock contrasted with the rustic character of the old cattle ranch. Those austere and simple farmhouses which had impressed W. H. Hudson and other foreign travellers with their poverty were replaced by more elaborate, and at times luxurious, rural residences such as those that astonished the French traveller Jules Huret around 1910.

In the big cities the transformation was even more noticeable. Buenos Aires was, like all the metropolises of the time, a city of contrasts: 'Buenos Aires has its Picadilly and its Whitechapel, which here is called "the rubbish-heaps . . ." it has its "palaces", but it also has its "tenements".' These were the contrasts between the northern and the southern part of the city, contrasts continuously denounced in the political speeches of the socialists of Buenos Aires.[11] The south and the north represented the city's two extremes, and these areas in particular made an impression on those who visited them. The most important phenomenon, however, was less spectacular: it consisted of the new districts formed by one-storey houses of a lower middle-class character which sprang up on innumerable plots on the unused land. However, even in 1914, some empty spaces were still visible, standing as a symbol of the closeness of the pampas to the very heart of the city.

Indeed, almost everything in the city was new. Little remained of the austere and provincial Buenos Aires of former times. The city was unrecognizable to anyone who had visited it in 1880. Increasing affluence was soon displayed in the refinement and opulence of public buildings. The big administrative buildings, the extensive parks with their costly monuments, the new avenues, the trams and the underground railway, all bore witness to this sudden collective enrichment. European customs and fashions were transplanted to the Río de la Plata region with an unusual speed, not only because they were brought by the immigrants, but also because there was an increase in the number of

---

[11] J. Huret, *En Argentine: de Buenos Ayres au Gran Chaco* (Paris, 1914), 30. For the Socialist view, see, for example, the pamphlet by Mario Bravo *La ciudad libre* (Buenos Aires, 1917).

Argentines crossing the Atlantic in both directions. Buenos Aires was changing as quickly as the composition of its population was transformed. In each of the twenty districts that made up the city, at least 43 per cent of the population was foreign-born. In the five most central districts, which were the most populous and active and where commercial establishments, theatres, cafés and administrative buildings were concentrated, the proportion of foreigners fluctuated between 54 and 62 per cent. 'Where is Spanish blood, one wonders. What is an Argentine?' the Frenchman Jules Huret asked in astonishment.[12]

But as well as traffic in people, goods and customs there was, of course, traffic in ideas. Buenos Aires at the turn of the century was receptive to all the scientific, literary and political currents of thought that were in vogue. This receptiveness was fomented by the rapid expansion of secondary and university education, and the creation of innumerable scientific and literary societies. In Buenos Aires, around 1914, hundreds of periodical publications were in circulation, many of them in foreign languages (Italian, English, French, German, Russian, Greek, Danish and Arabic), and several of them became vehicles for some of the new ideas that were entering the country.

Liberalism continued to be the predominant creed among the groups that directed cultural, social, economic and political life. In some groups, this liberalism reflected a certain tension between the optimism characteristic of the period and further intensified by the spectacular material progress of the country, and a certain scepticism caused by the memory of a recent past characterized by instability, conflict and violence. This scepticism was accentuated by the suspicion that the combination of a vast geographical area and the Latin race was not the best foundation for a solidly based stability. Such attitudes found expression in the anxiety to overcome the South American syndrome, as it was known, and in the belief that this would only be possible if the reins of power continued firmly in the hands of those who had governed the country since 1880. Also frequently found was that curious combination of admiration for certain European countries and an ardent patriotism that was created by the feeling of being the founders of a new Republic. This attitude was clearly demonstrated in foreign policy. Thus, for instance, at the First Pan-American Congress (1889) the Argentine delegation proudly and successfully challenged the attempt by

[12] Huret, *En Argentine*, 40.

the United States to set up a continent-wide customs union. During the negotiations with European creditors in the wake of the financial crisis of 1890, the foreign minister took an equally firm line. No less consistent was the policy on defence, which aimed at tilting in Argentina's favour the balance of power with Chile and with Brazil. In the last analysis, Argentine politicians did not attempt to hide the pride they felt at guiding the destiny of the country which, by the beginning of the twentieth century, had become the most powerful and prosperous in South America.

This brand of liberalism existed alongside another variant, popular in intellectual and political circles, and of a more decidedly optimistic and universalist character. This strand of liberalism was strongly influenced by Darwin, Spencer, Lombroso, and so on, and by nearly all the positivist and evolutionary theories then in vogue. These tendencies were to be reflected in official publications overflowing with statistics that proudly demonstrated the constant progress of the country. They were to be found also in some unexpected places, like the new and sophisticated Zoological Gardens whose construction was influenced by the ideas contained in Darwin's *Origin of Species*.

Such ideas, or the various combinations of them, did not suffer any serious challenge in the period before the first world war. During the discussion of the secularizing laws passed in the 1880s, the Catholic opponents of these laws proclaimed the same political and economic liberalism that underlay the ideas of the legislators who supported the government's proposals. Perhaps this is one of the reasons why the religious factor was only very sporadically a cause of political dissension in Argentina. Nor did the political opposition put forward ideas openly at variance with those prevailing among the ruling groups; not, at least, in the economic and social sphere, nor in that of existing institutions. In the case of the principal opposition force, the Radical Civic Union, criticism of the regime took on a strong moralistic overtone in reaction to what was considered to be a society excessively cosmopolitan and too obsessed with material welfare. The anti-positivist and nationalist reaction which began to emerge after 1900 can be seen in the speeches and documents emanating from the Radical Civic Union.

As we have seen, until about 1910–15 the labour movement was dominated by the anarchists. The Argentine anarchists, however, were significantly different from their European counterparts. Although both groups utterly rejected participation in parliamentary and electoral processes, and the intervention of the state in negotiations between employers and unions, in Argentina the prevailing doctrine was a kind of anarcho-syndicalism *avant la lettre* which concentrated its activities almost exclusively on the trade union. On the basis of the union the anarchists organized a series of co-operative, recreational and cultural activities which gave them a certain popularity in the working-class districts of Buenos Aires and Rosario. Nevertheless, in spite of their Bakuninist rhetoric, the Argentine anarchists were much more moderate than their European counterparts, and their more radical factions (including terrorists) found little acceptance in the Argentine milieu.

Much the same was true in the case of the socialists, who were moderate even in comparison with the contemporary currents of reformist thought that appeared in Europe. The Argentine socialists soon replaced a series of Marxist premises with ideas derived from the liberal and positivist tradition. At the same time, the political models which they most admired were the British and Australian labour movements, Belgian co-operativism and French radical-socialist tradition. Consequently, it is not surprising that when he visited Buenos Aires, the Italian socialist Enrico Ferri should have characterized his Argentine *confrères* as members of a 'Socialist party of the moon'.[13] Like the anarchists, the socialists did not question the basic foundations of the Argentine economy: they were supporters of free trade and ardent defenders of a strictly orthodox monetary policy. On both subjects, they were, in fact, much more emphatic than the politicians supporting the government. Alfredo Palacios, the first Socialist member of parliament to be elected in the Americas (1904), summed up exactly his party's economic ideology in rejecting the protectionist arguments put forward by the legislators who supported the government: 'While eternally protected industries enjoy the benefits of restrictive legislation, our true national wealth, namely stock raising and agriculture, is neglected.'[14]

The profound economic changes which occurred after 1870 had a pronounced influence on Argentine society, and, among other things, led to new social conflicts. However, these conflicts were in their turn conditioned by increasing well-being, the high rate of social mobility, and the success of an economic process that produced more beneficiaries

---

[13] Juan B. Justo, 'El Profesor Ferri y el Partido Socialista Argentino', *Socialismo* (Buenos Aires, 1920), 129ff.

[14] Quoted in O. Cornblit, 'Sindicatos obreros y asociaciones empresarias', in G. Ferrari and E. Gallo (eds.), *La Argentina del ochenta al centenario* (Buenos Aires, 1980), 595–626.

than victims. Argentina in 1914 bore little resemblance to the rest of Latin America, and, despite the Europeanization of many customs and ideas, it was also different from the Old World. It was in some ways similar to the new societies that had emerged on the plains of Australia and North America. But as we shall now see, the social situation was not mirrored in political and institutional life.

POLITICS BETWEEN 1880 AND 1912

The triumph of General Roca in the struggle of 1880 was followed by the formation of the National Autonomist party (PAN), the earliest nationwide political organization in Argentina. In addition, the National Army acquired a monopoly of force and became, with occasional exceptions, the firm support of the national authorities. In comparison with earlier periods, the new political stability was based on the universally recognized supremacy of the National Executive and a corresponding decline in the power of provincial leaders and *caudillos*. The central government maintained its control over the provinces by means of a graduated system of rewards and punishments, designed to achieve a delicate equilibrium between the need to obtain the support of the governing authorities and the desire to avoid the repetition of seditious acts. The provincial governors had a significant, though subordinate, role in the official coalition (PAN), and were rewarded with positions of prestige on a national scale. The sanctions were no less efficient. They consisted of federal intervention, which the Executive could decree even during periods of parliamentary recess (which could last as long as seven months). This was a powerful instrument for dealing with movements of disaffection. The role of federal intervention was defined thus by Osvaldo Magnasco, one of the most prominent politicians of the official party:

Federal interventions in this country, gentlemen, have invariably been decided on with one of these ends in view: to suppress a certain influence or to re-establish it, to set up a local government capable of guaranteeing the domestic position of the Executive, or to overturn a local government opposed to the central government.[15]

The constitution had facilitated presidential supremacy through such mechanisms as federal intervention. However, it had also placed

---

[15] Quoted in J. Irazusta, *El tránsito del siglo XIX al XX* (Buenos Aires, 1975), 169.

obstacles in its path: above all, the principle that forbade presidential re-election (a significant difference from, for example, the Mexico of Porfirio Díaz), and the control exercised over the executive by the judiciary and the Congress. The judiciary, especially, managed to maintain a degree of independence from the central powers. Further-more, the liberal principles of the constitution made possible the development of an extremely influential press which kept a close watch over the actions of the national authorities. This press, at least until the beginning of the twentieth century, had more importance in the formation of public opinion than did electoral activities. Ramón Cárcano was not far from the truth when he pointed out to Roca's successor Juárez Celman (1886–1890) that 'a newspaper for a man in public life is like a knife for a quarrelsome *gaucho*; he should always have it at hand'.[16] The turn-out at elections made matters easier: it was low in comparison to subsequent periods, though not so low when compared with that common in other countries of the world during these years. In normal circumstances votes were cast by between 10 and 15 per cent of the population eligible to vote (male Argentines of over 18 years of age; there were no literacy requirements). At times of great political enthusiasm (the years 1890–5, for example), turn-out might rise as high as 20 or 25 per cent of those entitled to vote. Moreover, the poll was much higher in the rural than in the urban areas.

If voting amongst those eligible was low, it was even lower as a percentage of the total male population of voting age. This was due to the enormous number of foreigners resident in the country, the great majority of whom had not acquired citizenship. The reasons for not doing so are unclear. In the first place, the foreigners had not immigrated with this objective in mind, and Argentine legislation did not establish discrimination of any kind with regard to their carrying on their activities in society. Moreover, if they did not become naturalized they could still count on the support of the consuls of their respective countries, some of whom, such as the Italian consuls, were extremely active in keeping the immigrants faithful to their countries of origin. Secondly, citizenship papers were not needed for petitioning and pressuring the authorities, since this could be done through employers' and workers' organizations. Besides, the anarchists and syndicalists attached no importance to the acquisition of citizenship papers. Finally,

16 Quoted by T. Duncan, 'La prensa política en la Argentina: Sud-América. 1885–1892', in G. Ferrari and E. Gallo (eds.), *La Argentina del ochenta al centenario*, 761–84.

the opposition parties, with the exception of the socialists, showed little interest in recruiting foreigners into their ranks.

At that time, political indifference was the characteristic attitude of the majority of the population. Voting was not obligatory (as it was after 1912); on the contrary, from his inclusion in the electoral register until polling day, the citizen had to show interest and diligence in order to be able to vote. Furthermore, the elections were more than once character-ized by fraudulent practices of various types, which were quite common at the time. Fraud did not, of course, take place systematically, because the apathy of the population made that unnecessary. It was, however, employed whenever the opposition overcame that apathy and threatened the stability of the governing authorities. There were various kinds of fraud, ranging from the most inoffensive tricks and the purchase of votes to the open use of physical violence. For this to be effective, however, those who indulged in it (sometimes the opposition) had to be able to count on the solid support of their political clientele and to have a proper organization.

This political organization had to supply men to fill the many varied appointments on the national, provincial and municipal administration, and it had to supply members of parliament and journalists to reply to the attacks of the opposition. However, it also had to win some popular support in order to be prepared for elections and even armed revolts, which remained an important feature of Argentine politics. For it was not only regular military forces which took part in armed revolts. On many occasions sizeable contingents of civilians also joined in. Until 1881 the provincial militias were the chief source of civilian involvement in revolts, especially in rural areas. These militias, which were generally led by political *caudillos* with military experience, were the main support of the provincial governments. Some of them, like the Santafesinos in 1880, even played an important part in national politics.

After the disbandment of the militias (1881), armed uprising with significant civilian involvement continued to occur. The revolution of 1890, which failed to overthrow the political system but which led to the fall of Juárez Celman, was organizationally a classic military-civilian uprising led by a political faction. Civilian involvement, however, was on a far smaller scale than in the bloody events of 1880. Nevertheless, during the provincial revolts of 1893 in Santa Fe, Buenos Aires, Corrientes, San Luis and Tucumán, large groups of civilians joined the combatants. In Santa Fe, many hundreds of immigrant farmers took up arms in defence of the revolutionaries. The number of people involved in these revolts was similar to the number of voters in the 1894 elections for the Santa Fe and Buenos Aires districts.

As a consequence of this violence, recruitment in politics had to be carried out with an eye to the possibility that recruits would be involved in fighting at great risk to their lives. It was for this reason that strong bonds of loyalty had to be formed between the leaders and their followers. Those responsible for cementing these bonds were not the national leaders, but the *caudillos* (bosses) of the rural districts or the urban areas. Such people held a key position in the political mechanism, because they were the real link between the regime and its clientele. The loyalty of this clientele was not freely bestowed, but was based on a complex system of reciprocal favours. The political boss provided a series of services which ranged from the solution of communal problems to the less altruistic activity of protecting criminal acts. Between these two extremes, there were small personal favours, among which obtaining jobs was paramount.

The *caudillos* were men of the most varied origins (small landowners or merchants, overseers of ranches and, more usually, ex-officers of the disbanded provincial militias) and, even though at times they held minor political appointments (as justices of the peace, deputies, etc.), they were usually content to exercise extra-official influence and power in their region. They were praised and vilified, and these two extremes represent, in a way, real facets of an extremely complex reality. Thus it could be asserted that 'to these *caudillos* the government . . . gives everything and permits anything – the police, the municipality, the post-office . . . cattle rustling, roulette, in short all kinds of assistance for their friends and persecution to their enemies'. On the other hand, the *caudillo* could be defined as 'the man who is useful to his neighbours and always ready to be of service'.[17] What is quite evident is that they possessed a great degree of independence, and that it was necessary to enter into intensive negotiations in order to obtain their support. In the words of one of the most influential *caudillos* of the province of Buenos Aires, on the occasion of the compilation of the list of candidates for the provincial elections of 1894:

What we conventionally refer to as the Provincial Union [the name of the PAN in Buenos Aires province] is composed of two parts: there is a decorative part,

---

17 Francisco Seguí, quoted in D. Peck, 'Argentine politics and the Province of Mendoza, 1890–1916' (unpublished D.Phil. thesis, Oxford, 1977), 36, and Mariano de Vedia, quoted in *ibid.*, 32.

made up of certain absentee landowners who reside in the city of Buenos Aires whose importance is more social and metropolitan than rural, and another part, the real militant electorate, made up of us, who are those who . . . have struggled in the province . . . We respect the decorative value of the other part, but we shall do so only if the real interests of the countryside, that is to say of the real provincial party, are taken into account . . .'[18]

Above this complex and extensive network of local bosses there were the provincial and national directorates of the official party, which was an equally complex and variable group of political leaders. These men were governors, ministers, legislators, and so on, and from their ranks emerged both the president of the Republic and the leader of the PAN, who were often one and the same person. From 1880 to 1916 this ruling group controlled national politics and, with very few exceptions, ruled the destinies of the Argentine provinces. The political opposition and certain more or less neutral observers accused it of being a monolithic and closed oligarchy which used any means to maintain its predominant position; a description which was, up to a point, correct, especially as regards the well-known political exclusiveness which the ruling group displayed. This picture, however, risks being somewhat stereotyped. Among other things, it takes no account of the fact that the ruling group that emerged in 1880 was, to a certain extent, the product of a significant change within the political leadership of Argentina. Carlos Melo, one of the first historians to observe this phenomenon, described it as follows:

At the same time, the conquest of the desert and the distribution of land . . . had increased the numbers of landowners by the addition of rough characters of humble extraction, and no less obscure soldiers rewarded for their military services . . . Both the new urban middle-class group and the new landowners were resisted by the patrician nuclei of old Argentine society, which explains why the former, in their aversion to the latter, gave their support to the president [Roca].[19]

The description of the new type of politician given by Melo is exaggerated, and expresses too rigid a dichotomy. However, it is a good description of a marked tendency and, at the same time, accurately reflects the way the ruling group was seen by its political opponents. This perception, which was quite clear in such places as Buenos Aires, Córdoba and Tucumán, was characteristic of the 1880s, and persisted until at least the middle of the following decade. It was a political phenomenon which reflected what was happening in the social sphere.

---

[18] *La Prensa* (Buenos Aires), 20 December 1893.
[19] C. R. Melo, *La campaña presidencial de 1885–6* (Córdoba, 1949), 22.

The political homogeneity of this ruling group should not be exaggerated. It was made up of people who represented regional interests which were often at variance. The history of the regime was marked by numerous internecine conflicts which had some influence on its final collapse. The periods of stability coincided with epochs of strong personal leadership, especially during the presidencies of Roca (1880–6, 1898–1904). On the other hand, instability predominated when the absence of strong leadership opened the field for all those opposed interests.

During this period, the term 'oligarchy' was used in its classic political sense. The PAN certainly counted among its members many who were prominent in social and economic life. However, many members of the elite were active in the opposition parties and were at times excluded from public life in consequence. Furthermore, the majority of the most prominent figures of the business world displayed a notorious indifference to politics, possibly because the contending groups did not differ very much in their conception of economic organization. One episode provides a good illustration of this phenomenon, because it is the only example of an explicit connection being established between the official faction and an important group of stock raisers in Buenos Aires province. During the election for provincial governor in 1894, the Provincial Union (the official party) was nicknamed the 'cattle party' on account of the well-known involvement in it of the Buenos Aires stock raisers. The Radical newspaper *El Argentino* predicted that the official candidate was going to have the following characteristics:

he will have to be somewhat *high life* (sic). He must above all have connections with the Jockey Club, because this appears to be an indispensable condition for a person who is to govern . . . This gentleman will have the advantage of being . . . a landowner, merchant, politician and financier . . .[20]

Those of the 'cattle party' did not spurn their nickname. Some members, such as Miguel Cané, adopted it with complacent pride: 'Yes, gentlemen, we are "cattle" and "sheep" because we are striving for the enrichment of every district of the province. As "cattle" and "sheep" we demand freedom for men, security for the cattle herds, and improvements in wool production . . .' At the same time, the official press would describe the opposition Radical party as 'pigs', clearly alluding to the support it received from the Agrarian League. However, the political

[20] *El Argentino* (Buenos Aires), 9 November 1893.

rhetoric of the period conceals the fact that the opposition parties (Radicals and *cívicos*) also numbered prominent Buenos Aires stock raisers among their members. The Agrarian League itself was made up of rural proprietors who were far from occupying the humble economic status suggested by the nickname 'pigs'. Finally, on this occasion the opposition was able to count on considerable support in other important financial and commercial circles, both national and foreign.[21]

The pre-eminence of personal rule also led to divisions within the ranks of the official party. Juárez Celman, for example, attempted to depose Roca from the leadership of the PAN and undermine the position held by Roca and his supporters both in the PAN and in the provinces. From 1889 onwards, the supporters of Juárez Celman also launched a bold political offensive against the Federal Capital, chief stronghold of the opposition. Their plan failed, however, because the financial crisis of 1890 created conditions favourable to the military revolt of the opposition. Yet it was not the opposition that benefited from the revolt, but rather Roca, who regained the position he had lost in the PAN, and Vice President Carlos Pellegrini, who became president (1890–2). The forces that supported Juárez Celman were not entirely defeated, and promptly regrouped into the Modernist party, thereby obliging Roca and Pellegrini to seek the support of Bartolomé Mitre, who had led the moderate wing of the revolutionaries and who expected to succeed to the presidency in 1892. In the event a weak compromise candidate, Luis Sáenz Peña, became president (1892–4). His period in office was characterized by unstable coalition cabinets and further armed insurrections organized by the Radicals. The resignation of Sáenz Peña because of ill health, his replacement by the pro-Roca Vice President José Evaristo Uriburu (1894–8) and the defeat of the armed revolts made possible a new consolidation of the power of Roca, which culminated in his election to the presidency for the second time (1898–1904). In 1901, however, Carlos Pellegrini, a national senator at the time, broke with Roca over the handling of the negotiations on the foreign debt. Roca found himself obliged to form a new coalition which in 1904 elected as president Manuel Quintana (1904–6), a former sympathizer of Mitre, and as vice president a Modernist, José Figueroa Alcorta. When Quintana

---

[21] Cané's speech in *La Tribuna* (Buenos Aires), 11 January 1894. The majority of the business community was in fact somewhat indifferent to political developments. For the attitudes of those who did participate in politics, see Ezequiel Gallo, 'Un quinquenio difícil. Las presidencias de Carlos Pellegrini y Luis Sáenz Peña (1890–95)', in Ferrari and Gallo (eds.), *La Argentina del ochenta al centenario*, 215–44.

died in 1906, he was replaced by Figueroa Alcorta (1906–10) who, with
the support of the dissident elements in the official party and a few
members of the opposition, destroyed the political coalition (especially
in the interior) on the basis of which Roca had enjoyed twenty-five years
of political predominance.

Roca fell by the very instrument on which he had based his
predominance: the enormous power of the presidential office. This
power was derived from two sources: a strongly personalist historical
legacy, and a national constitution which had granted very extensive
powers to the National Executive. To all this was added the fear of chaos
and anarchy which had been the legacy of the difficult decades before
1880. Roca clearly described the tremendous tension existing between
stability and order on the one hand and political freedom on the other. He
was aware of the countless defects which plagued Argentine democracy,
but he believed they were rooted in the age-old habits of the people. The
cure for political ills, therefore, had to be slow, gradual and firmly based
on consolidated and stable national institutions. In 1903, in one of his last
presidential addresses, he pointed out clearly what progress had been
made and what further steps had to be taken to crown the achievement of
the country's institutional organization:

In our brief and eventful existence as a nation we have travelled . . . through
civil wars, tyranny and disorder, an enormous distance, and today we can look to
the future without the uncertainties and anxieties of earlier times . . . Without
doubt there remain for us . . . many conquests to be made over ourselves, who
have such a propensity to set ourselves lofty ideals and to demand of the
government, political parties and constitutional practice the last word in
political wisdom which supposes a degree of perfection . . . which has still not
been attained even by peoples with a centuries-old history. More than on written
laws, a republican form of government is founded on public habits and
customs.[22]

Thus, Roca did not believe that a perfect representative democracy
could be achieved in haste. Towards the end of his life he once again
emphasized his old obsessions and strongly defended the guiding
principles of his political thought:

to defend . . . two essential things, which are always in danger: the principle of
authority and of national union against the forces, latent but always menacing,
of rebellion, anarchy and dissolution. For one must not harbour illusions
regarding the solidity of our organization, or of national unity . . . Anarchy is

---

[22] H. Mabragaña, *Los Mensajes*, IV, 66–7.

not a plant that disappears in half a century or a century, in ill-united societies such as ours.[23]

The opposition

Between 1880 and 1914 a variety of groups and parties made up the ranks of the opposition. Some had only an ephemeral life, like the Catholic groups during the 1880s, while others were confined exclusively to a particular province. Of the provincially based parties only two, the Socialists in the federal capital and the Southern League (later called the Progressive Democratic party) in Santa Fe, achieved any influence nationally. The traditional opposition to the PAN came from the forces defeated in 1880, especially the followers of General Bartolomé Mitre. These groups adopted various names (nationalists, liberals, *cívicos*, republicans) and survived until the end of the period. In 1890 the Civic Union was formed. This soon split into two factions, the National Civic Union (UCN) led by Mitre and the Radical Civic Union (UCR) led by Leandro Alem. Although the Radicals suffered from various cases of internal dissension, usually as a result of the attempts of some members to form coalitions with the official party or with the followers of Mitre, they soon became the principal opposition party. After the suicide of Alem in 1896, his nephew Hipólito Yrigoyen became the most prominent figure in the UCR and maintained that position until his death in 1933.

The opposition had no more activists than the government party. On the contrary, the PAN was better organized and had a political clientele, especially in the rural areas, which could be more easily mobilized. It was only during a few periods of political agitation that the opposition was able to mobilize its supporters. During the 1890–4 period, with comparatively honest elections, the numbers of voters rose significantly, and the opposition achieved partial victories in the most developed parts of the country (the capital, Buenos Aires province and the cereal-growing districts of Santa Fe). However, even in these districts the principal political forces were well-matched and enjoyed strikingly homogeneous social support. Only after the passing of the Sáenz Peña Law in 1912 (see below) would differences arise between the electoral strength of the official and opposition parties.

Nor were there significant differences between the leaders of the

---

[23] Quoted in J. de Vedia, *Como los vi yo* (Buenos Aires, 1922), 6off.

official and opposition parties, as we have seen. There were, of course, no differences with the UCN, an old and traditional Buenos Aires party. The UCR, in its early stages, had been formed by people who were prominent members of the traditional parties. It is true, however, that it had made possible the return to politics of individuals who, for one reason or another, had been excluded from public life. By 1912 this picture had changed somewhat, but the differences were still minor in character. Some time later, Federico Pinedo remarked on these differences, pointing out that:

it cannot be said that between one party and another, *especially up to 1916*, there was any marked difference, because the men of the different parties had the same conception of collective life and similar conceptions as regards economic organization, but there was, and this has perhaps become accentuated, a certain social basis – of category, if not of class – for political antagonism.[24]

The opposition, with a few exceptions, did not put forward programmes very different from those of the official party, and there were few differences as regards economic and social matters. In fact, with the exception of the Socialists in the labour field, the reforms proposed during this period came from the ranks of the PAN. In certain fields (such as tariff and monetary policy), it was also the official party that advanced the most heterodox proposals. The opposition always tried to focus the debate on political and constitutional issues and was more or less uninterested in any other topic. The Radicals themselves were conscious of the fact that the name of the party was perhaps too 'extreme' in view of the modest nature of some of its demands.

The opposition parties demanded honest elections, criticized the concentration of power and often launched bitter attacks against an administration which it considered to be excessively materialistic and, at times, corrupt. But they did not put forward any specific proposal in this field. The two proposals for electoral reform (those of 1904 and 1912) came from the official party. Instead, the opposition demanded that the constitution be implemented to the letter, and their declarations had a strong moralistic content. This is the impression given by both the moving protests of Sarmiento during the 1880s (until his death in 1888) against the 'arrogance' of power and the indifference of the citizenry ('this is a tolerated monarchy'),[25] and the fiery speeches of Alem from 1888 until his death in 1896 denouncing the concentration of power and

---

[24] Federico Pinedo, *En tiempos de la República* (Buenos Aires, 1946), I, 25.
[25] *Epistolario Sarmiento-Posse* (Buenos Aires, 1946), II, 419.

protesting at the limitation of provincial autonomy and political rights. A similar and even stronger impression is provoked by the abstruse writings of Hipólito Yrigoyen, with his clear-cut division of the world into an evil 'Regime' and a good 'Cause' (the UCR). The same could be said of the more cautious and prudent exhortations of Bartolomé Mitre, demanding a return to more austere practices of republican government. Even the moderate Socialist, Juan B. Justo, the founder of the party in 1894 and its leader until his death in 1928, followed a similar line with his ironical references to, what he derisively called 'Creole politics'.

The opposition was not, of course, entirely free of the defects (fraud, the influence of political bosses, etc.) which it criticized in the official party. Nor was personalism absent from their ranks. Such personalities as Mitre, Alem, Yrigoyen and even Justo played in the opposition parties a role very similar to that of Roca, Pellegrini or Roque Sáenz Peña in the official party. What the opposition challenged, basically, was a style of political life implacably oriented towards their exclusion. It is true that the vices of Argentine politics were also to be found in other countries at the time. However, even where this was the case, as in Spain, opposing forces were able to alternate in power. In Argentina this did not happen, except on the few occasions when divisions within the official faction obliged it to form coalitions, albeit unstable and ephemeral ones, with the more moderate elements of the opposition.

This style of politics affected the forms of action adopted by the opposition. There was a marked contrast between the virulence of its rhetoric and the moderation of its proposals and its programme. The Radicals eventually made 'Intransigence', their stubborn refusal to take part in any kind of agreement or political coalition, into a religious dogma. Furthermore, the opposition sometimes had recourse to armed insurrection as the only means of getting into power. For this purpose, it could count on the support of a few sectors within the armed forces which had not forgotten their old habits. The most serious incident was the Civic Union's revolt of July 1890 which as we have seen forced the resignation of Juárez Celman. Later, in 1892–3, there was a series of provincial uprisings, as a result of which the Radicals came to power for a short time in some provincial administrations. In 1905 the Radicals, now under Yrigoyen, attempted another insurrection, but when this failed they began to concentrate rather more on broadening their political base among the growing urban and rural middle class. Meanwhile, the revolutionary outlook of the Radicals and their almost mechanical propensity to indulge in armed insurrections were exploited with great skill by the governing groups, to demonstrate that there would be a future of chaos and anarchy if the Radicals ever got into power.

THE END OF THE REGIME, 1912–16

In 1916 the principal opposition party, the Radical Civic Union, came to power after winning the presidential elections of that year. This Radical victory was made possible by the electoral law proposed by President Roque Sáenz Peña (1910–14) and passed by parliament in 1912, which established universal, secret and compulsory suffrage for all male citizens over the age of eighteen. Furthermore, the electoral register and the control of elections were entrusted to the army instead of provincial police forces which had been too susceptible to pressures exercised by the government of the day. The so-called Sáenz Peña Law was a consequence of the infighting within the PAN and the final victory of the anti-Roca forces which since 1891 had been pressing for a change in electoral practices. It was also a Conservative response to the threat to stability posed by the conspiratorial activities of the Radical party and, to a lesser extent, by the growth of the Socialist party and the anarchist-led strikes. In the parliamentary debates on the Law in 1911 the official party was confident and certain of an electoral victory in 1916 and thus the legitimation of its dominance. And the elections did indeed show that the party was still an important electoral force. However, it was the leader of the UCR, Hipólito Yrigoyen, who was in the event elected president. What had gone wrong?

In the first place, the official party entered the electoral contest of 1916 in a weakened and divided condition following the confrontation between Roca and Pellegrini during Roca's second administration (1898–1904) and the anti-Roca presidency of Figueroa Alcorta (1906–10). The liberal sectors put forward the candidature of Lisandro de la Torre, the leader of a party which had originally belonged to the opposition, the Progressive Democratic party. This candidature was resisted by the strong Conservative provincial bosses, led by the most powerful, Marcelino Ugarte, who was governor of Buenos Aires province. The result was that the official party entered the contest of 1916 divided and with two candidates, which greatly diminished its chances of victory. The political coalition that had governed the country for 35 years was made up of extremely heterogeneous provincial forces, with marked centrifugal tendencies. Only the presence of strong personalities, especially that of Roca, had maintained the unity of this coalition. Roca died in 1914, and by 1916 so had his principal adversaries within the official parties, Pellegrini (in 1906) and Sáenz Peña (in August 1914). The latter was replaced in the presidency by Victorino de la Plaza (1914–16), who was an experienced politician but who lacked qualities needed for the arduous and complex task of uniting the party in 1916. In the second place, the beginning of the electoral cycle of 1912–16 coincided with the first downturn in the economy for almost twenty years. Thirdly, the Sáenz Peña Law led to an unprecedented political mobilization throughout the country. Voting increased threefold or fourfold in the parliamentary elections of 1912, 1913, and 1914, and rose still further in the presidential elections of 1916. Between 1912 and 1914 the Radicals obtained a number of governorships, and on two occasions (1913 and 1914) the Socialists won in the Federal Capital. What the opposition had been unable to achieve in a quarter of a century, the law achieved in the space of a few years.

The Radicals, united behind a strong candidate, quickly took advantage of the new situation. Radical committees were set up throughout the country, and groups of different origin joined this political force which appeared to have a chance of success. These committees were organized on fairly modern lines in the big cities and in some cereal-growing districts. In the rest of the country, their organization was a replica of the system of political bosses and personal favours which had characterized the Autonomist regime.

The Radicals triumphed in the most prosperous parts of the country. In the Pampa littoral, they won in the Federal Capital, Santa Fe, Córdoba and Entre Ríos. In this region the Radical votes were concentrated in the cities and in rural areas where cereal growing was most important. Although they did not achieve a majority, they also mustered significant support in the stock-raising areas. In the cities their votes came principally from the middle-class districts, although they also obtained support in the working-class districts and, to a lesser degree, in some upper-class residential areas. In the interior of the country, the Radicals won in the most developed provinces (Mendoza and Tucumán), and except for Santiago del Estero they were defeated in the areas which had developed least rapidly since 1888. The Radical electorate was, therefore, based on the intermediate sectors (both urban and rural) of the most advanced parts of the country, but there was a significant measure of support in all regions and among all social classes. These results were a reflection of the moderation, flexibility, and disinclination to make clear-cut definitions about ideology or political programmes that character-ized the leadership of the party.

The official parties found their greatest electoral support in the provinces of the interior and the stock-raising areas of the littoral. In the latter region, it was only in Buenos Aires province that the traditional conservative electoral organization was able to compete successfully with the Radicals. The populist nature of some of its *caudillos* enabled them to win even in some important cities such as Avellaneda. The most obvious of the political weaknesses of the conservatives was their poor electoral showing in the most advanced areas of the country, that is to say the city of Buenos Aires and the province of Santa Fe. Paradoxically, the official parties suffered their most crushing defeats in those areas which had benefited most from the economic boom that began in 1880.

The official parties and the Radicals together obtained over 85 per cent of the votes. The Socialists came a poor third, their votes being confined in practice to the city of Buenos Aires and some surrounding districts, where, however, they had to face strong competition from the Radicals. The moderate character of the Socialists enabled them to offset part of their losses in working-class votes with significant, though minority, support in the middle-class districts. In the rest of the country, the Socialists won a few votes in some cities, especially in those where there were important railway centres. In certain big cities, like Rosario and Bahía Blanca, some workers voted for the Radicals possibly at the instigation of trade-union leaders of syndicalist or anarchist persuasion. The Socialists polled very few votes in the rural areas, even where, as in Tucumán, there was an important sugar industry.

Thirty-six years of Autonomist rule produced a relatively stable political and legal system, thus providing one of the prerequisites for a rapid and sustained process of economic and social growth. In the end, however, it was the Radical opposition and its leader Hipólito Yrigoyen who profited from the momentous changes undergone by Argentine society since 1880. For the followers of Roca and Pellegrini, all that was left was the consolation of having presided over a political transition both peaceful and honourable.

The electoral reform of 1912 was followed by a period of almost two decades during which for the first time constitutional rule and political stability were combined with free and honest elections. Argentina's political ills were, however, only partially the result of its electoral legislation. They were rather the consequence of long-standing institutional habits and traditions that left little space for compromise and the sharing of political power. Yrigoyen was as staunch a believer in the power of the presidency and strong central government as Roca had been. He made even greater use than his predecessors had of the most powerful political weapon at his disposal (federal intervention). Thus the long-standing political traditions of exclusivist government and seditious opposition were not broken and the seeds for future instability were left untouched. In 1930 at a time of intense economic and political crisis the opposition, as in 1874, 1880, 1893 and 1905, chose to associate itself with a military coup rather than to abide by the rules of the democratic game. This time the coup was successful, and not only Argentina's experiment with democracy but almost 70 years of constitutional government came to an abrupt end.

Argentina in 1914

4

ARGENTINA IN 1914: THE PAMPAS, THE INTERIOR, BUENOS AIRES

On the eve of the outbreak of the first world war Argentina had enjoyed since 1880, apart from a quinquennium of depression in the early 1890s, almost 35 years of remarkable economic growth. The main impulse had been exogenous: foreign labour, foreign capital, and favourable foreign markets for its exports. In 1914 around one-third of Argentina's population of almost eight million, which the third national census showed had increased more than fourfold since the first census in 1869, was foreign-born; at least another quarter was composed of the descendants of immigrants from the past two generations. According to later estimates by the United Nations' Economic Commission for Latin America (ECLA), in 1914 foreign investments (around 60 per cent of them British), both public and private, accounted for half the country's capital stock, equal to two and a half years of the value of gross domestic production. Since 1900 foreign investment had risen at an annual rate of 11.41 per cent. British investors possessed around 80 per cent of the Argentine railway system, large tracts of its land, most of its tramways and urban utility companies, and some of its meat-packing plants and industries. ECLA again estimated that the annual rate of growth in the rural sector, already 7 per cent between 1895 and 1908, had risen to 9 per cent between 1908 and 1914. In the great compendium it issued on the Republic's affairs in 1911,[1] Lloyd's Bank of London pointed out that whereas until around 1903 the value of foreign trade in Argentina and Brazil was broadly equal, by 1909 Argentina's had grown by half as much again above its leading rival in the subcontinent. On the eve of the first world war per capita foreign trade in Argentina was almost six times the average in the rest of Latin America. It had attained a magnitude greater

---

[1] Reginald Lloyd (ed.), *Twentieth century impressions of Argentina* (London, 1911).

than Canada's and was already a quarter of that of the United States. The country had catapulted itself among the ranks of the world's leading cereal and meat exporters. It was the largest exporter of maize and linseed. It was second in wool, and third in live cattle and horses. If it ranked only sixth as a producer of wheat, it was still the third, and in some years the second, largest exporter. Despite the competition from cattle for the land, the expansion of wheat production after 1900 was faster than in Canada.

Apart from entrepôts like Holland and Belgium, no country in the world imported more goods per head of population than Argentina. Per capita incomes compared with Germany and the Low Countries, and were higher than Spain, Italy, Sweden and Switzerland. Buenos Aires, the federal capital, with its million and a half inhabitants, was proclaimed the 'Paris of South America'. Having grown at an average rate of 6.5 per cent since 1869, it was now, after New York, the second most populous city of the Atlantic seaboard. It was by far the largest city in Latin America, having for the time being left Rio de Janeiro, Mexico City, Santiago and the rest trailing far behind.

The euphoria of the years before the first world war was sometimes tempered by a sense that Argentina still had an enormous distance to traverse. Among the many European sophisticates who now visited the country, and eagerly debated its accomplishments, there was general agreement that the age of infancy was past; not so that of adolescence. Maturity beckoned in the shape of still greater ministrations of capital and labour. To have infused the Republic with a new population; to have constructed there one of the largest railway systems in the world; to have fenced in the pampas and brought 50 million acres under the plough; to have endowed Buenos Aires and Rosario with the most advanced port facilities; to have introduced into these and other cities from Bahía Blanca to Salta tramways, gas, water and electricity plants; these were undoubtedly considerable achievements. Yet it still left the country far short of fulfilling the destiny which General Roca and his successors had constantly invoked since 1880. This generation had looked to Argentina not merely as a leader in Latin America but as the antipodean counterweight to the United States. It dreamt of a Republic of 100 million people or more, imbued throughout with the same pulsating tempo as its eastern core.[2] Yet in 1914 a population of less than eight

[2] Cf. Carlos Pellegrini in Alberto B. Martínez and Maurice Lewandowski, *The Argentine in the twentieth century* (London, 1911), xv.

million inhabited a land mass equal to the whole of continental Europe between the Baltic, the Mediterranean and the Danube estuary. And the hand of change was for the most part visible only in the capital and its immediate pampas hinterland. Beyond this 500-mile radius most of the interior remained in a state of moribund backwardness.

The ambitions of the past generation were predicated upon the indefinite continuation of the present. But objectively there were already many grounds for doubting whether they would ever be realized. Already in 1913 a new depression had brought to an end the inflow of immigrants and foreign capital. These were signs of changing conditions in the outside world. In part they also suggested that Argentina was reaching saturation point in its capacity to absorb resources from abroad. For some time past the best land in Argentina had already been brought into production. Much of what remained would offer far more meagre returns to investors and pioneers alike. The old interior seemed no more likely now to follow the pampas into exporting than ever in its history. The most to be hoped for here was that growth on the pampas would continue to amplify the domestic market and in this way slowly awaken the regions beyond.

In 1914 there was as yet no alternative to the primary export economy. Despite the recent growth of manufacturing – by 1913 local industry provided one-third of Argentina's processed food products, one-eighth of its metals and one-sixth of its textiles[3] – there was as yet no conclusive evidence that the country had an imminent future as a fully fledged industrial power. Local manufacturing was heavily dependent upon the growth of domestic demand and incomes from the export sector and the inflow of foreign investments. At this point, despite the wide adoption of steam power, most industries were simple handicrafts employing little capital or machinery. Locally manufactured foodstuffs, for which raw materials were cheap and abundant, were of high quality. It now made little sense to import beers and table wines, or flour and Italian pastries. But these industries were again an outgrowth of the rural export sectors rather than completely convincing indicators of a new economy in formation. The metals and textile industries were much less firm. Local metallurgical plants used imported raw materials, and were thus highly dependent upon low ocean freights. The new textile industry in Buenos Aires also used a high proportion of imported raw material. Most of it

[3] Jorge Schvarzer, 'Algunos rasgos del desarrollo industrial de Buenos Aires', mimeo, CISEA (Buenos Aires, 1979).

still functioned on a mercantile 'putting-out' basis among female seamstresses. At this point the textile industry in Argentina was notably less developed than in Brazil. In 1911 Argentina had 9,000 spindles and 1,200 looms against an estimated one million spindles and 35,000 looms in Brazil.

In 1914 Argentina had few embryos of integrated heavy or capital goods industries. Its relatively scant reserves of coal and iron ore lay in far-flung and then inaccessible regions, mostly in the far south-west. To begin developing these would require an enormous new outlay of capital. Little of it would be forthcoming from abroad, at least not until the state or domestic investors took a lead, as they had done with the railways a half century before. Apart from sugar, wines and flour, recent mild and tentative experiments with tariff protection suggested that the country had no easy in-built capacity to lessen its dependence on imports. Limited markets narrowed the scope for the adoption of advanced technology and economies of scale among industrial producers. The home market was rich but still relatively small, while foreign markets were dominated by the industrial giants of the world. It was difficult to envisage here the linkages between industry and agriculture which prevailed in the United States. Nor did Argentine society have much in common with Germany, Japan or early-nineteenth-century Britain. The high standards of living of its new middle class were constructed upon an easy and painless inflow of foreign imports. They would not easily stomach high cost and for a time necessarily experimental national products. There was a real question at this point whether Argentina had the reserves of labour to sustain any major deepening and diversification of its industrial sector. In the pampas region there were some conditions, analogous perhaps to the classical agrarian revolution, expelling population from the land and the towns. The recent growth of manufacturing was in some degree an expression of this. However, this source of labour was limited, and there was none other like it either elsewhere in Argentina or in its contiguous states. The growth of the urban labour force thus largely depended on the country's attractiveness to emigrants from Europe. But if the attempt to industrialize were to lead to the compression of real wages, as it had done almost everywhere except the United States, Argentina was fast likely to become not an importer but a net exporter of labour. Lastly, it seemed quite beyond the bounds of possibility that the political structure could be remoulded to accommodate change of this magnitude. If at this point opinions were sometimes sharply divided on how much formal participation the system should admit, almost all sectors of the population were at one in their preferences for the present liberal institutions. To them was attributed the country's recent transformation. To abandon them would invite a return to the barren early nineteenth century.

In 1914 Argentina's immediate future thus seemed unlikely to be much of a departure from the immediate past. Yet now that easy expansion on an open land frontier was over, export earnings, and through them in large part the economy's capacity to remain prosperous, would be determined increasingly by world prices and conditions of demand in the meat, cereals and wool importing countries of Western Europe; Argentina could no longer respond to depression, as in the 1870s and the early 1890s, by simply increasing production on virgin land. A period of more modest growth than before thus loomed on the horizon.

THE PAMPAS

In 1914 Argentina was a country of startling regional contrasts. In the aftermath of the recent surge of growth, and with the exception of its drier periphery (like parts of Córdoba and the territory of La Pampa), or the less easily accessible areas (like Entre Ríos), the pampas region (Buenos Aires province, southern Santa Fe, eastern Córdoba, Entre Ríos, and the territory of La Pampa) was now markedly more advanced than the rest of the country. It was covered by a dense network of railways. Its landed estates were clearly demarcated by barbed wire, its landscape dotted with small towns, windmills, scattered homesteads and water troughs. According to the economist and statistician Alejandro E. Bunge, writing immediately after the first world war, this part of the country, including the city of Buenos Aires, had more than 90 per cent of Argentina's automobiles and telephones. Here were also no less than 42 per cent of the railways in the whole of Latin America. The Argentine pampas was the source of half the subcontinent's foreign trade, and the same area absorbed around three-quarters of the educational spending throughout Latin America.[4]

In the past two generations townships had sprouted in great abundance throughout the pampas, most of all along the railway lines.

[4] Alejandro E. Bunge, *La economía argentina* (4 vols. Buenos Aires, 1928–30), I, 104–23.

Some were originally the tiny hamlets, or the mere *pulperías*, from the days of Rosas or Mitre. Others, beyond the old frontier, were the result of planned colonization ventures by land or railway companies. Their chief functions were as rail-heads or local markets. They were also centres of small credit and banking operations or petty crafts and trades, many of them discharging these roles as landlocked miniatures of Buenos Aires. Many had grown at roughly the same rate as the population as a whole, at least doubling in size since 1890. They all had large congregations of immigrants in their midst. Many gave the appearance of being thriving civic centres. If most lacked the resources to construct paved roads or modern sewage and power facilities, they established their own newspapers, schools, hospitals and libraries. In 1914 most of the pampas towns were still of recent creation, and as yet none was conspicuously large. Azul, with a population of 40,000 in 1914, was the fourth largest township in the province of Buenos Aires after Avellaneda (an industrial suburb of the Federal Capital), La Plata (the provincial capital), and Bahía Blanca (the leading port of the southern pampas). In this province, an area the size of France and comparably endowed in resources, there were as yet only ten townships with populations in excess of 12,000. Its 50 or so other noteworthy urban centres were scarcely more than villages and subsisted, despite their rail links with the Río de la Plata estuary, as scattered and isolated oases among the farms and *estancias*.

In these and other respects the pampas apparently resembled frontier societies elsewhere at an early parallel stage of development. Yet there were some differences, and these threatened to undermine the capacity of the towns to continue growing from the rudimentary centres they were into the large cities their early pioneer inhabitants expected at least some would eventually become. Successive booms had failed to attract a large permanent and propertied population outside the towns in the country-side itself. In many areas the rural populace amounted to no more than a very thin sprinkling of agricultural tenants, cattle peons or shepherds and seasonal labourers. Where the beef herds were pre-eminent, there were no more than one or two persons per square kilometre. Wheat farming would on average sustain three or four. The highest population densities of the pampas were generally associated with maize cultivation, where there were up to fifteen persons per square kilometre. From 1900 farm machines were adopted on a fairly wide scale on the pampas, and by 1914 they amounted to almost a quarter of the capital stock in the rural sector. Nevertheless farming remained heavily dependent on manual labour. In harvest periods the population of the pampas as a whole would increase by around 300,000. In areas like Santa Fe or Córdoba, relatively close to the populated centres of the interior, the harvesters were often seasonal migrants from Santiago del Estero, Catamarca or San Juan. Many who flowed into the province of Buenos Aires before the first world war, and before the large-scale mechanization of agriculture in the 1920s, however, were short-term immigrants from Europe who usually returned there after the harvest. These 'swallows' (*golondrinas*) were a new embodiment of the rootlessness which had characterized pampas society since the beginnings of Spanish colonization; in them a quality formerly exemplified by the old *gauchos* was reborn. To an extent which seemed anomalous in this rich agrarian society, many farms and towns alike harboured a floating, semi-employed population. These conditions boded ill for the new towns of the pampas. A denser, wealthier and more widely rooted rural middle class, as opposed to these proletarian transients, would have promoted a broader market for local urban services, affording them greater opportunities for growth and diversification.

At root this was a commentary on the land tenure system and the survival of large estates into the twentieth century. In Argentina the estates had appeared in a sequence of waves after independence, following the opening of the frontier against the Indians and the distribution of the land by the state. After 1850 sheep-farming, economic depression and later agriculture had helped prune down many of them. Nevertheless this trend had been mitigated and many times negated by the enormous appreciation in land values from around 1860 onwards. Each successive boom made the possession of land, in as large portions as possible, an iron-clad guarantee of personal security and latterly great wealth. Yet the same inflation, combined with a poorly developed and frequently inequitable land mortgage credit system like the paper *cédulas* of the late 1880s, which usually enabled only those already with land to buy more, had recurrently diminished the range of potential buyers. Its chief casualties were many immigrant farmers with modest or meagre capital resources. Although by 1914 foreigners were in a great majority among the owners of industrial firms, they made up only a third of landowners.

Throughout the nineteenth century there was a body of opinion in Argentina hostile to large estates. It favoured their abolition and the adoption of homestead policies like those in the United States. Belgrano,

Rivadavia, Alberdi, Sarmiento and Avellaneda were each in varied ways representatives of this tradition. They had foreseen the state organizing colonization schemes on a large scale and granting land titles to farmer immigrants, but did not have the power and backing to realize this objective. This was not a country where Lincoln's ideal of rewarding the dispossessed with 'forty acres and a mule' had ever enjoyed a realistic chance of fulfilment. Nor was it entirely akin to Canada, Australia, or New Zealand, where the presence of a colonial state beyond the grasp of local vested interests had lent weight and authority to the pretensions of the small farmer interest. Since 1810 Argentina had been dominated by a shifting *mélange* of Creole landowners, merchants, and bevies of financiers and speculators. From the early 1820s into the 1880s they had pursued land policies which both favoured concentration and conferred upon themselves the greatest benefits from the opening up of the frontier. During the generation immediately before 1914 such monopolistic manipulation was less frequent than before. However, in the interval, the interplay of market forces had failed to dispel entirely the incubus of the past. According to the data in the 1914 census, elaborated by Carlos Díaz Alejandro, smaller farms in the pampas (i.e. between 500 and 1,000 hectares) accounted for only 23.5 per cent of the total land area. Farms of 1,000 hectares and more occupied 61 per cent. The largest 584 holdings in the pampas occupied almost one-fifth of the total area.[5] Landholding was less concentrated in the pampas than in most other parts of the country, but much more so than in frontier regions elsewhere. The mean size of landholdings in Argentina was 890 acres. In New South Wales it was 175 acres, in the United States 130 (and by comparison only 62 in England and Wales).

In many parts of English-speaking America and Australasia cattle and sheep had eventually surrendered a large part of the land to small-scale agriculture, bringing substantial change in land tenure and a higher density of land settlement. As late as 1900 there were still some who expected Argentina to follow a similar course, believing that here too temperate agriculture would eventually fulfil its propensity to construct a firm family-based society of independent yeoman farmers. There was some scattered evidence of this occurring during the 1890s. But in 1900 first British and later American-owned meat-packing plants began to appear. Encouraged by the demand for beef, and aided by the lending

5 Carlos F. Díaz Alejandro, *Essays on the economic history of the Argentine Republic* (New Haven, 1970), 152–62.

policies of the Buenos Aires banks, the landed classes reverted to cattle ranching, investing heavily in imported stock. Land sales which before had aided subdivision largely halted. Cattle encouraged a more extensive land use, and gave a renewed boost to the larger estates. Cattle were also an opportunity to employ less labour at a time when rural wage costs were tending to increase. In the early 1890s a high gold premium had created a wide disparity between wages paid in depreciating pesos and earnings from exports paid in gold. At the time the main effect of this was to boost agriculture. But since then the peso had appreciated strongly, bringing an increase in the relative price of agricultural labour. Yet the resurgence of cattle had no immediate impact upon output in the arable sector, which continued to climb. It first took the land from sheep. Sheep farming was driven out of the pampas and into Patagonia, the sheep population of the province of Buenos Aires declining from around 56 million in 1895 to only 18 million in 1915. However, there was now a much closer juxtaposition and intermingling between pasturing and arable farming on the large estates. The wide adoption of rotational practices, in which cereals or linseed were alternated with alfalfa and cattle, was a sign that arable farming had lost its earlier leading role in the rural economy and become subordinate to cattle ranching.

Most arable farming on the pampas was conducted under a tenancy or sharecropping system. In 1916 only 31 per cent of cereal farms were cultivated by their owners. In many cases the farmers themselves – many of them Italians – were willing accomplices in this arrangement, since it relieved them of onerous investment costs to develop their holdings. Nor was the status of tenant or sharecropper any necessary barrier to prosperity. But by and large the institutions of tenancy along with the recurrent inclemencies of nature – droughts, floods or locust inundations – prevented agriculture ever becoming a straightforward passport to prosperity. Years of exceptionally favourable prices would be closely followed by increases in land rentals or freight rates. Changes in the banking system in the aftermath of the Baring crisis in 1890 did little to facilitate the provision of adequate credit to the farmers, either for land purchases or to finance production. Many became chronically indebted to the landowners, to countryside storekeepers, or the great cereal export houses in Buenos Aires like Bunge y Born, Weil Brothers and Dreyfus and Co. These great oligopsonies also had the whip hand when it came to settling the prices paid to producers. Until the rural strike of 1912, the Grito de Alcorta, many tenants were bereft of even the protection of a written contract and were heavily dependent on the paternalistic goodwill of landowners. The adoption of rotational farming brought a sharp decline in the willingness of tenant farmers to make even minimal improvements on their holdings. One result of this was that the rough-hewn cottages and homesteads which were relatively commonplace before 1900, afterwards under rotational farming gave way to notably lesser quality dwellings, often no more than transient shacks. These were the results of 'sowing the land with *gringos*' (*sembrar con gringos*).

The end product of this was a rural society *sui generis*. Outside the shrinking traditional cattle *estancias*, few of its members resembled the archetypal prostrate tied peasantries of the rest of Latin America, groaning under the weight of time-worn seigneurial obligations. Many were genuine pioneers with the same acquisitive and energetic mentality as their peers elsewhere. Yet amidst all this was the legacy of the early nineteenth century, visible in the survival of many large estates, in an often uneven distribution of wealth and income, and in a relatively large floating population. In most of the pampas the family farm was much less prevalent than in English-language frontier communities elsewhere. During the past two generations the pampas had been laid open to the full force of capitalism. Many farms and *estancias* alike operated as highly efficient enterprises. On the other hand, the land tenure system, especially as it was now developing with cattle at the forefront, imposed limits on the capacity of the land to absorb and maintain population.

THE INTERIOR

If for some life on the pampas had its shortcomings, the opportunities it bestowed were usually infinitely greater than in the rest of the country outside Buenos Aires. One exception was the easily irrigated Río Negro valley. After its colonization by local and foreign land companies, among them a subsidiary of the Buenos Aires Great Southern Railway, this began to develop into a prosperous and middle-class fruit growing area, remitting its products to the city of Buenos Aires. There also seemed a promise of things to come in the territory of Chubut: in 1907, during an attempt to tap supplies of artesian water, rich oil deposits were discovered in the area known from this time forward as Comodoro Rivadavia. It was followed by further discoveries in Neuquén, to the south-west of Río Negro, at Plaza Huincul. But beyond these enclaves and the constantly struggling Welsh agricultural communities also in

Chubut, the vast Patagonian region in the south was underdeveloped. As yet it had evolved little beyond the naturalists' paradise encountered by Charles Darwin during the voyage of the *Beagle* some 80 years before. The great arid and windswept plateau contained nothing but vast sheep ranches, many of them the size of European principalities. In part such mammoth land concentrations illustrated that on average the pastures of Patagonia had only one-tenth of the sheep-carrying capacity of the province of Buenos Aires. It was also due to the manner in which the lands conquered by General Roca in the campaign of 1879 had been squandered by the national government. In 1885 no less than eleven million acres had been distributed among 541 officers and soldiers from the conquering expedition. The arrival of sheep soon afterwards brought only the barest stirrings of activity to the region; after 1900 the Argentine wool trade began to stagnate as it lost its earlier position as leader in the export trade. In 1914 the human population of Patagonia, about a third of the country's territorial area, was a mere 80,000, or 1 per cent of the total, much of it in the Río Negro region. Argentine-born settlers were relatively few. They were mainly simple shepherds, expelled from the province of Buenos Aires along with their flocks following the revival of cattle breeding, token military and naval personnel in garrisons along the Atlantic coast, and a demoralized sprinkling of government officials. Many Patagonian landowners were British, as were many of the farmers of the Río Negro valley. The area also had a marked Chilean influence. Land hunger across the *cordillera* had forced substantial numbers of peasants to retrace the paths of the Araucanian warriors and resettle in Argentine Patagonia. In Bolivia and Peru 30 years earlier a similar emigration of Chileans had led to war and the annexation of land by Chile. Chileans were thus regarded with some suspicion by the Argentine authorities. From time to time Patagonia, especially the Magellan Straits region, was the theatre of boundary disputes between the two countries.

At the other end of the country the north-east was an area of greater topographical and economic variety than Patagonia, but scarcely more developed. The great days of Entre Ríos had ceased after the death of its great *caudillo* Justo José de Urquiza and the suppression of the López Jordán rebellion in the 1870s. Entre Ríos now had railway connections with the Paraná river ports. However, outside some fairly small, often Jewish, agricultural colonies, it remained a peripheral cattle region, employing unimproved Creole herds to produce hides or jerked and salted beef. Most of Corrientes further north had a similar aspect, though here there was some Guaraní peasant agriculture like that across the border in Paraguay. In 1914 some 10,000 hectares of Corrientes was devoted to tobacco cultivation, mainly by peasant smallholders, though trade in tobacco with Buenos Aires was still negligible. There were more marked signs of progress in Misiones, which before had remained almost empty for more than a hundred years after the expulsion of the Jesuits in 1767. Like the Río Negro valley, Misiones had begun to attract capital and labour in the late nineteenth and early twentieth centuries. European colonists, particularly Germans and Poles, were moving into the region, cultivating forest clearings as others like them did across the border in Brazil. Similarly, the eastern Chaco region, particularly around the city of Resistencia, was becoming a small centre of cotton production.

Although during this period domestic sources provided only one-fifth of total national consumption, the main cash crop of the north-east was yerba maté. The contrast between farming on the pampas and conditions on the yerba maté plantations could not have been more striking. In this isolated corner of the Republic, it seemed, one immediately stepped back into the eighteenth century. Yerba maté production had arisen in Argentina for the most part in quite recent years, mainly in Misiones along with parts of Corrientes and the eastern fringes of the Chaco, in face of strong competition from suppliers in Paraguay and Brazil. Producers across the border relied on semi-forced labour. The Argentinians, large and small producers alike, were therefore obliged to copy these same practices. Monthly pay rates for seasonal labourers, known as *mensús*, were often under a third of those for unskilled workers employed the year round in Buenos Aires. The lot of the small permanent labour force was virtual imprisonment on the plantations. They were often held in tutelage by overseers and suffocated by debts to company stores, under outward conditions which most observers found indistinguishable from slavery.

Another industry of the north-east, in the northern reaches of Santiago del Estero, Santa Fe, parts of Corrientes and the Chaco, was the extraction of quebracho hardwood. Throughout this period the quebracho forests were decimated with reckless energy, mainly by British consortia. Only token attempts were made to replace the forest cover. Vast tracts became desolate, dust- or brush-covered wastelands. The timber of the north-western forests was largely employed for railway sleepers, and that of the east for its tannin content, which was shipped in bulk to Europe for the treatment of leather. During the first world war quebracho was also widely employed as a coal substitute on the railways. At that time the industry won some ill-repute on account of its labour practices. However, in normal times a free wage system sufficed to attract labour from among the Guaraní in Corrientes, some of the Chaco Indians, or from among workers from Santiago del Estero, who would often alternate between the quebracho industry and wheat harvesting in Santa Fe or Córdoba.

Outside the Mesopotamian plains of Corrientes and Entre Ríos the region most resembling them in character lay due west from Buenos Aires in Cuyo, especially the province of Mendoza. In the past generation this had become a flourishing area in which both production and population were increasing at a notably faster rate than in the rest of the interior. At the heart of the economy of Cuyo was viticulture. With the tariff protection they were given in the 1880s local wines established a firm position in the Buenos Aires market. Between 1895 and 1910 the area devoted to vines throughout Cuyo quintupled to 120,000 hectares. By 1914 annual wine production was approaching four million litres, and Argentina's production of wine exceeded Chile's, and was double California's. Vines were spreading quickly beyond Mendoza into San Juan, and into small pockets of Catamarca and La Rioja. The wine industry of this period had been largely created by immigrants, by French and Italians with the capital and expertise to organize it along efficient lines; almost alone of the regions outside the pampas Mendoza continued to attract a large number of Europeans. In Mendoza, however, the spread of viticulture was accompanied by a greater subdivision of the land than had occurred in the pampas. Small properties largely replaced the ancient cattle haciendas engaged in trading across the Andes with Chile. Prosperity on the land was reflected in an air of well-being and expansion in the city of Mendoza. By 1914 the city had a population of 59,000. This was four times that of the medium-sized provincial capitals of the interior, such as Santiago del Estero or Salta, and ten times that of the poorest, La Rioja and Catamarca. Both Mendoza and San Juan were becoming provinces of great political vitality. Behind this lay the changes in land tenure accompanying the transition from cattle to vines, land-grabbing among rival coteries of speculators, intense struggles for water rights, and disputes over the terms of credit, as the Buenos Aires banks established a financial stranglehold over the industry. Although the land tenure pattern in

Mendoza favoured smallholders, there was a fairly high degree of concentration in wine processing. Bickering over the prices paid to the cultivators by the *bodegas* which processed the grapes became another source of endemic conflict. By 1914 both these provinces had become centres of a flourishing local populism, which had undertones of neo-federalist hostility towards Buenos Aires.

The second growth centre of the old interior was Tucumán. Grasping the opportunities provided by its naturally moist climate, the coming of the railways in 1876 and the generous tariff privileges bestowed upon it by the national government, Tucumán had launched full tilt into sugar-cane production. By the early years of the twentieth century there were still some traditional activities, such as tanning, to be found here, but they were now vastly overshadowed by sugar plantations, which occupied four-fifths of the cultivated land area of the province. The most vital stage in the growth of sugar in Tucumán was between 1890 and 1895. During this period the earlier benefits of tariff protection were greatly enhanced by the discouraging effect of a high gold premium upon imports. At this point output increased tenfold. Growth was afterwards followed by overproduction in 1896 and a five-year crisis in which many small refineries were forced into liquidation. Between 1900 and 1914 output once more grew threefold, while imported sugar became an increasingly minimal proportion of total consumption. Between 1897 and 1903 government bounties made possible small exports of sugar cane from Tucumán, though this brief phase ended abruptly with agreements in Europe to cease admitting sugar subsidized in this fashion. Sugar in Tucumán advanced at roughly the same rate as vines in Mendoza, and by 1914 occupied a comparable land area. Later in the 1920s the cane-fields moved northwards into Salta and Jujuy. Before this northward dispersion, climatic variations in Tucumán frequently produced large annual oscillations in output. Domestic sugar distributors became adept at manipulating supplies to enhance their returns while minimizing recourse to imports. This was one of several reasons why the sugar industry gained ill-repute among consumers in Buenos Aires.

Like many similar semi-tropical agricultural activities of Latin America, the sugar industry was a diverse mix of modern, highly capitalistic elements and others which evoked a pre-capitalist past. With the exception of quebracho, fruit and sheep farming, and in their different way wines, sugar was the only activity of any substance outside the pampas to attract foreign capital. Many of the sugar refineries, or *ingenios*, were organized as joint-stock ventures with foreign shareholders, and employed imported, usually British, machinery. Cane production in Tucumán was again conducted mainly by smallholders. However, these were *mestizo minifundistas*, quite different from the vine growers of Mendoza. Eighty per cent of the Tucumán farmers operated on seven or eight hectares, and the rest often on less. Meanwhile the *ingenios* had long been under the control of what seemed an impenetrable oligarchy, able to dictate prices to producers and consumers alike, and allegedly possessing extraordinary wealth by virtue of its protected status in the national market.

Labour relations in the Tucumán sugar industry had features similar to those in the yerba maté region in the north-east. In the 1880s and the 1890s there were attempts to create a labour force of European immigrants. But horror stories of conditions in Tucumán percolated through to Buenos Aires, and this source of labour speedily evaporated. Immigrants were then replaced by primitive Indians dredged up from the forays of labour contractors in the Chaco, and by *mestizo* peasants from the south in Catamarca, La Rioja and Santiago del Estero. They were often inveigled into debt and then herded together by rail and cart into Tucumán. For the duration of the harvest these ingenuous and resourceless persons were encamped on the land often under the most extreme and deplorable conditions.

Many in Buenos Aires and abroad regarded the sugar industry as the very symbol of plantation-capitalist infamy. Even Lloyd's Bank, which sought to throw the happiest gloss on the Republic's affairs, called the industry a 'big, bad blot' on the country.

While the wealthy landowners and the big employers, the latter mostly of overseas nationality, are reaping increasingly rich rewards, those who perform toilsomely the actual labour that gives that reward are allowed to pass their lives in conditions that do not conform to the lowest standards of existence. The country that permits wholesale servile conditions among the bulk of its people must inevitably suffer from lack of that virility necessary for its continued progress along an upward path.[6]

By comparison with Mendoza or Tucumán, the rest of the interior languished in stagnation and backwardness. Railways constructed and operated by the national government, which now linked all the

[6] Lloyd, *Twentieth century impressions*, 346.

provincial capitals with Buenos Aires, failed to induce the changes which occurred elsewhere. Beyond the immediate radius served by the railways, goods were still transported by ox-carts or mules. In 1914 the age-old dream that parts of the region close to the *cordillera* would develop as mining centres was still unfulfilled. Many areas remained almost unchanged from the days of the Viceroyalty of the Río de la Plata in the late eighteenth century. Traditional haciendas held sway, sometimes co-existing with *minifundios*, the two together reproducing the classic social polarities of Andean America. Peasant communities were still subject to seigneurial levies. Peasant industries suffered from the incessant competition of imports and their own technological backwardness. With the exception of small sprinklings of petty merchants, many of them Levantines, the area had little new population. Its cities were still small, their crumbling and downtrodden aspect mirroring the indigence of their surroundings. Here provincial administrations and education required almost constant subsidies from Buenos Aires. Amidst all this were periodic outbreaks of political unrest. Local coups were common among feuding factions of landowners, each struggling to monopolize the paltry provincial budgets. Yet in other ways politics had changed during the past two generations. Violent revolt against Buenos Aires, so frequent before 1870 among the old Federalists, had now been completely suppressed. Along with this had also disappeared the peasant or *gaucho* insurrections from the days of 'El Chacho' Peñaloza, or Felipe Varela. There now appeared little political conflict rooted in social or regional antagonisms. Much of society appeared to drift along in contentedly ignorant, parochial equilibrium.

The bulk of the population of the interior was wracked by bronchial pneumonia, tuberculosis and a variety of gastric ailments. The infant mortality rate was double and often treble that of Buenos Aires. Illiteracy rates approached 50 per cent. The interior was also relatively empty, less so than Patagonia, but more so than the pampas. In 1910 it was estimated that only one per cent of the total land area was under cultivation. In the most backward parts, La Rioja and Catamarca, the distribution of a precious water supply from the small streams and rivers flowing down from the mountains was conducted according to the same time-worn rites of the eighteenth century. At the end of the nineteenth century there was a temporary revival in the old cattle and mule trades into Chile and Bolivia. In the Chilean case this was assisted by the growth of mining and the development of the nitrate fields on the Pacific coast. In Bolivia's it accompanied the resurgence of the Salta route to the Río de la Plata following the loss of Bolivia's access to the Pacific in the war with Chile in the early 1880s. For a time this revived the fortunes of the *llaneros* of La Rioja and Catamarca, and Salta's importance as a trade centre. Yet by 1914 this trade had either almost disappeared or shifted in the direction of Mendoza and Tucumán. Though they were thus falling under the orbit of the new centres of growth, the lesser provinces lingered on in a state of unspecialized semi-autarky. Santiago del Estero, whose growing population made it the chief source of internal migrants at the time, had as mixed an agricultural and pastoral economy in 1914 as it had 150 years before. Flood farming along the Río Dulce enabled the production of sugar, wine, cotton and tobacco; mules were still being bred for export to Bolivia. However, this was all very small in scale, faster development being constrained now as in centuries past by the high saline content of the soil. Until the advent of sugar on an important scale in the 1920s and 1930s, Jujuy in the far north-west had only minimal contacts with the markets to the south. Trade was largely confined to the surviving indigenous communities, which exchanged alpaca and llama wool for Bolivian salt and coca across a still scarcely acknowledged frontier. In some areas there had been retrogression. The old silver mines of La Rioja in the west were almost all closed, and sometimes even their whereabouts forgotten, in the aftermath of the fall in world silver prices at the end of the nineteenth century. Forces of tradition were everywhere stronger than those of change. Even the city of Córdoba, which had attracted substantial numbers of European immigrants, whose eastern and southern hinterlands were now part of the pampas economy and which boasted a substantial boot and shoe industry, obstinately refused to cross the threshold into the twentieth century. The city and its surrounding province was still governed by an unchanging oligarchy of local families. Social and political life centred around the university, an institution hidebound by conservatism, scholasticism and clericalism.

BUENOS AIRES

On the outbreak of the first world war nowhere in the provinces, not even other bustling commercial centres like Rosario and Bahía Blanca, could emulate Buenos Aires. In many aspects the city was still, as Sarmiento had depicted it, a lonely outpost of advanced European civilization on the outer limit of the vast, underpopulated, or backward regions to its rear. It was also a great vortex into which flowed much of the wealth of the new export economy. Buenos Aires lorded over its great hinterland first by means of its strategic position at the interstices of international trade. It dominated the fan-shaped railway system stretching out from the estuary of the Río de la Plata across the pampas and into the interior. Although towards 1900 it lost ground to Rosario and Bahía Blanca as an exporter, and was thereafter more important in the meat trade than in cereals, it upheld its traditional lucrative monopoly over the distribution of imports. More so than in any previous period in its history, it was the emporium of banking and finance. It also benefited from the survival of the large estates on the pampas; wealth that might otherwise have remained in the agrarian economy was in part transposed into the great stucco palaces which landowners, bankers and merchants had begun constructing from the early 1880s onwards. This city was also the hub of government, state spending and state employment. After the act of federalization in 1880 its earlier share of the revenues from trade may have slightly dwindled, but the total resources it gathered multiplied with the growth of trade, to be shared among its elites and its phalanxes of functionaries, construction workers and manufacturers. Buenos Aires had by this time been endowed with modern docking facilities for almost 30 years. Incoming visitors were no longer obliged to disembark into skiffs in order to reach the shore. Its great railway stations in Plaza Constitución or Retiro were near-replicas of those in London or Liverpool. With its networks of tramways and underground railway, its modern sewage, water, gas and electricity facilities, its solid and imposing central office blocks, its capacious avenues lined with jacarandas and sometimes paved in Swedish granite, it had become as well-endowed a city as almost any in the world at that time. In 1914 three-quarters of the children of Buenos Aires were attending primary school. Although tuberculosis was still estimated to kill around 20 per cent of the population, the epidemics of yellow fever or cholera which had decimated the population in the 1870s were the last of their kind.

In 1914 not all the territory designated as part of the Federal Capital in 1880 had been built upon. Agriculture and grazing were still to be found within its confines. But new construction, mostly single-storey, flat-roofed dwellings all laid out in the undeviating grid fashion created by the Spaniards, had advanced rapidly with the coming of the immigrants. The tramways had acted on land values in the city as the railways had outside. Between 1904 and 1912 property values had appreciated up to tenfold. The city was now divided into clearly demarcated residential zones, which corresponded to its principal class groupings. On the north side towards the estuary of the Río de la Plata were the homes of the well-to-do or *gente bien*. These stretched from the mansions of Barrio Norte and Palermo towards the city centre through Belgrano to the suburban weekend *quintas* of Vicente López, Olivos and San Isidro across into the province of Buenos Aires. In the centre and the west of the city were many middle-class neighbourhoods which reached as far as Flores. The south was the working-class and industrial zone. Here amidst the modest dwellings of Nueva Pompeya, Barracas, Avellaneda and parts of the Boca were already forerunners of the *villas miserias* of the 1940s and after. These shanty houses were often constructed of rough boarding, discarded packing cases, and simple galvanized zinc roofing. They were stifling cauldrons of heat in summer, and ice boxes in the chill and damp Río de la Plata winter. Many were periodically washed away in the fetid flood waters of the Riachuelo, the small river which divided the capital from the province on this southern side. In this period the more customary dwellings of the poor, housing around 150,000 persons, were the *conventillos* close to the city centre. A half century earlier the oldest of these two-storey, rectangular constructions, whose interiors contained large Spanish-style patios, had been residences of the well-to-do. After the epidemics of the 1870s and the first arrivals of immigrants the rich moved elsewhere. Their homes became tenements. Later others like them were built to house the immigrants. Where 50 years before the *conventillos* had housed a single extended family and its domestic servants, in the early years of the twentieth century they were occupied by as much as a score of families, eking out within a congested, insanitary and turbulent existence. There were often three, four or more persons to each dingy room; between 25 and 30 would share washing facilities and lavatories. Nevertheless, it was probably no worse than the alternatives: Milan, Genoa, Naples, Barcelona, Brooklyn, Philadelphia or Chicago.

One feature which distinguished Buenos Aires from many cities in the United States in this period was that the immigrants, with some exceptions like the growing Jewish community, from the start mixed very easily. The different national groupings created a great profusion of clubs, schools, hospitals and mutual aid societies. Yet few sought to perpetuate their national origins in separate ghetto neighbourhoods, this being due no doubt to the close linguistic affinities between Spaniards and Italians. Another difference between Buenos Aires and comparable cities elsewhere was that until the onset of the trade and financial depression of 1913 permanent unemployment was unusually low. Immigrants dissatisfied with their lot in the city needed merely to spend a summer harvesting in the fields to raise the necessary sum to return to Europe. Even so this left the city with its penniless indigents, especially women and children. From time to time newspapers would publish dramatic *exposés* of what they called the 'begging industry' in which would surface alleged practices such as the hiring of diseased or handicapped children for seeking alms.[7] The city was also crime-ridden, though not unduly so by the standards which prevailed elsewhere. There was no organized Italian Mafia in Buenos Aires. During these years, however, it won great notoriety on account of its white slave traffic. Beginning around 1903 large numbers of the unprotected pauper maidens of Genoa, Barcelona, Amsterdam or Warsaw were kidnapped and sold into a life of prostitution in Argentina. In 1913 there were 300 registered brothels in Buenos Aires, compulsory registration being the only gesture made by the authorities to control the spread of vice and those living from it. These were conditions which reflected the presence of large numbers of unmarried male immigrants among the city's population.

In the generation before 1914 all sectors of the social structure of Buenos Aires had at least doubled in size. Along with this came increasing complexity and diversity. At the apex of society was an elite composed of the great landowners and other large property owners, bankers, and those who controlled the main flow of foreign investment and trade. By 1914 this group had changed substantially by comparison with 50 years before. It no longer embraced only a few score Creole families, most typically descended directly from the Spanish Bourbon merchants of the late eighteenth century. It had become a larger and highly heterodox body with accretions from all the countries in southern and western Europe. On the one side there still remained the ubiquitous Anchorenas, or the Guerricos, the Campos, or the Casares, survivors from four or five generations past. But on the other were many more *parvenu* creations. Among those of more recent Italian background were men like Antonio Devoto, who gave his name to Villa Devoto, soon to become a noted middle-class neighbourhood in the western zone of the Federal Capital. In a manner now typical of the elite as a whole, Devoto

7 See, for example, the *Revista Popular*, March 1919.

had a multiple stake in land, banking, trade, public works contracts and manufacturing. Among his holdings of land in 1910 were 80,000 hectares and seven *estancias* in the province of Buenos Aires, 26,000 in Santa Fe on two *estancias*, another 75,000 in Cordoba among four, and 30,000 on one *estancia* in the more remote La Pampa territory. He also possessed extensive urban properties in central Buenos Aires, and he was the founder and president of the Banco de Italia y Río de la Plata. Others, like Luis Zuberbühler, a second generation Swiss-Argentinian, had comparable fortunes distributed among cattle *estancias*, land colonization companies, forestry and manufacturing. Similarly by 1914 Nicolás Mihanovich, who had arrived a penniless immigrant from Dalmatia about 50 years earlier, had a near monopoly on the coastal steamships plying between Buenos Aires and Asunción along the Paraná river or southwards to the Atlantic settlements of Patagonia.[8] Family appurtenances of the elite were scattered throughout professions like law, the military and public administration. Its members were separated in some degree by rival political affiliations and by clan-like family networks. But usually overshadowing these were the bonds formed by residential propinquity, and a sense of common class affiliation fostered by associations like the Rural Society or the Jockey Club. Much of the upper class lived with an ostentation which rivalled its counterparts in London or New York. Its mansions evoked Paris in architecture and magnificence. Their interiors often contained the most regal imported furnishings and *objets d'art*. Behind them lay great ornate patio gardens. During recent years members of the elite had become avid consumers of the most luxurious American or European limousines.

Observers of this leading sector of Argentine society generally acknowledged that it differed from its counterparts in Latin America in exemplifying a genuine sense of national identity. Georges Clemenceau had remarked, 'The real Argentine seems to me convinced that there is a magic elixir of youth which springs from his soil and makes of him a new man, descendant of none, but ancestor of endless generations to come.'[9] Others found the fierce national pride they encountered reminiscent of Manifest Destiny in the United States. Yet sometimes too what passed as nationalism was regarded as more akin to mere nativism, typical of a highly privileged group confronted by swelling tides of immigrants.

[8] Jorge Federico Sábato, 'Notas sobre la formación de la clase dominante en la Argentina moderna', mimeo, CISEA (Buenos Aires, 1979), 92–6.
[9] Quoted in Lloyd, *Twentieth century impressions*, 337.

While there were some who gave the elite credit for its success in promoting *haute culture*, most notably grand opera, more prurient observers criticized its apparent obsession with horse-racing and other games of chance as typical of a class whose fortunes were built largely on speculation in land. The more negative observers also found strong evocations of old Spain in the freedoms enjoyed by many men against the enforced seclusion of home and family. Women who were also members of the elite were sometimes active outside the home, especially in Catholic charity ventures. There was also a small feminist movement in Buenos Aires. Yet at a time when the suffragette campaign in Britain and the United States was reaching its climax, the accomplishments of most women here seemed unimpressive.

A second major social group in Buenos Aires was the middle class, which by this time had become by far the largest of its kind throughout Latin America. This was another indicator of the country's growing wealth. It also attested to the strong centralizing forces within it, which thrust into the narrow confines of the city a group which might otherwise have developed more widely outside. The middle class had a largely uniform immigrant background. Otherwise it was divided into two broad strata, each with a quite different status in society at large. Of the two the lower was composed of a growing number of petty industrial producers, shopkeepers and traders. According to the census of 1914 around four-fifths of this group in Buenos Aires was made up of foreigners. Its size – perhaps 15,000 to 20,000 strong – was another of the remarkable novelties of the past generation. Scattered throughout the city were multitudes of bakers, tailors, shoe and sandal makers, small brewers, chocolate, soap or cigarette manufacturers, printers, carpenters, blacksmiths and matchmakers along with a roughly equal number of street-corner shopkeepers (*almaceneros*). Most of the manufacturers among this group operated from workshops rather than factories. Outside the meat-packing plants, the flour mills, or a small number of textile and metallurgical firms, each unit usually had a work force no more than half a dozen strong, employing hand-tools rather than machinery, and often marketing its products in the immediate neighbourhood. This situation was not unlike that in many of the capital cities of Europe from London or Dublin to Constantinople. But in Argentina there was no domestic centre of heavy industry elsewhere to balance out light manufacturing. However fast local manufacturing grew after 1890, imports at least kept pace. It was therefore Manchester, Birmingham or

Lyons, and latterly Bremen, Essen and Detroit which serviced a major proportion of Argentina's industrial consumption needs. The manufacturers of Buenos Aires were as yet scarcely more than appendages to an economy still ruled by cereals and meat. The export sector, the commodities it embraced, the wealth which grew from it, closely influenced the development of domestic manufacturing; its access to raw materials and labour, and the growth of purchasing power in the markets it served. In 1914 the manufacturers occupied a relatively low standing in the community at large. They were weak and highly fragmented, and as yet commanded little political voice.

The upper segment of the middle class was entrenched among service and vocational occupations in the professions, in public administration or in white-collar positions in the private sector such as transportation. It differed from the manufacturers and shopkeepers in that its members were by this time mainly native-born. On the other hand many were no more than first generation Argentinians, and typically the upwardly mobile children of the manufacturing and commercial classes. In the introduction to the city census of 1910 it was mentioned that between 1905 and 1909 employment in manufacturing had increased from 127,000 to 218,000, or 71 per cent. However, the growth of service occupations from doctors, teachers, public officials to simple tinkers was from 57,000 to an estimated 150,000, or 163 per cent.[10] The middle-class component of this large and rapidly expanding tertiary sector owed much to the recent growth of the bureaucracy, both national and municipal. Expenditures of the national government, for example, were 160 million paper pesos in 1900. By 1910 they had climbed to 400 million. This was an increase in per capita terms from 30 to 58 pesos; a whole new stratum of government employees was its most visible result. By 1914 many members of this sector of the middle class, and those who aspired to join it, were deeply involved in the issue of higher education, since secondary school diplomas and university degrees were the normal prerequisites for admission into the professions and government. Unlike the manufacturers and traders, they had thus become a focus of political activism. In their strong support for the continuing expansion of both the bureaucracy and higher education, they found themselves repeatedly at variance with the elites. But otherwise these two sectors of society had much in common. Both were strongly conservative in economic policy.

---

[10] *Recensement général de la ville de Buenos Aires* (Buenos Aires, 1910), liii.

The middle class had little interest in domestic industrial development, preferring that consumption needs be satisfied cheaply and effortlessly through imports. Whenever its members could do so, they became avid buyers of land alongside the elites, though almost never farmers. In spite of their reputation for political radicalism, their interests and orientations thus indicated no promise of major change in, for example, the conditions which weakened the tenants on the land, or pushed the newly arrived immigrants into the urban *conventillos*.

In 1914 three-quarters of the Buenos Aires working class were immigrants and an overwhelming proportion of the rest were their children. The census of 1914 suggests that the working class made up perhaps two-thirds of the city's employed population, around 405,000 of a total male labour force of 626,000. Workers were employed in large numbers in commerce and the railways. There were other substantial congregations in public services, the tramways, the gas companies and so forth, or more humbly in sewage works and in refuse collection. Still more were employed in manufacturing, either in larger concerns like the meat-packing plants or in the small workshops to be found throughout the city. The structure of the working class was also influenced by the growth of service occupations. Perhaps as many as 20 per cent were employed in domestic service, among whom only about half at this time were women. A further fifth of the employed working-class population consisted of women and children. Among the large unskilled element within the working class immediately before 1914 a substantial portion drifted to and fro across the Atlantic, or alternated work in the city with seasonal harvest tasks outside. In past years, however, the working class too had become increasingly stratified. There were many highly skilled groups in the crafts, in construction, metallurgy or transportation. Some of the upper echelons exhibited the traits of an aristocracy of labour: a conspicuous moderation in political attitudes, a concern with wage relativities, or membership of a skill-based union brotherhood.

In 1914 Buenos Aires lagged conspicuously behind many of the cities of Western Europe, and for that matter its neighbour Montevideo across the Río de la Plata, in social legislation for the working class. There was no minimum wage law, eight- or ten-hour act, pensions or retirement provision. Nor were the state's shortcomings in this respect effectively remedied by co-operative and mutual aid societies or by the trades unions. But any dissatisfaction on this score was often overshadowed by others. In Buenos Aires the main bane of almost every worker's existence was housing. Many of the *conventillos*, as we have seen, were quite deplorable. In 1914 four-fifths of working-class families lived in one room. Otherwise conditions for the workers as a whole mirrored the broader features of the national economy. Imports, in this case mainly clothing, were often costly, partly on account of government tariffs which taxed some of the essentials of working-class consumption. On the other hand this was normally offset by the cheapness of most common foodstuffs and the availability of a nutritious diet. Generally real incomes among workers in Buenos Aires compared well with most Western European cities. The growth of a working-class culture in these years – the tango bars, the boxing and soccer clubs, the trades unions, and many other associations – suggests that a good proportion of the population had the income surplus and the leisure time for a quite rich and variegated existence. Even so there was much evidence of conditions which ranged from unsatisfactory to wretched. Among the large foreign employers of labour, the meat-packing plants were notorious for low wages and oppressive working conditions. Some of the worst abuses were perpetrated by small employers, most of them immigrants themselves. Wages in the city's small stores were at best paltry, and eighteen-hour shifts commonplace.

In 1914 Argentina had thus evolved into an extremely mixed and diverse society. Across the regions many highly advanced or sophisticated structures co-existed with others of immutable backwardness. Immediately before the first world war there were still high expectations that the imbalances would steadily recede as the present wave of growth continued. On this supposition the most pressing issue was political: the country required new institutions to arbitrate between new class and regional interests. To do this it was ready to jettison the oligarchic system of rule and launch itself on a quest for representative democracy. A preparedness for reform was due in some part to social tensions after 1900; at the same time it was also an expression of confidence in the country's ability to maintain its earlier momentum. Events were to show that this assumption was in part ill-founded. In 1914 there remained some areas of the country with an apparently promising future. The development of cotton in the north-east and oil in the south, for example, suggested means both to reduce the import bill and give further impetus to domestic manufacturing. On the other hand the pampas was nearing the peak of its development. In 1914 Argentina's potential for growth and in some respects its freedom of manoeuvre were diminishing. Instead of the earlier smooth upward curve of growth, the period which followed brought an alternating sequence of booms and slumps, more slowly rising consumption, and sometimes highly volatile short-term changes in income distribution among the different social sectors. Against this background came the attempt at democratic reform.

5

FROM THE FIRST WORLD WAR TO
1930

THE WAR AND POSTWAR ECONOMY

The decade and a half from the outbreak of the first world war to the onset of the world depression witnessed overall a continuation of Argentina's prewar economic prosperity based on the growth of its export sector. In 1929 Argentina was still the world's largest exporter of chilled beef, maize, linseed and oats, and the third largest exporter of wheat and flour. Comparing annual averages for 1910–14 with 1925–9, exports of wheat increased from 2.1 million tons to 4.2 million, maize from 3.1 to 3.5 million, and linseed from 680,000 to 1.6 million. Exports of chilled beef, which averaged only 25,000 tons between 1910 and 1914, increased to more than 400,000 between 1925 and 1929. Exports as a whole, which were valued on average at 4,480 million paper pesos at 1950 prices in 1910–14, increased to 7,914 million between 1925 and 1929. Per capita income in Argentina still compared favourably with most of Western Europe. Standards of living had risen, while illiteracy rates had again fallen. A substantial part of the population basked in prosperity and well-being. By 1930 there were 435,000 automobiles throughout Argentina, a substantially larger number than in many Western European countries, and a sevenfold increase from eight years before. Assisted once more by immigration, population rose by almost 4 million between 1914 and 1930, from 7.9 million to 11.6 million. In one sector, domestic oil, there was spectacular growth. In 1913 Argentina produced less than 21,000 cubic metres of fuel oil. By 1929 output had risen to 1.4 million.

On the other hand, growth was less rapid and less smooth than in the period before the first world war. During the whole 40-year period before 1910–14 gross domestic product at factor cost increased at an annual average of 6.3 per cent. Between 1910–14 and 1925–30 the rate fell to 3.5 per cent. Quantum exports grew at a rate of more than 5 per cent before 1914, and only 3.9 per cent after. The rate of growth of the land area sown to crops also fell from 8.3 per cent to 1.3 per cent. There was virtually no expansion in land use in the pampas: the increase was nil in Santa Fe, and minimal in Córdoba, Entre Ríos, and the province of Buenos Aires. Throughout this period population in the pampas continued to grow but at a notably lesser rate than before the war. Between 1895 and 1914 the growth of the rural population was around 1 million, but only 270,000 between 1914 and 1930. In the earlier period the annual rate of increase was 50,000, and in the later period only 22,500. There was also a pronounced fall in the rate at which new townships were founded. Advances in agriculture were less an expression of a growing rural population than of mechanization. Argentina was now a large market for imported farm machinery. Machines which amounted to 24 per cent of the capital stock in the rural sector in 1914 grew to around 40 per cent by 1929. By that year there were an estimated 32,000 combine harvesters, 16,000 tractors and 10,000 threshing machines in Argentina. To some extent increases in agricultural output during the 1920s were also due to substitutions in land use. A near doubling in the production of cereals and linseed between 1922 and 1929 was partly the result of a reduction in the cattle population by 5 million during these years, and the consequent decline in land acreages devoted to cattle and alfalfa fodder. The cattle stock was an estimated 37 million in 1922, but only 32.2 million in 1930. During the same period the land area devoted to alfalfa shrank from 7 to 5 million hectares. With mechanization there was also a decline in the acreage devoted to pasturing horses. On the other hand, the land area devoted to cereals rose from 11 to 19 million hectares. In 1921–2 cereals and linseed represented only 56.5 per cent of the cultivated area in the pampas, but by 1929–30 this had risen to 73.5 per cent.

After 1913 there was little new foreign investment for railway construction. Between that time and 1927 only 1,200 kilometres of new track were added, mostly branch lines or government-built lines in the interior. Between 1865–9 and 1910–14, the railways grew at an annual average of 15.4 per cent. Between 1910–14 and 1925–9 the increase fell to 1.4 per cent. British investment in Argentina ended completely during the war and the immediate postwar period, recovering to only a comparative trickle during the later 1920s. Overall the influx of foreign capital was only about a fifth of the prewar period, while the ratio of foreign over domestic capital diminished from 48 to 34 per cent between 1913 and 1927. Likewise immigration virtually ceased for a decade after 1913. And between 1921 and 1930 the net balance of migrants was only 856,000 compared with 1.1 million between 1901 and 1910. Population grew by an average of only 2.8 per cent in the immediate postwar period compared with 4.3 per cent in the period immediately before the war.[1]

Whereas between 1895 and 1913 there was steady upward growth, the period from 1913 began with depression (1913–17) which was followed by recovery and renewed boom (1918–21); then came another recession (1921–4) followed once more by expansion which continued to 1929.[2] The recessions had many of the features of those in the mid 1870s and early 1890s. They resulted from contractions in Argentina's export markets and a decline in its commodity export prices. From this came balance of payments crises, corrected eventually by falling imports, but at the cost of falling government revenues. The depression of 1913, as in 1873 and 1890, was exacerbated by a cessation of foreign investment. In 1914 the gold standard and peso convertibility schemes established in 1899 were abandoned. (They were restored afterwards for only a brief two-year period between 1927 and 1929.) The depressions of 1913 and 1921 both brought unemployment in the cities and the countryside alike, a fall in urban and rural land values, a spate of bankruptcies and severe credit squeezes. On the other hand during this period Argentina managed to avoid overseas debt crises like that in 1890. In 1913 around three-quarters of foreign investment was private, and the government was largely exempt from its earlier obligation to afford gold-based guaranteed minimum profits.

The depression of 1913 began when the Bank of England raised interest rates to correct a balance of payments deficit in Britain and to check financial uncertainty caused by wars in the Balkans. There was now a net outflow of capital from Argentina through interest and amortization repayments. The crisis deepened with a downward plunge in world cereal and meat prices, and with the failure of the 1913–14 harvest. Some months later, as matters appeared to be on the mend, the outbreak of war in Europe and the withdrawal of shipping from the high seas brought foreign trade almost to a complete standstill, obliging the

[1] Most of these figures appear in Carlos F. Díaz Alejandro, *Essays in the economic history of the Argentine Republic* (New Haven, 1970), chapter 1.
[2] The cycles are best followed in Guido Di Tella and Manuel Zymelman, *Las etapas del desarrollo económico argentino* (Buenos Aires, 1967), 295–420.

de la Plaza government to impose a financial moratorium throughout August 1914. The next year brought some improvement in exports. But by this time as Britain and France shifted to munitions production and an Allied blockade was imposed against Germany, there were growing shortages of imports, only partly remedied by supplies from the United States.

Depression persisted until the end of 1917. From then on export prices rapidly advanced under the stimulus of wartime demand. This was especially true of frozen and canned meat, enormous quantities of which were consumed by the Allied troops on the Western Front. Export earnings, around 400 million gold pesos in 1913–14, had almost tripled by 1919–20 to 1,100 million. Even so the rise of export prices was much less than that of imports: an acute world shortage of manufactured goods weighted the terms of trade heavily against the primary producers. The volume of Argentina's imports fell from an estimated 10 million tons in 1913, most of which was coal, to only 2.6 million in 1918. Yet their cost, inflated by the fourfold rise in shipping rates during the war, more than doubled from around 400 million gold pesos in 1913–14 to almost 850 million in 1919–20. As a neutral country throughout Argentina escaped the physical destruction of the war, including the depredations of submarines in the Río de la Plata. But it could not isolate itself from the highly disruptive economic effects of the war.

Until 1918 there was an uncharacteristically high rate of unemployment in Buenos Aires. In similar situations in the past it had been possible to 'export' unemployment by an outflow of former immigrants. Although after 1913 emigrants consistently exceeded new arrivals for the first time since 1890, the steep rise in shipping rates and the shortage of shipping impeded the operation of the normal escape mechanism, bottling up some of the unemployment in Argentina itself. In 1914 it was estimated that between 16 and 20 per cent of the labour force in Buenos Aires was unemployed. Despite emigration unemployment did not disappear entirely until 1918. The first three years of the war thus brought falling wages, a longer working day and extremely unpropitious conditions for trades unions. There were no strikes of any significance between the last year of prewar prosperity in 1912 and the end of 1916. The war further affected the public sector. After 1913 as imports fell, the De la Plaza government faced diminishing tariff revenues, its principal source of revenue. It was also obliged to employ a larger proportion of revenues in servicing the foreign debt. As had occurred in the mid 1870s and in the early 1890s, the depression thus compelled vigorous efforts to reduce current government spending. De la Plaza suspended public works schemes, and carefully trimmed the government's expenses in day-to-day administration. This fed unemployment. It also contributed to a heavy crop of business failures. Policies of the central government were matched by the provinces and the municipalities. All were obliged to cling rigidly to retrenchment and austerity.

The picture changed somewhat during the upward phase of the cycle between 1917 and 1921. At this point, which saw the steepest increases in export prices, the landed and commercial interests enjoyed an unprecedented bonanza. In 1918 it was reported that some of the meat-packing plants were earning a near 50 per cent return on capital invested. However, there was little immediate relief for other sectors of the population. In place of unemployment came rapidly rising inflation and a heavy redistribution of income against the middle and especially the lower classes. Except for rents, which emigration during the war helped keep fairly stable, inflation bit deeply into all the major components of popular consumption. The price of foodstuffs increased by 50 per cent between 1914 and 1918. The price of simple clothing goods, most of them normally imported, tripled. Domestic textile manufacturing, using mainly wool, afforded scant relief. It helped to reduce unemployment, though perhaps more among women than men, but failed to check rising prices. For many working-class families in Buenos Aires, between the plunge into depression in 1913 and the Armistice in November 1918, real wage levels as much as halved.[3] Falling unemployment and falling standards of living proved an explosive combination. Labour's earlier quiescence abruptly ceased. Between 1917 and 1921 trade unions in Argentina flourished on a scale unknown before and unrepeated until the mid 1940s; strikes, earlier so conspicuously absent, mounted in number, intensity and eventually in violence.

Meanwhile throughout the war imports and therefore revenues continued to fall. Pending changes in the taxation system to reduce the dependence on revenue from import duties, the government could alleviate its need to economize only by contracting new debts. This it managed to do to some degree by acquiring some short-term loans from banks in New York and floating bonds internally. Between 1914 and 1918, as new debts were contracted, the public floating debt almost

[3] *Ibid.*, 317. For details of the wartime inflation, see Alejandro E. Bunge, *Los problemas económicos del presente* (1919; Buenos Aires, 1979).

tripled from 256 million paper pesos to 711 million. However, total expenditure in 1918 at 421 million was roughly the same as in 1914, and not far above the figure of 375 million for 1916, the lowest throughout the period. This again changed dramatically after the Armistice when imports began to flow once more. From this point onwards public spending underwent a rapid increase. In 1922 it reached 614 million paper pesos, almost 50 per cent higher than in 1918.[4]

The postwar depression which began in 1921 led once more to unemployment, the collapse of the trade union movement, a decline in imports and another shrinkage in state revenues. In 1920 imports were valued at 2,120 million paper pesos, and only 1,570 million in 1922. Because of an increase in tariffs in 1920 revenues fell during the same period by only 20 million, from 481 to 461 million. However, since public expenditure climbed from 503 to 614 million, the government's floating debt also increased markedly from 682 to 893 million. Otherwise the chief effect of the postwar depression was upon the cattle sector, as the earlier great boom ended. After this came the shift back to arable farming.

During the late 1920s much of the real growth in the rural sector occurred beyond the pampas region. In the north-west Salta and Jujuy developed as sugar producers alongside Tucumán. In 1920 Salta and Jujuy contributed less than 16 per cent of national sugar output. By 1930 their share had risen to almost 26 per cent. The more northerly sugar region differed from Tucumán in that production was mainly conducted on large estates. From the 1920s, and into the following decade, it became common for the *ingenio*-owners of Tucumán to buy up estates northwards. Some they employed for cane production. Others they acquired apparently with an eye to capturing their peasant labour force for work on the plantations.[5] There was further growth of fruit production in the Río Negro valley, cotton, rice, peanuts and cassava in the Chaco, and fruits and yerba maté in Misiones. Domestic raw cotton output increased from an annual average of 6,000 tons between 1920 and 1924 to 35,000 tons in 1930–4. The increase in yerba maté was from 12,000 to 46,000 tons. Río Negro, Chaco and Misiones each grew quickly with an infusion of new European immigrants and the spread of small farming. These were each national territories administered from Buenos

---

[4] Figures on public accounts in David Rock, *Politics in Argentina, 1890–1930. The rise and fall of Radicalism* (Cambridge, 1975), 224.
[5] See Ian Rutledge, 'Plantations and peasants in northern Argentina: the sugar cane industry of Salta and Jujuy, 1930–43', in David Rock (ed.), *Argentina in the twentieth century* (London, 1975), 88–113.

Aires, and in this period the central government played a positive role in colonization. As a result by 1930 capitalist small-farming was established on a significantly wider scale than before the war. On the other hand all these regions were heavily dependent on cheap contract peasant labour. Large numbers of Chileans were brought on to the farms of Río Negro and Neuquén, and Paraguayans, *chaqueños* and *correntinos* to those of the north-east.[6]

After 1913 domestic industry grew overall at roughly the same rate as the economy at large, though increasing at a much faster rate after the war than during the war years. Taking the year 1950 as base 100, the index of industrial production was 20.3 in 1914 and 22.1 in 1918. However, by 1929 it reached 45.6. During the war the annual rate of increase in the index was 0.36, and after the war 2.10.[7] During the 1920s industry also diversified in some measure in fields such as consumer durables, chemicals, electricity and particularly metals. In the late 1920s the metallurgical industry surged forward. Between 1926 and 1929 the output index grew from 29 to 43 (1950 = 100).[8] Even so most of the total increase in manufacturing was again in light and traditional industries, continuing the pattern of the pre-1914 years. The textile industry meanwhile largely stagnated. The growth of manufacturing also failed to affect Argentina's high import coefficient, which remained roughly the same as in 1914, at around 25 per cent.

Of the much smaller volume of foreign investment which entered Argentina in the 1920s in comparison with the prewar period, the major source was now the United States. During this period American investment was almost double British. By 1930 it amounted to around one-third of British investment, having risen from an estimated 40 million gold pesos in 1913 to 611 million in 1929. Where before Americans had been interested almost solely in the meat business, they now became active as lenders to government, as exporters and as investors in local industry. Twenty-three subsidiaries of American industrial firms were established in Argentina between 1924 and 1933; other American goods were manufactured locally under licence. On the surface this suggested a growing maturity in the economy, and its ability to diversify beyond agrarian exports and to generate new sources of employment. Yet in the 1920s industry again grew without changing the

---

[6] For farming in the interior, see Jaime Fuchs, *Argentina: su desarrollo capitalista* (Buenos Aires, 1965), 217–24; also Ricardo M. Ortiz, *Historia económica de la Argentina, 1850–1930* (2 vols., Buenos Aires, 1955), II, 131–48.

[7] Di Tella and Zymelman, *Las etapas del desarrollo*, 309, 393.   [8] *Ibid.*, 391.

basic economic structure very much. Oil apart, relatively few backward linkages flowed from it. The machinery, still much of the fuel, the raw materials and technology of the American companies or domestic firms using American patents were largely imported. The overall result was thus to impose binding additions to the import bill, leaving manufacturing and urban employment as dependent as before on foreign earnings from exports.

Meanwhile the growth of imports from the United States led to strain in Argentina's relations with Great Britain. The value of imports from the United States was 43 million gold pesos in 1914. Afterwards this figure climbed to 169 million in 1918, and reached 310 million in 1920. The trend then continued throughout the 1920s. By 1929 American exports to Argentina were valued at 516 million gold pesos. During the war the Americans gained mostly at the expense of Germany, but then afterwards at the expense of the British, who in the 1920s found themselves under serious challenge in a market they had largely dominated for the past hundred years. The British share of the Argentine market fell from 30 per cent in 1911–13 to only 19 per cent by 1929–30, while the American share increased from 15 to 24 per cent. Although the British increased their exports of coal and railway materials to Argentina, they could not compete against the Americans in the goods for which demand was rising most rapidly: automobiles and capital goods for agriculture and industry. Such changes in the import trade were not followed by a parallel shift in exports: Argentina failed to acquire stable, growing markets in the United States. Despite a temporary increase during the war years, exports to the United States, which were 6.3 per cent of the total in 1911–13, remained at only 9.3 per cent in 1928–30. In the late 1920s, 85 per cent of Argentina's exports were still exported to Western Europe. Indeed the trend with exports was almost the direct inverse of imports. Although Argentina was now buying relatively much less from Britain, its exports to Britain grew from 26.1 per cent in 1911–13 to 32.5 per cent in 1928–30: the country was diversifying its sources of imports, but narrowing its markets for exports.

WAR AND POSTWAR POLITICS

Yrigoyen, 1916–22

Politically the years between 1916 and 1930 witnessed the first and also the most prolonged of Argentina's many abortive experiments with representative democracy. Along with neighbouring Uruguay, Argentina was the leader among the nations of Latin America in seeking to develop the political system and institutions most characteristic of advanced Western societies in the early twentieth century. In 1912 the old ruling class, prompted by its progressive wing led by Roque Sáenz Peña, who was president from 1910 to 1914, had reformed the political system largely in an effort to legitimize and stabilize its own authority. Since the emergence of the Unión Cívica Radical in the early 1890s, confidence in the durability of rule by oligarchy had been gradually undermined. After the failure of the 1905 insurrection the Radicals had begun to broaden their power base, attracting a large following among the burgeoning urban and rural middle classes. Operating semi-clandestinely they continued threatening to overthrow the existing order by force unless their demands for 'democracy' and the 'restoration of the constitution' were met. A second focus of disaffection was the Buenos Aires working class. After 1900 there was a string of sometimes violent general strikes led by militant anarchists. By the time of Sáenz Peña's election in 1910, many suspected anarchists had been gaoled or deported and the movement apparently broken. However, most of the conditions which had produced urban unrest remained unchanged. Manhood suffrage, the representation of minorities in Congress and an end to electoral fraud were offered by Sáenz Peña in his 1912 electoral reform law as a response to this dual threat to stability. In his view political order was essential for continuing economic expansion:

If our self-aggrandizement has begun, it is because we have been able to demonstrate the overriding power of the national government, inspiring a sense of security, peace and confidence. I shall not support oppression, but I condemn revolutions . . . I do not believe we can consolidate our present position, except by perfecting ourselves in a climate of order.[9]

Referring to the Radicals Ramón Cárcano, one of Sáenz Peña's supporters in Congress, declared:

For twenty years there has existed in the country an organized popular, dynamic party, which has had as its banner the liberty of the suffrage and openly supported revolution as the only way to fulfil its ideals . . . For a generation government and nation alike have been constantly having either to suppress rebellion or fearing that rebellion was imminent . . . A change in the electoral system . . . is to adopt at this critical hour the only policy the country is united

---

[9] Roque Sáenz Peña, *Discursos del Dr. Roque Sáenz Peña al asumir la presidencia de la nación* (Buenos Aires, 1910), 40.

on: the policy of disarmament, to eliminate abstention from the elections and rebellion; to incorporate each active political force into the electoral process.[10]

Beyond satisfying the Radicals the aim was to give moderate working-class associations, especially the Socialist party (founded in 1894), an opportunity to displace the anarchists. One conservative member of the National Senate in 1912, Benito Villanueva, suggested the need to 'open up an escape valve and allow two or three socialists into Congress, especially at this time of working class unrest when legislation on strikes is about to be discussed'.[11] Lastly, Sáenz Peña and his group also hoped to prod the oligarchic factions into creating a strong, united conservative party able to gather a large popular following. In 1912 there seemed every prospect that these objectives could be fulfilled. At the end of his term in 1916 Sáenz Peña would thus hand over to a progressive conservative like himself strengthened by having won the presidency openly and fairly at the polls. This would weaken the Radicals, also undercutting their main pretext for revolution. If it failed to domesticate the workers, it would strengthen the hand of government in the event of renewed conflict.

After 1912 events pursued a largely different course from the one anticipated. While the Socialist party built up a large electoral following in the city of Buenos Aires, it failed to capture control over working-class trade unions. Although anarchism continued to decline, a new syndicalist movement appeared in its place and in 1915 took over the main union federation, the Federación Obrera Regional Argentina. Meanwhile the Radical party underwent spectacular growth in all parts of the country. The conservatives, however, stagnated. Their efforts at self-democratization were only partially successful: unlike their chief rivals, they failed to create a united national movement. After 1912 they were split among the supporters of the governor of the province of Buenos Aires, Marcelino Ugarte, and the leader of the Progressive Democratic party based in Santa Fe, Lisandro de la Torre. In some measure this disunity was a symptom of economic depression; after 1912 falling land prices, credit restraints, and declining export earnings increasingly demoralized the conservative camp. Sáenz Peña did nothing to arrest the process of fragmentation and decay, and by the time he succumbed to cancer in August 1914 matters had been let slide too long to be easily remedied. Sáenz Peña's successor as president, the septuagenarian financier,

---

[10] *Diario de Sesiones*, Cámara de Deputados (1911), II, 160.   [11] *Ibid.*, Senadores (1911), II, 338.

Victorino de la Plaza, was soon caught up in the economic repercussions of the war; he had little opportunity for political manoeuvring. The unexpected result of the 1916 elections was thus a victory for the Radical party and its leader Hipólito Yrigoyen, though by the barest of margins.

Yrigoyen's election to the presidency in the first national elections under universal manhood suffrage in 1916 was widely recognized as portending a new era in the country's political development. The new ruling party embraced large segments of the population which before had enjoyed little real representation. They could be expected to push for innovations. But despite their defeat and their mistrust of Yrigoyen the conservatives were not unduly alarmed. In accepting electoral politics the Radicals appeared to have abandoned the idea of revolution. Yrigoyen had given no hint of a commitment to major change. Despite its substantial middle-class support, his party embraced a good portion of members of the elite. The recent election had done little beyond change the president. The conservatives themselves dominated Congress through their overwhelming majority in the Senate. They were firmly in control of many of the provinces. Their influence was similarly undiminished in other leading institutions: the army, the church, the Rural Society and elsewhere. They had created popular democracy by concession; what they had given they could also take away. Having won his position as much by courtesy of the old ruling class as by his own efforts, Yrigoyen enjoyed a highly conditional mandate: he was to uphold the status quo while reducing the level of popular unrest.

Hipólito Yrigoyen's first six-year term (1916–22) was far from the smooth transition to representative democracy the conservatives had hoped for. It was closely influenced by the wartime inflation which altered the distribution of income among the major social classes, and by the cycles of depression and prosperity which embraced the whole period between 1916 and 1922. Inflation, as we have seen, underlay a protracted outbreak of unrest among the working class of Buenos Aires and in parts of the country outside. Its main episodes were a general strike in Buenos Aires in January 1919 and a spate of rural labour agitation in Patagonia between 1920 and 1922. The economic cycles brought fluctuations in the influx of imports and therefore government revenues. Revenues in turn had a crucial bearing on the government's ability to enhance its popular support and to reduce the influence of the conservative opposition. They bore closely on its relations with the enfranchised upper tiers of the middle class, many of whose members were employed in public administration. Until 1919 the Radical government cultivated the middle class mainly by supporting change and expansion in university education. Afterwards it came to rely increasingly on patronage links. In the longer term Yrigoyen was pushed by a variety of forces into narrowing his political base which came to consist largely of the middle class. From this came class fissures in Argentine politics which had a close bearing on his overthrow in 1930.

At the beginning there was a strong air of continuity between the new Radical administration and its conservative predecessors. Yrigoyen carefully cultivated support from conservative bodies like the church, and his Cabinet was made up of members of the traditional elites. Most were affiliates of the Rural Society, the main guardian of the stock-raising interest. There was also continuity in international affairs, as Yrigoyen reaffirmed neutrality in the war. During his first months in office the new president persistently irritated conservative opinion by secretive political manoeuvres, and by a cavalier attitude to protocol, such as ignoring the accepted practice of being present at the opening of Congress. Yet for the most part on broad policy issues he behaved in a safe and conventional fashion.

The new government's legislative proposals, submitted to Congress in late 1916, were measures under public discussion for some time and were regarded as mild in content. The government requested funds for new colonization schemes on state lands, an emergency fund to assist farmers caught by a recent drought, a new state bank to provide better credit arrangements for agriculture, and the acquisition of shipping to attack the problem of high wartime freights. In 1918 it further proposed the introduction of an income tax. Yrigoyen's error in 1916 was to demand from Congress the large sum of 100 million paper pesos to execute these various measures. Conservatives immediately drew the conclusion that the funds would be employed for partisan purposes. Pleading the need for economy Congress gave them short shrift and rejected them. It was not so much that Congress was opposed to the measures themselves; it was unwilling to grant the executive financial independence – Yrigoyen would be less troublesome if the resources at his disposal were held to the minimum. Disputes of this kind over the sanctioning and disposal of public funds continued throughout his presidency, and were a chief source of the growing rift between the government and the conservative opposition. There were several years in which Congress failed to vote the annual budget, to which the government replied by carrying out expenditures by simple Cabinet resolutions. After 1919 this became Yrigoyen's chief method of increasing state spending. Constant wrangling between the Executive and Congress over financial matters was among the chief reasons for a somewhat barren legislative record before 1922. Yrigoyen's main achievement was the eventual creation of an agricultural mortgage bank in 1920 under Law No. 10,676. Under this legislation farmers were accorded more liberal credit terms for land purchases. The law assisted colonization efforts at the outer limits of the pampas and in the national territories.[12]

The president could only prevail over Congress by changing its composition and winning a majority. To do this he was obliged to control the provinces and supplant the conservative governors and their party machines. Like Roca, Pellegrini, and Figueroa Alcorta before him, Yrigoyen turned to federal intervention. Interventions in the provinces, and related election issues, were the source of some of the fiercest controversies during his first three years in office. The most serious came in early 1917 when Yrigoyen, ignoring Congress's claim that legislation was necessary in such matters, decreed intervention in the province of Buenos Aires against Marcelino Ugarte. Altogether during the six years of his government there were an unprecedented twenty federal interventions, fifteen of them by decree. However, most came after 1918, when the power struggle between Radicals and conservatives entered its more intense phase. Most were also employed in the backward interior provinces, where control over the executive and its store of patronage, jobs and credits, was the key to political dominance. Thanks largely to federal intervention, by 1918 the Radicals won a majority in the National Chamber of Deputies. What they failed to do was achieve control over the Senate, whose members enjoyed a long nine-year tenure, renewable by thirds triennially.[13]

Before 1919 the Radical government sought to strengthen its links with the middle classes by supporting the university reform movement, *La Reforma*, which began in Córdoba in 1918 as the climax to growing agitation for changes in higher education. At this time there were three universities in Argentina: Córdoba (founded in 1617 by the Jesuits), Buenos Aires (1821) and La Plata (1890). Attendance at these institutions

---

[12] See Roberto Etchepareborda, *Yrigoyen y el Congreso* (Buenos Aires, 1956); for agrarian legislation, see Ortiz, *Historia económica*, I, 57.

[13] See Rodolfo Moreno, *Intervenciones federales en las provincias* (Buenos Aires, 1924).

had grown from around 3,000 in 1900 to 14,000 in 1918. For a decade or more before 1918 there were rising tensions in Córdoba between the incumbent and unchanging clerical order and the new middle classes of immigrant background whose numbers were growing steadily in the student body. During the war years long-standing demands for improvements in the university's teaching, and the streamlining of its curricula, were radicalized by events outside the country – especially the revolutions in Russia and Mexico. The reform movement began in Córdoba with a succession of militant strikes and an outpouring of manifestos, organized by a new students' union, the Federación Universitaria Argentina. Demands were made for student representation in university government, the reform of examination practices and an end to nepotism in the appointment of the professorial staff. For much of 1918 the University of Córdoba and the city beyond were consumed in turmoil. In the following year the student strikes spread to Buenos Aires and La Plata.

The Radical government gave the students sustained support. In 1918 Yrigoyen sent to Córdoba personal delegates who were known to favour the reform movement. They implemented many of the changes the students deemed necessary, and sought to link the vague democratic ideals of radicalism and the diffuse body of doctrine emanating from the reform movement. Later the government carried out similar reforms in the University of Buenos Aires. Finally all three universities were given new charters supposedly guaranteeing their autonomy, but in fact bringing them more directly under the control of the central government. When in 1919 and 1921 new universities were created in Santa Fe and Tucumán, the same regime was implanted there. The Radical government's support for the university reform was long regarded as among its more positive and lasting achievements. Here Yrigoyen managed to challenge an area of privilege, and associate himself with democratization, without being circumvented by conservative opposition.

His much less fruitful contact with the Buenos Aires working class and the trade unions stemmed from the keen rivalries between Radicals and Socialists for a popular majority in the capital. The competition between the two parties began during the first elections held in the city under the Sáenz Peña Law in 1912, and persisted throughout the period under 1930. In 1912 the Socialists were already gaining upwards of 30,000 votes in the city. This number later doubled and then trebled as they established a stable position among the electorate. The Socialist party, however, was controlled by middle-class intellectuals and while its main voting strength lay among workers, it also attracted many white-collar groups and small businessmen. Its programme placed little emphasis on the socialization of property; it was mostly concerned with the protection of urban consumer interests. The party's main weakness, which stemmed in large part from the moderate stances it took, was its lack of backing from the trade unions. Before 1910 it was constantly out-manoeuvred by the anarchists, and afterwards by the syndicalists, who in 1915, as we have seen, took over the principal labour federation in Buenos Aires, the FORA. The chief aim of the Radicals was to exploit this fissure between the party and the union and swing voting union members over in their favour.

Competition for the working-class vote, already a leading issue in the presidential election in Buenos Aires in 1916, continued unabated when Yrigoyen assumed power. The Radical offensive began at the end of 1916 on the outbreak of a strike in the port of Buenos Aires. The strike was organized by a group known as the Federación Obrera Marítima (Maritime Workers' Federation), an association led by syndicalists. The syndicalists were a somewhat different species from their anarchist predecessors. For the most part they were not immigrants but native-born. They paid only lip service to the goal of class revolution, and were interested almost exclusively in wage questions. Yrigoyen saw in the maritime strike the opportunity to better his reputation among the working class, and to weaken the Socialists. When it began, the authorities responded with actions which suggested sympathy for the men's cause. They paraded their avoidance of police measures to quell it, as had been the usual practice up until that time. Instead several union leaders were brought before members of the government and urged to accept their arbitration. When a ruling was eventually forthcoming the strikers obtained a settlement which met most of their grievances.

Government intervention in this strike and others swiftly escalated into a major political issue. For a time it won the Radicals a measure of popularity among the trade unions and the voting working class which helped it to electoral victory against the Socialists. In the congressional elections of 1916 in the city of Buenos Aires, the Radicals gained 59,061 votes or 47.1 per cent of the total; in 1918 their vote increased to 74,180, 51.7 per cent of the total. But these electoral successes were at the cost of vehement conservative opposition, which moved quickly beyond

Congress and the press to encompass the major special interest associations led by the Rural Society. In 1917 and 1918 the strikes spread beyond Buenos Aires to the British railway companies. Here, largely due to the high cost of imported coal during the war, working conditions had deteriorated and wages had fallen. When the government again appeared to take the side of the men, opposition spread to British business interests, which branded the government as pro-German. Primed into action by leading British companies, the employers established a strike-breaking body, the National Labour Association, which pledged itself to all-out war against trade union 'agitators'.

For several months afterwards the labour front remained fairly tranquil. Then in early January 1919, working-class discontent suddenly revived with even greater intensity. This episode, known subsequently as La Semana Trágica, stemmed from a strike of metallurgical workers which began in early December 1918. The metallurgical industry had suffered perhaps more than any other during the war. It was entirely dependent upon imported raw materials at a time when prices had reached astronomical levels as a result of high shipping rates and world shortages due to arms manufacture. As the price of raw materials climbed, wages had fallen. By the end of the war the metallurgical workers were in a desperate position. The strike was a battle for survival. Violence immediately ensued, and the police were obliged to intervene. When the strikers killed a member of the city police force, the latter organized a retaliatory ambush. Two days later five persons were killed in an affray between the two sides.

At this the city erupted. Ignoring pleas for moderation from the syndicalists, the workers struck *en masse*, joining a great procession through the city in homage to the victims of the police attack. More outbreaks of violence followed. The affair ballooned at a speed which paralysed the government. As it hesitated, the army intervened. Led by General Luis F. Dellepiane, a former chief of police in Buenos Aires, military detachments, equipped with artillery and machine guns, appeared to quell the outbreak. Dellepiane accomplished his task with little difficulty. The strikers were quickly scattered. Soon all that remained of the movement were sporadic bread riots as food shortages enveloped the city.

While this was done Yrigoyen for the most part sat silently in the background. He was aware of a dangerous wave of opposition in military and naval circles. It sprang not only from his labour policies, but from his juggling with army promotions to favour Radical sympathizers and from his use of the army during recent federal interventions. By January 1919 there were some among the armed forces ready to overthrow him. In this climate the Radical government fell captive to a conservative reaction bent on exacting revenge for the recent disorders. In the strike's aftermath civilian vigilante gangs sprang up in large numbers. After perfunctory drilling and rifle practice from the army they were set loose on the streets. But soon their activities centred upon the city's Russian-Jewish community. Its members became prime targets in the belief that the general strike was the prelude to a Bolshevik revolution, part of an alleged world conspiracy directed from Soviet Russia for the overthrow of capitalism. In Argentina, as in other parts of the Americas and Western Europe infected by similar fears, this suspicion was groundless. Nevertheless the reaction it provoked claimed the lives of up to two hundred victims. Xenophobia together with anti-labour, anti-communist and anti-semitic sentiments were employed by the conservatives to overcome the isolation and disunity which had cost them the election of 1916. They had conjured up a large popular movement, which included many Radicals, and the support of the army made it a parallel and potentially competing focus of authority against the government. As the violence finally subsided, the vigilante groups organized themselves into an association styling itself the Liga Patriótica Argentina (Argentine Patriotic League).

In March 1919 a vital senatorial election was held in the Federal Capital. This the Radicals managed to win, but by a margin of only 3,000 votes out of a total of 99,000 cast. In scarcely a year their share of the vote had dropped from more than 51 per cent to less than 40 per cent. The convervatives, however, represented by the Progressive Democratic party, increased their vote from 9,030 to more than 36,000. This expressed a strong swing away from the Radicals among the middle classes in Buenos Aires. It was both a vote of censure against the government for the recent strikes and a strong gesture of support towards the conservatives.

In late 1920 there was another major spate of unrest – this time in Patagonia. Beginning in the towns it mushroomed outwards among the great sheep ranches. To enforce the strike in the more outlying areas its adherents organized themselves into armed bands. Skirmishes with the ranchers promoted anxious petitions to Buenos Aires for assistance. Alleging that the strike was a cover for Chilean annexationist plots in the region, the Patriotic League demanded action. Once more Yrigoyen was unable to resist. A military expedition was raised to suppress the strike. In a long campaign throughout 1921 and 1922, punctuated by a flood of reports of army brutalities, the strike was broken.[14]

This saga of labour unrest repeatedly revealed the fragility of Yrigoyen's authority. In a bid to reconstruct his support, he turned to populism and patronage. After mid 1919 as imports and revenues recovered, state spending began its steep upward ascent. The stream of federal interventions in the provinces became a torrent. By opening up the bureaucracy to his followers, and rewarding them in the provinces, Yrigoyen rapidly recovered his personal popularity. In late 1919 an attempt to impeach the president from the Senate was filibustered into oblivion by the Radicals, while the strike in Patagonia became in part a means to divert the attentions of the army and the Patriotic League away from politics in Buenos Aires. In the congressional elections of early 1920 the Radicals again beat back the challenge of the Socialists and the Progressive Democrats, the latter's share of the vote declining substantially. After this the conservative electoral challenge rapidly dwindled. (In 1922, as in 1916, they entered the presidential election campaign divided: the Progressive Democrats mustered only 5.8 per cent of the vote, and a new conservative group formed to contest the presidential election, the National Concentration, obtained another 12.2 per cent.) In the country at large by 1922 the Radicals had a political organization which gave them the edge over all their opponents combined. But Yrigoyen's liberal use of federal intervention, and his heavy spending policies as revenues began to decline again during the postwar depression, brought renewed heavy conservative criticism. In rewarding his middle-class clientele, Yrigoyen also provoked frictions with the patrician wing of his own party. Conservatives and Radical dissidents alike bitterly attacked the president's 'personalist' leadership, accusing him of fomenting financial chaos and of promoting corrupt and incompetent party hacks to key positions in government. There were predictions of breakdown unless the slide into 'demagogy' were halted. In 1916 the conservative interests accepted Yrigoyen in the belief that he

14 The story of Patagonia has been told in dramatic and fascinating detail by Osvaldo Bayer, *Los vengadores de la Patagonia trágica* (2 vols., Buenos Aires, 1972).

would protect continuity and stability. In most areas there was undoubtedly continuity: the reform achievements of the Radicals were insignificant. On the other hand in 1922 stability seemed as distant as at any time during the past 30 years.

Alvear, 1922–8

To the great relief of his opponents, in 1922 Yrigoyen's term came to an end. His successor, elected by a large majority of the provinces and by a plurality of the popular vote against conservative and Socialist opposition, was Marcelo T. de Alvear, a member of one of the country's oldest and wealthiest families. The new president assumed power at the height of the postwar depression. The economic cycle again overshadowed some of the chief issues he faced: the crisis in the beef industry, tariff reform and the public debt. The first of these was chiefly significant as an illustration of the power now wielded by the meat-packing plants in Argentine politics. The second showed that nineteenth-century attitudes towards the tariff and industrial protection still largely prevailed in the 1920s. Meanwhile, Alvear's handling of the public debt issue closely influenced politics throughout the 1920s. It underlay the division of the Radical party in 1924, Alvear's growing weakness as president, and Yrigoyen's resurgence as a popular leader in readiness for the presidential elections of 1928.

The appearance of American and British meat-packing plants after 1900, and growing exports of high-quality chilled beef, induced major changes in cattle ranching in Argentina. In many parts of the pampas, particularly the province of Buenos Aires, there was heavy investment in improved stock, especially shorthorns. At the same time specialization developed among the ranchers between breeders and fatteners. During the war, however, these trends abruptly ceased. The chilled beef trade was suspended, while exports of frozen and canned beef rapidly increased; the shift towards a lesser quality meat made it no longer essential to use a high-grade stock, nor to fatten it on special pasture before slaughter. Between 1914 and 1921 all ranchers, regardless of the quality of their stock, serviced the frozen and canned meat business, and benefited in roughly equal measure from the boom. Several new meat-packing plants were created in Zárate, Concordia and La Plata. Prosperity reached beyond the province of Buenos Aires into less central cattle regions such as Entre Ríos and Corrientes, where the herds were mostly traditional Creole breeds. At the same time urban interests from Buenos Aires and Rosario, equipped with lavish bank credits, were drawn into ranching on a large scale. Between 1914 and 1921 the cattle stock in Argentina increased by around 50 per cent, from 26 to 37 million.

The boom ended in 1921 when the British government ceased stockpiling supplies from Argentina, abolished meat control and began to liquidate its accumulated holdings. In Argentina there were fewer than half the cattle slaughtered for export in 1921 as there were in 1918. Prices also halved. Production of frozen and canned beef declined precipitously and all but disappeared. Afterwards what little trade remained was again, after this seven-year lapse, dominated by chilled beef. For a time all sectors of the cattle economy, from humble alfalfa farmers to the great meat-packing plants like Armour and Swift, suffered from the depression. But because of the vertical organization of the industry, the losses it occasioned were not distributed evenly. Some could protect their margins in some degree by forcing down the prices they paid to the sectors below which serviced them. This power and freedom of manoeuvre belonged most of all to the meat-packing plants. Cattle ranchers with shorthorn stock could also avoid the full impact of the depression by reverting to the chilled beef trade, while the specialist fatteners could follow the lead of the meat-packing plants and cut the prices they paid to breeders. Besides the breeders the main victims of the depression were the cattle owners of Entre Ríos and Corrientes, who had made the mistake of over-investing in Creole stock, and the gamut of wartime speculators, equally overloaded with useless herds, and now facing crippling outstanding mortgage obligations.

At the height of the crisis a segment from among the cattle breeders won control over the Rural Society. This prestigious institution was employed to bring pressure on the government to intervene against the meat-packing plants. They were accused of operating a buying pool to safeguard their own profits. To counter this monopsony the Rural Society proposed the creation of a locally owned packing plant paying higher prices than the American and British buyers. Other measures were conceived to assist ranchers overstocked with Creole cattle. They recommended a minimum price for cattle by the criterion of weight rather than pedigree, and secondly to exclude the foreign meat-packers from supplying the domestic market, thereby reserving it for those with inferior stock. In 1923, with support from the government, legislation was passed by Congress which incorporated most of these proposals, but the attempt at regulation failed in a spectacular fashion. The packers replied by imposing an embargo on all cattle purchases, an action which quickly reduced the ranchers to confusion and division. Soon afterwards the government shelved the entire scheme and no further action was taken. The breeders were obliged to ride out the depression without government assistance.

Alvear's proposals to Congress in 1923 for changes in the national tariff have sometimes been depicted as a strong shift towards protectionism to encourage domestic manufacturing. This was certainly the president's declared aim in the preamble to the measure. He suggested reducing duties on imported raw materials required by the metallurgical industry, and secondly extending the protection afforded sugar and wines in the 1880s to cotton, yerba maté and temperate fruits. However, the impact of this on manufacturing overall was slight. In so far as this part of the measure was protectionist it was largely a continuation of late-nineteenth-century policies. Its chief significance was for agricultural areas like the Chaco and Río Negro which the government was attempting to colonize. Beyond this Alvear also recommended a uniform 80 per cent increase in the tariff valuations of imports. Here the change was not in duties themselves, but in the assessed customs values of imports. Upon these a variable schedule of duties was applied. The increase in the valuations, which Congress trimmed to 60 per cent, was in addition to one of 20 per cent carried out under Yrigoyen in 1920. An 80 per cent increase spread over three years seemed large, but in fact barely compensated for the inflation in import prices during the war. It was, as we have seen, a change in the tariff valuations, not for the most part in the duties themselves; the latter afforded the real opportunity to guide the development of the domestic economy. All this achieved was roughly a return to 1914 eight years after the original valuations had been made. Because of inflation the valuations, which were originally around 25 per cent of real values in 1906, had fallen to an average of only 9.4 per cent in 1921. The tariff reform of 1923 was thus protectionist to only a very limited degree. Its main objectives were different: to increase government revenues while at the same time reducing imports during the postwar recession, to assist colonization schemes, and to guard against a repetition of the events of 1920 which brought a spate of dumping by foreign manufacturers. Among these goals the increase of revenues was the most important. Alvear's message to Congress in 1923 described the present tariff valuations as a 'flagrant injustice', and the cause of 'an unsatisfactory decline in national revenues'.

Perceptions of the tariff issue and domestic industry in the early 1920s were strongly coloured by events during the past decade. Between 1913 and 1920, first with the depression and then with the war, local industry had enjoyed unprecedented, if also quite involuntary, protection. Yet in the eyes of the postwar generation all that appeared to have been achieved was uncontrollable inflation, unjustifiably high returns to pools of profiteering businessmen at the expense of consumers, and a crop of strikes which had been on the point of provoking a workers' revolution. Against this it was essential to return to the stability of the prewar period. Views towards national industry were largely the same as they had been for most of the nineteenth century. Protection was only justifiable for national products which would quickly become price competitive with imports, for the most part agricultural goods; the rest were 'artificial': to foster them through protection would induce chronic inefficiencies in the economy. If they helped employment and reduced the need for imports, they would also inflate prices and depress overall consumption. The tariff reform of 1923 probably had little impact on industry during the 1920s, which grew mainly with the arrival of new immigrants and the beginnings of American investment. If industry overall enjoyed any significantly greater protection in the 1920s than before 1914, this was probably due as much as anything else to the hidden surcharge on imports resulting from the depreciation of the peso between 1921 and 1926.

As a complement to his changes in the tariff, Alvear also tackled the issue of government spending and the public debt. In 1923 his minister of finance, Rafael Herrera Vegas, prophesied 'national ruin' with 'the payment of 1000 million of floating debt and 604 million of budget expenditure'.[15] Both he and Alvear determined to halt the slide, which had been taking place since 1919, towards what they acknowledged was financial anarchy. However, fiscal austerity was extremely unpopular among the rank and file members of the Radical party. For them, high state spending was not only a matter of career opportunities and social mobility but a means of escape from the depression. To control state spending it was essential to clear Yrigoyen's appointments from the

---

[15] Quoted in Rock, *Politics in Argentina*, 225.

administration, many of which were made immediately before the presidential elections in 1922. Regardless of the dangers and its likely effect on his relations with Yrigoyen, Alvear committed himself to this task. He abandoned his predecessor's disputed practice of authorizing expenditures by simple Cabinet resolutions, and restored full congressional supervision over financial affairs. Between late 1922 and 1924 there was a spate of campaigns against administrative corruption, and a long succession of purges and dismissals. By 1925 a semblance of greater order prevailed. With its tariff changes and recovery from the depression, the government's revenue position greatly improved. Although overall Alvear failed to arrest the upward trend in public spending, he eventually matched revenues with expenditures, and managed to slow down the growth of the floating debt.

But this cost him dearly with his party. Under the impact of the purges and swingeing spending cuts Alvear's control over the party swiftly collapsed. In the middle of 1924 the Radicals divided into two irreconcilable bands. One, the majority in Congress and in the constituency committees, renounced Alvear and reasserted their allegiance towards Yrigoyen. They now styled themselves Yrigoyenistas. The rump became the 'Antipersonalist' Radicals, adopting this title to express their opposition to Yrigoyen. The latter group was composed mainly of the party's conservative and patrician wing, and many provincial Radicals alienated from Yrigoyen on account of his use of federal interventions against them after 1919. After 1924 came an embittered struggle between the two factions for supremacy. Politics, not policies, now dominated the Alvear administration. The Yrigoyenista majority in the Chamber of Deputies torpedoed his legislative programme. At first the president aligned himself with the Antipersonalists, but in 1925 in an effort to reunify the party he broke with them, refusing to accept their demand for a federal intervention against the Yrigoyenistas in the province of Buenos Aires. In July 1925 Vicente Gallo, the Antipersonalist minister of the interior, resigned. Without Alvear's support the Antipersonalist challenge quickly flagged. It was soon just another conservative faction, little more than a coalition of provincial groupings dominated by its branch in Santa Fe.

Alvear's reluctance to embrace the Antipersonalists and to use the powers of the president to favour them left the way open for Yrigoyen. After 1924 his followers rapidly reconstructed their party organization. By the time of the interim congressional elections in 1926 Yrigoyenista party committees were flourishing in the cities and the countryside alike, attracting enthusiastic support from a wide variety of popular groups. During this period Yrigoyen's followers revealed themselves as peerless practitioners in the arts of popular mobilization. They deluged the country with propaganda through the press and also the radio. They sought support indiscriminately, making no effort to build a party of compatible interest groups. Helped by the return of prosperity in the mid 1920s, they cultivated expectations throughout the voting population of a return to the spoils bonanza of 1919–22, intimating that all sectors of the population would share in its fruits. At the same time they sought to glorify their leader's person, dwelling upon his virtues as a popular leader, while magnifying and inflating his past achievements. By 1928 Hipólito Yrigoyen enjoyed a popularity unknown in Argentina's past history. He was poised for a triumphal return to the presidency.

Nevertheless, as the election approached, Yrigoyen still had many powerful enemies. Their animosities towards him increased as he again became a contender for power. His position was weak in some of the provinces where Antipersonalists and conservatives were in control. Here memories lingered of the flood of interventions during his past administration, which were remembered as violent and arbitrary usurpations of provincial rights. Opposition against him of this type was no longer confined to provincial landowning oligarchies. In Mendoza and San Juan, under the leadership of the Lencinas and Cantoni families, the opposition had democratized itself to become localist replicas of Yrigoyen's own popular movement. There was still bitter antagonism towards him among the conservatives who had fanned the flames of chauvinism, anti-semitism and anti-communism between 1919 and 1921. Opposition was again undisguisably manifest in the army. Once more rumours of a military *coup d'état* were in the air. Towards the end of Alvear's term reports surfaced of an army plot to prevent his return to power, orchestrated by the minister of war, General Agustín P. Justo.

Among these different groups Yrigoyen was repeatedly denounced for the irresponsible and what seemed patently demagogic manner in which he was manoeuvring his present popular following. His main supporters, the job-hunting middle classes, were regarded by conservative groups as irredeemably corrupt. Yrigoyen now seemed an altogether more dangerous proposition than in 1916. Following the party split of 1924 there were no longer the earlier checks against him which the more conservative wing of radicalism had always in some degree exercised. He was suspected of plotting a popular dictatorsnip. By this time an interminable succession of election defeats had left the conservative opposition with little remaining confidence in the Sáenz Peña reform. It had failed to produce the type of government they wanted. If some conservatives, Justo for example, would have been content with government by the Antipersonalists, others had recently undergone a further marked shift to the right. They were admirers of Mussolini's Italy and Primo de Rivera's Spain, and advocates of military dictatorship. But with Yrigoyen nearing the zenith of his popularity, there was little that could be done. An attempt to forestall his return to power ran the risk of provoking civil war. At this juncture there was no guarantee that the conservatives would emerge from it the victors. The conservatives had to wait.

Oil and international relations

During the election campaign of 1928 the Yrigoyenistas emerged with an issue which proved crucial in carrying their leader back into the presidency: a state monopoly over oil. This nationalist campaign also focused against American oil interests, particularly against Standard Oil of New Jersey. Here it became bound up in the wider question of relations between Argentina and the United States.

The oil campaign of the late 1920s began some twenty years after the discovery of the rich Patagonian oil fields at Comodoro Rivadavia in 1907, and other smaller ones in Neuquén, Mendoza and Salta. The peculiarities of the history of oil in Argentina were the state's leading part in the industry from its very beginnings, and the early strong determination to prevent oil resources falling into the hands of alien interests. In 1910 legislation was passed establishing a state reserve over a 5,000 hectare area in Comodoro Rivadavia, from which all private claims were for a time excluded. Soon afterwards the state itself commenced drilling operations in Comodoro Rivadavia. Private interests were initially confined to the smaller oil fields in Neuquén and the provinces. Sáenz Peña was a strong supporter of efforts to develop national oil, largely because strikes in Britain immediately before the war appeared to threaten imports of coal. On the other hand, before the war there was little conflict between this small state enterprise and foreign oil companies. At this point the latter showed little interest in developing production in Argentina, and had a stake in the country only as importers. In these early years the industry's progress, with the state sector acting as leader, proved somewhat disappointing. Hopes of reduced imports, which came mainly from Texas and Mexico, were not fulfilled. Before 1914 local production was barely 7 per cent of total consumption. Congress was unwilling to grant sufficient funds. Other difficulties common to ventures of this kind outside industrial countries were encountered in obtaining skilled personnel and equipment. During the war there was an embargo on the export of drilling and refining equipment from the United States. Although attempts to increase domestic production won growing support during the war from the navy and the army to satisfy defence needs, progress did little to alleviate the crisis caused by declining imports of British coal. Furthermore, of the still small total output of crude oil, only a fraction could be refined.

The fuel crisis during the war eroded some of the more extreme prejudices against foreign capital. The sentiment grew that it was a necessary evil to ensure more rapid development. This opinion appeared to be shared by the first Radical government. Between 1916 and 1922 Yrigoyen was perhaps less nationalistic on the oil question than his immediate predecessors. He registered no opposition against the presence of a private sector, most of it in foreign hands. Under his government private companies increased their share of total production from a diminutive 3 per cent to 20 per cent. He used Comodoro Rivadavia as a source of political patronage. Any efforts at reform he made here, as in so many other cases, fell foul of a hostile Congress. His most significant step was the establishment in 1922, shortly before his departure from office, of a supervisory and managerial board for state oil, the Dirección General de los Yacimientos Petrolíferos Fiscales (YPF). Under Alvear, when more favourable conditions for the importation of equipment appeared, the industry began to revive. He appointed a vigorous and committed military administrator to lead YPF, General Enrique Mosconi, at the same time granting them both a good deal of autonomy. Under Mosconi many of the state industry's early difficulties were resolved. In 1925 a large refinery was opened at La Plata. YPF also established its own retailing network, producing and distributing petrol and paraffin. In the immediate postwar period oil in Argentina at last began to attract keen interest among the major companies from abroad. In these years the growth of the YPF was overshadowed by that of the private sector, which by 1928 had increased its share of production to almost 38 per cent. Yet the growth of production was unable to keep pace with domestic demand. Despite a tripling in the total output of crude oil between 1922 and 1928, imports of coal also increased by one-third, and imported oil almost doubled. In 1928 domestic oil fields still supplied less than half of total domestic fuel consumption.

By the late 1920s, long before the Yrigoyenista campaign, there was thus a tradition of state involvement in the oil industry. It was grounded upon nationalist sentiments, which frequently crossed party political lines. Equally, Argentina was the first country outside Soviet Russia to form a vertically integrated state-owned petroleum industry. However, commitment to this had not been carried to the point of excluding private or foreign shares in the industry. In the interests of increasing output and ensuring efficiency, the policy of each government was to permit the growth of the state and private sectors alike. Intervention mainly took the form of protecting the state sector's share of the market and preventing the regular export of oil. After the war this permitted several foreign companies to construct sizeable operations in the country which eventually became the source of the lion's share of production. By 1928 private companies provided one-third of the output from Comodoro Rivadavia, two-thirds of that from Plaza Huincul in Neuquén, and the whole of that in the smaller fields in Salta and Mendoza.

Among the private companies Standard Oil was by this time the most prominent. It now had interests in almost every sphere of the industry. It was still, as before the war, the leading importer of oil, and controlled the main channels of internal distribution. It had substantial interests in refining, and despite YPF by far the largest share in sales of paraffin and automobile fuels. But its activities which now drew most attention were its drilling operations in the province of Salta. Standard Oil established itself here by carefully wooing the provincial authorities, which controlled subsoil rights in the province as the national government did in the national territories of the south. During the 1920s Salta was still under an oligarchy of landowners, the most powerful of them now in sugar. Until recent years the province had been heavily stricken with poverty. With the terms it offered, Standard Oil had little difficulty in amassing a vast area to which it held exclusive exploration and drilling rights. The oil fields in Salta were acquired with the aim of linking up with an overlapping field the company possessed in Bolivia. It intended to lay out a transnational sphere of influence in this corner of South

America. The position it commanded in Buenos Aires would give it the outlet for the exports it intended to develop from Bolivia, and, if it could do so, from Salta itself.

During the 1920s, confronted by a now embittered and highly publicized conflict for supremacy between the private oil interests and YPF, public opinion in Buenos Aires retreated into its prewar hostility towards foreign capital. In typically zealous and ebullient fashion the Yrigoyenistas plunged into a campaign to win political dividends from the prevailing popular mood. In July 1927 they issued a pledge to bring all the nation's oil fields under state control, and to extend this monopoly to refining, subproducts and distribution. They laid the issue before the electorate with characteristic panache, unceasingly cultivating popular aspirations for undisputed local control over national assets and latent resentments against foreign business. Oil nationalization was depicted as the sovereign remedy for the nation's ills. Grandiose promises were delivered that the revenues from oil, once under national control, would permit the cancellation of the foreign debt, and render all future borrowing superfluous. Domestic manufacturers would be endowed with a limitless source of cheap power, which would permit a miraculous and painless transition to an industrial society. A state oil monopoly would make possible the elimination of all other forms of taxation, finally relieving the popular sectors of the irksome duties on imports which inflated the cost of living.

Nationalization soon commanded enormous popularity among the middle classes: once geared to the oil flow, state revenues would no longer be subject to the unpredictable ebb and flow of foreign trade; afterwards there could be virtually no limits to the expansion of the public sector and the bureaucracy. The issue also blended in closely with Yrigoyen's wider struggle against the Antipersonalists and the conservatives: the situation in Salta was portrayed by his followers as the black alliance of Oligarchy and Imperialism, which a state monopoly would shatter. If Yrigoyen could vest control over oil in the hands of the national government, and take it away from the provinces, he would destroy one of the major props of the opposition. With the oil royalties in their own hands, the Yrigoyenistas felt confident of perpetual supremacy.

The nationalist component of this campaign was directed against Standard Oil alone. It largely ignored British oil consortia, such as Royal Dutch Shell. The latter's manoeuvrings were conducted with less fanfare, and had so far attained less success than Standard Oil's. But behind the scenes they were scarcely less ambitious in scope. In recent years control over Argentine oil had become as much a British as an American objective. Standard Oil, however, was the target because of its ill-advised local affiliations with the Salta oligarchy, because of its international ill-repute – and quite simply because it was an American company. Here the oil issue impinged closely on the wider field of international relations, and also upon relations between Yrigoyen and the conservative power groups.

Moreover, anti-Americanism emanated not from the middle classes, nor from the Radical party, but from the landed and exporting interests of the pampas and from the conservatives. Its origin lay principally in long-standing disputes over trade. Although since around the turn of the century, first with Texas oil and afterwards with automobiles and many capital goods, the Americans had built up a large share in the Argentine market, Argentina had failed to develop reciprocal exports to the United States. At the behest of the American farm lobby, Republican administrations in the United States continually kept most of its goods out. Argentina protested vigorously, frequently, but unavailingly against American policy. By 1914, despite the coming of the Chicago meat-packers, Argentina had still failed to establish a market in the United States for its beef exports. The Americans were prepared to accept only its second-rank goods, such as hides and linseed. During the first world war Argentina's exports to the United States increased tenfold in value. However, soon afterwards in 1922 the Frodney-McCumber Tariff restored and in some measure extended the earlier policy of exclusion.

In the 1920s, in face of its still weak position in the American market, Argentina relied heavily on its exports to Britain. But the longer-term stability of this connection was threatened by the growing shift in Argentina's imports from Britain to the United States. By the late 1920s Argentina's trade surplus with Britain roughly matched its deficit with the United States. In Britain, however, there was now a growing campaign in favour of imperial preference. If this were adopted in the effort to reduce Britain's trade imbalances, it would give British dominion producers – Canada, Australia, New Zealand and South Africa – the share in the British market previously accorded to Argentina.

These issues bore closely on the question of Argentine oil and relations with Standard Oil of New Jersey. In 1926 the Coolidge administration in the United States imposed an absolute ban on imports of dressed beef from the Río de la Plata region. It was done ostensibly as a protection against foot-and-mouth disease. But the measure provoked an infuriated response in Buenos Aires as another act of discriminatory protection. Instantly the search began for means of retaliation: Standard Oil stood conveniently at hand. On Yrigoyen's part the campaign against Standard Oil was an act of considerable political astuteness. It enabled him to ride with the popular tide, but also to pose as a champion of wider national interests and the pampas landowning elite. On the other hand in approaching the oil question it was essential to avoid giving any offence to the British, who might seize on this as the pretext to commence commercial reprisals themselves. It was thus Standard Oil alone which bore the brunt of the campaign against foreign capital. Having eliminated Standard Oil, Yrigoyen evidently intended giving the British the role of the main importers of oil and the equipment required by YPF. This would help reduce the trade surplus with Britain, and improve Argentina's bargaining position in face of imperial preference.

THE MILITARY COUP OF 1930

In 1928 Yrigoyen regained the presidency with around 60 per cent of the popular vote, almost 840,000 against the combined opposition's 537,000. As he reassumed office in October the adulation he received recalled the honours bestowed upon the emperors of Rome. Yet this moment, the acme of a public career which now spanned more than half a century, proved his last personal triumph. Less than two years afterwards, in September 1930, his reputation in ruins, he was ignominiously ejected by a military *coup d'état*.

Hipólito Yrigoyen returned to the presidency at the advanced age of 76. He was suspected in some quarters of senility, and two years later this emerged among the pretexts for overthrowing him. The truth was that in 1928 he reappeared with a much more carefully defined strategy and purpose than twelve years earlier in 1916. He was aware that whatever his apparent popular support, the survival of his government rested upon his ability to keep at bay the conservative and military opposition. The oil question had still to be resolved; his return to office amounted to little more than an auspicious beginning in the battle for its control. His supporters had submitted legislation in favour of nationalization to Congress in 1927. The measure had passed through the popularly elected

Chamber of Deputies where the Yrigoyenistas had a majority. But it was then simply ignored in the Senate, where the voices of the interior provinces led by Salta and Yrigoyen's other opponents remained dominant. Here the president had the same problem which had bedevilled his previous administration. To push the legislation through he required a majority in the Senate. To win senatorial elections he needed to control the provincial legislatures; national senators were elected by them and not by popular vote. This meant more federal interventions to clear out the incumbent regimes, but at the risk of exacerbating the resurgent federalism in the interior. At this time elections to the Senate were pending in Mendoza and San Juan. These were the centres of *lencinismo* and *cantonismo* where, as in Salta, opposition to the administration was particularly virulent and entrenched. The new government thus gave much of its immediate attention to politics in the Cuyo provinces. Here it was quickly embroiled in an embittered and often violent struggle for supremacy. The issue was resolved in two climactic episodes. At the end of 1929 the leader of the Mendoza opposition, Carlos Wáshington Lencinas, was assassinated by Yrigoyenistas. The year after, following an acrimonious and almost interminable debate, the president's supporters successfully impugned the election of Federico Cantoni and one of his personal supporters as senators for San Juan. Thus in mid 1930 the Yrigoyenistas were close to final victory. They had quashed the most extreme opposition in the interior. They also stood on the brink of a clear majority in the Senate. Their intention was to resubmit the oil legislation when Congress reconvened in 1931.

During 1929 and for a time into 1930 Yrigoyen was also successful in keeping at bay his conservative opponents in Buenos Aires, adroitly cultivating their sympathies on the matter of trade relations with Britain and the United States. In 1927, soon after the United States had banned imports of Argentine beef, and while the political confrontation with Standard Oil was at its height, the Rural Society led a campaign to promote favourable treatment for imported British goods. Its slogan, 'Buy from those who buy us', was quickly adopted by the new administration. When Herbert Hoover, as president-elect, visited Buenos Aires in late 1928 on a trade promotion tour of the Latin American republics, he met with a hostile reception and was virtually insulted by Yrigoyen himself. However, the following year a British trade mission received a quite different welcome. To its leader, Lord

D'Abernon, Yrigoyen intimated his wish to offer a 'moral gesture' to Britain in acknowledgment of the 'close historical ties' between the two countries. Without seeking an undertaking for compensatory increases in Argentina's exports to Britain, he promised numerous concessions to British firms and British goods in the Argentine market. Among them was an undertaking to acquire all future supplies for the state railways in Britain, by-passing the normal practice of seeking international tenders.

Several aspects of Yrigoyen's second administration thus suggest a carefully calculated and sophisticated strategy slowly undergoing realization and enjoying considerable success. The president was managing to steer a viable middle course between the aspirations of his popular followers on the oil question and the concern of the elites on international trade. This was done at the expense of the Americans and the provinces. Had the government been able to continue in these directions, it would have had very little to fear from the army. In 1929 there were few signs of the confusion, incompetence or paralysis which gripped it in the year which followed, and for which it was most remembered. What transformed these first relative successes into failure, whence matters slid swiftly towards collapse and catastrophe, was the great depression in the wake of the Wall Street crash. It struck in Argentina at the end of 1929, after two years of slowly falling commodity prices and diminishing gold reserves. As the downturn accelerated, Yrigoyen's government responded with orthodox anticyclical measures of the type employed by the conservatives in 1913–14. It abandoned peso convertibility and it sought new loans in Britain and the United States to avoid difficulties with the foreign debt. These were reasonable if uninspiring responses. They expressed the initial expectation in government and banking circles that the crisis would be short lived. The rapid erosion of the government's authority began when it was obliged to curb state spending. Here Yrigoyen finally paid the price for his break with the elites, his tilt towards the popular sectors, and the methods he had countenanced since 1924 to attract their support.

On Yrigoyen's return to power his supporters had immediately launched themselves on a campaign to take over the bureaucracy. By mid 1929 all departments of the administration had become virtual employment agencies serving the political ends of the government. The regime was soon saturated in petty corruption. State spending immediately assumed an upward course. In 1928 there was a 10 per cent fall in revenues against the previous year, but spending increased by 22 per cent. In 1929 the gap increased still further. In this year revenues improved by 9 per cent, but spending accelerated by a further 12 per cent. In 1930, as revenues again declined to around the 1928 level, spending was running at around 23 per cent higher than that year.[16] At length the government was obliged to contemplate economies. By the time the coup came in September there were signs that the upward climb in spending was beginning to level off. However, retrenchment and austerity came precisely at the moment when, with growing unemployment and falling incomes, the demand for relief was increasing. In 1930 Yrigoyen fell into a trap similar to that he had set for Alvear in 1922. Depression swiftly unhinged the government's party and popular backing. Yrigoyen's followers were demoralized, and they soon began to defect in growing numbers.

In the congressional elections of March 1930 the Yrigoyenistas' share of the vote shrank by 25 per cent by comparison with 1928, from 840,000 to a little over 620,000. In the city of Buenos Aires the Yrigoyenistas lost an election for the first time since the party split of 1924. Here they were defeated by the Independent Socialist party, a newly formed offshoot from the old Socialist party now aligned with the conservatives. In the months which followed disillusionment with the government became inflamed opposition. Events in the Cuyo provinces, often ignored before, were now a matter of daily, intense debate. The press conducted long and detailed exposés of administrative corruption. The students, who after *La Reforma* were among Yrigoyen's most vocal supporters, plunged into demonstrations against him. Rival factions of Yrigoyenistas and a right-wing organization known as the Republican League fought openly for control of the streets. The Cabinet disintegrated into warring factions. Reports of the president's senility were bruited with growing insistence.

At last Yrigoyen's most inveterate opponents, many of them nursing grievances against him for more than a decade, had the opportunity to gather the force to overthrow him. The leader of the military coup, General José F. Uriburu, behind whom was General Justo, had long been prominent in denouncing Yrigoyen's intrigues among the army promotion lists. He had been a chief opponent of Yrigoyen's labour policies in the postwar years. During the 1920s he had imbibed fascist and corporatist doctrines. He was contemptuous of the Sáenz Peña Law.

[16] Detailed figures in Carl E. Solberg, *Oil and nationalism in Argentina* (Stanford, 1979), 149.

He was also a member of the Salta oligarchy which had pursued the deal with Standard Oil. The uprising of September 1930 elicited active support from only a minority in the army. But this was enough to achieve its purpose. As Yrigoyen resigned, a vicious struggle for the succession among members of the Cabinet laid bare the total bankruptcy of his administration. Few of Yrigoyen's supporters came to his assistance. Some joined the mobs which ransacked and burned his home in Buenos Aires.

The coup of 1930 was an entirely domestic affair. If Standard Oil had an obvious interest in securing Yrigoyen's downfall, there is no evidence it did so. The coup was greeted in Washington with some sense of expectancy and with a hope for better relations with Argentina, yet subsequent developments during the 1930s left them unrealized. Any possible American influence on events in 1930 was negated by the presence of the British. They were among Yrigoyen's last supporters, reluctant to rejoice in his downfall. It seemed that their hopes of trade concessions would perish with him. After his fall, Hipólito Yrigoyen was banished to the island of Martín García in the estuary of the Río de la Plata where he spent much of what remained of his life. (He died in 1933.) In this now frail, sometimes morally fallible, though never completely ill-intentioned figure, representative democracy in Argentina had lived and died. With his departure, politics in Argentina assumed new directions. The middle classes were cheated of their expectations of perpetual supremacy. The conservatives returned to power under the protection of the military, and remained in power for more than a decade, until the military coup of 1943 and the rise of Perón.

6

ARGENTINA, 1930–1946

The year 1930 opens the gateway into modern Argentina. The military coup of September 1930 brought the collapse of constitutional government and initiated the long sequence of weak democracies, punctuated by coups d'état and military dictatorships, that remained the cardinal feature of Argentine politics into the 1980s. The plunge into depression in 1930 permanently shifted the path of economic development. Hitherto Argentina had subsisted as an informal dependency of Great Britain, supplying Britain with meats and grains and serving as a leading British market for coal, manufactured goods and, at least till 1914, capital exports. Beginning in 1930 the Victorian structure, already under growing pressure since the outbreak of the First World War, began to totter. From the depression came a decline of agrarian exports and an expansion of manufacturing – conditions that impaired the stability of the Anglo-Argentine relationship as they transformed the components of the Argentine economy. Social change of equal magnitude, and with the same enduring consequences, paralleled the economic shifts. The population of Argentina grew from 11.8 million in 1930 to 15.3 million in 1946, but the rate of growth declined. Falling rates of growth were a consequence of a substantial decline in the birth-rate, from 31.5 per thousand in 1920 to 24.7 per thousand in 1935, which contemporaries conventionally blamed on the depression. (In contrast death-rates fell only slightly, from 14.7 per thousand in 1920 to 12.5 per thousand in 1935.) Declining population growth was also a result of the end of mass European immigration. Foreign-born men still represented 40 per cent of the male population in 1930, but only 26 per cent in 1946. It was no longer Spanish and Italian immigrants but internal immigrants who fed the continued expansion of Buenos Aires as mass migration from the land and the provinces greatly accelerated during the 1930s and 1940s.

The year 1930 also marked the acceleration of a profound ideological shift — the decline of liberalism and the rise of nationalism — that later coloured the texture of Argentine politics. A nationalist awareness began to emerge before 1930 among segments of the intelligentsia. But after 1930 nationalism evolved into a political movement, complementing and intensifying the other changes in government and institutions, economy and society and forming part of a complex, mutually reinforcing process of change.

In the 1930s echoes of the past combined with precursors of the future. In September 1930 'democracy' fell and 'oligarchy' returned, sustaining itself first through the army and then, for a decade or more, by electoral fraud. The conservative oligarchy of the 1930s marked a regression to the political system that had prevailed before the electoral reform of 1912 and the Radical victory of 1916, as successive governments again sought to exclude much of the eligible population from political activities. But as in 1900–12, the 1930s witnessed slow liberalization, and by early 1940 under President Roberto M. Ortiz politics seemed about to re-enter the democratic phase that began in 1912. In other ways, too, the 1930s recalled the past. At the centre of conservative economic policy during the depression stood the Roca–Runciman Treaty of 1933, an effort to protect the historic commercial and financial links with Britain that the nineteenth-century oligarchy had created. In other respects, however, conservative responses to the depression soon branched out in innovative directions. Led by the Central Bank in 1935, new institutions were established to manage the economy, and 'devaluation', 'exchange control' and 'deficit financing' entered the lexicon of economic policy-making, where they have remained ever since.

The conservative regime confronted the depression with striking success. Recovery commenced as early as 1934, and by the end of the decade Argentina had regained the prosperity of the 1920s. Yet oligarchical rule prevailed for a shorter period than the Radical rule which preceded it (1916–30), for in the early 1940s new political forces emerged and swiftly overwhelmed it. The collapse of conservatism in June 1943, following a second military coup, stemmed partly from the Second World War, which brought a crisis in international relations and economic policy after 1939. In mid-1940, as Nazi Germany swept through France and Belgium, the conservatives' attempt to revitalize the old European linkages ended in abrupt failure. Faced by a rapid fall in foreign trade, conservative leaders made vigorous efforts to create a new, yet essentially similar, relationship with the United States. But in treaty negotiations with the United States in 1940–1, Argentina failed to win its chief objective: the opening of the United States market to its meat and grain exports.

Internal conditions also strongly conditioned political change. After 1940 the rural sector underwent a major shift from farming to stock-raising, as cattle and pigs took over much of the land on which tenant farmers had once raised their crops and seasonal labourers harvested grains. Industry, meanwhile, was expanding and drawing the population displaced from the land into the cities. By the end of the war internal migration was radically changing the physical distribution and the occupations of a substantial part of the population. These changes helped to undermine the political base of conservatism by reducing the dominance of agrarian producers, while enhancing the weight of sectors dependent upon, or sympathetic towards, urban manufacturing.

If retrenchment and recovery became the keynote of the 1930s, revolution entered the agenda of the early 1940s. By 1942 the conservative regime, now under Ramón S. Castillo, who had reversed Ortiz's attempts at liberalization, stood divided and drifting. From abroad it faced growing U.S. opposition to its policy of neutrality in the war and its reluctance to join the pan-American alliance, stances it had taken, at least in part, in response to the reluctance of the United States to co-operate on trade. Domestically, the government faced similar opposition from a variety of interest groups and political organizations, some of them former conservative supporters. But its most serious challenge came from the ultra-right-wing *nacionalistas*, who were grouped in several different factions and enjoyed little popular support but who were becoming increasingly entrenched in the army.

The military coup of June 1943 unleashed the Nationalist Revolution: commitments to expunge all ties with 'imperialists', to pursue state-sponsored industrial development led by a new weapons industry and to establish an authoritarian political system to root out 'communism' and 'liberalism'. Led by the *nacionalistas*, Argentina embarked on radical reform and profound political change. Yet the corporatist military dictatorship sought by the *nacionalistas* of 1943 failed to materialize. By contrast, 1943–6 marked the rise of Juan Perón, culminating in his election as president. Backed by a newly created mass working-class movement, the *peronistas* swept into power on a programme of industrialization and social reform. Perón's victory in 1946 and the triumph of 'national populism' thus became the major consequence of the war, and Perón himself, the champion of 'economic sovereignty' and 'social justice' and the enemy of 'oligarchy', 'colonialism' and 'communism', embodied the ideological transition of the early 1940s.

POLITICS UNDER URIBURU AND JUSTO, 1930-8

The revolution of September 1930 sprang from deep personal animosities towards Hipólito Yrigoyen, president of the republic from 1916 to 1922 and again from 1928, on the part of conservatives. In 1930 few conservatives opposed 'democracy' as a political system. They remained more concerned with the way democracy had functioned under the Radicals. They analysed politics in Aristotelian categories: under Yrigoyen, 'democracy' had slid into 'demagogy' and 'tyranny'; the venality of the *yrigoyenista* party bosses and committees had stifled democracy's mission of achieving 'true representation'. Behind these perceptions stood a good deal of patrician snobbery. 'Obsequious cliques' and a 'low circle of inept flatterers' had dominated and eventually destroyed Yrigoyen's regime. The fallen president himself was 'low caste', the illegitimate son of an 'unknown Basque', who long ago embarked on his political career in the gambling halls and cockpits of the Balvanera District of Buenos Aires, where in the 1870s he had been chief of police. Yrigoyen's accomplices were men like himself, a 'low breed on the lookout for profit and self-enrichment' and responsible for democracy's other great failure, its 'flattening of due rank (*avasallamiento de las jerarquías*) at the caprice of the mob'.[1] In 1937, as he campaigned for the presidency, Roberto M. Ortiz declared that the 1930 revolution had 'terminated a system of misgovernment which substituted for the rule of law the arbitrary caprice of a demagogue, who subordinated the general interest of the nation to disorderly appetites stimulated by the pressure of the lowest of the masses'.[2]

Conservatives had long hated Yrigoyen. They had made every effort to destroy his reputation before the 1928 election, and soon after the election they began plotting to overthrow him. Their opportunity to do so arrived with the depression. *Yrigoyenismo* was built on patronage and held together by the flow of state spending. Controlling the middle class in this way worked well during periods of economic expansion, such as in 1928 and most of 1929, when revenues were growing. But it failed instantly in an

[1] See Carlos Ibarguren, *La historia que he vivido* (Buenos Aires, 1955), pp. 318, 368, 400, 428.
[2] Quoted in Felix Weil, *Argentine Riddle* (New York, 1944), p. 63.

economic crisis like that beginning in late 1929. At this point Yrigoyen fell victim to a contest for rapidly shrinking resources between the exporting and propertied interests, most of them conservatives, and the urban middle class, which was mostly Radical. As the depression struck, the former demanded drastic government spending cuts to reduce pressure on credit and interest rates and to enable the banks to respond more effectively to hard-pressed landowners and merchants. The middle class reacted by demanding still higher government spending to protect employment and to arrest the fall of urban incomes. In 1930 the government struggled desperately to surmount these conflicting pressures. Eventually it started to reduce spending, but not fast enough for conservatives and much too fast for Radicals. Thus, as opposition from the landed and commercial interests intensified, Yrigoyen's popular support also disintegrated.

Apologists for the 1930 coup commonly depicted the army as simply the instrument of the popular will, acting on the people's behalf: the revolution, declared Carlos Ibarguren, 'fue el ejército hecho pueblo, y el pueblo hecho ejército' (the army transformed into the people, and the people transformed into the army).[3] As Felix Weil later recalled:

Nobody . . . raised a hand to defend the legal government. The workers were disinterested, apathetic, no strike was called, no demonstration was held, no plant or shop closed. . . . With so many government employees, especially police and military officers, unpaid for some time, the military and civil bureaucracy did not mind exchanging the legal but insolvent, vitiated government of a senile, dreamy, insincere reformer for a general's government which could be expected to be favored by the banks, pay salaries on time and reward its followers handsomely.[4]

In this atmosphere it became easy to mount a coup with remarkably little organization and with a minimum of military force. The coup of 6 September 1930 was an almost exclusively military action. General José F. Uriburu, its leader, who had participated in the failed insurrection against Juárez Celman in July 1890, explicitly forbade civilian involvement on the grounds that civilians had caused defeat forty years before. Leaders of the ultra-conservative Liga Republicana, whose members had sporadically fought the *yrigoyenistas* in the streets during the past year, played a part in urging Uriburu to stage the revolution but no active role in the uprising itself. The function of civilians therefore consisted of laying the ground for

[3] Ibarguren, *La historia*, p. 380.
[4] Weil, *Argentine Riddle*, p. 39.

the coup through street demonstrations, inflammatory speeches and a massive onslaught by the opposition press during the weeks before.

The revolution itself entailed little more than a few hundred officer cadets marching from the military garrison at Campo de Mayo to take possession of the Casa Rosada, the seat of government, in the centre of Buenos Aires. Uriburu had made no effort to organize movements in the provinces or to make detailed plans to seize communications centres and major installations. Elaborate preparations proved quite unnecessary. Yrigoyen himself, having got wind of the insurrection, fled to La Plata. When troops there refused him support, he resigned and was placed under arrest. As they entered central Buenos Aires, the cadets were resisted by a handful of snipers, most of them firing from the roof of the Congress building; these exchanges produced a few casualties on both sides. But this opposition was quickly overcome, and the cadets proceeded down the Avenida de Mayo to the Casa Rosada. There the vice-president, Enrique Martínez, attempted to negotiate with the rebels, but having failed, he too resigned.

After seizing power, the revolutionaries proclaimed a provisional government with Uriburu as its head. The new regime consisted almost entirely of civilians, mostly ageing conservatives who had last served in office before 1916 under Roque Sáenz Peña or his successor, Victorino de la Plaza. The provisional government immediately began purging Radicals from the administration, the provincial governments and the universities, but it soon became apparent that the new regime was sharply divided into two factions and held together only through shared opposition to the *yrigoyenistas*. Uriburu himself led the first of the factions, supported by Matías Sánchez Sorondo, the minister of the interior, and by Carlos Ibarguren, who became 'intervenor' (*interventor*) of Córdoba. To many, Uriburu's faction comprised Argentina's 'fascists', those bent on imposing a system like Mussolini's. Uriburu not only persecuted the Radicals; he also coolly shot a pair of anarchists convicted on charges of sabotage. He encouraged the formation of the Legión Cívica Argentina, whose members wore Fascist-style uniforms and adopted the Fascist salute.

Yet Uriburu himself persistently rejected the label 'fascist' and dismissed fascism as a 'foreign doctrine' that was 'inappropriate' to Argentina. Instead he aimed for a 'true democracy', free of the *yrigoyenista* bosses and committees. Indeed, this aspiration appeared to make Uriburu not a fascist but a liberal, because 'democracy', as a right-wing critique charged, identified him with 'the language and the ideas of the French Revolution' – the foundation of modern liberalism.[5] In fact, neither fascism nor liberalism but Catholic scholasticism provided the chief inspiration for Uriburu's political ideas; his conception of democracy was closer to the ancient Greek idea than to its modern practice in the Americas or Western Europe. The scholastic foundations of Uriburu's ideas appeared most clearly in a manifesto he published in February 1932 which he described as the 'doctrine of the September Revolution'. This document – replete with ironies in view of Uriburu's conduct as president – echoed precepts of St Augustine, St Thomas Aquinas and their successors:

The supreme authority's reason for being. . . . is . . . the accomplishment of the collective welfare. . . . Any government that fails to serve that end, either through abuse of its authority or by abandoning its responsibilities, is a tyrannical government. . . . The tyrannical government is a seditious government because in sacrificing the common good it compromises the unity and tranquillity of society, which exists for the simple reason of ensuring the welfare of its members. . . . And every seditious government ceases, by definition, to be a government, so that an organized revolution which overthrows it by an act of force is quite legitimate as long as its objective is to restore the collective welfare.[6]

For Uriburu the whole purpose of the revolution was to establish a better system of representation, and thus to avoid the tyranny of an 'egotistical minority' like the *yrigoyenista* bosses, so that 'genuine representatives of real social interests may act within the State . . . and prevent electoral professionalism from monopolizing the government and imposing itself between the government and the living forces (*las fuerzas vivas*)'.[7] Drawing on current corporatist theory, Uriburu therefore suggested that associations (*gremios*), not parties, be represented in Congress. He and his supporters described this idea as *nacionalismo,* since it would, they claimed, unify and harmonize the constituent parts of the nation. The *uriburistas* therefore campaigned for constitutional reform, concentrating on changing Article 37 of the Constitution of 1853: the composition and functions of the Chamber of Deputies. Once he had achieved this reform, Uriburu appeared ready to call elections and retire. At least for a time he hoped to pass on the presidency not to a fascist but to Lisandro de la Torre, a veteran liberal-conservative who had been among his comrades during the 1890 revolution and his friend ever since.

[5] See Comisión de Estudios de la Sociedad Argentina de Defensa de la Tradición, Familia y Propiedad, *El nacionalismo: Una incógnita en constante evolución* (Buenos Aires, 1970), p. 29.
[6] *Crisol,* 14 February 1932.
[7] Quoted in Carlos Ibarguren, Jr., *Roberto de Laferrère (periodismo–política–historia)* (Buenos Aires, 1970), p. 32.

Uriburu failed both to accomplish constitutional reform and to stage his own succession. His supporters consisted mostly of conservative lawyers and academics. However, most of the army and the *fuerzas vivas*, the great ranchers and merchants who dominated the economy and provided the main civilian base for the revolution, supported the second faction in the provisional government. Led by General Agustín P. Justo, this faction aimed to create a popular conservative party of the type Sáenz Peña had envisaged in 1912 and that would keep the *yrigoyenistas* from regaining power. Its members wanted a conservative economic policy to protect the export economy, defending the linkages with Britain and Western Europe. The faction is thus best labelled 'liberal-conservative', and it differed from the *nacionalistas* led by Uriburu in opposing constitutional reform and corporate representation, which, like Uriburu's other opponents, it viewed as potentially fascist. At root the dispute between 'liberals' and 'nationalists' concerned the structure of the state. The former opposed the type of mediatory state set above society that the corporatist theoreticians envisaged. They wanted government by class, government controlled by themselves – the major producer and commercial interests.

The critical moment in the contest between the two factions came in April 1931 when Sánchez Sorondo as minister of the interior arranged an election in the province of Buenos Aires, intending to use it to demonstrate Uriburu's popular support and to strengthen him against Justo. The plan totally misfired when the election brought a large and quite unanticipated Radical victory, which observers attributed in part to a recent ill-advised increase in the price of postage stamps. From this time forward, as Uriburu's standing crumbled, the Justo group controlled the provisional government, which now set the date for presidential elections for November 1931, Uriburu's role being reduced to little more than that of keeping the Radicals in check. After defeating a Radical revolt in July 1931, the president arrested most of the leading Radicals, and in September he banned their candidates from appearing on the November ballot.

In this way Justo successfully manoeuvred his way towards the presidency. By November 1931, having carefully maintained his standing in the army and among the *fuerzas vivas*, he headed the newly formed 'Concordancia', a coalition of parties with three main branches: the old conservatives, who now called themselves the National Democrats, although they were mostly regional oligarchs; the Anti-Personalist Radicals, who had split from Yrigoyen in 1924; and the Independent Socialists, who had broken away from the Socialist Party in 1927. Justo's only opponents in

November 1931 consisted of a coalition between Lisandro de la Torre's Progressive Democrats and the orthodox Socialists led by Nicolás Repetto. Of an electorate of 2.1 million, 1.5 million voted. The Concordancia's vote totalled a little more than 900,000, and that of the Progressive Democrat–Socialist alliance a little less than 500,000. Three months later, in February 1932, Justo assumed the presidency, as Uriburu departed for Europe, where he died a victim of cancer a short time later.

The 1931 election restored the presidency to the same interests, in particular the pampas landowners and exporters, who had controlled the government before 1916. Justo had gained power thanks to the army's backing and that of the *fuerzas vivas* and because of the ban on the Radicals. Electoral fraud heavily tainted this election. Immediately after the poll, de la Torre, Repetto and the Radicals detailed cases of brazen fraud throughout the country. In some parts the police had robbed the opposition voters of their ballots as they waited in line to cast them; the records of those who had voted were shown to contain numerous falsified signatures, which meant that the Concordancia's vote contained many names of persons who had not actually voted. Opposition supporters had sometimes seen forged stamps and seals on ballot boxes, which suggested either that these boxes were bogus or that boxes had been opened before the official count, checked and 'adjusted' when necessary to ensure that their contents yielded the desired results. In numerable cases, fake ballots had been used, and in still more, dead men had voted.

Electoral fraud, endemic until the Sáenz Peña law of 1912, was no novelty in Argentina. Fraud had persisted under the Radicals, particularly in rural areas, although they had usually practised it in indirect ways, more through covert intimidation than by direct falsification. But in the 1930s, beginning in November 1931, fraud again became ubiquitous in politics and a practice conservatives sometimes openly admitted to: this, they claimed, was a 'patriotic fraud', an unhappy necessity to keep the Radicals at bay. Notorious examples included the election for governor in the province of Buenos Aires in 1935 in which the supporters of Manuel Fresco ensured victory by forcibly preventing the Radicals from voting, by switching ballot boxes and by replacing the real vote with another concocted in the conservative clubs. In an election in Corrientes in 1938 more men voted than were registered; in Mendoza in 1941 conservatives armed with rifles manned the voting booths and watched each ballot being cast. Among the many forms of electoral bribery during this period, one of the most common consisted in offering voters sealed voting envelopes containing already marked ballots, which the voter would then smuggle into the voting booth and use to cast his vote. To prove that he had accomplished the mission, he would emerge with the ballot card and the envelope he had been given inside; after handing it over, he would be paid for his services. In the 1930s the working-class city of Avellaneda, just outside the capital, had one of the worst reputations for political corruption. Here, in what some called the 'Argentine Chicago', conservative political bosses led by Alberto Barceló were alleged to be heavily involved in gambling, prostitution and racketeering, some of the profits of which were used to control elections. Throughout the 1920s the conservatives had complained repeatedly about the bosses, the committees and the corrupt patronage techniques the Radicals had used. Yet after they regained power in 1931, the conservatives themselves swiftly resorted to still cruder versions of the same methods.

The three parties that formed the Concordancia gradually fused, losing any separate identity. By 1934 the Independent Socialists and the Anti-Personalists had disappeared; the main function of both these parties had been to enable a small handful of political leaders to shift to the conservatives and to take office under the Justo government. From the Independent Socialists, for example, came Federico Pinedo, twice minister of finance during this period, who sponsored several of the Concordancia's major economic reforms.[8] A second prominent Independent Socialist was Antonio de Tomaso, a talented minister of agriculture, whose career ended on his death in 1934. But most of the Concordancia's leaders were Anti-Personalists: Justo himself; Roberto M. Ortiz, who became Justo's successor as president; and Leopoldo Melo, whom Yrigoyen had defeated in the 1928 election and who now served as Justo's minister of the interior. Throughout the 1930s the true conservatives remained a minority in the government. The most prominent was Ramón S. Castillo, the last of Justo's ministers of justice and public instruction, who in 1938 became Ortiz's vice-president and then president himself in 1940.

Thus, the more progressive figures substantially outnumbered the reactionaries in the government, and although for some time their preponderance did nothing to abate electoral fraud, it gave the Justo regime a relatively benign and tolerant quality that contrasted strongly with the repressive political atmosphere prevalent under Uriburu. Justo himself spent much of his time maintaining his position in the army, seeking to

---

[8] See below, pp. 190–1, 211–15.

isolate some diehard *uriburistas* led by Colonel Juan Bautista Molina, who were continually hatching plots to overthrow the government. Throughout the 1930s the army remained a critical political force that Justo kept firmly under control and out of politics through a skilful strategy of appointments and promotions.

On taking office in 1932 Justo lifted the state of siege that had prevailed since the 1930 revolution. He released and offered amnesty to Uriburu's political prisoners, among them Hipólito Yrigoyen, who until his death in July 1933 made feeble efforts to rally his supporters for a come-back. Justo reinstated the university professors whom Uriburu had dismissed because they were Radicals. He sharply curbed the activities of the Legión Cívica, the paramilitary organization sponsored by Uriburu. The legion, now under the leadership of retired general Emilio Kinkelín, commanded little significance after 1932, although it managed to survive into the early 1940s. The legion's fate illustrated the skill with which Justo repeatedly isolated and weakened his potential opponents. As Justo demilitarized the regime, he adopted a new technocratic style of government that entrusted certain areas of policy to the hands of specialists. The most famous of these specialists was the young Raúl Prebisch, who became a leading member of the team headed by Pinedo which conceived and implemented the major economic reforms of the 1930s.

Justo experienced few difficulties with organized labour since, at the height of the depression, workers struggled primarily to avoid unemployment. The government mediated a telephone workers' strike in 1932 and did the same in subsequent labour disputes. This approach contrasted with events under Uriburu, whose government at one point threatened to shoot three convicted taxi-drivers unless it obtained an obsequious statement of support from leading trade unionists. The Justo regime sponsored a substantial body of labour legislation that included indemnities for dismissal and curbs on Saturday afternoon working, a measure known as the 'English Saturday' (*sábado inglés*). Even so, this government never flinched from using repression against the unions, Justo continuing the deportations of 'agitators' that had begun after the Residence Law of 1901. The government increased the powers of the police, and it established a Special Section to deal with labour issues.

In 1930 the labour movement had formally united in the Confederación General del Trabajo (CGT), which fused the two leading confederations of the late 1920s, the Socialist Confederación Obrera Argentina (COA) with the syndicalist Unión Sindical Argentina (USA). Although printers for a time dominated the CGT's leadership, the sole union of any importance was the railwaymen's union, the Unión Ferroviaria, which provided about 40 per cent of the CGT's affiliates. Economic liberals led the Unión Ferroviaria; they supported free trade, renewed foreign investment and – their only departure from free-trade concepts – workers' protection against dismissal and redundancy. Throughout the 1930s fewer than one-fifth of the workers in Buenos Aires belonged to trade unions. Most unions at this point upheld at least informal links with the Socialist Party, although small anarchist and syndicalist groups survived. A syndicalist, Antonio Tramonti, headed the CGT until his overthrow in the union split of 1935, which left most of the unions under the dominance of José Domenech, a Socialist who guided the CGT into a more explicitly political, and specifically anti-fascist, stance. During the late 1930s the CGT directed most of its energies towards the defence of the Spanish Republic during the Civil War. Communist influence in the unions remained negligible until the creation in 1936 of a new construction workers' union, the Federación Obrera Nacional de la Construcción (FONC) in response to the Comintern's directive to Communists worldwide to erect an independent Communist-led trade union movement. By 1939 the FONC had become the second largest union in Argentina, and it led the way in unionizing the low-paid, unskilled workers, mostly of rural migrant origin. Despite the growth of the FONC during the late 1930s, the Communist Party had not developed much since its creation in 1920 and still consisted of little more than a handful of intellectuals and labour leaders whose political influence remained relatively small.

Persuasion and manipulation became the distinctive traits of the Justo regime. For a time it achieved political stability but at the cost of growing public disillusionment and indifference. The government never succeeded in freeing itself from the stigma of its origins, which lay in electoral fraud. Justo's apparent strength derived substantially from the weakness of the government's opponents, from the absence of an effective opposition presenting genuine alternatives to its policies. During the 1930s the old Socialist Party again failed to expand much beyond its traditional bulwark in the federal capital. The socialists never fully recovered from the defection of the Independent Socialists in 1927 and the death of the party's founder, Juan B. Justo, in 1928. Under an ageing leadership headed by Nicolás Repetto, the Socialist Party remained the largest party in the capital, where electoral fraud was less common than elsewhere, but its programme remained much the same as it had been twenty-five years before. As dedicated as ever to its constituency of working-class consumers, the party operated on much the same general liberal assumptions as the government. The appeal of the Socialists lay in their secular, hard-headed appraisals of public issues; what they now lacked was the energy and the evangelism they had displayed under Juan B. Justo in their earlier years as they challenged the old oligarchy. In mid-1936 a measure of the old style finally returned as the Socialists, side by side with the CGT, plunged into campaigns to support the beleaguered Spanish Republic, but by the time the republic finally succumbed to Franco's forces in early 1939, Argentine Socialism too was fast becoming a spent force.

Also in rapid decline was the Partido Demócrata Progresista, which by the mid-1930s amounted to scarcely more than the person of its leader, Lisandro de la Torre. At this point, de la Torre had been prominent in politics for more than forty years from his base in Rosario, where he had long served as a spokesman for the farmers and small ranchers of the littoral. Admired for his oratory, his integrity and his colourful, forceful personality, de la Torre upheld mostly conservative ideas. But throughout his career, which began in the 1890 rebellion against Juárez Celman, he had been a firm democrat who detested electoral fraud. Because of his outspoken support for democracy, de la Torre never commanded much support among more traditional conservatives, apart from Uriburu in 1930 (whose offer of the presidency he had rejected).

In 1935 de la Torre served as a member of a congressional commission investigating the meat trade, and in that capacity he provoked one of the greatest political scandals of the Justo presidency. During the early 1930s the British and American meat-packing plants reacted to falling prices by organizing a pricing pool to safeguard profits at the expense of their suppliers. Thus, whereas the prices the meat-packers paid to ranchers for livestock declined from an average of thirty-four cents per kilo in 1929 to only seventeen cents in 1933, between 1930 and 1934 meat-packers' profits ranged from between 11.5 and 14 per cent of capital investments. In 1935 the commission substantiated charges that an illegal pool had been created. But in a dissenting opinion de la Torre went far beyond his colleagues' somewhat muted criticisms and issued other accusations of numerous accounting and tax frauds by the meat-packers. One company, Vestey Brothers, had been discovered attempting to smuggle its accounts out of the country in a container labelled 'canned beef'. In addition, de la Torre declared, members of the government led by the minister of agriculture, Luis Duhau, had connived at these evasions and personally profited from them. Congress debated de la Torre's allegations, as each side traded

insults, amidst bitter denials from members of the administration. As the
tension rose, an unknown spectator attempted to shoot de la Torre, but
succeeded in mortally wounding Enzo Bordabehere, his junior Senate
colleague from Santa Fe. After this, de la Torre faded rapidly from politics,
and within a few years he took his own life.

Throughout the 1930s, indeed almost till the eve of the 1946 election,
Radicalism remained the largest of Argentina's political movements, and
only proscription, fraud or internal dissent kept it from the presidency.
Soon after the 1930 revolution much of the energy and élan the Radicals had
displayed during the 1920s returned as they embarked on a sometimes violent attempt to regain supremacy. By April 1931 the Radicals had regained
a popular majority in the province of Buenos Aires; in July they attempted
armed rebellion, an adventure some of them repeated, again without success, in 1933. Following the coup d'état, Radicals incessantly denounced
the imprisonment of Hipólito Yrigoyen, most of which took place on the
island of Martín García in the middle of the Río de la Plata, and when Justo
finally released Yrigoyen, scores of Radicals paid daily homage to him at his
home in Buenos Aires. Yrigoyen's death in 1933 provoked a demonstration
in Buenos Aires that ranked among the greatest in the city's history.

If at the time of his death Yrigoyen had regained much of the popularity
he had enjoyed at the beginning of his second government five years
before, after his overthrow, continually ailing, he had become little more
than a nostalgic symbol. In April 1931 former president Marcelo T. de
Alvear returned to Argentina from his second home in Paris and now
became, with Yrigoyen's blessing and in spite of their past differences, the
party's acknowledged leader, a position he retained until his death in
1942. Alvear, the scion of a great patrician family that to all outward
appearances embodied the very 'oligarchy' Radicalism had pledged to
destroy, had hitherto lacked a personal power base in the party. But his
standing immediately rose in 1931 when he publicly repudiated Uriburu
and then cheerfully submitted to arrest and imprisonment at the hands of
the provisional government. In all likelihood had the Radicals escaped
proscription and fraud during the election of November 1931, Alvear as
their intended candidate would have regained the presidency.

Yet as party leader throughout the following decade, Alvear failed to
maintain the momentum and energy of 1931. He now continued his
attempts as president to bring the party committees and its bosses to heel
and to mould the party, as the Anti-Personalists had sought to do, into a
popular conservative movement around a clear set of programmes rather

than around the search for patronage or single issues like the oil nationalization campaign of 1927–30. In this quest Alvear again failed, and as
time passed he became an increasingly antiquated figure whose much-
rumoured secret deals with the government made him resented by many of
the party's rank and file. Nor did Radicalism change much after Alvear's
death when leadership passed to Honorio Pueyrredón, a man of similar
disposition and background.

Under colourless and uninspiring leadership, the Radicals therefore
drifted. Until 1935 they refused to contest any elections and readopted
'abstention', one of Yrigoyen's tactics from the party's early days that was
intended to highlight and protest electoral fraud. When abstention was
finally abandoned in 1935, the combination of fraud and the need to
rebuild the party organization left the Radicals electorally weak for several
years. Socialists dominated the capital into the early 1940s, and conservatives, under leaders like Alberto Barceló and Manuel Fresco, controlled
the province of Buenos Aires. The great stronghold of Radicalism now lay
in Córdoba under Amadeo Sabbatini, long Alvear's rival for control of the
national party. The Radicals, like the Socialists, appeared bereft of any
new ideas. Although they continued to demand oil nationalization (an
issue that Uriburu and Justo simply ignored), they too remained overwhelmingly liberal in outlook, nostalgic for the 1920s and, except for
fringe groups, the opponents of any major reform. The Radicals remained
long on moral imperatives but frequently short on substance, plagued by
incessant internal rivalries. In 1944 Felix Weil could discern no real
difference in outlook between Radicals and conservatives:

Dissension is even more prevalent among the Radicales [*sic*] today. They still have
no constructive platform, and their need for an authoritative leadership is greater
than ever since Alvear's death. Opposition to the conservatives is not a powerful
enough factor to unify a demoralised party, particularly since it is difficult to
distinguish between the glittering generalities of the Radicals and those of the
conservatives. The conservatives stand for 'moderate progress and honest government', and the Radicals a 'tempered program and clean government'. Neither of
them means it.[9]

ECONOMY AND SOCIETY IN THE 1930S

The revolution of September 1930 occurred as the Argentine economy was
hit by the world depression. In 1930–1 export earnings fell by one-third,

---

[9] Weil, *Argentine Riddle*, p. 6.

from an average of about a billion (U.S. billion) pesos during the late 1920s to only 600 million in 1931. Gross domestic product (GDP) slid 14 per cent between 1929 and 1932, with grain output declining by 20 per cent and manufacturing by 17 per cent. Following the suspension of the gold standard on the closure of the Caja de Conversión in late 1929, the peso depreciated by about 25 per cent by late 1931. Argentina escaped the worst afflictions of the depression, such as the 20 to 30 per cent unemployment rates among industrial workers in Germany and the United States and the catastrophe that struck Chile as foreign markets for copper disappeared almost completely. Even so, the crisis hit farming severely and provoked a wave of bankruptcies in the cities as manufacturing and commerce declined. By early 1931 bankruptcies were triple the rate of mid-1929, reaching a peak in the aftermath of the poor harvest of 1930. From 1929 to 1933 the wholesale prices of Argentina's major exports – grains, linseed and meat – declined by roughly half. Real wages fell by an estimated 10 per cent.

The provisional government of 1930–1 took immediate and energetic action on public spending and foreign trade. In 1930, after two years of rapidly growing government spending under Yrigoyen, the budget deficit had climbed to the high rate of 6.5 per cent of GDP. By 1931 the public debt had reached 1.3 billion pesos – an increase of more than 50 per cent since 1929. Rapidly falling revenues in the wake of the depression compounded the new government's difficulties in curbing the upward expansion of the public debt. The government responded with severe cuts in spending, which fell from 934 million pesos in 1930 to 648 million in 1932. Massive lay-offs among the personnel of the public administration – about twenty thousand in all – became the chief weapon in the fight to reduce spending, Radicals being the main victims. In a bid to contain the fall in revenues, the government raised taxes and in 1931 introduced an income tax that aimed to lessen dependence on tariff duties as a source of public finance. The budget deficit had fallen to 1.5 per cent of GDP by 1932.

In 1930 both the value of exports and, because of harvest failures, the volume of exports fell. Imports, however, contracted more slowly, and import prices fell much less steeply than export prices: terms of trade, taking 1937 as base 100, stood at 97.6 in 1928 but only 63.2 in 1931. The result was a severe balance-of-payments deficit which drained the country of its gold reserves and threatened its ability to service the foreign debt. In an effort to curb imports the Uriburu government raised tariffs, which now became more important as trade regulators than as instruments of taxation.

In October 1931, following the example of numerous other countries, Argentina imposed exchange controls. These measures proved at least temporarily successful, since by mid-1932 the balance-of-payments deficit had been eliminated. By 1932 imports by volume stood at scarcely 40 per cent of the 1929 figure.

Servicing the foreign debt in the early 1930s proved far less difficult than it had during the early 1890s. One reason was that the depreciation of the peso provoked a corresponding contraction in the gold or hard currency profits of foreign companies, many of which therefore ceased making remittances abroad in the hope that exchange rates would eventually improve. The British railway companies, for example, lost an estimated £6 million in this way between July 1930 and July 1932. Delayed remittances helped reduce the balance-of-payments deficits and the resources required to service the foreign debt. A second reason was that in the early 1930s public foreign indebtedness remained light by comparison with that in the early 1890s. Thus, out of a total foreign investment of 4.3 billion pesos in 1934, only 900 million constituted public debts. Although servicing the foreign debt absorbed around half the total gold reserves in 1930–1, Argentina was able to avoid a foreign debt default.

In Argentina the early depression years are better characterized as a period of dislocation than as one of collapse. Despite falling export prices, farm output and farm export volumes declined severely only in 1930 and then recovered to the levels of the late 1920s. In the cities the depression struck the food and drink, the metallurgical and the small-household-goods industries, but left construction and especially textiles unscathed. Visible unemployment remained remarkably light, at perhaps 5 to 6 per cent. In 1933 the British commercial attaché in Buenos Aires calculated unemployment at a mere 2.8 per cent. A year later his successor remarked that 'in comparison with the rest of the world, Argentina may be said to be free of any serious unemployment problem'.[10] Official statistics may have seriously underestimated real unemployment, however. They failed to take account of women workers, who made up perhaps one-fifth of the total, and they defined unemployment, quite misleadingly, as a percentage of the total population as opposed to the total labour force.

Apart from 1930, 1933 proved the most severe year of the depression, as world prices plummeted to their lowest levels in forty years and to

[10] H. O. Chalkley, in Department of Overseas Trade, Great Britain, *Economic Conditions in the Argentine Republic* (London, 1933), p. 146; Stanley G. Irving, in Department of Overseas Trade, Great Britain, *Economic Conditions in the Argentine Republic* (London, 1935), p. 174.

scarcely 50 per cent of those in 1929. This produced another serious balance-of-payments deficit that pushed the Justo government into taking new measures to deal with the crisis. In 1933, in an effort to promote exports and help farmers, the government encouraged the renewed depreciation of the peso, which by the following year had slipped to only 60 per cent of its 1929 value. A second measure of 1933 extended the income tax introduced two years before. As a result, import duties that had provided 54 per cent of revenues in 1930 accounted for only 39 per cent by 1934.

In 1933 the government also modified the system of exchange controls introduced in 1931. The original regulations were designed to check the depreciation of the peso and to ensure the availability of funds to service the foreign debt. At that point the government obliged exporters to sell to it the foreign exchange from their transactions, which it afterwards resold in open auction. The reforms of November 1933 established a review procedure for all remittances of foreign exchange by private parties and began classifying imports by a scale of priorities. The measures limited the number of possible purchasers of foreign exchange from the government by introducing permits. Those who lacked permits had to buy foreign exchange on a free market at much higher prices. With these changes the government could regulate not only the volume of imports, but their content and their source. Giving importers of British goods far more exchange-control permits than those who wished to import U.S. goods, for example, proved an effective means of channelling trade towards British goods.

After the exchange control reforms were introduced, the government began to make large profits from its foreign exchange dealings, which by 1940 totalled about 1 billion pesos. Some of these revenues helped service the foreign debt, but most were employed to subsidize rural producers. Regulatory boards, or juntas, were created to administer the subsidies. Starting with the *junta de cereales* in 1933, similar entities appeared soon after to deal with meat, cotton, milk and other products.

The economic reforms of late 1933 were accomplished under Federico Pinedo, who became minister of finance in succession to Alberto Hueyo, an orthodox figure who had been successful in controlling the balance-of-payments deficits, reining in public spending and avoiding default on the foreign debt. Pinedo, by contrast, proved imaginative and innovative, thanks largely to his team of technical advisers led by Raúl Prebisch. In 1934 Pinedo consolidated the public debt, a measure that fostered lower interest rates and shifted investment away from high-yield government bonds. But the Central Bank created in 1934 became the great monument of the Pinedo ministry. Hitherto the banking system had suffered from undue rigidity, with credit tight during harvest periods, banks competing for loans from the Banco de la Nación, a private entity that had some primitive central banking functions and with interest rates therefore tending to rise rather than fall during depressions. The Central Bank offered new methods for regulating the economy through control over the money supply: buying and selling government securities, rediscounting and changing reserve requirements. The Central Bank geared the supply of credit to the ebb and flow of business activity and gave the government greater control over exchange rates and foreign trade. Although it eventually became an instrument of deficit financing, this was not its original intention. Deficit spending, the Pinedo group believed, would intensify imports and therefore balance-of-payments deficits, while provoking inflation.

Pinedo's measures in 1933 and 1934 established many of the basic instruments that later governments refined and built upon in creating a centralized, directed economy. The Roca–Runciman Treaty of 1933 embodied the other, regressive side of conservative economic policy during the depression. The treaty followed Britain's adoption of imperial preference at the Ottawa Conference the year before. Under imperial preference, Britain would seek to import as much as it could from the Empire, while excluding imports from other countries in return for enjoying privileged access to imperial markets. Imperial preference threatened Argentina, because at Ottawa the British faced strong Australian and South African demands to import meat from these sources at the expense of supplies from Argentina. Rumours surfaced that Britain intended to apply 5 per cent monthly cuts on imports of Argentine meat, reducing purchases by as much as 65 per cent during the first year.

From the start it seemed unlikely that the British intended to carry through the proposal to this extent, since imperial suppliers appeared incapable of increasing production and exports fast enough to meet British demand. At the same time, cutting meat imports from Argentina posed a potential threat to Britain's exports to Argentina and risked retaliation against British investments and British companies. In 1933 the British were searching for bargaining power, seeking means to compel Argentina to buy more British and fewer American goods and to correct the trading pattern that had arisen during the 1920s when Argentina had sold large quantities of goods to Britain while continually increasing its imports from the United States, leaving Britain with a growing trade deficit.

During the early years of the depression, the British had also been irritated by the restraints on remittances by British companies in Argentina that arose from exchange controls and the depreciation of the peso.

The Argentine government responded to the threat against meat exports by despatching a negotiating team to London led by the vice-president, Julio A. Roca, Jr. In May 1933 Roca and Walter Runciman, president of the British Board of Trade, signed a trade treaty, which was followed in late September by a treaty protocol and an agreement on tariffs. The treaty specified that Britain would continue to import the same quantity of Argentine meat as it had from July 1931 to June 1932, unless a further substantial fall in consumer prices made it necessary to apply new restrictions to safeguard retailers' profits in Britain. Britain agreed that Argentine-owned meat-packing plants would supply 15 per cent of meat exports to Britain, a concession that sought to counter Argentine complaints about the foreign meat-packers' pool. Allowing exports from *frigoríficos* that were owned co-operatively by the cattle ranchers would, it was argued, help maintain cattlemen's profits. Finally, Britain undertook not to impose tariff duties on imported Argentine grains.

Since Britain did not import Argentine grains in large quantities, the treaty related principally to beef and amounted to an agreement to maintain beef imports at the relatively low levels of 1931–2. In return, however, Argentina agreed to reduce duties on almost 350 British imports to the level of 1930 before the Uriburu government's tariff increases and to refrain from imposing duties on goods such as coal that traditionally entered free of duties. In addition, Britain won an agreement that the remittances by British companies would now be paid by means of subtractions from Argentina's export earnings from its trade with Britain; any remittances that remained 'blocked' in Argentina would now be treated as interest-bearing loans. In the Roca–Runciman Treaty Argentina committed itself to the 'benevolent treatment' of British companies, granting them favourable terms to acquire imports under the exchange-control regulations. The treaty exempted the British railway companies from contributions to recently established pension schemes for their workers. The treaty made no specifications on shipping and therefore left the great bulk of Anglo-Argentine trade in the hands of British shippers, giving Britain an almost exclusive share of the invisible earnings from trade.

The Roca–Runciman Treaty enabled Argentina to maintain meat exports at the level of 1931–2, but little else. The concessions to the local meat-packing co-operatives proved meaningless, since British shippers avoided doing any business with them, and because they were unable to attract ships, the co-operatives could operate only in the domestic market. Britain, by contrast, regained the conditions for trade it had enjoyed before the depression. Since the British also gained preferential access to scarce foreign exchange, they won what amounted to the dominance in trade with Argentina, now protected by treaty, that they had enjoyed before 1914. The British won highly favourable terms for making remittances, including protection against the future devaluation of the peso. The Roca–Runciman Treaty also struck hard against the United States. Importers of American goods were now obliged to surmount the tariff wall created in 1930 and to purchase expensive foreign exchange on the parallel market.

Originally scheduled to be in force for three years, the Roca–Runciman Treaty was renewed and extended in 1936. On this occasion the British gained an authorization to levy new taxes on imported Argentine meat. In return for reducing freight rates, the British railways received still more favourable terms for making remittances. They gained an undertaking that the state railways would not be granted subsidized rates that undercut British rates, along with promises to curtail new road-building that took traffic away from the railways.

Despite all of Argentina's concessions in 1933 and 1936, Britain did little more than protect its existing trade in the 1930s. Although U.S. exports fell steeply, Britain's share, which stood at slightly less than 20 per cent in 1927, remained less than 24 per cent throughout the 1930s. Moreover, although Britain had gained better terms for remittances from Argentina, total earnings by British companies fell sharply during the depression, so that profits remained still far below the levels of the 1920s. In 1929–35 tonnages transported by the British railways fell by 23 per cent, but revenues fell by 40 per cent. Half of the British investors who held stocks in Argentine railways received no dividends during the 1930s; average share quotations of the railway companies in 1936, for example, stood at scarcely 10 per cent of those in the late 1920s. As an illustration of the financial distress of the British railways, in 1937 the Central Córdoba company volunteered its own expropriation by the government and its incorporation to the state lines.

The financial difficulties of the British railway companies resulted not only from the depression but from increasing competition from road transport. Throughout the 1920s Argentina had imported a large number of cars, buses and trucks, mostly from the United States. In 1932, despite bitter opposition from the railways, the Justo government inaugurated a road-building programme. Most of these new roads were constructed in the littoral, where they competed directly with the British railways. The growth of road transport became still more conspicuous in the cities, where the obsolescent British tramways faced an ever-growing challenge from the *colectivo* buses, which proved invariably cheaper, faster and more flexible. In 1929 the tramways earned 43 million pesos, but in 1934 only 23 million. In 1935, as preliminary negotiations began for the renewal of the Roca–Runciman Treaty – which it judged a propitious moment to act – the largest of the British tramway companies in Buenos Aires, the Anglo-Argentine, submitted a plan to the government to place the city's transportation services under a single entity, the Corporación de Transportes.

Establishing the Corporación de Transportes amounted to a thinly disguised plot to subject the *colectivos* to the control of the tramways, which would then try to destroy them. Under the scheme's provisions, all parties providing transport services in the city would be obliged to join the Corporación, receiving shares and voting power according to the size of their capital assets. Under this scheme the tramways would become dominant, since the *colectivos* were often shoe-string businesses operating heavily on credit. In 1935 the Anglo-Argentine Tramway Company further petitioned that the Corporación de Transportes receive a minimum 7 per cent profit guarantee, the type of subsidy that had been widely used before 1890 to attract British investment to Argentina. Since it feared retaliation against meat exports as the Roca–Runciman Treaty fell due for renewal, the Justo government felt obliged to agree to the creation of the Corporación, despite strong opposition from both the *colectiveros* and consumer interests led by the Socialist Party. But having done this, the government failed to follow up with the substance of the plan. It avoided any attempt to force the *colectivos* into the Corporación and repeatedly denied requests from the tramways to charge higher rates. On this score, the Justo government succeeded in outmanoeuvring the British, although simultaneously it was sustaining severe political damage on the issue of the meat-packers' pool at the hands of Lisandro de la Torre.

Economic growth had resumed in Argentina by 1934, and recovery continued at an accelerating pace throughout the late 1930s except for a recession in 1937–8 when the harvest failed. Grains led the recovery of the mid-1930s. In 1936–7 Argentina recorded its highest-ever volume of grain exports, as farmers gained a more than 20 per cent increase in prices over 1933. By 1937 Argentina remained the world's seventh-largest producer and second-largest exporter of wheat; it also produced half the world's linseed. The devaluation of the peso in 1933, which boosted grain exports during following years, triggered substantial inflation; the cost of living in Buenos Aires rose by about 25 per cent from mid-1934 to mid-1936, at which point inflation served as a symptom of economic recovery. Rising prices helped foster the construction boom in Buenos Aires during the late 1930s. In 1939, after several years of rising public spending and a 20 per cent rise in 1939 alone, Argentina had a budget deficit of 2 per cent of GDP.

During the early 1930s the manufacturing industry was depressed along with the rest of the economy, although the slide had been less severe than in other sectors. Manufacturing then recovered swiftly, and from the mid-1930s it began to outpace all other sectors, growing at more than double the rate of agriculture. Several conditions favoured industrial growth during the 1930s. Tariffs, bilateral trade, exchange controls and devaluations both restricted imports and distorted their composition, making local producers more competitive in the domestic market. Throughout the 1930s Argentine manufacturers could acquire second-hand machinery at knock-down prices from bankrupt industrial firms abroad. Cheap labour became increasingly plentiful as a result of migration from country to city.

The 1914 census had counted 383,000 'industrial' workers. In 1935 there were 544,000; by 1941 the number had climbed to 830,000; and by 1946 it was more than a million. In the early 1940s the manufacturing sector produced a variety of goods, of which textiles and processed foods, followed by chemicals, metals and cement, were most prominent. Most industries produced finished consumer goods. The absence of any heavy industry reflected limited local supplies of basic raw materials like coal and iron-ore and the unhelpful network of communications that remained heavily biased towards agricultural exporting. Credit shortages also constrained more diverse industrial development. Beyond all this, Argentina's manufacturers sometimes behaved more like speculators than entrepreneurs and long-term investors. They often appeared to believe that manufacturing might yield short-term profits with minimal investment, but it could not be relied on in the longer term except in a very few instances. Such attitudes derived in part from memories of the war and immediate post-war years; industry had flourished in 1914–18 but had then collapsed as imports resumed after the war. During the 1930s similar expectations prevailed; only the depression prevented the resumption of imports, and when it passed, foreign competition would again strangle local manufacturers. All these conditions helped preserve most industrial units as small-scale, low-investment concerns. Figures from 1939 showed that 60 per cent of 'industrial firms' had ten or fewer employees, and 75 per cent fewer than fifty. Two-thirds of industry in 1935 embraced food and drink and textiles. Side by side with these numerous small firms, however, stood a handful of very large concerns whose size derived from monopoly and from an abundant supply of cheap raw materials. Among them were the great Bemberg consortium, which dominated the brewing industry; Torcuato Di Tella, whose company, Sociedad Industrial Americana de Maquinarias (SIAM), produced a variety of appliances under licence from the United States; and Miguel Miranda, the rags-to-riches canned foods giant who in the late 1940s under Perón became Argentina's chief economic planner. Foreigners still occupied a prominent position in Argentine manufacturing as they had done before 1914. Part of the sudden surge in industrial growth at the end of the 1930s, for example, could be traced to the tide of Jewish refugees who arrived with whatever capital they could retrieve as the Nazis extended their grip over Central Europe. Another striking feature of the manufacturing sector in Argentina was its overwhelming concentration in the city of Buenos Aires and its immediate surroundings. The 1939 figures showed 60 per cent of industrial firms, 70 per cent of industrial workers and about 75 per cent of industrial wages in Buenos Aires.

Some of the expanding industries of the 1930s and 1940s, particularly textiles and manufactured foods, had been established for a generation or more. Among the industries that produced novel goods like electrical bulbs and rubber tyres stood several that sprang up as subsidiaries, mostly of North American companies. United States exporters set up operations in Buenos Aires because of the high tariffs and the discriminatory use of exchange controls after 1933. If U.S. investment as a whole was dwindling during the depression and war years, private investment in these manufacturing subsidiaries increased by U.S. $30 million between 1933 and 1940. By the later 1930s fourteen subsidiaries of U.S. companies appeared, employing a total work-force of fourteen thousand.

However, industry in the 1930s meant principally textiles, which continued to grow during the early 1930s, although manufacturing as a whole was contracting. The number of textile factories increased from twenty-five to thirty between 1929 and 1934, and the workers they employed from eight thousand to twelve thousand. In 1930 domestic textile producers provided only 9 per cent of total consumption. By 1940 the domestic producers' share of the market rose to almost half, and by 1943, as imports fell steeply during the war, it climbed to more than four-fifths. By the mid-1930s Argentina became self-sufficient in cotton knit-ted cloth and in the coarser counts of cotton yarn. A silk-weaving industry developed. During the 1930s and 1940s textiles achieved an annual growth rate of 11 per cent, compared with about 6 per cent in manufactur-ing as a whole.

Throughout this period textile producers enjoyed exceptionally favour-able conditions. Foremost among them was an abundance of wool, as wool exports collapsed during the depression. Woollen textiles accounted for about three-quarters of total production until the late 1930s. As early as 1934 several wool manufacturers in Buenos Aires were working with twelve-month advance orders. Simultaneously, raw-cotton production was increasing rapidly, as cotton acreages grew from 258,000 acres in 1924 to 706,000 in 1934 and 832,000 by 1940. Small farmers in the province of Chaco in the Far North, most of them close to the city of Resistencia, supplied more than four-fifths of raw cotton. In 1933 the government introduced a subsidy for cotton growers financed by the profits of ex-change control, and this *junta de algodón,* one of Pinedo's regulatory boards, helped maintain the upward expansion of cotton production.

Besides access to cheap raw materials, textiles enjoyed other advantages. Policies adoped during the depression – higher tariffs, exchange controls and devaluations – tended either to reduce imports of textiles or to change the relative prices of domestic goods and imports. The Roca–Runciman Treaty, for example, helped to reduce the inflow of cheaper textiles from countries like Japan and Italy in favour of relatively expensive British goods, in a way that increased the competitive edge of local producers. While supply conditions were changing, demand for textile products remained relatively constant and inelastic, and as imports fell the profits of local producers increased, boosting output. Like the rest of manufactur-ing, the textile industry benefited from the growing abundance of cheap labour, becoming perhaps the largest employer of women. The industry also benefited from the practice of requisitioning cheap second-hand ma-chinery from abroad; the number of cotton spindles, for example, in-creased fivefold in 1930–6. Of all these favourable conditions, the ready supply of cheap raw materials was the most crucial. Other sectors of manufacturing, like metallurgy, which remained dependent on imported raw materials, grew at a slower rate during the 1930s than during the 1920s. The new textile industry displayed the same general features as industry at large. In 1936 some 225 firms were in operation, but the top 10 employed almost half the total labour force.

Mass migration from the land to the cities accompanied the rise of manufacturing. Internal migration did not begin during the 1930s, but the pace now rapidly increased. Having contributed an average of roughly 5 per cent to the growth of Buenos Aires and its suburbs between 1914 and 1935, the migrants' share rose to 37 per cent in 1937–47, reflecting also the much lower rate of foreign immigration during the 1930s and 1940s. Between 1937 and 1943 an average of 70,000 migrants entered the city of Buenos Aires and its suburbs each year, but in 1943–7 the rate climbed to 117,000. Migration played a major part in sustaining the expansion of Buenos Aires, whose population, 1.5 million in 1914 and 3.4 million by 1936, had grown to 4.7 million by 1947. Recent studies of internal migration have attempted to gauge movements out of the country-side, as opposed to additions to the urban population. These figures suggest not only that the rate of mobility was much higher than earlier estimates had indicated, but also that migration began to increase mark-edly during the early depression years rather than in the late 1930s. Nonetheless, the older view that migration intensified during the 1940s and after remains unchallenged. Alfredo E. Lattes' calculations, for exam-ple, show rural flight at about 185,000 during the quinquennium 1930–4, 221,000 between 1935 and 1939 and 446,000 during the years 1940–4. Throughout the 1930s and 1940s almost two-thirds of the migrants came from the pampas region, and mostly from the province of Buenos Aires, rather than from the interior. Lattes estimates that Greater Buenos Aires attracted 1.1 million migrants between 1935 and 1947, of whom two-thirds came from the pampas provinces and Mendoza. By the early 1950s the position changed substantially, but before then, it seemed, most migration occurred over relatively short distances and often consisted of first a movement from the land into adjacent small towns followed by a later shift into the metropolitan area.[11]

Manufacturing pulled population into the city; agricultural conditions expelled it from the land. The depression struck an agrarian society whose basic features had changed little during the past generation. In the pampas

[11] Alfredo E. Lattes, 'La dinámica de la población rural en la Argentina', *Cuadernos del CENEP*, no. 9 (1979).

the rural population still consisted mostly of tenants and day-labourers who were employed on large estates on terms that often made their lives extremely insecure. Land tenure was hardly different from what it had been in 1914. In the province of Buenos Aires slightly more than 300 families owned one-fifth of the land, and only 3,500 families half the land. In both Buenos Aires and Santa Fe, the two leading pampas provinces, large farms of more than 1,000 hectares embraced two-thirds of the land area. An agricultural census in 1937 revealed that only 20,000 landowners, in a total rural population of about 1.5 million, owned 70 per cent of pampas land. During the early 1930s landowners who were threatened by the depression had incorporated their holdings to attract new capital and to prevent their alienation or subdivision.

During the early depression years, the government made some efforts to improve conditions for the farm population, particularly for the tenants. Legislation in 1932 established minimum five-year contracts for farm tenants and insisted that tenants be reimbursed for improvements they had made on the lands they farmed. In 1933, as farm prices on the international markets plummeted, the government imposed a moratorium on farmers' debts. Unless they found their rents increased, farmers also gained some protection from the depreciation of the peso after 1929 and from grain subsidies provided by the *junta de cereales*. From the standpoint of production at least, these measures helped to maintain agricultural output, which continued to climb up to the record harvests of 1937.

Yet there were other signs that the farmers remained unhappy and their position uncertain. In the 1930s farm tenants still suffered from the conditions that observers had criticized continually over the past fifty years: credit remained inadequate, and much of it still came from the often rapacious local storekeepers (*pulperos*) rather than from agricultural banks; farmers lacked storage facilities for their grains and therefore had to release their crops as they harvested them, forcing prices to fall; farmers remained in the hands of the railways for transportation and dependent on the goodwill of the monopolistic 'Big Four' grain exporters in Buenos Aires. Among the large grain exporters the biggest, Bunge y Born, now exported almost one-third of the total grain crop and served as broker in the financing of half the country's grain between harvesting and exporting. Only two firms handled almost three-quarters of all grain shipments. On the land the continuing practice of itinerant tenancy and reliance on a seasonal labour force fostered weak family structures, a low marriage-rate, a low birth-rate and a high rate of illegitimacy.

These adversities had plagued farmers for decades. But in the 1930s came hints that conditions were deteriorating still further. As more and more *estancias* underwent incorporation, landowner absenteeism – another perennial complaint of farmers – grew. Relations between landlords and tenants became still more impersonal, and the paternalistic links that had sometimes bound them together diminished. Despite the 1932 legislation most tenants continued to work without written contracts, and notwith-standing import shortages during the depression, farming continued to be mechanized, the number of harvesters growing from 28,600 in 1930 to about 42,000 by 1940. Increasing mechanization meant less need for seasonal labourers, and it tended to force out marginal small farmers. In 1934 the British commercial attaché referred to 'the growing number of tramps [who are] a matter of serious concern to owners of camp property and to the railway companies'.[12] Farmers suffered their greatest blow after mid-1940 with the collapse of agricultural exports during the war. But even before 1940 at least fragmentary evidence suggested widening in-come differentials between countryside and city that may have spurred internal migration.

THE RISE OF NATIONALISM

During the 1930s Argentine politics began to undergo the shifts and realignments that were to culminate in Perón's rise to power. Of the new political currents of this period, nationalism became the most central and significant. Nationalism had complex roots that stretched back into the early nineteenth century, but the sudden proliferation of nationalist ideas after 1930 accompanied the depression. Nationalism emerged as a major ideological force in 1934 with the publication of *La Argentina y el imperio británico: Los eslabones de una cadena, 1806–1933* by Rodolfo and Julio Irazusta. This book attacked the mentality of the liberal-conservative ruling class that had conceded so much, the Irazustas claimed, in the Roca–Runciman Treaty out of a misplaced sense of gratitude and loyalty to Britain for British support during the struggle for independence. The Irazustas dismissed this idea as myth: if Britain had ever supported the independence movement, it had done so only to capture Argentina as a commercial and investment market and to establish a new form of colonial domination to replace that of Spain.

[12] See Chalkley, *Economic Conditions in the Argentine Republic* (1935), p. 174.

Within the nationalist movement at large there appeared two separate strands, which were ultimately united by Perón. The first was the popular nationalist thread that had first surfaced during the oil campaigns of the late 1920s. In seeking to extend state control over raw materials like oil and to exclude foreigners, the campaign aimed to stem the outflow of wealth that foreign control allegedly induced and to develop new areas of employment. In 1935 this *yrigoyenista* brand of nationalism re-emerged in a small organization of young Radicals known as the Fuerza de Orientación Radical de la Juventud Argentina (FORJA). The FORJA embodied two main principles: popular democracy ('Argentina's history', declared its first manifesto in June 1935, 'shows the existence of a permanent struggle by the people for popular sovereignty') and anti-imperialism ('We are a colony; we want a free Argentina').[13]

For a decade, until many of its members defected to join Perón in 1945, the FORJA became one of the chief irritants to Alvear within Radicalism. 'Forjistas' intensified the anglophobia that the Irazustas had helped create. In his widely read *Ferrocarriles Argentinos,* published in 1940, Raúl Scalabrini Ortiz, a fringe member of the FORJA, depicted the British railway companies as corrupt exploiters and agents of British colonial domination. During the Second World War anti-imperialism led the FORJA into a staunch defence of neutrality against the pro-Allied position taken by Alvear and most other Radicals. But powerful and effective though its campaigns became, the FORJA had limitations as a full-blown anti-imperialist movement. Its overriding concerns and objectives lay in transferring property or resources controlled by foreigners to natives. Like the Radicals at large, the FORJA tended to ignore the deeper and ultimately more challenging issues like industry and social reform, and its chief role, fully in keeping with the Radical tradition, was to promote the interests of the 'statist' middle class that the Radicals represented.

Nacionalismo, a movement of the extreme Right of more complex origins and content than the FORJA, became the second nationalist current of the 1930s. The *nacionalistas* originally comprised Uriburu's small band of civilian supporters in 1930–2 who had supported his attempt to reform the system of congressional representation and created paramilitary groups like the Legión Cívica. In some measure *nacionalismo* echoed nineteenth-century federalism. Its members detested Buenos Aires as an agent of internal

---

[13] Quoted in Arturo Jauretche, 'De FORJA y la década infame', in Alberto Ciria (ed.), *La década infame* (Buenos Aires, 1969), p. 91.

domination over the provinces and as a symbol of 'corrupt materialism', while idealizing the provinces, rural areas and rural people as incarnations of virtues they regarded as characteristically hispanic and Argentine. Principally a literary movement in its formation period before 1930, *nacionalismo* had assimilated various ultra-conservative influences from Europe, of which the most important were Spanish clericalism and the doctrines of Charles Maurras, the French monarchist. These European influences shaped its basic ingredients of anti-liberalism and anti-communism. At the heart of *nacionalismo* lay a conviction that liberalism and popular democracy represented a mere prelude to communism. A liberal political system, declared Roberto de Laferrère, one the leading *nacionalistas* of the 1930s, 'allows all sorts of seditious propaganda. A powerful Communist organization has arisen among us. . . . Democracy hands us over unarmed to these forces of extreme socialism and anarchy'.[14]

Enemies of the *nacionalistas* attacked the unfounded exaggerations and the paranoia that underlay such claims and dismissed *nacionalistas* as 'creole fascists'. Indeed, the movement contained many fascist elements and imitations. Its members venerated dictatorship in the same terms as Mussolini ('to impel actions . . . [to] silence dissent, . . . [to] do constructive works'] and made a cult of will, intuition and virility, searching for the 'grandeur of life . . . through a leap into strenuous discipline'.[15] Like fascism, *nacionalismo* thrived on crusades against mythical anti-types. It regarded both liberalism and communism as Jewish in origin, contending that Jews simultaneously controlled world capitalism and the world revolutionary proletariat. Typical of *nacionalista* writing was the attack on the 'Jewish nihilist, the exploiter but also the secret director of the world proletariat . . . the God-less and nation-less Jew, who is infiltrating the minds of our young proletarians'.[16]

Throughout the 1930s the *nacionalistas* led muck-raking assaults against prominent Jewish families. Such attacks became closely associated with their dogmatic belief that in Argentina the city exploited the countryside, since in *nacionalista* propaganda urbanism often became synonymous with Jewry. Typical of their anti-Semitic campaigns were denunciations of the monopolistic grain export houses based in Buenos Aires, most of which were Jewish-owned. The *nacionalistas* were by no means alone in attacking the export houses, since they had long been a favourite target of

[14] Ibarguren, Jr., *Laferrère*, pp. 69–70.
[15] See Comisión de Estudios, *El nacionalismo*, pp. 110–11.
[16] Federico Ibarguren, *Orígenes del nacionalismo argentino, 1927–1937* (Buenos Aires, 1969), p. 398.

all who supported the farm interest. But the *nacionalistas* stood out on account of their violent racism. The Jewish Bemberg family became another of their major targets: its head, Otto Bemberg, the *nacionalistas* contended, had manoeuvred to secure a monopoly in the brewing industry and used his profits to buy up foreclosed lands from bankrupt farmers and ranchers.

Nacionalismo therefore contained echoes of Fascist Italy and some of Nazi Germany, coupled with a mystical ruralism and an aggressive defence of the smaller ranching interests and their peon dependants. In other respects *nacionalismo* developed as an offshoot of Spanish conservatism and as a weaker version of the Spanish nationalist movement that waged the Spanish civil war under Franco. In the early 1930s Argentina underwent a Catholic revival that reached a climax during the Congreso Eucarístico Internacional held in Buenos Aires in 1934. At this point militant priests and lay Catholics came to exercise a dominant role in the movement and to shape its central ideas. At the heart of *nacionalismo* lay an organic concept of society that was rooted in antiquity and Catholic scholasticism. Like Uriburu's 1932 manifesto, the *nacionalistas* regarded the purpose of government as that of serving the 'public' or 'common good', and they defined human society in the spiritual and corporatist terms that stood at the core of conservative Catholicism, rejecting liberalism because it treated humanity in falsely individualist terms and communism because of its atheism and materialism.

But the great peculiarity of *nacionalismo* that largely explains its importance after 1940 was its juxtaposition of the most reactionary attitudes with a commitment to progressive reform. Among the major influences on *nacionalismo* were the papal encyclicals of 1891 and 1931, *Rerum Novarum* and *Quadragesimo Anno*. Both documents contained bitter attacks on liberalism and socialism, but they also posed the issue of 'social justice', a better ordering of relations among the social classes to achieve the age-old Catholic quest for an organic, 'harmonious' society. By the mid-1930s, as they fulminated against 'liberals' and 'communists', the *nacionalistas* were proclaiming a concern for the working class and social reform. 'The lack of equity', declared La Voz Nacionalista, 'of welfare, of social justice, of morality, of humanity, has made the proletariat a beast of burden . . . unable to enjoy life or the advances of civilization'.[17] In 1937 one of the most stridently anti-Semitic groups, the Alianza de la Juventud Naciona-

---

[17] La Voz Nacionalista, *El nacionalismo argentino* (Buenos Aires, 1935), p. 5.

lista, coupled demands for a ban on Jewish immigration and the expulsion of Jews from public offices not only with 'social justice' but with what it described as 'revolutionary' land reform to destroy 'oligarchy'. The *nacionalistas* stood out among the first proponents of industrialization and the nationalization of foreign-owned public services. Proposals among them to develop a national steel industry appeared as early as 1931. In 1932 a *nacionalista* newspaper attacked the American-owned Unión Telefónica as a 'foreign firm that monopolizes a public service and that ought to have been nationalized some time ago'.[18]

Nacionalismo was not a political 'party', a designation its members totally rejected because 'party' implied the liberal proposition that a mere segment of the community could uphold an identity separate from society at large; 'parties', said the *nacionalistas,* 'split' an indivisible entity: the nation. Equally, the *nacionalistas* refused to take part in any elections, since they regarded electoral practices as another derivative of liberalism. Throughout the 1930s the movement consisted of a dozen or so factions, often competing and squabbling among themselves and headed by members of the intelligentsia, whose chief activities were disseminating propaganda, holding public meetings and staging occasional street demonstrations. By the end of the decade, in addition to the publication of numerous newspapers and periodicals, the *nacionalistas* had turned to 'historical revisionism', the rewriting of Argentine history to attack what they saw as the distorted historical vision of the liberal establishment, the heroes of liberal historiography, the British, and above all to rehabilitate the figure of Juan Manuel de Rosas as the great model of political leadership they aspired to. 'It's a foul lie', declared Marcelo Sánchez Sorondo, 'that we owe our historical being to liberalism. To liberalism we owe only the handover of our frontier lands, and the tutelage of foreigners'.[19] Rosas' governments, by contrast, exemplified the 'collaboration of each element of society: leader, enlightened minority and mass'.[20] Soon after after 1930 the *nacionalistas* had therefore renounced the *uriburista* aspiration for 'true democracy' in favour of a commitment to autocratic corporatism under a military leader. In spite of this shift, it remained the duty of the government to promote both the 'common good' and 'social justice'.

During the 1930s these right-wing sects began to achieve an influence

---

[18] *Crisol,* 21 February 1932.
[19] Marcelo Sánchez Sorondo, *La revolución que anunciamos* (Buenos Aires, 1945), p. 35.
[20] See Tulio Halperín Donghi, *El revisionismo histórico argentino* (Buenos Aires, 1971), p. 14.

that far outweighed their number – a few hundred activists. The *naciona-listas* played a major part in shaping the incipient anti-imperialist move-ment, as it gathered adherents not only from the Right but also the Left and Centre. Anti-imperialism in Argentina developed on a web of conspir-acy theories of the type that were fundamental to the political tactics and techniques of the ultra-Right. In much anti-imperialist propaganda, for example, the British, and later the North Americans, came to be viewed in much the same terms as the *nacionalistas* painted the Jews, as covert and malign conspiratorial forces. Thus, Raúl Scalabrini Ortiz, who was an ostensible leftist, castigated the British in the same terms and language as one of the *nacionalistas'* anti-Semitic tracts: 'We have in our midst an enemy who has won world dominance through the astuteness and skill of its indirect manoeuvres, through its acts of ill-faith, through its constant lies'.[21]

In the 1930s the nationalist movement remained mostly civilian and, despite the activities of Molina, Kinkelín and a handful of others, had as yet failed to penetrate the army on a large scale.

ARGENTINA ON THE EVE OF THE SECOND WORLD WAR

On the eve of the Second World War Argentina was in much the same prosperous and promising situation it had enjoyed on the eve of the first. Only the recent expansion of industrial Buenos Aires and the growing outward movement of population from the pampas suggested any striking contrast with conditions thirty years before. The country upheld its re-gional diversity, along with the structural lopsidedness that concentrated a disproportionate share of population, wealth and resources in and around Buenos Aires. Since 1914 new regional growth centres, such as the Chaco cotton belt, had emerged beyond the pampas, but in other respects the interior remained largely unchanged: Patagonia as an empty land of vast sheep farms, the Río Negro valley as an area of small-scale fruit farmers, Mendoza and San Juan as wine producers and Tucumán as the source of sugar. In the Far-North-east and Far North-west persisted the forced labour practices that had long provoked the denunciations of reformers in Buenos Aires. The interior remained extremely poor and largely bereft of

[21] Raúl Scalabrini Ortiz, 'De: Politica británica en el Río de la Plata', in Ciria (ed.), *La decada infame*. p. 198.

population. In 1941 the combined incomes of nine interior provinces amounted to only 1 per cent of total taxable incomes throughout the nation, and the per capita incomes of Catamarca and Santiago del Estero, two of the poorest provinces, stood at only 10 per cent of those in the city of Buenos Aires. Diseases caused by malnutrition remained endemic in the interior, most of all among the Tucumán sugar workers, who continually fell victim to malaria, impetigo and even leprosy. In Tucumán, as in much of the interior, 50 per cent of births were illegitimate.

Despite recent industrial development the vast middle class of Buenos Aires had undergone little change during the past generation and remained heavily bunched in services, the professions, commerce and public administration. In 1944 Felix Weil described the middle class as

rather shapeless mass of independent handicraftsmen, merchants, general store owners, clerks and agents of export and import concerns, employees of public utilities, and innumerable beneficiaries of the political patronage system who live off salaries and stipends of all kinds. Since there was no large-scale industry until industrialization took an upward swing after 1930, there was no place for an independent middle class. What there was, were the remains of a colonial economy coupled with the political system of spoils. This mass is necessarily amorphous in politics and political philosophies. It easily becomes the object of manipulation by political machines.[22]

Throughout the 1930s successive conservative governments had deliberately cut the middle class's access to power and the spoils of office. Although the schools, academies and universities administered by the middle class upheld the city as a centre of high culture, they were often a breeding-ground for blocked social aspirations and cumulative frustrations. Observers in addition to Weil commented on the overcrowding of the professions and on the falling marriage- and birth-rates and rising suicide-rates of the middle class in this period. In a piece entitled 'Esplendor y decadencia de la raza blanca' (Splendour and decadence of the white race), published in 1940, the economist Alejandro E. Bunge urged his countrymen and countrywomen, 'particularly the more materially blessed ones', to practise 'Catholic marriages' and to rear large families. 'From now on', he declared, 'with all our vigour, our patriotism and with a selfless Christian spirit, we should seek to restore the acceptability of large families and the idea that children are a blessing'.[23]

[22] Weil, *Argentine Riddle*, p. 4.
[23] Alejandro E. Bunge, 'Esplendor y decadencia de la raza blanca', *Revista de Economía Argentina*, no. 259 (January 1940), pp. 9–23.

By early 1940 many observers were beginning to take note of the economic and social changes of recent years. But little of this was reflected in government policy. During the 1930s conservative leaders frequently acknowledged that the restrictions they had imposed on imports and their attempts to rechannel foreign trade would foster industrial growth, but they remained far from adopting a deliberate commitment to industrial development. By and large their outlook had changed little since the nineteenth century: some industrial growth, they argued, would strengthen the balance of payments and help stave off industrial unrest as it created new jobs. The American economist George Wythe exaggerated in 1937 when he declared, 'The new road of [industrialization] has been accepted from which there is no turning back.'[24] The Central Bank painted a more accurate picture in 1938: 'The country's capacity for industrialization is limited . . . and if we increase purchasing power by too much, production will fail to increase, and prices will rise . . . with all its unfortunate consequences on the cost of living'.[25]

Members of the government and bodies like the Central Bank wanted not to intensify industrial development, but to try to restore the conditions that had prevailed before 1930. Their policies thus favoured exporting interests and sought to revive foreign investment. Policy-makers emphasized repeatedly the obstacles to industrial development: the risk of inflation, meagre and inaccessible supplies of coal and iron-ore, inadequate power and transportation facilities, capital shortages and the restricted size of the domestic market, which impeded economies of scale. Outside the small band of economic nationalists, these views prevailed among other organized political groups, including a large majority of the Radicals.

By the late 1930s industrial expansion commanded greater interest among the trade unions as they perceived that new industry meant new jobs. Some, like the *nacionalistas,* argued that a policy of progressive income redistribution should accompany support for industry, since more money in the hands of wage-earners would widen markets and intensify industrial growth. However, ideas of this kind commanded little support among industrialists themselves, who continued to view low wages as the key to high profits. Typical of this outlook was that of the Federación Argentina de Entidades del Comercio y la Industria, which conducted an unrelenting war on trade unions for 'disrupting' labour markets. Some

[24] Quoted in Vernon L. Phelps, *The International Economic Position of Argentina* (Philadelphia, 1938), p. 7.
[25] Quoted in Eduardo F. Jorge, *Industria y concentración económica* (Buenos Aires, 1971), p. 172.

industrialists, however, had now begun to support protection. Protectionist ideas slowly gained favour after 1933, when the Unión Industrial Argentina, the largest and most powerful of the urban employers' associations, led a campaign against foreign dumping. The union's later campaigns attacked anomalies in the existing tariff, which, it alleged, often imposed higher duties on industrial raw materials than on finished goods. But among all these groups, unions and employers alike, no concerted or sustained effort had emerged to promote industrial development.

Early in 1938, Agustín P. Justo's six-year tenure as president came to an end. At this point, in the Indian summer of pre-war prosperity, not only were nationalist influences growing but sharp differences had emerged within the ruling Concordancia between reformers and reactionaries. The presidential election of 1937, which the Concordancia again won easily thanks to extensive fraud, mirrored this cleavage: the presidency passed to Roberto M. Ortiz, a reformer, but the vice-presidency went to Ramón S. Castillo, leader of the conservatives.

As the self-made son of a Basque grocer, Ortiz became the first president-elect whose background was among the urban middle class of immigrant descent. Ortiz had made his living and his fortune chiefly as a lawyer for several British railway companies and was therefore extremely unpopular among the *nacionalistas*. Having been a Radical deputy during Yrigoyen's first term (1916–22), Ortiz joined the Anti-Personalists in 1924, serving as minister of public works under Alvear and then as minister of finance under Justo. As his past career suggested, Ortiz was an anti-*yrigoyenista* democrat with impeccable liberal-conservative credentials: 'liberal' because of his links with the British and his pledge to end electoral fraud ('I am a sincere believer in the benefits of democracy', he said on accepting the nomination for the presidency in July 1937), and 'conservative' because of his fear of *yrigoyenista* 'mob rule'. Castillo, by contrast, came from Catamarca, one of the most underdeveloped western provinces, the bastion of an oligarchy of *hacendados*. He had served many years as dean of the law faculty of the University of Buenos Aires until becoming Justo's minister of justice and public instruction.

With the accession of Ortiz, tension grew between the national government and Manuel Fresco, governor of the province of Buenos Aires. Fresco was a former conservative, who like Ortiz himself had past ties with the British railways but who now posed as a *nacionalista*. Fresco continually attacked 'communism', persecuted those he saw as its adherents and sought the friendship and patronage of Mussolini during a visit to Rome in 1938. But he also emerged as a champion of social reform. Under Fresco the government of Buenos Aires Province organized large-scale public works that included public housing schemes and a large road-building programme. He sponsored labour legislation for both urban and rural workers, and he made some attempts to build a network of trade unions controlled by his administration. From the federal capital, Fresco was seen as a fascist.

The Ortiz administration began cutting federal funds and subsidies to the province, forcing Fresco into large budget deficits and eventually into curtailing his activities. Finally in March 1940 Ortiz decreed a federal intervention in Buenos Aires to unseat Fresco, whom he accused of plotting fraud in the forthcoming gubernatorial election. Soon afterwards Ortiz carried out interventions in other provinces, among them, to the extreme annoyance of his vice-president, Catamarca. In the congressional elections of May 1940 the Radicals scored their greatest victory of more than a decade and now regained a majority in the Chamber of Deputies. By early 1940 Argentine politics thus seemed to be following the same course as that after the election of Roque Sáenz Peña in 1910. Led by Ortiz, the Concordancia, like the conservatives of thirty years before, had pledged itself to restoring democracy. And, as before, democratization opened the door to the Radicals.

ECONOMY AND POLITICS, 1940–3

At the very time it appeared so strong, liberal Argentina stood on the brink of collapse. In May 1940 Germany invaded and occupied Western Europe, and after evacuating its battered forces from the beaches of Dunkirk, Britain imposed a naval blockade against the Continent. The German conquests and the blockade dealt a blow to the Argentine economy that was even more severe than that of 1929–30. Trade plummeted instantly: in 1940 exports shrank by 20 per cent. In 1938 40 per cent of Argentina's exports went to Western Europe, but by 1941 the proportion had fallen to only 6 per cent, nearly all to neutral Spain and Portugal. Britain imported most of Argentina's meat, and the British market remained open, but the Continent now became inaccessible to most of Argentina's grains, with the result that agriculture and farmers, rather than cattle and ranchers, suffered by far the more serious effects of the war. By late 1940 shipping in Argentine ports had fallen by half. Both exports and imports sank to levels below the low point of the depression.

The disruptive conditions that emerged in late 1940 persisted throughout the next four years of war. In 1937 Argentina had exported 17 million
tons of grains, but managed only 6.5 million tons in 1942. Agricultural
prices averaged only two-thirds of those of the late 1930s. Within agriculture as a whole the war damaged maize most severely, since before the war
about 90 per cent of maize went to continental Europe. During the late
1930s maize exports averaged more than 6 million tons but in 1941–44
only 400,000 tons. By 1941 coal imports were only one-third those of
1939, and by 1943 they were one-sixth. By 1942 oil imports were half
their 1939 level, and by 1943 half again.

Immediately before the war, Argentine importers had made few efforts
to stockpile supplies of machinery, raw materials or spare parts, so that it
now became necessary to improvise with existing materials. Denied their
normal coal supplies, the railways resorted to burning quebracho logs, as
they had in 1914–18, and then, as timber supplies dwindled, they
turned to burning surplus maize. By 1944 grains provided about one-
third of the country's energy needs. As imported oil supplies fell,
Yacimientos Petrolíferos Fiscales (YPF) made great efforts to increase
production and eventually managed to double output from the wells at
Comodoro Rivadavia. Even so, oil shortages forced the widespread use of
linseed as a substitute. Falling imports offered great new opportunities to
Argentine manufacturers, and permanent shifts soon became common in
the factories of Buenos Aires. Yet industrial growth occurred at a somewhat lower rate during the war than in the late 1930s, since industrialists
now fell foul of recurrent power shortages and of their inability to obtain
needed supplies abroad. At the same time, urban unemployment remained all but non-existent as both manufacturing and services steadily
absorbed new workers, including a large number of women. Repair work
became the largest component of the new service sector, as an army of
versatile mechanics sought to maintain ageing machinery, cars, lorries
and thirty-year-old rolling stock.

The collapse of agricultural exports after mid-1940 had some beneficial
effects on the urban economy, since it meant cheap bread and a relatively
stable cost of living. But on the land, agriculture's decline produced
turmoil. During the war two processes operated simultaneously: farming
declined but ranching expanded as Britain steadily increased its meat
imports. A massive shift from agriculture to cattle ensued as the cultivated
area shrank by more than 3 million hectares during the war years. Land
used for wheat declined by an estimated 8.4 per cent, but that for maize

by more than 40 per cent. The maize surpluses helped to intensify the move into livestock, since they induced the growth of pig farming, an activity that doubled in size during the war. To some extent the growth of forage crops, alfalfa, barley and oats, which serviced the cattle economy, and some new industrial crops led by sunflowers compensated for the decline in the old grain staples. But the overriding trend was the move from grains to cattle. Between 1937 and 1947 the cattle population of the pampas increased by 25 per cent, or 3.5 million, whilst the human population fell by about half a million. Government attempts to arrest the outflow of population, such as the controlled tenant rents introduced in 1942, proved completely ineffectual in stemming the flight from the land.

By contrast, conditions in the interior now began to diverge from those in the pampas. Producers there responded to the rapidly expanding internal market centred in Buenos Aires by increasing production. Growth was especially marked in areas like the Chaco where virgin land remained available. Elsewhere in the settled peasant regions of the North-west and the North-east, increasing market production raised demand for labour and thus for a time helped draw population into the region. However, growth also increased demand for a relatively fixed supply of land and thus in the longer term provoked an expansion of the market-producing haciendas at the expense of subsistence-oriented peasant smallholdings. The final result was a process of peasant encirclement and the beginnings of an eventually acute latifundio–minifundio polarization that in the 1950s and afterwards provoked a second, still greater wave of flight from the land. In this way the interior, and no longer the pampas, eventually emerged as the main source of internal migrants.

In late 1940 the conservative government sought to respond to the fall in trade through a Plan de Reactivación Económica, better known as the Pinedo Plan, since its chief author was Federico Pinedo, serving a second term as finance minister. The plan was conceived on the assumption that in the following year, 1941, exports would remain at levels below those of the depression. If this happened, the result would be 'industrial crisis, unemployment and misery in the cities, a general collapse of all business, that would provoke social consequences of unforeseeable scope'.[26] Pinedo therefore proposed, New Deal style, to use government spending as a

---

[26] See 'El plan de reactivación económica ante el Honorable Senado', *Desarrollo Económico*, 19, no. 75 (1979), p. 404.

countercyclical device to revive demand, minimize inflation and safeguard employment. Above all the measure was concerned with the 'social consequences of unforeseeable scope', a phrase that would be readily understood as a reference to the labour unrest of the First World War that had climaxed in the 'revolutionary strike' of January 1919.

The Pinedo Plan marked Argentina's entrance into the field of comprehensive economic planning. First, it proposed to assist the farm sector by extending the crop-financing schemes administered by the juntas that Pinedo himself had created seven years before. The government would now expand its grain purchases from the farmers and offer higher prices, while urging landowners to show restraint on land rents in order to leave tenants with adequate profits. Second, the plan sought to foster faster industrial growth and to start exporting industrial products. It proposed a new state-backed credit fund for industry and the introduction of 'drawbacks' (*reintegros*), a scheme long sought by the Unión Industrial, that provided for the reimbursement of exporters of manufactures for the tariff duties they incurred when importing raw materials or capital goods. To complement these measures the government would attempt to conclude free-trade treaties with other nations in Latin America in order to create new markets for manufactures and assist producers in achieving economies of scale. Third, the plan proposed to finance the expansion of the construction industry, which the government believed capable of providing more than 200,000 new jobs. Through government-assisted construction schemes, cheap houses would be offered with long-term mortgages to workers and employees.

In 1940 the government remained extremely sensitive to the charge that it was leaning towards deficit financing and therefore risked inflation. The plan, Pinedo declared, would be financed not by printing money but from international loans, and expenditures would be directed into productive activities rather than into mere subsidies for the unemployed. The Pinedo Plan manifested far greater concern for agriculture than for industry since the sums allotted for credits to industry totalled only one-sixth of those destined for farmers. Thus, the shift towards industry remained relatively small. Government, Pinedo declared, would support only 'natural industries'. This phrase had been in common usage among liberals for the past seventy years, and it meant that only industries that employed a substantial quantity of local raw materials and could be expected to establish themselves competitively would receive government support. Pinedo expected that industry would continue to have a secondary role in the economy. When he argued the measure before Congress, he talked of farm exports as the 'master wheel' of the economy; manufacturing and construction would become 'lesser wheels' at their side.

The Pinedo Plan offered a formula for controlled change and a measure of diversification that would contain the effects of the war and minimize unrest and dislocation. But it remained only a plan, since by the time it appeared the country had fallen into political crisis. In July 1940 the diabetic president Ortiz, now a victim of bouts of blindness, was forced to leave office and to hand over power to the arch-conservative Castillo. For a year, until Ortiz finally resigned, Castillo was only acting president. But soon after taking over, he began reversing the policy of liberalization embarked upon earlier in the year. By September 1940 Castillo had partly reorganized the cabinet, and to the rising anger of the Radicals he began organizing elections in the provinces that Ortiz had placed under 'intervention'. Fraud heavily tainted several of these elections, most of which the conservatives won. Having so recently been convinced that they were at last on the road to regaining power, the Radicals now found themselves in danger of being cheated by Castillo. A bitter spate of party conflict followed, and the Pinedo Plan became its main victim. Although the conservative-dominated Senate accepted the plan, the Radical majority in the lower house prevented it from being brought to the floor. Radicals rejected Pinedo's appeal for a 'patriotic accord' to deal with the economic emergency until they gained redress for the recent elections.

The Pinedo Plan failed owing to the long feuds between Radicals and conservatives that Castillo had reignited. Yet even if politics had not prevailed, the plan contained certain assumptions and expectations that from the start made its success problematical. During the following months, executive decrees implemented many of its proposals for dealing with agriculture, but they did little to resolve the farm crisis or to halt the rising flood of migrants pouring into Buenos Aires.

The Pinedo Plan also raised the now-critical issue of relations with the United States. The plan's aim of promoting industry rested on the assumption that Argentina could continue to import the capital goods and raw materials that it lacked. Yet in order to import it had to export or, alternatively, secure a large, continuous flow of foreign loans and investment. Currently, with the closure of the European markets to its grains, only Britain survived among its largest markets. But as Britain mobilized for war, it ceased to be able to export to Argentina any of the goods useful to local industry. As a result throughout the war Argentina's export earnings accumulated in Britain as 'sterling balances'. By the end of 1942 the sterling balances had climbed to 295 million pesos, and a year later to 714 million. By December 1944 the balances were estimated to be more than a billion pesos, or some £80 million. The British undertook to protect the sterling balances from any future devaluation of the pound; but with the hope of repaying the debt in exports after the war, they kept the balances 'blocked' in Britain, completely beyond Argentina's reach. On several occasions the British refused Argentina's requests to use blocked funds to redeem part of its own debt to Britain or to exchange them for the assets of British-owned firms in Argentina; these companies, led by the railways, usually purchased most of their supplies in Britain and therefore helped British exports. Moreover, the British would never allow Argentina to convert its sterling balances into dollars, since this would mean a return to what in British eyes were the highly unfavourable trade practices of the 1920s, when Argentina's earnings on sales to Britain had been used to increase purchases in the United States. By 1940 Argentina found itself locked into the bilateral relationship with Britain that it had so eagerly sought in 1933, but in a way that was quite useless to Pinedo's goal of 'economic revival'.

In the plan of 1940 both Pinedo and Raúl Prebisch, still his chief adviser, anticipated the United States developing as a substitute supplier of the goods needed by local industry and as a new market for Argentina's exports. 'The great market of the United States', the plan declared, 'offers enormous opportunities. There is no logical reason why our producers should not take advantage of it'.[27] For a brief period in late 1940 Pinedo tried to orchestrate a pro-U.S. campaign in Argentina and to promote the idea that closer links with the United States would bring a flood of prosperity. Pinedo's calculations transcended purely short-term goals. To conservatives like Pinedo, Argentina now stood at a historical crossroads. The old link with Britain no longer functioned and indeed might collapse completely if, as now seemed very likely, Britain suffered invasion and defeat by Germany. A new relationship with the United States not only would resolve the trade issue, but in doing so would also safeguard the political dominance of the class of ranchers and merchants that underpinned liberal-conservatism. For these reasons Pinedo now pleaded for 'close and complete co-operation' with the United States.

However, at this critical moment Argentina again failed to surmount

27 'El plan de reactivación económica', p. 423.

the barriers that for almost a century had persistently impeded all efforts to create any stable and durable ties with the United States. During the past decade relations between the two countries had often been cool, as the United States extended its protectionist measures against goods from Argentina. In 1930 the Hawley–Smoot Act strengthened the restrictions on most meat and grain products from Argentina, raising tariffs on meat, corn and wool and imposing new duties on hides. In 1935 all imported farm goods that undersold American equivalents were banned completely. In 1936 came new duties on Argentine tallow. Throughout the 1930s the United States employed sanitary regulations, ostensibly directed against the spread of foot-and-mouth disease, to exclude other goods from Argentina. Both Uriburu and Justo made intermittent but unavailing protests against such policies, while the United States refused Justo's suggestion of a bilateral treaty between the two countries. In retaliation the conservatives, like the Radicals in the late 1920s, sometimes harassed American companies like Standard Oil, while employing exchange controls to exclude U.S. imports. Throughout the 1930s imports from the United States thus remained at a mere fraction of imports in the 1920s; at the same time, Argentina's exports to the United States halved.

The trade conflicts of the 1930s sharpened the latent anti-U.S. currents in Argentina. Argentines now ignored or attacked the Roosevelt administration's Good Neighbor policy, which renounced armed interventions by the United States in Latin America, and they saw the pan-American movement sponsored by the United States as an example of *maquiavelismo yanqui,* the real purpose of which was to promote U.S. control throughout the South American continent. After 1935 Argentina participated, at times reluctantly, in the succession of pan-American conferences sponsored by the United States, and when towards the outbreak of war the United States attempted to create a pan-American defence alliance, the Ortiz government gave the idea only half-hearted endorsement. Trade and diplomacy had become inextricably linked. By late 1939 at least some Americans were beginning to recognize the main source of Argentina's uncooperative behaviour. 'Winning the friendship of Argentina', declared John W. White, an American diplomat in Buenos Aires, 'is largely a matter of trade and economics'. 'We must reconcile ourselves', he continued, 'to some commercial sacrifices for the sake of our political and military safety, and permit the importation of Argentine products'.[28] But in

[28] John W. White, *Argentina: The Life Story of a Nation* (New York, 1942), pp. 21, 311.

1939–40, all Argentina gained from the United States was a credit from
the Export–Import Bank of New York for the purchase of U.S. goods.
Following the Lend-Lease act of January 1941, the United States began to
provide arms to its Latin American allies led by Brazil, but it gave
Argentina lowest priority, denying it military supplies almost completely
because of its stance on hemispheric defence.

Against this discouraging background, but as part of the strategy of the
Pinedo Plan, the Castillo government finally embarked on formal trade
negotiations with the United States, seeking through a trade treaty – the
first with the United States for almost a century – the concessions that
had been so long denied. For a time members of the government, the
political parties and even some of the trade unions became enthusiastic
converts to pan-Americanism, as they contemplated a large flow of funds
and goods from the United States. But when this treaty was concluded in
October 1941, it proved a complete disappointment, since each side made
only token concessions. The United States offered little more than to lower
tariffs on the goods from Argentina it already imported, such as linseed
and cattle hides. The only new goods to be admitted from Argentina were
some rare minerals, such as tungsten, which was required by U.S. arms
manufacturers, and some dairy products and wines that the United States
had before imported from France and Italy. But the door remained shut to
Argentina's great staples, its meats and grains. The United States thus
gave the impression that this treaty was simply a wartime expedient that
marked no major shift in traditional U.S. policy.

The failure of the October 1941 treaty with the United States signalled
the approaching end of the liberal-conservative plan to achieve economic
recovery and thus maintain political dominance. For more than a year,
since Ortiz's forced leave of absence in July 1940, the balance of power in
the Concordancia and the government had been changing. Early in 1941
Pinedo had resigned following accusations instigated by the *nacionalistas* of
his involvement in corrupt dealings with the British railway companies.
In March the liberal-conservative foreign minister, José Luis Cantilo, had
also resigned, leaving the ultra-conservatives led by Castillo himself to
dominate the government. But Castillo was becoming increasingly isolated, and he responded by bringing men with *nacionalista* sympathies into
the government. Among them was the new minister of foreign affairs,
Enrique Ruiz Guiñazú, who was widely known as a sympathizer with
General Franco's Spain.

Nacionalismo was thus ceasing to be a movement on the fringe of politics. As fresh *nacionalista* organizations sprouted and their propaganda intensified, the *nacionalistas* began to pull the country in several new directions. The first was towards 'economic sovereignty', which meant principally greater industrialization and the nationalization of foreign companies that performed public services. The second became what was called 'active neutrality', which meant as one propagandist succinctly defined it in January 1941, 'We are not neutral, we are against everyone'.[29] The third was a new emphasis on 'social justice'. In late 1939 *nacionalistas* were complaining that

in Santiago del Estero the people lack water. [Elsewhere] there is no bread. In the south children fail to attend school for lack of clothing. But in Buenos Aires a committee made up of two ex-presidents, a vice-president, senators etc. . . . . all of them Argentines collect funds for the war hospitals in France.[30]

By 1941 these sentiments had taken a more aggressive form. Now the *nacionalistas*, declared the Alianza Libertadora Nacionalista, aspired to 'the leadership of the proletarian masses, to bring them into harmony with other elements of society towards the conquest of justice and the grandeur of the Nation'.[31] A typical *nacionalista* program in 1941 listed the following demands: 'economic emancipation' to enable the country to regain 'all its sources of wealth' from foreign control; the creation of 'large markets of internal consumption' through 'industrialization'; the redistribution of 'uncultivated land so that it would be worked' (*para su trabajo*); 'functional representation'; 'just wages'; the reintroduction of Catholic education in the schools; defence against 'threats to national unity' (a euphemism for anti-Semitism and anti-communism); and measures to ensure the country's 'military preparedness'.[32] These ideas were commonly expressed in the slogans 'Sovereignty', 'Nationalization', 'Social Justice'.

Many observers viewed all this as symptomatic of the rise of Nazi-Fascism in Argentina. Years later Raúl Prebisch urged his audience not to underestimate Nazi influence in Argentina in the 1930s. 'I have seen it; I experienced it myself while in the Central Bank. The penetration of Nazism in the Army, in certain newspapers, aided by the resources of the German embassy was a highly disturbing element in Argentina'.[33] In-

---

[29] *El Fortín*, January 1941.
[30] *La Maroma*, October 1939.
[31] Quoted in Comisión de Estudios, *El nacionalismo*, p. 50.
[32] Estatutos del Consejo Superior del Nacionalismo (Buenos Aires, 1941).
[33] Raúl Prebisch, 'Argentine Economic Policies since the 1930s – Recollections', in Guido Di Tella and D. C. M. Platt (eds.), *The Political Economy of Argentina, 1880–1946* (London, 1986), p. 146.

deed, just as fascists lurked among the *nacionalistas* in the 1930s, so now did Nazi sympathizers, among them the staff of *El Pampero,* a new newspaper in Buenos Aires whose editor, Enrique Osés, received subsidies from the German Embassy in return for publishing Nazi war bulletins and some Nazi propaganda. Some looked to Germany in 1940–1 to provide the kind of relationship that the Pinedo group had sought with the United States. At the same time, many *nacionalistas* regarded Germany and Nazism with hostility. To the Catholic hispanophile groups, Nazism symbolized 'four hundred years of apostasy' that had begun with the Reformation, and local pro-Nazis reminded one *nacionalista* (referring to Carlos de Alvear, one of the leaders of the Argentine independence movement) 'of the posture of some of the men during the May Revolution [of 1810], who contributed towards our independence from Spain only to make us depend on the English'.[34] In September 1939 a Nazi diplomat in Buenos Aires remarked to his superiors in Berlin, 'The anti-British sentiment . . . must not be construed as pro-German. . . . The new Germany is viewed as anti-cultural [*sic*] . . . because of its supposed threat to the Catholic Church'.[35]

Rather than expressing an expansion of Nazi-German influence, *nacionalismo* emerged in the train of rising anti-U.S. sentiment and in the vacuum left by the defection of the liberal-conservatives from the Concordancia. At the end of 1941, following the failure of the approach to the United States, Argentina found itself starved of foreign markets and foreign supplies. Moreover, it faced what it perceived to be a military threat from Brazil, which the United States was now arming faster than any other country in the region. Prompted by the *nacionalistas,* Argentina's response grew increasingly spirited and recalcitrant. As it reaffirmed neutrality and refused to bend to U.S. pressure to join the pan-American alliance, it began seeking ways to conquer its economic and military isolation.

In late 1941 *nacionalista* influences became stronger and more entrenched within the army, where a growing fascination with a national arms industry emerged, which in turn provoked much stronger support than before for industrial development. The industrial promotion schemes of the past, such as those of the Pinedo Plan, had stressed *selective* industrialization, ventures that would aim for competitive efficiency and seek economies of scale through exporting. What was now taking shape was

[34] Ibarguren, Jr., *Laferrère,* p. 94.
[35] Quoted in Stewart Edward Sutin, 'The Impact of Nazism on Germans of Argentina' (Ph.D. dissertation, University of Texas, 1975), p. 68.

the commitment towards *total* industrialization that would be army- and state-directed. Under army pressure, the government created the Dirección General de Fabricaciones Militares to develop armaments. A year or so later Colonel Manuel S. Savio produced blueprints for a steel industry that he proposed would be state-financed and state-directed.

Throughout 1941 and 1942 Castillo clung to power despite his narrowing base of support and the steady growth of opposition led by the Radicals. Although some *nacionalistas* like Ruiz Guiñazú had been drawn into the government, a majority of *nacionalistas* rejected the regime as 'liberal', 'oligarchic' or 'electoralist'. With Congress controlled by the Radicals, the government began to rule almost exclusively by decree. The Japanese attack on Pearl Harbor in December 1941 was the pretext first for the imposition of a state of siege and then for the use of the police to stop (usually pro-Allied) demonstrations and to muzzle the press. But failing to staunch the opposition, Castillo was compelled to cultivate the army. At regular intervals he conducted lavish banquets attended by military chiefs. Crisis and an atmosphere of decay now pervaded the country. The American observer John W. White perceived the 'problems of 1942' as

reactionary government of force in the hands of a minority party, an over-specialized grain economy with an almost helpless dependence on foreign markets, an unhealthy concentration of population in the cities, an exploited farming class that was not settled on the land it worked, a falling birth rate, and a high rate of illegitimacy and illiteracy.[36]

To compound Castillo's difficulties, relations with the United States sharply deteriorated as Ruiz Guiñazú led an attempt to foster neutralism, at the expense of pan-Americanism, in other parts of Latin America. In February 1942, at the pan-American conference in Rio de Janeiro, the main purpose of which was to persuade the Latin American nations to break diplomatic relations with the Axis and Japan, Ruiz Guiñazú consistently opposed the United States, and although he failed to erect a 'southern bloc' outside the pan-American alliance, he did succeed in preventing an agreement to break relations. The resolution that emerged in Rio merely 'recommended' rupture, but left it to each country to determine its own course of action. Led by Secretary of State Cordell Hull, the United States retaliated by imposing on Argentina a total arms embargo, by halting credits from the Export–Import Bank and by cancelling supplies of oil tankers and machinery.

[36] White, *Argentina*. p. 292.

After the Rio conference, the United States began to label the Argentine government 'fascist' and 'pro-Axis'. In Buenos Aires there were recurrent rumours of an impending invasion by Brazil and of a planned occupation of Comodoro Rivadavia, the chief oil source, by U.S. marines. But as this pressure mounted throughout 1942, Castillo found unexpected support from Britain. In the early 1940s the United States and Britain had quite different objectives with regard to Argentina. The former was concerned chiefly with forging a united military and political front throughout Latin America, and it viewed Argentina as an obstacle to this end. Britain, however, became increasingly dependent on Argentine meat and resisted any course of action that threatened its meat shipments. In addition, Britain's extensive commercial and financial interests in Argentina made the British reluctant to allow Argentina to drift totally into the U.S. orbit, as seemed likely to happen if Argentina committed itself fully to pan-Americanism. Since 1940 Britain had been apprehensive of U.S. attempts to secure control of British companies in Argentina. A U.S. proposal that year, for example, suggested that Britain pay Argentina for its meat in the securities of British companies, which Argentina in turn would transfer to U.S. ownership to pay for imports from the United States. As a result opinion in Britain often favoured a neutral Argentina. If Argentina's neutrality risked allowing Axis spies to transmit intelligence on British shipping movements, it would help to protect the meat ships that sailed under the Argentine flag from German submarines.

From early 1942 the State Department pursued evidence to support its view that Argentina's neutrality merely masked an underlying support for the Axis. It exposed the subsidies to *El Pampero* from the German Embassy; it accused the government of favouring German propaganda against the Allies and of seeking to destroy pro-Allied organizations; it discovered that the government was dealing with German firms and that visas had been granted to persons suspected of being German spies. But the British Foreign Office often took a different line. It sometimes acknowledged the practical difficulties of administering neutrality in a country in which most of the belligerent powers possessed substantial business interests and sizeable expatriate communities. The British appeared to recognize the absence of a general commitment to the Allied cause in Argentina. By and large public opinion favoured democracy and feared totalitarianism, but clouding such sympathies were the lingering animosities towards Britain that stemmed from the Roca–Runciman Treaty and the deep-seated hostilities towards the United States. Throughout 1942 and early 1943 the

British view, if based on British self-interest, offered a more accurate picture of affairs in Argentina than that of the United States: rather than secretly supporting the Axis, Castillo in fact supported no one. He had no constructive foreign policy at all and aimed merely for a holding operation till the war ended, hoping, it seemed, that at that point Argentina could restore its pre-war relationship with Western Europe and that U.S. pressure would diminish.

In the middle of 1943 Castillo faced yet another domestic political crisis, and this time he failed to surmount it. In April Castillo's refusal to endorse the claims of Rodolfo Moreno, the governor of Buenos Aires Province, to succeed him split the Concordancia. A month or so later it became known that Castillo intended Robustiano Patrón Costas, a leading Tucumán sugar baron and an old-style conservative from the far interior like himself, to become the next president. Within days the news of Castillo's intentions had triggered a military coup d'état which, on 4 June 1943, swept the regime aside with the same ease that the army had dealt with the Radicals in 1930. Once again troops marched into the centre of Buenos Aires to occupy the Casa Rosada, while for a few hours Castillo made futile efforts at resistance from a naval destroyer in the Río de la Plata on which he had taken refuge.

THE RISE OF PERÓN, 1943–6

The coup of June 1943 differed from that of September 1930 in arriving unannounced, without the open civilian unrest that had foreshadowed the fall of Yrigoyen; the population at large appeared taken by surprise. Yet the coup had been in the wind for months. At the time of Castillo's fall, the Concordancia was only a shadow of its original form, and for some time the government had survived thanks only to the army. In two respects the 1943 coup resembled that of 1930: it was conceived and executed by the army alone, and its leaders were divided into 'liberals' and 'nationalists'. The former, initially more substantial in number and rank, aimed to re-create a government like Ortiz's, free of the fraud they expected would accompany the election of Patrón Costas and backed by the great liberal interest groups, or *'fuerzas vivas'*. The liberals could be expected to reach a speedy agreement with the United States, which now meant, before all else, breaking relations with the Axis. The *nacionalistas,* by contrast, were still committed to resisting the United States, to maintaining neutrality and to supporting the development of a national arms industry.

At the heart of the *nacionalista* faction was a secret association of military officers, the Grupo Obra de Unificación (GOU), consisting of only a score of active members, about half of them colonels or of lower rank. The GOU was obsessed with Communism. Before the June revolution, its members seemed less concerned at the prospect of another conservative government elected by fraud than with the possibility that a Communist-controlled popular front would emerge to contest the November elections. The election victory of a popular front, its members claimed, would bring disaster on the scale of the Russian Revolution or the Spanish civil war. The GOU considered it its duty to awaken the army at large to this danger: thus its 'task of unification'. Members of the GOU appeared to be *nacionalistas* in uniform, constantly discussing 'international conspiracies'. The international Masonic movement, for example, was 'a Jewish creation . . . a fearful secret organization, international in character . . . a kind of Mafia writ large. . . . Among its works were the French Revolution, the Spanish Civil War. . . . It is anti-Catholic, and therefore by definition anti-Argentine'. The Rotary Club was a 'network of international Jewish espionage and propaganda in the service of the United States'. And the Popular Front was 'a pseudo-democracy, a vulgar gathering of fellow-travellers (*comunizantes*) serving at the behest of Judaism . . . an openly revolutionary organization trying to repeat the pattern of Spain where the moderates fell and became Communist puppets'. The *nacionalistas,* by contrast, were 'the purest forces, those with the most spiritual awareness within the panorama of Argentine politics'.[37] The close links between the GOU and the *nationalistas* can be illustrated by one remarkable statement purporting to justify the revolution of 1943 and the imposition of military dictatorship, which took the form of a lengthy quotation from St Augustine:

When a people is moderate and serious by custom . . . and esteems the interest of all above private interest, that law is just that allows it to elect its own magistrates. But when little by little it starts to place private interest above the common good, and if corrupted by ambitious men, it lapses into selling its votes and handing over government to the depraved, it is just that the man of goodwill, even though it be a single man possessing the influence or the necessary force, may take away the right of choosing government, and may submit the people to the authority of one man.[38]

---

[37] Quotations from Robert A. Potash (comp.), *Perón y el G.O.U.: Los documentos de una logia secreta* (Buenos Aires, 1984), pp. 101–2, 103, 199, 200.

[38] Quoted in ibid., p. 235.

The titular leader of the June coup d'état was General Arturo Rawson, popular and well connected in both the army and navy and able to unite the two forces against Castillo in a pledge to root out government corruption. But having assumed the presidency Rawson was immediately deposed by his military colleagues following wrangles over the composition of the new cabinet. Into Rawson's place stepped General Pedro Ramírez, who until just a few days before the coup had been Castillo's minister of war. The strength of Ramírez's claim lay in his secret links with the GOU, whose members had in fact sworn allegiance to him, but also in his appeal to liberals and Radicals: in months past there had been hints that the Radicals planned to make Ramírez their candidate in the November elections.

Ramírez's cabinet consisted almost exclusively of members of the armed forces, whose exact political affiliations remained as yet unclear but were in fact divided almost equally into liberals and *nacionalistas*. The one civilian member of the cabinet was Jorge Santamarina, the minister of finance, a liberal widely known as a scion of the *fuerzas vivas* or, as the GOU described him, 'one of them'.[39] At least outwardly the new government appeared to be under liberal control; the U.S. State Department quickly welcomed the coup and hastened to recognize Ramírez, while the German Embassy burnt its secret files the day after the coup. Certainly at this point the liberals controlled foreign policy through Admiral Segundo Storni, the foreign minister. Early in July Ramírez informed the United States that Argentina could be expected to break diplomatic relations with Germany in August. At this point, too, Ramírez, despite his links with the GOU, seemed ready to call early elections, apparently anticipating that he would become the candidate of a coalition headed by the Radicals.

Within a month of the coup, the two factions were engaged in a battle for full control of the military regime, the liberals campaigning to remove the *nacionalistas* from the government with the slogan 'Put the generals before the colonels', the *nacionalistas* counterattacking with their campaign to prevent Ramírez from naming a date for elections, which they argued would bring the Popular Front, and thus the Communists, into power. There were numerous disputes between the two sides over lower-level government appointments, as each struggled to stack the administration with its own appointees. Finally, in early September the liberals attempted to break the deadlock by enlisting the support of the United

[39] Ibid., p. 220.

States. In the celebrated 'Storni letter' the foreign minister, writing to Cordell Hull, intimated that the regime was now ready to break relations with the Axis, but he asked Hull first to lift the arms embargo. Storni argued that lifting the embargo would represent a goodwill gesture by the United States to demonstrate its willingness to restore the strategic balance in South America, removing what Argentina perceived as the military threat from Brazil. The obvious purpose of this request was to trigger a wave of pro-Americanism in the army, which the liberals could then exploit to outmanoeuvre and destroy the *nacionalistas*. But Hull ignored this crucial opportunity to intervene in ways that would further U.S. interests. Against the wishes of his senior advisers led by Sumner Welles, the under-secretary for Latin American affairs, he curtly rejected Storni's request, demanding that Argentina break relations with the Axis without any prior quid pro quo from the United States. In his reply Hull recalled Argentina's behaviour during the Rio de Janeiro conference eighteen months before, when it had systematically defied U.S. policies. The Storni letter thus did nothing to help the liberals; rather it vindicated the *nacionalistas*, strengthening the argument they had made persistently since 1941: the United States was hostile towards Argentina, and therefore Argentina's only recourse was to strike out alone. Within days of Hull's reply reaching Buenos Aires, all the liberals including Storni had resigned from the Ramírez government, to be replaced by *nacionalistas*. Among the new appointments the most significant were those of General Edelmiro Farrell as vice-president and of Gustavo Martínez Zuviría, the notorious anti-Semite novelist 'Hugo Wast', as minister of justice and public instruction. The stage was cleared for the *nacionalista* revolution and the rise of Perón.

Ysabel Rennie's comments on the coup d'état in June 1943, written soon after the event itself, amounted to a highly perceptive view of the future course of Argentina's politics:

When time has lent perspective, this event will be seen for what it was: economically, politically, socially, the most important event . . . since the [revolution of 1890]. For this blow, struck swiftly, and without warning, marked the end of a society, an economy and a way of life. With it were buried the Argentina that lived from beef alone, the Argentina of the Enlightened Oligarchy, liberal Argentina, the free trader, and the hopes, the power and the predominance of the landed aristocracy.[40]

40 Ysabel Rennie, *The Argentine Republic* (New York, 1945), p. 344.

Her judgement was, however, more appropriate to the months immediately following the coup than the coup itself. It was in October, not June, that the most decisive political shift occurred before the final climax of February 1946 when Perón won election as president.

Once the *nacionalistas* had gained full control over the Ramírez junta in October 1943, they moved swiftly to consolidate themselves at home and abroad. They refused any further discussion with the United States on breaking relations with the Axis, and the United States replied by freezing the assets of Argentine banks in the United States. The *nacionalistas* reiterated 'active' neutrality and recommenced the search for allies in Latin America. By late 1943 Argentina had built up a substantial export trade in manufactured goods in Latin America, which Ramírez sought to consolidate by concluding commercial treaties with several neighbouring Latin American states. The regime also began dabbling in its neighbours' politics; in an episode that again created serious friction between Argentina and the United States, a coup d'état in Bolivia in December 1943 brought a neutralist, pro-Argentine regime into power, to which for some time Argentina alone extended diplomatic recognition.

Internally the regime ceased to pretend that it would soon call elections. As a result it began to face growing opposition led by the Radicals. The regime responded with a blend of *nacionalista*-style enactments, repression, incipient populism and a growing flood of propaganda. A 20 per cent reduction in farm tenants' rents and a freeze on urban rents were imposed. The tramways in Buenos Aires, led by the Anglo-Argentine Tramway Company, were forced to cut fares, and the hated Corporación de Transportes was abolished. The regime nationalized the British-owned Primitiva Gas Company. The regime stepped up the drive against corruption and carried out a new wave of purges. It placed the provinces under military *interventores* and extended censorship of the press. At the end of 1944 it abolished all political parties, contending that they had failed to represent 'authentic public opinion' effectively. In the meantime members of the government delivered speech after speech replete with *nacionalista* slogans like 'Honesty, Justice, Duty'; Ramírez himself lauded, in particular, the rural working-class population, 'uncontaminated', as he put it, 'by the exotic ideas of the cities'.

Martínez Zuviría began his term as minister of justice with a speech urging measures to 'Christianize the country. . . . We should increase the birth-rate, not immigration; we must ensure labour's fair share of rewards, and put every household under a decent roof; we have to root out doctrines based on class hatreds and atheism'.[41] To the Church's great approval Martínez Zuviría reimposed religious teaching in the schools for the first time in sixty years and then led a search for 'Communists' in the universities, closing them when students replied with strikes. Anti-Semitic policies were also pursued. Although rumours that the government had set up concentration camps in Patagonia proved false, it suppressed several Jewish welfare associations, dismissed some Jewish teachers and cancelled the citizenship of some naturalized Jews. The *nacionalista* press waged a long campaign against Bemberg, the brewing tycoon. In April 1944 the government took control of the grain export trade and nationalized grain elevators and warehouses, measures that some viewed as anti-Semitic since they were directed against the Big Four grain export houses. Finally, there was another spate of attacks on Communists, this time among the trade unions. Immediately after taking power in June 1943 the government had dissolved a Communist-led faction of the CGT that had succeeded in splitting the federation the previous March. At this point too it destroyed the FONC, the Communist-dominated construction workers' unions. Strikes of meat-packing workers in Buenos Aires in late 1943, denounced by the government as Communist-led, were met by mass arrests. Several trade unions, including the railway organizations, had already been placed under government control through the device of *intervención*.

Much of this government behaviour manifested the negative and purely reactionary face of *nacionalismo,* its exotic blend of prejudices against 'liberalism', 'capitalism', and 'communism', its habit of romanticizing rurality, its blind antipathies towards the 'foreign' and its menacing anti-Semitic impulses. Yet *nacionalismo* remained committed to 'social justice', the purpose of which was to reconstruct the organic national community. This other face of the movement also showed itself within less than a month of the palace revolution of October 1943 with the appointment, on 28 October, of Colonel Juan Domingo Perón as head of the Departamento Nacional del Trabajo. Those close to the regime immediately recognized the great significance of his appointment. Perón, said *Cabildo,* now the leading *nacionalista* daily newspaper, would bring 'weight and efficiency to labour problems', because he knew the 'true needs of the workers' organizations', and would support the unity of the trade union movement, 'always

[41] *Cabildo,* 15 November 1943, 1 January 1944, 2 November 1943.

trying to avoid and solve [*sic*] conflict'. Perón's task was the 'organization of the trade unions'.[42]

Although not as yet a member of the cabinet, and quite unknown to the public, Perón thus emerged in the front ranks of the *nacionalista* regime. He had been among the founders and leaders of the GOU, active in the 'task of unification' campaign in the army, in the conspiracy against Castillo, as a supporter of Ramírez against Rawson in June and more lately as one of the chief figures in the battle between liberals and *nacionalistas*. Of Perón's past career, which since early adolescence he had spent in the army, the most striking feature was his long experience with military politics. Immediately before the 1930 revolution Perón had played a secondary role as an intermediary between the Uriburu and Justo factions, although he had avoided being identified with either of them. Immediately before and after the outbreak of war in 1939, on official missions in several European countries, he had become familiar with the Mussolini and Franco regimes and witnessed the fall of France. Perón enjoyed some standing in the army for his organizational talents and for his academic expertise on the subject of the role of the army in modern society. His views on this issue were typical of the *nacionalistas*. Unlike liberals, who regarded the army in a negative guardian role as a mere adjunct to the state, Perón and the *nacionalistas* saw it as the very epicentre of the national community, charged with leading and mobilizing society. As a member of the GOU Perón had avoided the anti-Semitic and crude xenophobic tirades of his fellow officers, but had distinguished himself as an extreme anti-Communist, apprehensive of Communist intrigues to fashion the Popular Front, and above all fearful of Communist influence in the trade unions. Perón's involvement in labour issues preceded his appointment to the Labour Department. He had been actively seeking contacts in the unions since the June coup d'état, especially in the 'intervened' Unión Ferroviaria, which was now administered by his close personal associate and friend Colonel Domingo Mercante.

By the end of 1943 the various sub-themes of 'social justice' had become subjects of almost daily debate in right-wing, Catholic and *nacionalista* circles in Argentina. For several years past the Alianza Libertadora Argentina had conceptualized social justice as a system of state-controlled trade unions. After the coup of June 1943, while in a typical vein demanding measures against 'Communists' and 'Jews', the Alianza urged the forma-

---

[42] Ibid., 28 October 1943, 30 October 1943.

tion of a 'state-protector of the Argentine working class'.[43] In 1943 the prestigious *Revista de Economía Argentina* devoted great attention to the recently issued Beveridge Plan in Britain and judged the formation of a 'welfare state' the best way to prevent a Communist revolution. Other *nacionalistas* perceived the working class under their control and tutelage as the instrument for carrying them to power: 'The conquest of the state begins with the conquest of the multitude', Marcelo Sánchez Sorondo had declared in May 1943.[44] Most of these ideas of mass mobilization and working-class tutelage sprang from European fascism. But the *nacionalistas* who looked for outside inspiration to create their programmes and strategies no longer had to focus on the now rapidly collapsing Fascist regime in Italy: a model lay much closer at hand in Getúlio Vargas' Brazil: 'Vargas has given an extraordinary impulse to workers' rights in Brazil. He started this activity with the creation of the ministry of labour. . . . The way they deal with this matter in Brazil . . . invites us to consider this as a basis for study and ideas'.[45]

Perón's take-over of the Labour Department in October 1943 could thus be seen as the execution of a long-established *nacionalista* strategy that Perón adopted with the full knowledge and support of his colleagues in the military junta. He made several quite explicit statements of his intentions and objectives, the first in an interview with a Chilean journalist, Abel Valdés, scarcely two weeks after he took office. Throughout this interview Perón made constant reference to *nacionalista* concepts that bore on working-class issues, as he also employed classic *nacionalista* phrasing and vocabulary:

Our revolution is essentially spiritual (*espiritualista*). In Argentina the wealth of the people [ought to stay] in our hands, so that each Argentine may receive the best return on his labours. I myself am a trade unionist (*sindicalista*), and as such I am anti-Communist, but I also believe that labour should be organized in trade union form, so that the workers themselves, and not the agitators who control them, are the ones to reap the benefits of their labours.

His aim, Perón declared, was to

improve the standard of living of the workers, but without tolerating social conflict. . . . I shall not allow free rein to the agents of destruction and agitation, who are often not even Argentines but foreigners. I have working class issues completely under control, and not by force but agreement (*conciliación*). . . .

[43] *La Razón*, 8 June 1943.
[44] Sánchez Sorondo, *La revolución que anunciamos*, p. 246.
[45] *La Razón*, 8 June 1943.

Don't believe we are anti-capitalist. Not at all. [But] international capitalism is quite mistaken if it believes it can conquer the national spirit in Argentina, which this government incarnates.[46]

Thus, in Perón's words the *nacionalistas* were attempting a *spiritual* revolution: the term, borrowed from Spanish conservatism, was among the most common in the lexicon of *nacionalismo*. The *nacionalista* revolution meant keeping the national wealth in the country and giving labour its due share; the purpose of trade union organization was to keep 'agitators' at bay and to improve living standards without provoking class conflict. Perón's remarks on 'international capitalism' also echoed the *nacionalistas*, and his hints that capitalists should make concessions to prevent labour from becoming revolutionary paraphrased the great papal encyclicals *Rerum Novarum* and *Quadragesimo Anno*. Again Perón had avoided explicit anti-Semitic remarks, but his simultaneous strictures against communism and 'international capitalism' adopted the general suppositions and the outlook on which anti-Semitism in Argentina was based.

The Valdés interview marked the first occasion on which Perón had exposed himself to the public at large. His air was one of confidence; his performance was appealing and provoked Valdés himself into making a memorable forecast: 'My general impression is that the present Argentine government is united, powerful and strong. . . . Another of my impressions is that . . . Colonel Juan Perón may very soon become the supreme chief (*el caudillo máximo*) in the Argentine Republic, and who knows for how long'.[47] Soon after, in an open letter to Ramírez, Perón modestly denied that he aspired to anything beyond his current position, but it was clear to all that he was rapidly gaining personal impetus and political stature.

At the end of November, in a decree signed by all eight members of the cabinet, the government replaced the Labour Department with the Secretaría de Trabajo y Bienestar Social, a measure which brought Perón, as its head, into the cabinet. In a lengthy preamble to the decree, Perón outlined his plans with respect to labour still more explicitly. The Secretaría de Trabajo, said the preamble, would serve as an 'organization that centralizes and controls', to produce 'greater harmony between the productive forces: to strengthen national unity through a greater measure of social and distributive justice . . . conceived in the Christian way in the

---

[46] *Cabildo*, 11 November 1943.
[47] Ibid., 11 November 1943.

light of the great encyclicals'. Speaking to a group of workers a few days after, Perón declared: 'I am a soldier in the most powerful unionized association (*gremie*) of all: the military. And I therefore advise you that to achieve the same cohesion and strength that we have, always remain united'.[48]

As Perón spelled out his intentions towards the unions, there were some immediate signs of labour's willingness to collaborate. In December 1943 the Secretaría de Trabajo reached an agreement on pay and fringe benefits with the Unión Ferroviaria, which amounted to conceding to the union virtually everything it had demanded but had been continually denied since 1929. Soon after this, union leaders led by the CGT's secretary, José Domenech, hailed Perón as 'Argentina's Number One Worker'. Perón ended the year with a public appeal to businessmen to volunteer a Christmas bonus to their workers in the shape of an extra month's wage. The campaign to further 'social justice' continued into 1944, as the *nacionalista* press, led by *Cabildo*, declaimed Perón's achievements as it fulminated against what it would characteristically describe as the pernicious canker (*ingerte*) of Manchester liberalism'.[49] In February 1944 Perón gained new prominence when he placed himself at the head of relief operations following a devastating earthquake that levelled the city of San Juan. At this point, too, Perón began his soon notorious relationship with the actress Eva Duarte, who was among a team of popular entertainers involved in the San Juan relief campaign.

Soon after the San Juan disaster, however, a new foreign affairs crisis suddenly overshadowed Perón's activities among the trade unions. Following the Storni letter affair the United States had intensified its economic boycott and renewed its propaganda campaign against Argentina, both of which had been briefly suspended since Castillo's overthrow. The campaign reached a climax in December 1943 following the coup d'état in Bolivia, amidst reports that Argentina was involved in a similar conspiracy to overthrow the government of Uruguay. The *nacionalista* regime now redoubled its efforts to create an arms industry, but in a desperate effort to relieve its immediate military weaknesses it began plotting to buy arms from Nazi Germany. This move proved a disastrous blunder, since Osmar Hellmuth, Ramírez's secret agent, was arrested by the British in Trinidad en route to Spain and Germany, and the British passed on information

[48] Ibid., 30 November 1943; *La Razón*, 10 December 1943.
[49] *Cabildo*, 12 January 1944.

about his activities to the State Department. The Hellmuth affair finally provided the United States with what appeared to be concrete proof of Argentina's collusion with the Axis, and armed with this evidence the State Department immediately threatened to make it public, placing Ramírez in an untenable position. He soon surrendered, and on 26 January decreed the break in diplomatic relations that the United States had demanded unsuccessfully since 1942.

Except to the handful of those familiar with the details of the Hellmuth case and its consequences, the diplomatic break lacked any rational explanation and seemed an unintelligible capitulation to U.S. pressures. The break in relations therefore precipitated an immediate political crisis that came to a head in the second week of February, as the government sought to silence a rising flood of criticism from the *nacionalistas* by suddenly dissolving and banning all the *nacionalista* associations. After the ban came a spate of cabinet resignations, which included that of Colonel Alberto Gilbert, who as foreign minister became the immediate scapegoat for the Hellmuth mission, and that of Martínez Zuviría, who left the government in protest against both the diplomatic break and the ban on the *nacionalistas*. But then as the *nacionalistas* fought back, Ramírez himself was ousted on 25 February by his critics, who forced him to take a temporary leave of the presidency that soon after they made permanent. The Hellmuth affair had thus brought down Ramirez and others, but left the *nacionalista* regime as a whole quite unshaken, as the United States acknowledged when it refused the new government diplomatic recognition. The episode marked another crucial stage in the rise of Perón. As Vice-president Farrell replaced Ramírez as president, he relinquished the position he had hitherto held as minister of war to Perón, at first temporarily but soon after permanently. Thanks to the fall of Ramírez, Perón now controlled two cabinet posts.

Under Farrell, Argentina continued to be estranged from the United States, and although meat shipments to Britain continued, the United States maintained a virtual blockade on supplies to Argentina. The regime replied to its forced isolation by launching a vast military mobilization of men and resources. By late 1945 it had tripled the size of the army, while increasing the military's share of government spending from 17 per cent in 1943 to 43 per cent in 1945. As the army grew, its personnel were deployed into road construction; new experimental industrial plants were formed under army control and supervision; the army led eager searches for industrial raw materials in the Andean region. In April 1944 the government established a Banco Industrial, charged with financing industries deemed of national interest, which meant primarily the state corporations producing armaments.

Rapid militarization in 1944, which started principally as a response to U.S. pressures, thus quickly became an instrument of economic policy, a means to funnel resources into industrialization. Militarization corresponded to the basic tenets of *nacionalismo,* which regarded the army as an instrument for reshaping society. But an overtly authoritarian structure was now taking shape. As it expanded the armed forces, the government imposed still more restrictions on the press and in April 1944 inflicted a five-day ban on *La Prensa.* At the end of July Farrell officiated over a great torchlit gathering in the Avenida Nueve de Julio in Buenos Aires. To an audience estimated to be a quarter of a million he issued a 'Declaration of Sovereignty':

Today . . . the entire people of the Republic . . . has understood the fundamental truths of nationalism (*nacionalismo*). . . . [This demonstration] reveals the existence of a powerful national movement (*fuerza*), seeking ends that are purely national, and which therefore cannot be a political party, because it does not defend the interests of any 'part' against any other part, but the grandeur of the whole nation.[50]

Still more *nacionalista* edicts flowed from the government, among them a 'peon's statute', which in setting minimum wages for rural workers exemplified the long-standing concern of the *nacionalistas* with the rural population. In mid-October Farrell presided over a ceremony that symbolically 'consecrated' the armed forces to 'the Virgin', an act meant to evoke the 'union of the Cross and the Sword' that formed the *nacionalista* vision of the Spanish conquest of the Americas.

Thus, despite the confusion of the Hellmuth affair, the *nacionalista* regime continued to gain momentum and to acquire an increasingly aggressive character. After the fall of Ramírez, Perón rededicated himself to his activities in the Secretaría de Trabajo and was now busily weeding out opponents in the unions, principally Socialists. By June, having eliminated its leader, Francisco Pérez Leiros, he had gained control of the large metal-workers' union, the Unión Obrera Metalúrgica. Unmistakeable signs now appeared that he had started to mobilize a vast popular constituency. In March 1944 a large number of railwaymen demonstrated on his behalf. For the first time ever the CGT joined the annual parade of 25 May

[50] Ibid., 29 July 1944.

to commemorate the revolution of May 1810. Throughout this period Perón remained in constant touch with trade union leaders, promising, exhorting and if necessary threatening them. His message remained the same as in late 1943: he urged unity, and he constantly promulgated the classical Catholic precept of 'social justice':

. . . the new social policy . . . is based on the need . . . to avoid a situation where some men are unduly rich and others unduly poor. The wisdom of the ancients *'in medio veritas'* continues to be valid. . . . Truth stands at the mean, at a due balance being maintained in the sharing of wealth so as to eliminate the absurd polarization . . . between the class of the wealthy and powerful and the class of beggars . . . a healthy balance . . . understanding and conciliation between the classes. . . . In his speech . . . Perón mentioned all the points that comprise the Christian concept of social justice contained in the great papal encyclicals.[51]

From his other position as minister of war, Perón actively supervised the expansion of the army, while increasing his own power and prestige within it. As minister he controlled communications between the government and the military, and he fully exploited his power over supplies, patronage and promotions at a time when the military budget was growing at an accelerating pace. Perón emerged as the foremost ideologue of the *nacionalista* proposition that the role of the army was to direct public policy and to construct a new society. On 11 June 1944 he delivered his most powerful speech to date, in which he advanced his concept of the 'nation in arms'. War, Perón declared, was an inevitable consequence of the human condition. But each nation's best deterrent against it was to become militarily strong, and military strength required the mobilization of all available resources; mobilization in turn meant industrialization and 'social justice'. 'Si vis pacem, para bellum', he proclaimed: 'If you wish peace, prepare for war'.[52]

In the United States Perón's speech was attacked as 'totalitarian', and it brought a further cooling of relations. Henceforth, the State Department referred frequently to the Argentine regime as 'Nazi'. But in Argentina itself the speech served to advance Perón's political standing. Thousands of trade unionists responded to the attacks on Perón in the United States with popular demonstrations. Capitalizing on his ever-growing stature, less than a month after the speech Perón provoked a conflict over spheres

[51] Ibid., 25 June, 1944.
[52] *La Prensa,* 11 June 1944.

of authority with General Luis Perlinger, who as minister of the interior had become his leading rival in the junta. In this conflict Perón proved irresistible, carrying the rest of the government along with him in a demand that Perlinger resign. When Perlinger did so, Perón acquired yet a third office, the vice-presidency, which had been vacant since the fall of Ramírez in February.

Within scarcely a year of the June 1943 coup d'état against Castillo, Perón had unquestionably become the leading figure in the military regime; Farrell retreated into the role of figurehead president. In the middle of 1944 Perón faced only two remaining adversaries: the U.S. State Department and an amorphous but large mass of domestic opponents, led by the Radicals and the *fuerzas vivas*, beneficiaries of the old liberal economy threatened by government policies of state-directed industrialization and social reform. For the rest of 1944 the State Department showed little interest in Argentina. The economic sanctions remained, but the United States proved unable to take further action against Argentina, mainly because of British opposition. By late 1944 domestic opposition to Perón was increasing, but it remained extremely disunited and unfocussed. The liberation of Paris in August provoked large street demonstrations in Buenos Aires which turned into an angry outburst against the regime for its 'Nazi sympathies'. Spokesmen for the still-banned political parties occasionally issued demands for elections, and the 'peon's statute' provoked a flood of criticisms from ranchers' and farmers' associations led by the Sociedad Rural Argentina. At the end of the year Perón became embroiled in a bitter dispute with the Unión Industrial Argentina, the chief industrial employers' organization, when he instituted an obligatory year-end workers' bonus, the *aguinaldo*, which the year before had been purely voluntary. But the nature of Argentine politics was being rapidly transformed: each time Perón's opponents, at home and abroad, struck out against him, his trade union and working-class followers immediately responded to support him.

As he erected his popular alliance, Perón benefited from various conditions that helped make labour responsive to his appeal. First, an industrialization policy that increased urban employment inevitably proved popular among a rapidly growing working class. Second, although between 1941 and 1945 the total number of *workers* affiliated in unions with the CGT increased relatively slowly from 441,000 to 528,000, or by 17.7 per cent, the number of *unions* affiliated with the CGT increased during the same period from 356 to 969, or by 285 per cent, a trend that illustrated the spread of trade unionism into the new small-scale manufacturing sectors. As a result, as it began its operations, the labour secretariat had a mass of potential contacts to which it could attach itself throughout the labour force. Employers, however, confronted by a sellers' labour market and separated from one another by enormous differences of scale, found it difficult to unite themselves in common resistance either to the unions or to Perón. Third, unlike the period 1914–19, which saw a steep decline in real wages, the years 1939–45 witnessed a slow increase in real wages, principally because of the growth of new industrial jobs and abundant cheap grains. In 1940 average real wages stood at roughly the same level as they had in 1929 and grew by 10 per cent by 1944. Strikes occurred much less frequently during the early 1940s than they had twenty-five years before. Between 1940 and 1944 the incidence of strikes, measured by man-hours lost, remained at only one-third that of 1915–19, although the labour force had roughly doubled between the two periods. Thus, during the Second World War, not only was labour less militant than it had been twenty-five years earlier, but the unions tended to be less concerned with wages than with fringe benefits such as sick pay, bonuses, paid vacations and accident compensation.

Fringe benefits were easier to deliver than wage increases, and were exactly the type of rewards the Secretaría de Trabajo could arrange. Equally, it proved much easier to deal with labour when the main issue concerned relatively superficial improvements to already fairly acceptable conditions, rather than the survival of desperate workers, often at the point of rebellion, as had been the case twenty-five years before. Perón's basic techniques were to enforce labour legislation that already existed, to support wage increases in sectors where unions were already organized and to promote new unions where none existed. Perón gained some advantage from the purge of Communist union leaders soon after the June 1943 coup. The Communists were the union leaders likely to have resisted him most tenaciously. Yet they remained few in number, and the government constantly exaggerated their influence. Nor was their standing among workers very secure, since throughout the war they had avoided militant stances that might affect the war effort. Although many union leaders in 1943–5 resisted dealing with Perón and attempted to keep their distance, rank-and-file pressures frequently forced them into contact with the Secretaría de Trabajo. By late 1944 the Secretaría had begun to deal only with unions that possessed *personería gremial,* or full legal standing conferred by the government. But to gain this status, unions had to be controlled by leaders acceptable to Perón, which meant those willing to follow his orders.

On the international front, after Cordell Hull's resignation as secretary of state in November 1944, responsibility for Latin American affairs in the State Department passed to Nelson Rockefeller, the new under-secretary. Supported by numerous manufacturing associations in the United States that regarded Argentina as a large potential post-war market, Rockefeller now led an attempt to win greater co-operation from Argentina through concessions. Soon after November the United States re-established diplomatic relations, lightened the trade and financial embargoes and hinted at its willingness to terminate the wartime ban on arms sales to Argentina. This new-style diplomacy had several, almost instant positive results. In February 1945 Argentina became a signatory to the Act of Chapultepec, which pledged inter-American co-operation on mutual defence and trade. Finally, towards the end of March Argentina declared war on Germany and Japan. At this point, with Germany's capitulation scarcely a month away, the declaration of war was only token, but in making the gesture Argentina ensured its admission to the United Nations, while suggesting a readiness for quite different future relations with the United States. For a fleeting period it thus seemed that the aspirations of the Pinedo Plan of late 1940 might ultimately be accomplished under the military junta.

However, the new approach to Argentina under Rockefeller ceased abruptly after mid-April when Truman replaced Roosevelt as president and the State Department underwent yet another reshuffle. Although Rockefeller remained at his post for some time, control over policy towards Argentina passed to Spruille Braden, one of the leading critics of Argentina's wartime neutrality and of the current Argentine government. As the war in Europe ended, the United States at last freed itself of British restraints, and led by Braden it now directed its energies into a campaign to sweep Perón and the *nacionalista* regime aside. In May Braden was designated ambassador to Argentina, and by June he was touring the country attacking the government and demanding immediate elections; he urged Washington to afford no further assistance to Argentina 'until such time as the Nazi militaristic control of this country has been replaced by a constitutional and cooperating [*sic*] democracy'.[53]

In the meantime, Perón had continued to expand and consolidate his

[53] Cable of 11 July 1945. Quoted in Bryce Wood, *The Dismantling of the Good Neighbor Policy* (Austin, Tex., 1985), p. 96.

alliance with the trade unions. In his most prominent speech of this period he defined his goal as the 'peaceful revolution of the masses':

> If we fail to carry out the Peaceful Revolution, the People themselves will take the road of Violent Revolution. . . . And the solution to the whole problem is social justice towards the masses. . . . Naturally this is not a popular idea among rich men. . . . But they are their own worst enemies. Better to offer 30 per cent now, than within years, or perhaps even months, to risk losing all they have, including their ears.[54]

Indeed, the message was not popular among 'rich men', and in mid-1945 Spruille Braden's activities swiftly rekindled the opposition to Perón that for some months past had remained largely dormant. In June a 'Manifesto of the *Fuerzas Vivas*' attacked the government's social reforms, but this document was closely followed by a counter-manifesto from the trade unions 'in defence of the benefits won through the Secretaría de Trabajo y Bienestar Social'.

Finally, on 19 September, after three months of growing tension, thousands upon thousands of Perón's opponents gathered in the streets of Buenos Aires in a 'March of the Constitution and Liberty'. Five days later General Arturo Rawson, the one-day president of June 1943, led an unsuccessful coup d'état from Córdoba. At the end of September the navy pronounced in favour of a return to civilian rule. Soon after, the government itself split between the opponents of Perón led by General Eduardo Avalos and Perón's supporters. On 9 October Avalos succeeded in forcing Perón into resigning his multiple posts in the government. Three days later he was imprisoned on the island of Martín García. It seemed now that under challenge, *'peronismo'* had collapsed and that Farrell would soon concede the chief demands of the liberal 'constitutionalists': set a date for elections, while ceding control to a caretaker government headed by the justices of the Supreme Court.

Then came what Sir David Kelly, the British ambassador, described as an 'incredible comedy'. With victory in its grasp the movement to destroy Perón faltered. In the days that followed his fall, bickering within the liberal coalition delayed the efforts of Juan Alvarez, the chief justice of the Supreme Court, to organize a caretaker government. Other conflicts arose between the leaders of the coalition and the army. If the latter, led by Avalos, had eventually bent to pressure and sacrificed Perón, it stopped

[54] Quoted in Darío Cantón, 'El ejército en 1930: El antes y el después', in Haydée Gorostegui de Torres (ed.), *Historia integral Argentina*, vol. 7 (Buenos Aires, 1970), p. 11.

short of further steps that would have meant the collapse and termination of the 1943 revolution. Within the army, partly out of concern for future reprisals but also because of an unwillingness to surrender its new powers in both the government and the economy, resistance quickly grew to the plan to hand over the government to the Supreme Court. As the deadlock continued, events suddenly took a decisive turn when on 17 October thousands of workers marched into the centre of Buenos Aires to demand Perón's release from imprisonment. Had the army wanted a new government dominated by the liberals, it might have acted quickly to prevent the workers' march. Not only did it permit the march, but it allowed Perón, who two days earlier had returned to Buenos Aires from Martín García, having convinced his captors that he required medical treatment, to address the vast crowds gathered in the Plaza de Mayo from the Casa Rosada. He proclaimed an 'indestructible union of brotherhood between the people [and] the army'.[55] After 17 October the Avalos faction in the Farrell government resigned; Perón and his supporters returned to power.

To all contemporary observers the workers' march occurred quite spontaneously. Yet Perón had obviously planned an event of this sort as part of his strategy for political survival. While taking leave of his staff on 10 October, he urged an attempt to rally popular support. After his fall, his leading associates led by Domingo Mercante toured the industrial and working-class areas of the city, urging action on his behalf. Many workers had already begun to strike by 13 October, after numerous employers had refused to observe Perón's enactment that the 12th, the 'Dia de la Raza', be treated as a workers' holiday. Attempts by workers to cross the Río Riachuelo, which divided the federal capital from the province of Buenos Aires, began on 16 October. The great march of 17 October owed virtually nothing to the CGT, whose leaders met only on the evening of the 16th as the demonstrations were reaching a crescendo. Even then the CGT voted to support action by the slender margin of 21 to 19. Above all the '*17 de octubre*' appeared to be an exhibition of established behaviour, since for the past year or more unions and workers had grown steadily accustomed to responding to threats against Perón through popular mobilization.

The events of September–October 1945 demonstrated the extent to which in only two years Perón had totally transformed Argentine politics: he had rendered the fifty-year-long feud between the Radicals and the

<hr/>

[55] The literal translation of this phrase reads 'brotherhood between the people, the army and the police'. See Felix Luna, *El '45* (Buenos Aires, 1971), p. 295.

conservatives an anachronism; he had precipitated the working class into politics, while virtually eliminating the traditional working-class parties, in particular the Socialists; he had divided the country into the *'peronista'* supporters of 'economic independence' and 'social justice' and 'anti-*peronista'* defenders of the old liberal order. In November, although it continued to resist making way to a government under the Supreme Court the junta announced elections for February 1946. By December 1945 Perón's opponents had finally overcome their internal differences and united in a Unión Democrática (UD) to contest the elections. The Radicals dominated this coalition, but alongside them stood a disparate mélange that included remnants of the conservative National Democratic Party, the Socialist Party and the Communist Party. The UD represented the closest analogue that appeared in Argentina to the Popular Front against which the GOU had mobilized in 1943. But the UD lacked the main ingredient of the Popular Front: the support of the organized working class. Behind its reformist façade, the coalition subsisted on little more than the impulse to oppose Perón. Nevertheless, led by José Tamborini, a former Radical with a political background similar to that of Roberto M. Ortiz, the UD remained confident of a sweeping electoral victory.

For Perón the crisis of September–October 1945 had ended in a nearby miraculous escape from political oblivion and yet, despite the 17 *de octubre*, not in any final victory. He now faced the challenge of contesting an election against a coalition that comprised nearly all of the political parties with little organization of his own. He had the support of the unions in Buenos Aires, but almost none beyond. In less than five months he had to build a national coalition. First, Perón secured the support of the Partido Laborista, a new working-class party backed by the unions that was modelled roughly on the British Labour Party. Second, after numerous earlier failures during 1944 and 1945, Perón finally managed to win over a substantial minority of Radicals. Hortensio Quijano, the leader of the dissident Radical faction, the Unión Cívica Radical–Junta Renovadora, which now supported Perón, became his running mate and helped project the movement into the provinces. Among the other Radical defectors to join Perón in late 1945 were several leading members of the FORJA, along with some of the conservative *nacionalistas* led by the Alianza Libertadora Nacionalista. In the provinces Perón added further to his following by attracting a few conservative local political bosses who had last tasted power under Castillo and who remained opposed at all costs to the Radicals. Finally, Perón enjoyed support from the Church, as he undertook to retain the religious teaching in the schools that Martínez Zuviría had reintroduced in 1943 and continually reminded Church leaders that Communists formed part of the UD. In late 1945 *'peronismo'* thus mushroomed swiftly beyond its Buenos Aires trade union base into a heterogeneous movement with new sources of support in the provinces and the rural population.

As the election of February 1946 approached, having begun far behind his opponent Tamborini, Perón was gaining ground rapidly. Then only days before the election the U.S. State Department issued a 'Blue Book: A Memorandum of the United States Government [to other Latin American governments] With Respect to the Argentine Situation'. Spruille Braden, now assistant secretary of state, had instigated the preparation and distribution of this document, the aim of which was to show 'how Nazi agents in Argentina . . . had combined with totalitarian groups to create a Nazi-Fascist state'.[56] The report presented materials collected by the United States during the war that sought to show that members of successive governments in Argentina and senior military personnel, including Perón himself, had colluded with the Axis. It repeated the charges that Argentina had tolerated or encouraged German espionage and propaganda; it cited the pro-Axis speeches of military leaders, dealings between governments and German firms and loans by German banks to Argentine politicians.

The 'Blue Book' was received on almost all sides in Argentina as a crude foreign ploy to influence the elections. It instantly rekindled nationalist sympathies, crippled the UD and gave Perón a major issue with which to rally the electorate. In an interview with a Brazilian journalist, Perón sarcastically thanked Braden 'for the votes he has given me. If I carry two-thirds of the electorate, I shall owe one-third to Braden'.[57] In the run up to the election the *peronista* campaign rang with the cry of 'Braden or Perón!': surrender to U.S. pressures or a bold commitment alongside Perón to a programme of revolutionary change. When the vote was counted, Perón had won 52.4 per cent against Tamborini's 42.5 per cent (1.49 million votes against 1.21 million), with the rest of the vote being won by minor parties. But having carried eleven of fifteen provinces, including the federal capital, Perón gained an overwhelming majority in the electoral college. He would now take office as president on 4 June 1946, the third anniversary of the 1943 coup.

[56] Quoted in Wood, *Dismantling of the Good Neighbor Policy*, p. 113.
[57] Quoted in Enrique Díaz Araujo, *La conspiración del '43* (Buenos Aires, 1971), p. 95.

The 1946 election showed that the bastions of *peronismo* lay in the capital and in two of the three principal littoral provinces, Buenos Aires and Santa Fe. In all three jurisdictions the *peronista* alliance captured more than 50 per cent of the popular vote. Within the littoral only Córdoba fell to the UD, thanks to a hastily arranged and fragile alliance between Radicals and conservatives. *Peronistas* gained a majority in Mendoza and Tucumán, the leading wine and sugar provinces, both of which had a large number of rural and urban workers, and in the most backward provinces of the West and North, which held large peasant communities: Catamarca, La Rioja and Santiago del Estero. In the eastern cities, above all Buenos Aires, the Partido Laborista won the vote of almost the entire working class, both the 'new' workers composed of migrants employed in new manufacturing and services and the 'old' proletariat that before had voted Socialist.[58] In the capital and its main suburbs led by Avellaneda, *peronismo* thus emerged as an overwhelmingly working-class movement, gathering support from only a small minority of other sectors. But elsewhere Perón's support was much more mixed and included numerous rural groups that had often supported conservative candidates. The dissident Radical Junta Renovadora faction supporting Perón played an important part in the election by taking votes from the orthodox Radical (Unión Cívica Radical) ticket.

In 1946 Argentina thus embarked on Perón's revised, popular version of the Nationalist Revolution. Until late in 1940 there had been few hints of the imminence of this great transition. That the shift occurred partly reflected the accident of Ortiz's retirement and early death, since if Ortiz had survived, the conflicts between Radicals and conservatives that undermined Castillo might have been much less acute. Yet the change of president alone did not release the forces that destroyed liberal-conservatism. Equally significant for its collapse were the Second World War and the failure to reach agreement with the United States, which provided the *nacionalistas* with the opportunity to spread their alternative vision of Argentina's future.

---

[58] The distinction between the 'old' and 'new' working classes and their contribution to Perón's electoral support in 1946 is documented and debated in Peter H. Smith, 'La base social del peronismo', and Gino Germani, 'El surgimiento del peronismo: El rol de los obreros y de los migrantes internos', in Manuel Mora y Araujo and Ignacio. Llorente (eds.), *El voto personista: Ensayos de sociología electoral argentina* (Buenos Aires, 1980), pp. 39–164.

Twentieth-century Argentina

7

ARGENTINA SINCE 1946

THE *PERONISTA* DECADE, 1946 – 55

On 24 February 1946 General Juan Domingo Perón was elected president of Argentina in an open poll. This victory was the culmination of his dizzying political rise, which had begun a few years earlier when the military revolution of June 1943 put an end to a decade of conservative governments and brought to power a clique of army colonels with fascist sympathies. The emerging military regime had been groping its way between the hostility that its authoritarian and clerical tendencies had awakened in the middle and upper classes and the diplomatic quarantine organized by the United States in reprisal for Argentina's neutral position in the Second World War. Through clever palace manoeuvring Perón became the regime's dominant figure and ended the political isolation of the military elite by launching a set of labour reforms that had a powerful impact on the working class, whose numbers had swelled with industrialization and urbanization since the mid-1930s. In Perón's vision, the function of these reforms was to prevent the radicalization of conflicts and the spread of Communism. But the Argentine bourgeoisie did not fear an imminent social revolution, a fear which, at other times and in other places, had facilitated the acceptance of similar reforms. As a result, they joined the anti-fascist front organized by the middle class, imbuing political cleavages with a visible class bias.

In 1945, the new climate created by the imminent triumph of the Allied forces led the military authorities to look for an institutional solution. Perón, after trying with limited success to obtain the backing of the tradi-

We would like to express our thanks to Guido di Tella, whose manuscript on the economic history of this period helped us greatly, although the final responsibility for this work is ours alone. The chapter was translated from the Spanish by Elizabeth Ladd.

tional parties, decided to launch his presidential candidacy by appealing to the popular support he had developed when in office. In October 1945, this mass following proved decisive when a military plot instigated by the opposition was on the point of interrupting his political career. A popular mobilization, organized by the unions and abetted by Perón's supporters in the army and the police force, succeeded in releasing him from jail and reinstating him in the electoral contest. Perón's candidacy was sustained by the unions, which were the main force behind the newly established Labour Party, together with dissidents from the Radical Party organized in the Junta Renovadora. The opposition centred on the Unión Democrática, a coalition of centrist and leftist parties which had considerable backing from the business community and the U.S. government. Perón took full advantage of these circumstances to present himself as a champion of social justice and national interests and to win the elections held in February 1946.

Formed over a relatively brief period from sectors of different origins, the *peronista* coalition was on the verge of disintegration once the elections were over. At the center of the conflict were the union leaders of the Labour Party and the dissident radical politicians of the Junta Renovadora. According to constitutional law, representatives to the Senate were elected indirectly by the provincial legislatures. Before the elections, labour and the junta had agreed to share the seats in the Senate equally, but after the poll, the politicians used specious arguments and bribery in an effort to oust the labour leaders in the Senate and the provincial cabinets. In this conflict Perón decided to support more docile elements from the traditional parties and lessen the influence of labour. A few days before assuming the presidency in June, he ordered the dissolution of the parties of the electoral alliance and called for the creation of a new party, invoking the need for cohesive movement in order to govern with effectiveness and unity. The leaders of the Labour Party, which was more insistent on its own autonomy than was the Junta Renovadora, debated what course to follow for several days. Finally, arguments in favour of unity won them over. They were promised a representative place in the new party in exchange for the renunciation of their old political ambitions. The potential benefits entailed in their inclusion in the official political order promised more than did the defence of independence, which would place them on the margins of the nascent *peronista* Argentina.

Thus, labour's brief resistance ended in the middle of June 1946. Perón appointed the organizers of the new party from among the recently elected legislators. Although there were a few union men, the majority were middle-class politicians. This tendency would become accentuated over time. There was no place in the scheme of the new organization for sectors which had a power base independent of the party itself.

In January 1947, when the organizers of the new party approached Perón to approve the name 'Partido Peronista', they explicitly sanctioned another and more decisive feature of the political structure of the movement. Personalism was an almost inevitable consequence of a movement formed in such a short period of time out of the convergence of heterogeneous forces. Moreover, Perón was careful to avoid being influenced by the forces that supported him. Article 31 of the statutes of the Partido Peronista, approved in December 1947, empowered him to modify all decisions made by the party as well as to review all candidacies. Although Perón owed an obvious ideological debt to the authoritarian tradition in which he had been trained, conflict within the triumphant bloc of 1946 also imposed a strong and centralized leadership role upon him. Anarchy was, in fact, the distinctive feature of the *peronista* movement during the first years. Only the constant exercise of authority by Perón himself neutralized the general lack of discipline among his followers.

Shortly after taking office Perón resolved local problems, beginning in the province of Catamarca, by replacing local authorities with an official appointed by the central administration. This mechanism of control, provided for in the constitution, was amply used during the first year – in Córdoba in 1947, La Rioja, Santiago del Estero and Catamarca again in 1948 and Santa Fe in 1949. Even Corrientes, the only province where the opposition had triumphed in 1946, was subjected to intervention in 1947.

Perón also attacked the last bastion of the survivors of the Labour Party. In November 1946 Luis Gay, former president of the party, was elected secretary-general of the Confederación General del Trabajo (CGT) and tried to follow an independent line. The controversial visit of a delegation of U.S. labour leaders gave Perón an opportunity to accuse Gay of plotting to withdraw CGT support from the government and joining the inter-American union movement promoted from the United States. The accusation unleashed a violent campaign against Gay in the official press, and he had to resign in January 1947. A few of his close associates resigned with him, but the majority chose to adapt to the new order. Led by figures of second rank, the CGT henceforth became an agency of official directives within the labour movement.

Step by step, Perón quelled those independent forces he had been obliged to tolerate during the election campaign. Besides the Partido Peronista and the CGT, the other fundamental pillar of the regime was the armed forces. The open breach between the military and the democratic opposition in 1945 had allowed Perón to pursue the presidency. After he was elected, he once again presented himself as a man of arms in an effort to gain the support of the military establishment. However, he sought to define his relations with the military on strictly institutional bases, and although many officers served in the government, the institution as a whole was not involved. Perón set as an objective the neutrality of the officer corps; to achieve this he addressed himself above all to the satisfaction of their professional demands.

These were the years of expansion and modernization in the armed forces. As a result of the boom in military investment following the 1943 coup, military spending represented 38.4 per cent of the national budget by 1945. The percentage decreased to 20.6 in 1951, but even this was well above the pre-war level of 18.2 per cent, and Argentina continued to earmark more of its budget for defence than did any other Latin American state. The enlargement of the officer corps at a faster rate than the increase in enlisted men (the number of generals doubled between 1946 and 1951) and the purchase of modern equipment permitted the armed forces to tolerate the regime during the early years.

This political exchange would not have been possible without some degree of identification by the military with the general principles of Perón's government. Nationalism, industrialization and social justice were congruent with deeply rooted beliefs among the officer corps. In addition, a prudent manipulation of internal rivalries and the distribution of favours helped to isolate the least trustworthy elements and reward the loyalty of the most faithful. Confined to a professional role that yielded tangible benefits, the armed forces were progressively integrated into the *peronista* regime.

The Church also contributed to the consolidation of the new regime. It had played a positive role even during Perón's election campaign of 1946. Harassed by anticlericalism among the traditional political forces, the ecclesiastical hierarchy, imbued with anti-liberal ideology, welcomed Perón's consistent homage to the social doctrine of the Church. On the eve of the election it circulated a flyer recommending that people not vote for candidates whose programmes and attitudes contradicted the Catholic message. This warning obviously applied to the Unión Democrática, which objected to the military government's 1943 decision to include religious instruction by decree in the schools. Once in power, Perón transformed the decree into law. Later, official activity in the field of social welfare and education cooled the bishops' enthusiasm, since they found it difficult to reconcile their support of Perón with their traditional links to the upper class. Nevertheless, they refrained from making these reservations public, in an effort to achieve peaceful coexistence with the new political order.

With the backing of the army and the Church, and the loyalty of a popular mass soon corralled under a centralized leadership, the new regime had established secure foundations. But Perón also decided to reinforce his government through bureaucratic and repressive mechanisms. The first victim was the Supreme Court, which had resisted Perón's social reforms from the beginning. In September 1946, its members were accused in Congress of, among other things, having recognized as legitimate the de facto governments that arose out of the military coups of 1930 and 1943. Eight months later they were dismissed as part of a general purge of the judicial power. Another stronghold of resistance in 1945, the university, went through a similar process with the expulsion of thousands of professors. In 1947 training schools run by opposition parties were closed, and economic groups linked to the regime began to buy up the national radio broadcasting system. In 1951 the expropriation of one of the most traditional papers, *La Prensa,* and its transfer to the CGT led to a virtual state monopoly over the mass media. Those who survived with a degree of independence took care not to challenge openly the proselytizing tone used by the official media to praise the policies of the regime.

With this gradual suppression of public freedoms, the political opposition found itself limited to the congressional sphere. However, the narrow margin of votes that had granted victory to the *peronista* coalition was transformed by electoral legislation into an overwhelming government majority. The application of the Sáenz Peña law, which awarded two-thirds of the electoral seats to the majority and the remaining third to the leading minority party, gave the *peronistas* control not only over executive power but also over the lower house, with 109 deputies out of 158. Furthermore, thirteen of the fourteen provincial governments went to the *peronistas,* and this gave them control of the Senate.

The psychological shock the opposition forces experienced following defeat in the elections was magnified when they realized that they had practically disappeared from the political map. The Partido Demócrata and the *antipersonalista* Unión Cívica Radical (UCR), which had governed between 1932 and 1943, were reduced to three deputies and two senators.

The Socialist Party, whose presence in Congress had been continuous since 1904, did not have a single representative; nor did the Communist Party. Only the Radicals had managed to survive, although they were reduced to forty-four deputies.

The regime's authoritarian tendencies hardly encouraged a reduction of political antagonisms. The small, militant opposition bloc would not declare a truce with the official movement, but its criticism did not extend beyond Congress, and even there it was silenced by the pressure of the large *peronista* majority. In the congressional elections of 1948, the 52 per cent obtained by the *peronista* coalition in 1946 rose to 57 per cent, concentrating political power even more.

Its legitimacy guaranteed on the internal front, the new government sought to re-establish relations with the United States. A few weeks after taking office, Perón sent Congress the Act of Chapultepec (March 1945) to be ratified, making official Argentina's re-entry into the inter-American community.

Simultaneously, he permitted himself a gesture of independence in renewing relations with the Soviet Union, which had been suspended since 1917. This was followed by the deportation of a number of Nazi spies and the state's acquisition of German- and Japanese-owned companies. In June 1947 President Truman announced his satisfaction with Argentina's conduct. At the long-delayed inter-American conference convened in Rio de Janeiro in September 1947, Perón's foreign minister, with a very different attitude than that of his predecessor at the previous conference in Rio in 1942, signed the Hemispheric Security Treaty. The reward was the lifting of the arms embargo by the United States.

At the end of the war, Argentina found itself free of external debt and in possession of substantial reserves of foreign currency, benefiting from high demand and high prices for its food exports and a growing industrial base. Within this framework, the *peronista* administration implemented an economic policy with three major objectives: the expansion of public spending, giving the state a stronger role in production and distribution; the alteration of relative prices to encourage a more egalitarian distribution of national income; and the progressive accumulation of a system of incentives that rewarded activities oriented towards the internal market and discouraged production destined for international markets.

This combination of state intervention, social justice and an inward-looking economy was not an isolated experience in Latin America in the 1940s. It is true that in the Argentine case, characterized by a tight

internal labour market and a very active union movement, the egalitarian
bias was more marked than in other countries of the area. Nevertheless,
the leading role of the public sector in the accumulation of capital and the
growing emphasis on the internal market constituted, almost without
exception, a regional version of the Keynesianism in vogue in the countries of the Centre in the West.

The *peronista* economy was not the product of a deliberate economic
strategy. The social bases of the regime influenced its economic choices.
Between the project for industrialization for national defence, based on
essential industries and sponsored by army officers during the war, and the
continuation of light industrialization, Perón chose the latter alternative,
which was more congruent with a progressive distribution of income. In
only three years – between 1946 and the beginning of 1949 – real income
increased more than 40 per cent. This alteration in relative prices, almost
without national or even international precedent, led to a rapid expansion
of consumption and an industrial growth that reached 10.3 per cent in
1946, 12.1 per cent in 1947 and 6.9 per cent in 1948. In this context
optimism in the business community overcame the apprehension generated by the bold income policy and union power, paving the way for
prolonged euphoria in the stock market and a wave of investment by
private business. The idea that capitalist profit could increase at the same
time that salaries were rising ceased to be a paradox extolled by the official
line and became a widespread conviction.

The rapid growth of public stock and restrictions on the flow of foreign
trade were not decisions rationally derived from an original economic
strategy. It is true that from 1946 the *peronista* government carried out a
policy of nationalization of public services (railroads, telephones, merchant marine, airlines, gasoline, etc.). These decisions, together with the
growing share of the budget allocated for the social welfare policy, led to a
progressive extension of state activity and to a leap of around 30 per cent
in public spending. It is also true that due to the policy changes and the
establishment of quantitative restrictions on imports – especially after
1948 – the economy was turning inwards and being exposed to a low level
of international competition.

Nonetheless, there seemed to be no alternative to these developments,
either from the government's point of view or from that of the main opposition. Both the government and the opposition were convinced of the imminent outbreak of World War III, which they expected to eradicate international trade. They also had a certain amount of distrust, common in Latin

America, for the leadership of private capital in the development process. From these premisses both sides agreed that the construction of a strong, extensive state and the protection of national enterprises – intrinsically weak in the face of foreign competition – were prerequisites for economic growth and, above all, for the maintenance of a high level of employment. Furthermore, the generalized statism in the majority of Western countries, the tense calm of the Cold War and the slow expansion of commercial opportunities in the world market for Argentine industry seemed to support the prevailing analysis.

The economic policy of *peronismo,* with its nationalist, Keynesian and distributionist features, was possible thanks to a combined set of favourable circumstances which would not be repeated in Argentine economic history. After nearly two decades of commercial crisis, the sudden improvement in the prices of agricultural exports and, consequently, in the exchange rate allowed the new prosperity to be financed with foreign currency and opened a channel for the redistribution policies needed to consolidate the *peronista* regime. The reserves of foreign funds accumulated during the war – a large proportion of which were not convertible – also permitted the financing of the nationalization of public services.

Moreover, the relative abundance of easily collected fiscal resources meant that the new level of public spending could be reached and maintained without major difficulties. The creation of the Instituto Argentino para la Promoción y el Intercambio (IAPI), an entity that had a virtual monopoly over foreign trade, provided the government with indirect access to the principal source of capital accumulation and permitted the diversion of the rise in export prices to benefit the public sector. To this end, IAPI bought grain from local producers at a price fixed by the authorities and sold it on the international market at higher prices. The resources obtained through this mechanism, together with the forced savings that came from a pensions system that had a large surplus and a broad battery of direct and indirect taxes that fell heavily on the highest income brackets, contributed to the justifiable image of a rich and generous state.

Finally, the nationalization of the finance system and the notable expansion of its deposits, which was due in good measure to the economic rise of small savers who benefited from the redistribution of income, permitted an increase in the flow of subsidized credit towards public and private enterprises. This credit policy was an important part of the *peronista* economy since it encouraged capital investment and reduced working capital, offsetting the effects of the higher cost of labour through financial profits.

Thus, the *peronista* economy was facilitated by the exceptional evolution of the international post-war market, growing fiscal income and the opening of institutionalized saving to the masses. This pattern of development, which was based on the purchasing power of the state and on high salaries, but which, since it was oriented towards the internal market, could ignore the inevitable costs in terms of efficiency and competitiveness, lasted barely three years. Nevertheless, these were the years that stamped an enduring profile of the economics of *peronismo* in the collective memory.

Between 1946 and 1948, Argentina had to face the obstacles to its foreign trade raised by boycott which the U.S. government had imposed as a consequence of Argentina's neutrality in the Second World War. It had begun as early as 1942, and until the end of the 1940s Argentina was treated under U.S. trade policy as an enemy nation. A partial fuel embargo was applied, and Argentina was denied other vital imports, over and beyond the restrictions imposed by the war. From 1946 to 1949, the focus of the boycott shifted from a deprivation of critical industrial inputs to an effort to reduce Argentine exports, which would force political concessions out of a regime perceived as unfriendly. When relations were normalized in 1947, the U.S. government's economic persecution of Argentina continued in a covert form, through the Economic Cooperation Administration (ECA). This powerful agency, which was in charge of distributing Marshall Plan funds to its European beneficiaries, discouraged purchases of Argentine foodstuffs while encouraging purchases from some of its competitors, such as Canada and Australia. This policy was against State Department guidelines, and its effects were sufficiently damaging to elicit the informal admission of U.S. officials that the agency's discrimination had contributed to Argentina's scarcity of dollars, paving the way for a future economic catastrophe. Because these obstacles to dollar-earning exports coincided with Great Britain's unilateral declaration of sterling inconvertibility in August 1947, the situation became progressively more difficult to manage.

Yet the Argentine landowners demonstrated considerable flexibility in the face of the new regime. Perón contributed to this by choosing a member of the Sociedad Rural as minister of agriculture. Furthermore, he made sure that the veiled threats of land appropriation made during the electoral campaign were soon shelved. The organization representing rural owners made peace with the new president and kept its institutional structure intact. The Unión Industrial met a different fate. The industrial entrepreneurs challenged the new administration by appointing an anti-collaborationist leadership to run the association. The price of their audacity was the government's decision to put an end to the Unión's independence. Little by little, however, businessmen accommodated themselves to the new situation when they realized that official policy would not go so far as to confiscate the profits of the economic boom, and their initial open resistance was transformed into enforced conformity.

The unions continued to recruit new members with official support. The 877,300 workers unionized in 1946 grew to 1,532,900 in 1948. In most sectors of the urban economy the rate of unionization climbed by 50 to 70 per cent. The greater union impact ran parallel to the extension and unification of the institutions that regulated labour relations. During previous years, labour laws had reflected great imbalances of strength within the labour movement; the working conditions enjoyed by, for example, railroad employees were unknown in other sectors. Perón's labour policy put an end to this type of union elitism. From 1946 collective bargaining penetrated deeply into the labour market; the retirement system was extended to employees and workers in industry and trade; and paid vacations and unemployment compensation were introduced. Official tolerance and a state of nearly full employment translated into a surge of union activism. In 1945 strikes in the city of Buenos Aires affected 50,000 workers; in 1946 the number of strikers increased to 335,000; and in the following year nearly 550,000 workers were involved.

The social climate that accompanied the development of the regime needed constant invigilation, for which Perón found the ideal partner in the person of his own wife. Eva Duarte had been born in a lower-middle-class household in the province of Buenos Aires, the illegitimate daughter of a rancher who refused to acknowledge either her or her brothers. At the age of fifteen she came to Buenos Aires, attracted by the glamour of the city, and played small roles in unmemorable radio plays and soap operas until she met Perón in 1944. Eva rapidly assimilated the rudiments of a political education given by the extroverted military officer who professed admiration for her. In 1946 Evita – as she was called – was twenty-seven years old, and it was soon obvious that she was hardly inclined to accept a decorative role as the first lady of the regime. While Perón concentrated on the tasks of government, Evita set out to champion the cause of the underprivileged, to whose service she brought a vibrant and deliberately brutal rhetoric that inflamed her followers and provoked fear and hatred among her enemies. As she wrote in her autobiography:

Because I know the personal tragedies of the poor, of the victims of the rich and the powerful exploiters of the people, because of that, my speeches often contain venom and bitterness. . . . And when I say that justice will be done inexorably, whatever it costs and whomever it may affect, I am sure that God will forgive me for insulting my listeners, because I have insulted out of love for my people! He will make them pay for all that the poor have suffered, down to the last drop of their blood![1]

Evita's meddling first became visible from her office in the Ministry of Labour, where she meted out rewards and punishment, teaching the union leaders the iron discipline of the new regime. Later she reached out to the most marginal sectors of the population, the urban sub-proletariat and the most backward classes of the provinces, for whom the new labour rights had only limited significance. She created a network of social and health services for them through the Eva Perón Foundation, which replaced and far surpassed the religious charitable organizations of the upper class. Developing into an effective instrument of proselytization among the poorest sectors, the foundation extended its activity to every corner of the country with shipments of sewing machines, bicycles and soccer balls. Evita later found another crusade to which she could dedicate her energies in the political condition of women. she led the campaign for women's suffrage and, once it was established by law in 1949, organized the women's branch of the official party. Through Evita's intervention, *peronismo* continued the political mobilization begun in 1945; new sectors were added to the regime's vast popular following, complementing and at the same time restricting the role of the unions within it.

Economic prosperity, popular support and authoritarianism combined to ensure the development of the regime, which sought to entrench itself through the constitutional reform of 1949. A constitutional assembly in which Perón's followers had a comfortable majority introduced modifications into the liberal charter of 1853. Some of these measures consolidated the advances in civil and workers' rights. An article based on the Mexican Constitution established state ownership of energy resources, but the most significant political modification was the repeal of the provision that prohibited the consecutive re-election of the president.

[1] Eva Perón, *La razón de mi vida* (Buenos Aires, 1951), p. 122; quoted in Marysa Navarro, 'Evita and Peronism', in F. Turner and J. E. Miguens (eds.), *Juan Perón and the Reshaping of Argentina* (Pittsburgh, Pa., 1983), pp. 15–32.

Once the reform was passed, a campaign was begun to re-elect Perón in 1951. The unions proposed that Evita join him on the presidential ticket, but the military commanders disliked the idea and advised Perón to refuse. The president yielded to the military veto, and Evita announced that she was withdrawing her candidacy. Perón's landslide victory in the elections of November 1951, with Hortensio Quijano as his running mate for a second time, dashed all hopes of overcoming *peronismo* through the electoral route. The official slate captured 4,580,000 votes, while the candidates of the Radical Party, Ricardo Balbín and Arturo Frondizi, who had been denied access to the mass media, received 2,300,000 votes.

In voting by a margin of 2 to 1 for Perón, the electorate effectively authorized him to continue along the authoritarian path. In 1952, Congress, in which the forty-four opposition deputies had been reduced to fourteen, raised *peronista* ideology to the status of national doctrine under the name of *justicialismo*. This 'new philosophy of life, simple, practical, popular and fundamentally Christian and humanist', had as its 'supreme goal' to 'guarantee the happiness of the people and the greatness of the Nation through Social Justice, Economic Independence and Political Sovereignty, harmonizing spiritual values and the rights of the individual with the rights of society'.[2] Its obligatory imposition on officials and citizens eliminated every trace of pluralism in political life and condemned the other parties to a virtually clandestine existence.

Once *peronismo* considered itself to be the only national movement, its relations with the rest of society were destined to change. One of the most important changes after the beginning of Perón's second term in June 1952 was the reorganization of the links between the state and the network of social interest groups. The corporatist order erected by Perón was congruent with his ideology; it promised a harmonious society free of class strife. The new equilibrium among social forces permitted the establishment of an 'organized community', the main competing components of which were brought together to operate as an organically independent whole under the state. After the 1951 elections, the incipient corporatist order was extended in successive steps. The CGT was joined by the Confederación General Económica (CGE), an umbrella organization for the economic establishment, and soon afterwards by the Confederación General de Profesionales, the Confederación General Universitaria and the Unión de Estudiantes Secundarios.

---

[2] See Alberto Ciria, *Política y cultura popular, la Argentina peronista* (Buenos Aires, 1983), p. 64.

Ideological motives were not the only factors that inspired the new architecture of the regime. There was also a desire to construct a political order that would be less centred on the working and popular sectors and would clearly assign the role of arbiter to the state. The creation of a new power structure also changed the position occupied by the armed forces, which had already begun to lose the relative autonomy they had enjoyed between 1946 and 1949. Perón had demanded increasing integration of military institutions into the official political movement, winning over high-ranking officers with new favours and privileges. Perón's electoral strength had convinced the political opposition that the ballot box held no future for them, and, supported by a number of retired military men who were victims of the 1945 purges, they made a number of vain attempts to overthrow the president. However, their luck appeared to change in 1951 due to military discontent in the face of clear evidence that Perón was preparing to be re-elected and that, even more serious, Evita would be his running mate on the presidential ticket. This threat helped to overcome the reluctance of the high military command, which began to discuss the removal of Perón. But first, tactical differences and personal rivalries, and then the withdrawal of Evita's candidacy, hindered the gestation of a co-ordinated uprising; the retired general Benjamín Menéndez launched an isolated attempt, which was rapidly suppressed. Perón's re-election by 62 per cent of the vote provoked a retreat by the conspirators and cleared the way for an intensification of political control over the armed forces. From 1952 onwards, attempts to replace constitutional subordination to the chief of state with loyalty to Perón's personal leadership became more overt. The military establishment yielded to the new demands, but their discontent remained alive, particularly in the middle ranks.

The reorientation of the military with respect to *peronismo* was part of a broader process. Because of their standard of living and social background, members of the officer corps shared the anxiety with which the middle class followed the overwhelming presence of the masses in public life. The speed with which social change had occurred dampened the traditionally progressive spirit of the urban middle class. Older countries had passed through structural changes similar to Argentina's with the intensification of industrialization, but these changes had been absorbed into the institutions more slowly, making the transition to mass democracy less abrupt. In Perón's Argentina everything seemed to happen at the same time: the growth of the working sectors, the development of the unions, the expansion of social welfare and, on a more profound level, the loss of the deference that the old order had expected from the lowest strata of society.

This subversion of traditional patterns of power and prestige was aggravated by a disquieting question: How far was *peronismo* going to go? When would Perón deem the historic reparation to the popular masses – a product of his intervention – to be complete? For the urban middle class to understand that behind such an aggressive policy lay a sincere respect for the bases of the existing order, it would have needed a perceptiveness of which, under the circumstances, it was scarcely capable. Motivated by a profound aversion to the plebeian tone that coloured the regime's accomplishments, the middle class became the moving force of the conservative opposition. A civil resistance movement began to take shape, at first surreptitiously, consisting of small, symbolic gestures of rebellion.

On 26 July 1952 Evita died, a victim of cancer. With her died the figure who best represented the *peronista* movement for the popular masses but also much of what was intolerable to its adversaries. The feeling of profound collective grief at her passing inaugurated, ominously, Perón's second term in office. With the key element of popular activism gone, the government now seemed to be a bureaucratic machine lacking the political attraction of the first years and exhibiting the vices associated with an over-confident power; at the beginning of 1953 Perón's intimate circle was involved in a scandalous case of corruption. They supported the president's efforts to rectify matters, but the resulting public trial ended dramatically with bombings that caused injuries and deaths. The immediate answer of the *peronistas* was to burn the Jockey Club, the traditional seat of the upper class, and to destroy the headquarters of the opposition parties. A wave of mass arrests followed these events, dealing a rude blow to the embryonic resistance movement.

Perón seemed to realize the need to dissipate the political tension. The doors of the presidential palace were opened to the opposition leaders. In the event, it was the Radicals who came to talk; ten years after the revolution of 1943, the electoral support of both the conservatives and the Socialists had practically disappeared. The Radicals, who had broadened their appeal by presenting their programme as the only alternative to *peronismo,* were little disposed to reach an entente that, if successful, would entail a retreat from their role as a zealous opposition. The government was also reluctant to compromise. Towards the end of 1953, an amnesty was declared, but its beneficiaries discovered that being out of jail made little difference, since the restrictions on political activity were maintained in full force.

By then the economic prosperity which had accompanied the establishment of the *peronista* regime was dissipating. The first signs of a deterioration in the economy were evident as early as 1949. After four consecutive years of surpluses, the trade deficit reached U.S. $160 million, due largely to a decline in the terms of trade. The index of the terms of trade (1935 = 100) was 133 in 1947 and 132 in 1948. By 1949 it slipped back to 110, and in 1950 to 93. At the same time, inflation, which had been 3.6 per cent in 1947, increased to 15.3 per cent in 1948 and 23.2 per cent in 1949. The expansion in public spending and the resulting growth in the fiscal deficit completed a picture of growing difficulties.

Although consciousness of the dawning crisis was growing among the members of the government, they did nothing beyond correcting relative prices, and lacking a policy of fiscal austerity, they vacillated for some time between continuity and change. For a growth model that had, from the beginning, been based on the leadership of the public sector and cheap credit to finance internal market expansion and high wages, stabilization had a very high cost for the level of internal market activity, employment and salary levels.

For these reasons, the first measures were partial and quite ineffective. Miguel Miranda, who had presided over economic affairs during the bonanza years, was replaced by Alfredo Gómez Morales, who was charged with taking a new direction. His first steps were a moderate devaluation of the currency and a rationing of credit for both the private and public sectors. Nonetheless, the interest rates charged by the Central Bank on special credit lines continued to be negative, and real wages were kept at the high levels of previous years. The results of this first stabilization trial, maintained from 1949 through 1950, were therefore ambiguous: the boom was interrupted as the economy entered a recessive phase, but relative prices and the existing distributive model were not modified.

The peak of the crisis came in 1951, endangering the survival of an economic strategy that had succeeded thanks to exceptional internal and external circumsances. During 1951 and 1952 the terms of trade continued to fall, placing the country in a situation of external strangulation that would later repeat itself frequently but which at this stage dashed official optimism about the evolution of international markets. The trade balance was U.S. $304 million in deficit in 1951 and $455 million in deficit in 1952. At the same time, inflation again accelerated, reaching a rate of more than 30 per cent in 1952. In that year the government decided on a turnabout in economic policy, revising its initial priorities. The new strategy favoured stability over the expansion of economic activity and consumption, agriculture over industry, private initiative and foreign capital over public sector growth.

Convinced that the distributionist struggle was the principal cause of inflation, the government imposed a social truce on business and the trade unions. The instrument for this was a wage and price freeze for two years, from May 1952 to May 1954, after wages were first readjusted. A Comisión de Precios y Salarios, formed by representatives of the CGT, business and the government, had the mission of controlling the progress of the social accord and studying wage increases based on labour productivity. The acceptance of wage restrictions by workers was facilitated by the control of prices and by subsidies granted to foodstuffs and public utility costs.

The priority given to the anti-inflation policy and the clear awareness of the social support that sustained the regime led Perón to dispense with the option of a new devaluation, although it represented a quick way to eliminate the balance-of-payments deficit. The exchange rate was kept constant in real terms, because devaluation would shift income to the farmers but at the cost of increasing food prices in the internal market. In order to manage the external disequilibrium, the authorities first resorted to a mechanism that had been selectively employed since 1948 – quantitative import restrictions. These restrictions had been used in December 1950, when the outbreak of the Korean War appeared to signal a third world war and led to the purchase of imported goods that could become scarce in the immediate future. In 1952 these had to be drastically reduced whilst a serious drought caused Argentina to import wheat for the first time in its history.

Once devaluation was ruled out as an option, agricultural production was stimulated by means of a reorientation of subsidies. The IAPI, which had hitherto served to transfer resources from the countryside to the urban centres, now subsidized the prices received by farmers for crops that were exported. The key to this operation was a more restrictive monetary policy towards industry and a fall in public investment.

This policy of adjustment and austerity had both benefits and costs. Inflation began to decline, reaching a low of 3.8 per cent in 1954. Imbalances in public finances were reduced to 9.8 per cent of GDP in 1949 and a little more than 5 per cent in 1952. At the same time, industrial production fell by 7 per cent in 1952 and by 2 per cent in 1953. Real wages fell by 25 per cent in two years. In spite of these costs the foundation for a rapid and surprising economic reactivation was laid. This recuperation also rested on a more moderate credit policy, greater financial assistance to the agricultural sector and a more restrictive incomes policy.

The reorientation of economic policy included a new role for foreign investment. At the time, Argentina was almost self-sufficient in finished manufactured goods. The demand for imports was concentrated on fuels and raw materials and capital goods required by a more diversified industrial sector than had existed before the war. The problems of supply and the obstacles to industrial modernization created by the hard-currency scarcity led Perón to call for foreign investment. This change in the statist and nationalist ideology for the regime began in 1953 with a new, more permissive foreign investment law that was followed by agreements with various companies, including Mercedes Benz and Kaiser Motors. The most audacious initiative occurred in the area of petroleum exploitation, a sacred bastion of Argentine nationalism, to which an attempt was made to attract a subsidiary of Standard Oil Company. Selling his new policy to a group of trade union leaders, Perón said:

And so, if they work for YPF [the state oil company] we lose absolutely nothing, because we even pay them with the same oil they take out. It is a good thing, then, that they come to give us all the petroleum we need. Before, no company would come if it weren't given the subsoil and all the oil it produced. Now for them to come, why shouldn't it be a business deal, a big one, if we are spending each year upwards of $350 million to buy the oil we need when we have it under the earth and it doesn't cost us a cent? How can we go on paying this? so that they will get profits? Of course they are not going to work for the love of the art. They will take their profits and we ours; that is just.[3]

The opening to foreign capital implied, if not an abandonment, at least a modification of many aspects of *peronista* foreign policy. This had been inspired by what came to be called the Third Position, an effort to find a place between the two rival blocks growing out of the Second World War. Influenced by the current of non-alignment among countries which had achieved independence in the post-war decolonization process, the Third Position was, above all, an instrument used by Perón to negotiate the price of his support to the United States on international issues. After

---

[3] *La Nación*. 17 September 1953; quoted in Robert Potash, *El ejército y la política en la Argentina. 1945–1962* (Buenos Aires, 1981), p. 225.

1953, this policy was progressively substituted by an open quest for good relations with the new Eisenhower administration.

The crisis that brought about the downfall of Perón had its origins less in the economic situation than in political conflicts that he himself unleashed. In fact, the Argentine economy from 1953 to 1955 was in good shape, compared with the emergency of 1952. The annual inflation rate, after having climbed to more than 30 per cent fell to 4 per cent in 1953 and to 3.8 per cent in 1954. After the abrupt decline of 1952, industrial real wages increased, although without regaining the level reached in 1950. The same occurred with company earnings. Economic activity recovered with a cumulative growth in gross domestic product (GDP) of 5 per cent between 1953 and 1955. The foreign trade balance was positive in 1953 and 1954, although it was in deficit at the end of 1955. Unresolved issues remained. Despite the excellent performance of 1953, agricultural production was unable to increase its volume of exportable surpluses. At the same time, the re-evaluation of the local currency and the lag in public utility prices constituted factors of repressed inflation. But the economic picture did not show signs of an imminent crisis. Moreover, the rapprochement in relations with the United States and the opening to foreign capital had galvanized the image of the *peronista* regime overseas.

The most direct cause of the military conspiracy that put an end to the *peronista* regime can be found in the government's confrontation with the Church. For the armed forces, the ecclesiastical hierarchy's support for official policies had provided confirmation of the culturally conservative character of *peronismo*. Yet at the end of 1954 a succession of governmental initiatives began to undermine the interests and the influence of the Church in national life. Among them were the elimination of state subsidies to private schools, the legalization of brothels and the suppression of religious teaching in public schools. What was behind this sudden offensive against the Church?

This issue has provoked innumerable questions, because Perón never clearly explained the causes of the conflict. It has been suggested that the reason might have been Perón's anger with the Catholic hierarchy's abandonment of political neutrality in deciding to support the creation of a Christian Democratic Party; others claim that the conflict lay in the search for a new element of cohesion in the *peronista* movement at a time when the regime had to shelve its economic nationalism. Whatever the explanation, it is certain that Perón set in motion a conflict that escalated beyond his control and precipitated the end of his regime.

The legal reforms were supported by a massive anticlerical campaign in the official press. Perón irritated the bishops by lavishing official attention on the clergy of other religious sects, even the spiritualists. During the first half of 1955 the confrontation took on a more threatening tone when a new constitutional reform was announced establishing the separation of church and state. In the face of these attacks the Church hierarchy opted for caution, but the militant Catholic sectors closed ranks and converted the churches into tribunals of moral and political protest. The most diverse groups of the anti-*peronista* opposition came to their aid, sensing that the conflict was an occasion for reviving the resistance movement. Flying new colours, the 1945 alliance of the middle class, conservative circles and students took over the streets once again. On 11 June 1955, the day of Corpus Christi in the Catholic calendar, a long procession made its way through the centre of Buenos Aires, challenging the police prohibitions.

The events of the next three months would reveal a new phenomenon: a Perón lacking the political brilliance that had previously enabled him to deal with the most difficult situations. The day after the procession of Corpus Christi, the government accused the Catholics of having burned a national flag and deported two clergymen, accusing them of anti-government agitation. A civil protest of 16 June was followed by an attempted coup d'état. Sections of the navy and the air force rose in rebellion, bombing and strafing the vicinity around the presidential palace and claiming numerous victims. That night, the uprising quelled, the principal churches in the city's centre were sacked and burned by *peronista* vigilantes.

The shock produced by these acts of violence, unprecedented in recent history, cast a shadow over Perón's victory. Furthermore, the CGT's intervention in supplying arms to the workers created justified alarm among the military leaders who remained loyal to the regime. A few days after these sombre events, on the advice of the high command, Perón initiated a policy of conciliation. The state of siege was lifted, the most abrasive members of the cabinet – in particular, the ministers of education and the interior, who were openly associated with the anticlerical campaign – were replaced and opposition leaders were invited to discuss a political truce. Perón declared to his followers that 'the *peronista* revolution is over' and promised to be, from then on, 'the president of all Argentines'.

But the call for pacification, which was aimed at isolating the resistance movement, did not have the desired effect. In fact, it further fuelled the civilian and military opposition. Political leaders, who were permitted access to radio broadcasting for the first time in twelve years, availed themselves of the government's concession to make it clear that they were unwilling to compromise. Arturo Frondizi, speaking in the name of the Radical Party, pledged to accomplish, in peace and liberty, the economic and social revolution that Peronism was renouncing and, with the confidence of a winner, promised a generous pardon to the regime's collaborators.

The failure of the truce prompted Perón to shift tactics. On 31 August, in a letter to the Partido Peronista and the CGT, he revealed his decision to leave the government in order to guarantee peace. Predictably, the unions organized a large demonstration of support. The Plaza de Mayo saw a new version of 17 October 1945. Following a prepared text, Perón told the crowd that he was withdrawing his resignation and then delivered the most violent speech of his political career. He began by saying that he had offered peace to his opponents but that they did not want it, and concluded by authorizing his followers to take the law into their own hands:

With our exaggerated tolerance, we have won the right to repress them violently. And from now on we establish as permanent rule for our movement: Whoever in any place tries to disturb order against the constituted authorities, or against the law and the Constitution, may be killed by any Argentine. . . . The watchword for every *peronista*, whether alone or within an organization, is to answer a violent act with another violent act. And whenever one of us falls five of them will fall.[4]

This unexpected declaration of war overcame the resistance of many undecided military officers. An initiative by the CGT also helped precipitate the dénouement. Shortly after Perón's harangue, it let the army know that it was placing the workers at the army's disposal so that together they could protect the regime. The military leaders, who had been uneasy for some time over the prospect of the creation of workers' militias, promptly rejected the offer. On 16 September, the decisive military revolt finally broke out. Rebel troops under General Eduardo Lonardi occupied the garrisons of Córdoba, and the rebellion spread through the rest of the country with various degrees of success. Superior in number, the forces loyal to the government nevertheless lacked the will to fight. For five days, the outcome of the conflict hung in the balance, until the loyal commanders received a message from Perón saying that he was ready to

---

[4] *La Nación*, 1 September 1955; quoted in Potash, *El ejército y la política*, p. 268.

negotiate a solution but that he refused to resign. The confusion was cleared up the next day when Perón sought refuge in the Paraguayan Embassy. On 23 September, while the CGT begged the workers to stay calm, a crowd thronged the Plaza de Mayo, this time to hasten the swearing in of General Lonardi as provisional president of the Argentine Republic.

THE *REVOLUCIÓN LIBERTADORA*, 1955–57

The members of the political and economic coalition who backed the armed movement in 1955 shared the objective of dismantling the system of authoritarian controls created by Perón. But there were few points of convergence when it came to the profile of the new social and economic order that would emerge from the urgent task of reconstruction.

The spokesmen for the old elite, who were linked to the countryside and the export economy, used the period of debate following Perón's fall to convey a crude and simple message: the origin of the country's problems lay in *peronismo*'s mistaken effort to subvert Argentina's 'natural' economy. They proposed a revision of the policies that had led to the creation of an over-protected industrial base, that discouraged rural producers and that fostered a premature and excessive incorporation of workers into the consumer market. In its place, they sought a return to the economic strategy based on free trade and its comparative advantages, which had stimulated Argentina's impressive growth until 1929. In the short run, it was a matter of adjusting the economy so as to offset the growing deficit in the balance of payments, using measures like large devaluations to reduce imports and promote agricultural exports, severe monetary and credit restrictions and a reduction in wages to bring internal consumption into line with the country's financial limitations. In the longer term, the aim was to re-create Argentina's pre-war economic structure and social balance of power.

After a decade of industrial growth and prosperity, social mobility and the extension of political participation, this was not a very viable alternative. The *peronista* experience had certainly not been able to modify the structural underpinnings established by the conservative political class in the 1930s: it was based on light industrialization, complementary to an agro-export country. However, by converting what had been a stopgap policy after the crisis of 1929 into a more permanent programme and by reorienting national resources towards the extensive substitution of imported manufactures, *peronismo* contributed to the deepening of differentiation within the existing economic and social structure. Alongside the landowning sectors, the large foreign and agrarian capitalists and the old commercial and bureaucratic middle class, a vast industrial world began to consolidate itself, weak in economic power, dependent in its productive capacities, but powerful in its impact on employment and urban life.

When the spokesmen for the old elite tried to promote their strategy in 1955, they met with resistance, not always co-ordinated but always disruptive, from this urban–industrial complex that had been nourished at their expense. If at the beginning of the 1950s it was evident that light industry oriented towards the internal market was losing its impetus for expansion, by 1955 it was equally clear that a return to pre-war Argentina was politically untenable. The transformations in society and the economy had not eradicated the old hierarchical order but had superimposed it on the new industrial, participatory order. Thus, landowners, businessmen, middle class, working class – every sector – nourished a compact knot of interests and managed to become entrenched in their own distinct institutions. Although no one of them by itself was able to steer the process of change, each was, nevertheless, powerful enough to prevent the others from doing so. After 1955, policy alternatives were played out against this background of negative pluralism.

The overthrow of Perón, far from being guided by a concerted military and political plan, was the result of isolated efforts by different and opposing military and political leaders. The crumbling of the anti-*peronista* offensive, which placed even the armed victory itself in jeopardy, led to a political crisis during the first days of the Revolución Libertadora. The unanimity with which the revolutionaries celebrated the end of the *peronista* regime vanished as soon as it became necessary to decide the political direction of the transitional period. Each of the leaders of the conspiracy desired to steer the new political process. The post-revolutionary stage was thus shaken by a silent internal struggle within the military establishment. The crucial bone of contention was what attitude to take towards the *peronista* movement.

One sector, that of nationalist affiliation, favoured a policy of co-optation. Under the slogan 'No winners, no losers', formulated by President Lonardi, they hoped to garner the political heritage of the deposed regime through co-operation with the leaders of *peronista* unionism. This policy was, from the beginning, resisted by another sector, which, in the name of democracy, declared itself adamantly against the enemies of democracy, whom they understandably identified as Perón's followers. The two factions had, nevertheless, one thing in common: the conviction that *peronismo* would not survive as a political force after the fall of the regime that had created it. For the nationalists this meant channelling the movement and purging its excesses under new leadership. In this spirit, President Lonardi named a *peronista* union lawyer to the Ministry of Labour. Those to whom gestures of conciliation were directed responded favourably and thereby managed to secure the survival of their organizations: to this end they exhorted their followers to avoid conflict and agreed to renew the union leadership through elections under the supervision of the Ministry of Labour.

The nationalists' political project never got off the ground. Everything about it aroused distrust in the majority of those who had gathered together to accomplish the Revolución Libertadora. Some of the nationalist military officers had remained loyal to the overthrown regime until the last minute; their political advisers were prominent Catholic intellectuals of anti-liberal sympathies. Attempts by a number of them to use the forces that had supported Perón for their own benefit understandably provoked suspicions of a return to the political situation that had just been brought to an end. Less than two months after the successful armed uprising, concerted pressure from within the military and from politicians led to the resignation on 13 November of President Lonardi, together with that of his nationalist entourage. The revolution would resume its course under the leadership of a new president, General Pedro Eugenio Aramburu, in pursuit of democratic regeneration.

The driving force behind this campaign was the conviction that Argentina had spent the past ten years in a totalitarian nightmare. Its mission was therefore to convince the masses who had been deceived by Perón's demagoguery to abandon their old loyalties and join, as individuals, the family of democratic parties. In the state of emergency, the Revolución Libertadora made use of repression and proscription to accomplish its task of political re-education. After an aborted attempt at a general strike, the CGT and the unions were placed under government control, the Partido Peronista was officially dissolved and a decree imposed to prohibit the use of *peronista* symbols or even the mention of the very name of the man who had been, and from exile continued to be, its undisputed leader.

The firm attitude shown in dealing with the *peronistas* was not extended to the economic problems inherited from the previous regime. During the last part of his government, Perón had already recognized the need to alter the country's economic course. The corrections he introduced in agrarian policy and in the area of foreign investment pointed to a new direction which his political commitments prevented him from pursuing. The Revolución Libertadora did not have any better luck. Hindered by internal conflict in the anti-*peronista* front, it too left the decision up to the future constitutional authorities. One of the Lonardi government's first measures was to ask Dr Raúl Prebisch to assess the economic situation and recommend a policy. Prebisch's report evaded the dilemma of agrarian versus industrial nation, which some nostalgic sectors wanted to reopen, and concentrated on continuing the process of industrialization. Nevertheless, in order to solve the problem of the balance-of-payments deficit, he advised a price policy favouring agricultural exports.

The less controversial measures of the programme were adopted without delay. The peso was devalued, bank deposits were denationalized, the country joined international financial organizations like the International Monetary Fund (IMF) and the World Bank and controls on foreign trade were eliminated at the same time that the IAPI was dissolved. Policy concerning foreign capital had been one of the most controversial issues under Perón. The political opposition that had criticized Perón for the more liberal attitude of his last few years was not inclined to abandon its nationalist bent, and it influenced the military government to cancel its negotiations with the California Petroleum Company. Consequently, foreign investment was negligible.

Policies to stimulate the rural economy collided with declining international prices for Argentine exports. In spite of a higher volume of exports, the dollar value increased by only 7 per cent between 1955 and 1958. In addition, the abolition of import controls caused an explosion in the demand for foreign currency, which had been repressed for a long time. This pressure was especially noticeable in the demand for imported motor vehicles, which doubled in volume between 1955 and 1957.

The military government's decision to call elections soon relieved it of the need to impose abrupt changes in the social equilibrium, which would have adversely affected the democratic regeneration of the *peronista* masses. The desire to avoid a serious deterioration in income levels limited the economic swing in favour of the rural sector and postponed the attack on the imbalances in the structure of production. Business responded to wage increases by raising prices. After a decline in the last years of Perón's regime, inflation accelerated again and in 1957 the cost of living rose by 25 per cent. That year saw another attempt at stabilization, which was moderately successful but did not prevent a decline in real income.

The contradiction between its economic objectives and its political objectives, the diversity of the views of the members of the cabinet, which included spokesmen for the business community as well as members of the Radical Party, set the Revolución Libertadora on a vague economic course which did not permit it to resolve the problems it had inherited.

General Aramburu's government did not suppress – as other military governments would in the future – union activity and collective bargaining. Its labour plan stressed, rather, the eradication of *peronista* influence in the labour movement. In April 1956 a decree was passed excluding from union affairs all leaders who had occupied posts between 1952 and 1955. Proscription and imprisonment were the measures by which the unions were purged, so as to return the unions and the exercise of their rights to the workers.

However, the union elections held at the end of 1956 and the beginning of 1957 witnessed the beginning of a return to *peronismo*. The decision to participate in these elections was the occasion for an outbreak of a conflict between Perón and the new generation of *peronista* union leaders. From exile, Perón ordered a boycott of the elections and the subordination of the old union leaders, some of whom had formed a clandestine organization. Ignoring these instructions, the new leaders who had emerged after 1955 chose to participate and gained control of a number of important industrial unions. Invoking their *peronista* identity first and foremost, the new leaders won the political support of the majority of workers. During 1957 the individual strikes typical of 1956 were followed by more concerted actions. In June and July two general strikes again brought the presence of *peronista* unionism to centre stage.

The political debut of the new labour leaders took place in the congress called by the government to normalize the CGT in August 1957. An alliance of *peronistas* and Communists won the majority of seats, which provoked the suspension of deliberations. The *peronista* delegates to the aborted congress then met at what was called the '62 Organizations', under which label they continued as a central entity of Argentine political life.

Significant though they were, the advances made by *peronista* unionism were still limited compared with the losses it had suffered. Its inclusion within the state had grown till 1955, but now an insurmountable breach opened between *peronista* unionism and government institutions. The only option that seemed viable was to fall back on its isolation, on the defence of its symbols and beliefs, and to radicalize its struggles. From exile in Paraguay, Panama and Venezuela, Perón initially shared this attitude. But there was another way, which began to take shape in the platform of the principal party of the anti-*peronista* coalition, the Radical Party.

Yrigoyen's old party had not survived the traumatic experience of 1946 undamaged. Since then, one of the internal factions, the intransigent wing, had repudiated the conservative bias of the Unión Democrática and, exploiting the crisis that followed the electoral defeat, progressively displaced the old moderate leadership. In 1954 the intransigents managed to elect one of their own as president of the National Committee: Arturo Frondizi, a lawyer who that year delivered in his book *Petróleo y política* a message of a strong nationalist and anti-imperialist tone. While the moderate faction openly rejected the *peronista* regime, the intransigents tried to position themselves to its left, questioning, not its objectives, but its weakness in addressing them, particularly in the field of policy towards foreign capital and international relations.

The success of the policy of de-Peronization conceived by the Revolución Libertadora depended on the ability of the democratic front to remain united behind the condemnation of Perón and his policies. Under these conditions there remained no alternative for Peron's followers but to join ranks with the traditional political parties. The elimination of General Lonardi left the political stage open for the Radical Party, which threw itself into the conquest of the *peronista* masses. This new attempt at co-optation designed by Frondizi broke the unity of the democratic front. From the first days of President Aramburu's government, the Radical Party stood on the side of the opposition in order to present itself as the new champion of national, popular interests. Thus, Frondizi denounced the regime's economic policy as a plan orchestrated by the oligarchy and imperialism, and seeking to gain the sympathy of *peronista* workers, he demanded an end to the persecutions and the continuance of the structure of one union for each branch of activity that had existed until Perón's overthrow. Frondizi's political strategy soon became obvious to all: to make himself the heir of the Revolución Libertadora and to be the politically viable alternative for the proscribed *peronista* masses.

To achieve this he first had to gain support for his positions within the Radical Party, where his attitudes aroused the justified suspicions of the moderate sectors. After a few months dominated by internal conflict, the party met in November 1956 to nominate candidates for the next presidential elections. The moderates and one faction of the intransigents decided to walk out of the assembly, but Frondizi managed to keep together the necessary quorum and was nominated candidate for president. Shortly afterwards the division was made official: in January 1957 the dissident sectors joined together as the Unión Cívica Radical del Pueblo (UCRP), while the sector victorious at the party convention renamed itself the Unión Cívica Radical Intransigents (UCRI).

This crisis had repercussions in the ranks of government, which continued to worry about Frondizi's political manoeuvres. In a gesture openly favourable to the UCRP, whose most important leader was Ricardo Balbín (once a leader of the intransigent wing, but now opposed to Frondizi's ambitions), President Aramburu offered Balbín three cabinet positions – among them the key portfolio of minister of the interior. President Aramburu's decision made it clear where the danger lay for the future of the Revolución Libertadora but was an implicit confession that he could not confront it with his own forces. The conservative political sectors, who best expressed the interests of the military government, carried no significant electoral weight. This phenomenon, which would be a constant in post-1955 Argentine political life, led the military to give its support to Balbín's party, with whose *yrigoyenista* rhetoric it had little in common. The *peronismo*–anti-*peronismo* conflict would thus be waged behind the men and traditions of the now-fragmented Radical Party.

The first instance of the confrontation for which Argentines were preparing themselves was the election for the Constitutional Assembly in July 1957. The military government called these elections to make official the repeal of the constitutional reform instituted by Perón in 1949, but its other objective was to measure the electoral importance of the various political forces before the coming presidential elections. During the electoral campaign Frondizi bent over backwards both to attract the *peronista* electorate and to neutralize the campaign for the casting of blank ballots mounted by local *peronista* leaders. The electoral results indicated that the number of blank ballots was larger than the number of votes received by any of the parties. The 2,100,000 blank ballots were, however, less than half the number the *peronistas* had obtained three years before. With a small difference, the UCRP came in second while Frondizi's party received 1,800,000 votes; the votes captured by the Conservative and Socialist parties barely exceeded half a million. In spite of having achieved considerable electoral support, the UCRI had to resign itself to having failed in its policy to co-opt the *peronista* electorate.

When the Constitutional Assembly began its deliberations, the representatives of the UCRI kept their promise to boycott it. Very soon they were followed by the representatives of other minority parties; even a

faction of the UCRP decided to leave. From the beginning mutual recrimi-
nations between Radicals and Conservatives dominated the Assembly's
sessions. In this atmosphere, the reforms to the charter of 1853, again in
force after the repeal of the *peronista* constitution of 1949, were few and
limited.

The Constitutional Assembly soon lost its importance, and the parties
got into the full swing of political campaigning for the upcoming presidential elections. Meanwhile, the economic situation had escaped the control
of the military government. One economic minister after another proved
unable to put a stop to rising prices or to attract foreign investment. One
obsession guided the behaviour of the leaders of the government: to hand
over power to the future constitutional authorities. But this did not
preclude the temptation to influence who those authorities would be.
Thus, official support was openly given to Balbín's candidacy; he was
summoned to play the role of the anti-*peronista*, in spite of his efforts to
present himself as a progressive politician.

Frondizi's political future, by contrast, could not have been more uncertain. The *peronista* electorate had not been responsive to his overtures,
while the anti-*peronista* sectors seemed to take him too seriously. In an
effort to break out of his isolation, Frondizi moved pragmatically in
several directions. The elections for the Constitutional Assembly had
clearly revealed the vitality of the proscribed movement: if the *peronista*
masses would not listen, it was necessary to negotiate with Perón.
Frondizi's emissaries left in great secrecy for Caracas, where the exiled
leader lived under the protection of Marcos Pérez Jiménez's dictatorship,
and promised him an end to political proscriptions and the restoration of
the union legislation that had been in force during the *peronista* regime, in
exchange for his support for UCRI's candidate.

While these negotiations were taking place, Frondizi maintained that
the Argentine dilemma was not *peronismo* versus anti-*peronismo*, as the
leaders of the Revolución Libertadora claimed, but industrialization versus
underdevelopment. Under this watchword, Frondizi called for the formation of a national popular front formed by the working sectors, the national bourgeoisie, the army and the Church. The ideology of this new
alliance of classes, convoked in the name of economic development and
political integration, was the invention of a group of dissident leftist
intellectuals, headed by Rogelio Frigerio, who gathered round the UCRI
candidate and relegated the party militants to secondary roles.

A novelty in Argentine political life, this convergence between intellectuals and political leaders was accentuated by Frondizi's own personality. More a teacher than a politician, he adopted a dry, technocratic language, making no concession to the traditional political rhetoric of which Balbín, his rival, was a master. This image of rationality, the very attempt to modify the terms of the political conflict that divided the country, made an impact on the modern middle class and captured the imagination of the new generation that had come of age after 1955. To these forces Frondizi tried to add more decisive sources of support. He appealed to the nationalist sector displaced in November 1955 in an effort to gain some influence in the army, and at the same time he tried to pacify conservative public opinion by coming out for the Church's position in favour of freedom of education and against divorce. The fundamental key to this complex political operation was, however, Perón, who, two and a half years after his fall, continued to be the arbiter of Argentine political equilibrium.

Finally, from the Dominican Republic, where General Trujillo extended him hospitality as the Venezuelan dictatorship of Pérez Jiménez was brought to an end, Perón withdrew his authorization to cast blank ballots and came out openly for a yes vote on Frondizi's candidacy. On 23 February 1958 the *peronista* masses went to the polls and followed Perón's instructions. Twelve years after 1946, they again sealed the fate of the elections, this time rewarding Frondizi's virtuoso politicking with 4,100,000 votes, as against 2,550,000 for Balbín. But 800,000 blank ballots were also counted, certifying the existence of alienation and political resistance that not even the exiled leader's own orders had been able to alter.

THE PRESIDENCY OF ARTURO FRONDIZI, 1958–62

Although Frondizi's victory had been a landslide, its significance was far from clear. The jubilation with which Perón's partisans celebrated the results of the election cleared up some of the questions, identifying the true artificer of the victory, but this only led to malaise in military circles. Sectors of the army and the navy insinuated the possibility of not recognizing the credentials of the candidate elected with the *peronista* vote. Rushing to congratulate Frondizi on the same day of his triumph, President Aramburu blocked this manoeuvre and sought the necessary support to honour the word of the 1955 revolutionaries to set the country on the road to democracy.

Given the electoral verdict, this would have to be, however, a tutelary democracy. The elections of 1958 ended the optimism with which the armed forces had launched into the dismantling of the structures of the *peronista* regime. In the face of a political reality that resisted change, they decided to respect it formally, regroup themselves in their headquarters and from there influence the future administration.

With the barely concealed resistance of the military and the open opposition of the UCRP, who had seen a sure victory vanish, the president-elect set about keeping the many promises made during the electoral campaign. If he perhaps had entertained the possibility of institutionalizing the winning coalition in a political movement that would transcend the old cleavages, this fantasy was short-lived. The contradictory nature of the aspirations of those who had voted for him were badly suited to such a project. But what really made it impossible was the distrust that surrounded Frondizi's person, which was shared by the temporary allies he had recruited during his ascent to power. Frondizi more than justified this distrust when he revealed the major outlines of his political plan, the true extent of which was not made known to his adversaries and his backers until 1 May.

The new president's first measures were aimed at paying back his debt to Perón: the repeal of the decree that prohibited *peronista* activities; the enactment of an amnesty law; the annulment of a decree (passed in the last moments of the military government) that had turned the CGT over to a group of non-*peronista* unions; the return of several important unions under state control to *peronista* leaders; the re-establishment of the monopoly union system in force until 1955; and a general wage increase. The revision of the Revolución Libertadora's anti-*peronista* policy stopped short, however, at one crucial aspect: the decree that dissolved the Partido Peronista was not revoked, so the *peronistas,* even though they could once again act and diffuse their ideas, remained unable to compete in elections.

The policy of conciliation towards *peronismo* carried out from May to July 1958 was accompanied by denouncements and accusations by anti-*peronista* civilian and military groups, who saw in it a confirmation of their worst fears. In August, there was an equally hostile reaction within the ranks of the winning coalition to the decision to authorize the granting of academic degrees by private universities. Conceived by the previous military administration but later abandoned to avoid conflict, the new legislation figured among the promises made by Frondizi to the Church. Allowing religious instruction in a field until then reserved to the state stirred up deep-rooted beliefs in the student movement and revived anticlerical sentiment in important segments of the middle class. Large crowds gathered in the streets to defend the lay tradition, while Catholic opinion took the same route to demand freedom of education. Congressional approval of the controversial initiative put an end to the conflict, but not to the hostility of the student movement towards the government.

The measure which had the greatest repercussions was revealed on 25 July when Frondizi announced the beginning of the 'oil battle'. The former nationalist intellectual told a surprised radio and television audience that he had signed several contracts with foreign companies for the mining and exploitation of oil:

The main obstacle to the advance of the country is its strict dependence on the importation of fuels and steel. This dependence weakens our capacity for self-determination and puts in danger our sovereignty, especially in the event of a worldwide armed crisis. Actually, Argentina imports about 65% of the fuel it consumes. Of 14 million cubic meters consumed in 1957, approximately 10 million came from abroad. Argentina has been forced to become simply an exporter of raw materials, which are exchanged for oil and coal. The country works to pay for imported oil, oil that we have under our feet. Argentina cannot continue on this road, which has been converted into a dangerous slope towards domination.[5]

Frondizi thus took up the policy which the *peronista* regime had attempted, with little conviction, in its last days. The goal was now, as then, to reduce the demand for imported fuel, capital goods and supplies that weighed so heavily in the balance-of-payments deficit. The 'oil battle' would be only the beginning of a new attempt at import substitution, which aimed to develop basic industry and build a more highly integrated industrial structure.

The leitmotif of Frondizi's principal adviser, Rogelio Frigerio, was a forced march towards industrialization, by any means and at any price. In spite of the growth of light industry since the mid-1930s, Argentina continued to be a food-producing country and an importer of fuel, machinery and supplies for local manufacture. The cause of Argentine underdevelopment and dependency lay, according to Frigerio, in the position the country occupied within the international division of labour. From this angle, industrialization, particularly the establishment of steel production, petrochemical complexes and oil refineries, would modify the pattern of development based on the export of primary materials and thus be the key to national liberation.

[5] Arturo Frondizi, *Mensajes presidenciales* (Buenos Aires, 1978), p. 133.

The old dream of economic autarchy encouraged by the military during the Second World War was reappearing in a new language. The necessary accumulation of capital had then conflicted with the political needs of the *peronista* regime, which chose a more limited course of industrialization compatible with the redistribution of income. Facing the same equation, Frondizi decided to finance the industrial effort with foreign capital. Argentina was able to take advantage of a novel phenomenon: investment by multinational companies in Latin American industry. To this end the Argentine government, like others on the subcontinent, offered to foreign investors a market closed by high protectionist barriers, with optimal possibilities for expansion, guaranteed by a pre-existing demand and an oligo-political control of its terms.

To justify this heterodox project without abandoning his espousal of nationalism, Frondizi maintained that the source of the capital was not important as long as it was used, with appropriate direction by the government, in areas of strategic importance for national development. The prejudice against foreign capital, he insisted, only consolidated the structure of underdevelopment by leaving the oil underground and postponing the integration of the industrial apparatus.

While the fruits of the new strategy ripened, Frondizi, aware of the fragility of the power he had been handed, launched a series of drastic and irreversible changes in the management of the country's economy. To appease the expectations and demands awakened in the electoral campaign he declared a general wage increase a few days after taking office. This was followed by more flexibility in monetary and fiscal policy, all of which aggravated the economic situation and prepared the stage for a serious crisis of inflation and in the balance of payments. The warning signals of the crisis did not seem to alarm either the president or his economic advisers, who felt confident that they were about to introduce major structural changes. Their attention was attracted more towards winning *peronista* goodwill for their overall economic strategy.

Even at this stage, to speak of *peronismo* was to speak of *peronista* union leaders. Perón's exile and the absence of a legal party created a situation in which the union organizations, in addition to their professional functions, were transformed into the natural spokesmen of the *peronista* masses. This displacement of representation of the political movement towards the union leaders had important consequences in the institutional life of Argentina. In the short run, it allowed the government to negotiate measures such as the new union law in exchange for a neutral attitude towards the abandonment of aspects of the program of 23 February which were, in any case, the very ones that the *peronista* regime had tried to jettison in its last days.

For the leaders of the 62 Organizations, the end of the military interregnum opened the possibility of recovering lost positions, both those of symbolic character associated with their full recognition in the political system and those of a more concrete character embodied in control over the resources of the union machine and the CGT. However, the rapprochement between *peronista* unionism and the government did not last very long. Eight months after Frondizi took office a crisis took place, in spite of efforts on both sides to prevent it.

Several factors contributed to this crisis. In September labour contracts were prorogued for another year, which implied a virtual freeze on wages, and it was made known that regulation of the right to strike was under study. This was more than the 62 Organizations were willing to tolerate in silence; in mid-October they demonstrated their discontent in what would be the first general strike of the constitutional period.

The government was under pressure from both directions. Every move that tended to pacify the *peronista* unions provoked the alarm of their civilian and military adversaries. In light of the attempt to attract foreign capital, this conciliatory attitude was even more contradictory. Frondizi believed he had found a way out of the dilemma by supplementing the search for compromise with the *peronista* labour leaders with exemplary gestures accompanied by political firmness. The oil workers' strike at Mendoza was the first test. Arguing that the conflict was part of an insurrectionary plot, Frondizi imposed martial law for thirty days and sent many union militants to jail. The 62 Organizations, in turn, called a new forty-eight-hour general strike. The government and the unions seemed to be marching towards a final confrontation. The rupture, however, was avoided. No doubt the willingness of the 62 Organizations to reach an agreement was influenced by fear of a breakdown in the order through which they hoped to consolidate their positions.

Frondizi's boldness was not limited to the abandonment of the ideological causes with which he had identified for such a long time. He also tried to change the relationship of the forces within the military establishment in an attempt to diminish the influence of sectors that were hostile to him. For this daring enterprise he sought the support of nationalist officers and those who had been excluded from active duty. At the beginning of September the president and his secretary of the air force tried to recommission an officer discharged by Aramburu in 1957. The resistance by the bulk of leaders and officers provoked a state of rebellion in the air force, which stopped only when the president withdrew his controversial decision and agreed to replace his secretary of the air force. At the price of a severe weakening of his authority, Frondizi had to acknowledge that the stability of the government was dependent on the maintenance of the inherited distribution of power.

For their part, Argentina's military leaders redoubled their vigilance over the government's activities. The spokesmen for these concerns was the former president, General Aramburu, who supported constitutional order but demanded the removal of Frondizi's *eminence gris*, Frigerio, from his position as secretary of socio-economic relations. Frigerio was deeply distrusted in military circles because of his leftist origins, his political rise on the fringes of the party structure and the role he was playing in the negotiations with the *peronistas*.

The president apparently acceded, and on 10 November he relieved Frigerio of his official functions but, demonstrating that duplicity which so infuriated his enemies, a little later let him in again through the back door as a member of his intimate circle.

Under these circumstances, strong rumours of a coup d'état began to circulate. The presumed existence of a secret pact between Frondizi and Perón, denounced by the opposition parties and denied with little success by the administration, engendered deep doubts about the stability of the government. Uncertainty about Frondizi's real intentions converted the hypothesis of a military uprising into a broadly debated possibility. The conspiratorial atmosphere the country had lived through on the eve of Perón's fall took over political life again. As before, one could hear, now in the voice of Balbín, the defence of revolution as the natural right of a society faced with a totalitarian threat. However, this campaign of the civil opposition collided with the scruples of the military, still undecided whether to put an end to the incipient constitutional experiment.

In this context, the leaders of the 62 Organizations decided to lift the November general strike. Although they only received promises from Frondizi, the *peronista* unionists decided to stop the workers' mobilization so as not to provide new excuses for a military take-over. The continuity of the truce between the government and the unions required that both be able to control their own decisions. It was soon evident that neither Frondizi nor the leaders of the 62 Organizations were in any state to do so.

On 29 December the stabilization plan reached with the IMF was announced. Its purpose was to obtain financial assistance to alleviate the balance-of-payments crisis inherited by Frondizi and made even more acute by his economic management. Its principal measures included an anti-inflationary monetary policy, stimuli to exports and new investment and the abolition of the system of controls and subsidies.

In the short run the consequences of the plan were predictable. Salaries fell by 25 per cent and GDP declined by 6.4 per cent. Exchange rates were unified and there was a 50 per cent devaluation, which spurred a rise in prices of such proportions that towards the end of 1959 the inflation rate was twice that of the previous year. The real devaluation amounted to 17 per cent, helping to transform the trade deficit of 1958 into a modest surplus in 1959.

The new economic policy left no room for negotiation with the unions. However, the confrontation took place long before its effects were fully felt. The incident that led to the rupture was Frondizi's decision to dislodge the workers by force from the Lisandro de la Torre meat-packing plant, which they had occupied in protest against its privatization. The policy of rapprochement with *peronista* unionism suffered a rude blow when Frondizi called in the army to neutralize the workers' protest. Having indebted himself to the military, the president was now obliged to respond to its disapproval of a policy that continued to restore the union structures to *peronismo*. In the following months the labour policy was revised, the minister of labour (a former labour leader and collaborator of Frigerio) resigned, the scheduled union elections were suspended and important unions which a short time before had been put in the charge of *peronista* leaders passed again into state control.

The new attitudes were not limited to labour policy. Frondizi mollified the military with other gestures: in April he prohibited the activities of the Communist Party, expelled several Soviet diplomats and replaced the government appointees most closely identified with Frigerio, who had to resign again. This did not save him from a serious political crisis in June 1959, when Perón, confirming the suspicions of many, gave the press in Santo Domingo copies of the alleged pre-election pact with Frondizi. Annoyed with his former ally, Perón thus offered a new excuse to anti-Frondizi and anti-Perón sectors to challenge the military's loyalty to the constitutional authorities. Frondizi's denials convinced no one. On the fourth anniversary of the anti-Perón uprising of 16 June 1955, a group of retired military men flew to Córdoba to lead a rebellion of local troops. But the attempt had no repercussions whatever. Although they were harshly critical of Frondizi's attitudes and policies, the high command still preferred to avoid extreme measures.

The crisis of June 1959 had a surprising outcome. In order to improve his deteriorating image in power circles, the president undertook a spectacular cabinet reorganization. On 24 June he offered Alvaro Alsogaray, a persistent critic of the government, the posts of Economy and Labour. A fervent defender of private enterprise and the market economy, Alsogaray seemed an impossible choice for Frondizi; but this decision was one more proof of the president's lack of political prejudice, which alarmed his supporters and surprised his enemies. Alsogaray's credentials were certainly the most apt for soothing the military and implementing the plan of austerity formulated with the IMF.

Under this program, 1959 was a year of sharp economic recession. Argentina had never before experienced such a strong effort to apply monetarist mechanisms. To the drastic decrease in the general liquidity of the economy was added the rapid rise in the cost of living provoked by the removal of price controls. In contrast to the experience of 1956, when negotiation allowed the unions to defend real wages successfully, the union offensive now collided with a solid defence of the official programme of capitalist modernization. The world of big business and the military establishment suppressed their reservations about the origins of the government, and at the moment of confrontation with the unions they gave it their full support.

Wages fell 30 per cent – it would take ten years for them to recover – and business regained the incentives suspended during the *peronista* decade of distributionism. Throughout 1959 labour conflicts were accompanied by a wave of terrorist attempts against businesses in an unprecedented exhibition of frustration and rage. The collapse of the strikes of 1959 brought the cycle of mobilizations begun in 1956 to a close. The mandays lost to strikes were more than 10 million in 1959, nearly 1.5 million in 1960 and only 268,000 in 1961. Under the impact of repression and economic hardship there began a process of demobilization and demoralization of the rank-and-file militants who had been the nucleus of the renaissance of *peronista* unionism.

The subjection of his economic policy to the orthodox monetarism recommended by Alsogaray did not relieve the president of new military anxieties. From the middle of 1959 until March 1962, Frondizi had to govern under the strict vigilance of the military chiefs. During this period, the armed forces acted according to their belief that the president could be pressured to adopt the policies they considered essential; it was neither necessary nor desirable to remove him from office. The most important figure in the exercise of this overbearing tutelage was General C. Toranzo Montero. Named commander-in-chief of the army after the crisis of June 1959, Toranzo Montero began to fill the high command with men he trusted and who, like himself, were convinced that the ideals of the Revolución Libertadora were at risk. When his plans were impeded by Frondizi's secretary of war, who ordered him to quit his post, Toranzo Montero declared himself in rebellion. On 3 and 4 September the country waited, expecting a battle between the tanks deployed throughout the centre of Buenos Aires. The clash was averted when Frondizi acceded to the rebel general's demands and sacrificed his secretary of war, an act which created acute reservations among his cabinet colleagues. To the consternation of the governing party, Frondizi henceforth had to coexist with a military caudillo whose authority emanated from a successful challenge to his presidential powers.

The preoccupations of the army led by Toranzo Montero closely reflected the new political climate provoked by the impact of the Cuban Revolution. The triumph of Fidel Castro in 1959 was initially interpreted by the anti-*peronista* press as being in line with the democratic crusade that had overthrown Perón. Then, following the rapid radicalization of the regime in Havana and the deterioration of relations with the United States, this positive attitude began to give way to a growing alarm about the new model of Latin American revolution. Because of his recent stay in Washington as Argentine delegate to the Inter-American Defense Board, Toranzo Montero was in an advantageous position to personify the anxiety of military circles throughout the continent. Accordingly, he began to reorganize the armed forces on the basis of an anticipated revolutionary war.

In March 1960 Frondizi capitulated to the wishes of the military and instituted the Conintes Plan, which assigned control of the anti-terrorist struggle to the armed forces, subordinated the provincial police to their control and authorized the trial of civilians by military courts. The intrusion of military power in areas of civil jurisdiction produced predictable conflict. Thus, the military commander of the region of Córdoba accused the local governor of complicity with terrorism and demanded his removal. Frondizi yielded to the demand and forced his followers in Congress to decree the intervention in the province of Córdoba.

This and other manifestations of a policy that increasingly reflected an attitude of capitulation on the part of the government led Toranzo Montero to challenge Frondizi's authority openly. In October 1960 the high command of the army circulated a memorandum accusing the government of tolerating the Communist presence in cultural and educational institutions, of exploiting the resentment of the *peronista* masses against the military and of administering state enterprises corruptly and inefficiently. The military's hard line created widespread fear that the precarious balance upon which Frondizi's government had survived would now collapse.

Such conflicts did not have exclusively negative consequences for political stability. Frondizi astutely found ways to exploit them in strengthening his ability to remain in office. His message was to persuade public opinion that the alternative was a slide towards civil war. To give some basis to his warnings he began to lift the restrictions that weighed on the unions, started negotiations to legalize the CGT and allowed more *peronista* activities. Frondizi hoped that this incipient threat would turn the anti-*peronista* sectors to his side and restore the backing he needed to resist the pressure of his civilian and military enemies.

At the beginning of 1961 the president took a step forwards in the search for greater autonomy by succeeding in removing Toranzo Montero, who resigned after failing to sway military opinion against official policy. Thus, after three difficult years in office, Frondizi now had greater liberty to set his government on course.

In addition, without offering any explanation, he removed Alsogaray, who had shown unexpected pragmatism but never been welcome in Frondizi's cabinet. Nevertheless, Alsogaray was replaced by another figure from the local financial establishment who did not substantially modify the policy established by the agreements with the IMF. After the sharp depression of 1959, the economy grew at a 7 per cent rate in 1960 and 1961. The key element in this reactivation was investment. Consumption remained stable because of salary containment and the austere fiscal policy, but this was more than compensated for by the mobilization of capital provoked by import substitution. Thanks to the increase in investment in the highly protected markets of automobiles, tractors, heavy chemicals, steel and oil, the expansion of global demand allowed a reduction of the extensive idle capacity created by the recession of 1959.

The success of the programme of reactivation was not independent of the backing of the international financial community. The financing of the investment push came from foreign savings, whether through short- or

long-term loans or direct investment. Foreign indebtedness helped overcome the restrictions on the capacity to import that derived from the
negative behaviour of exports. In spite of the devaluation of 1959, the
trade balance was negative again by about U.S. $200 million in 1960. The
flow of external funds helped to raise credit in the private sector without
compromising the goals of the monetary policy agreed on with the IMF.

In addition, the economic recovery was initially accompanied by a sharp
reduction in inflation. When Alsogaray was appointed, prices were rising
at an annual rate of 127 per cent; by April 1961, when he stepped down,
the rate had fallen to 9.5 per cent. His successor followed the same line,
but he could not prevent prices from rising by 21 per cent in January
1962, when, on the eve of the election, the government relaxed the
austerity policy. These fluctuations in both the economy and political life
took place in a very sensitive context. The central role of foreign capital in
the economic recovery had introduced an element of great instability in
the official programme. Keeping the confidence of the foreign investors
and bankers required a climate of political peace that Frondizi could not
ensure for long.

Foreign policy was the second front where Frondizi tried to take advantage of his increased freedom of action, following an independent line in his
treatment of the Cuban question. By August 1960, at a meeting of Latin
American foreign ministers held in Costa Rica, Frondizi had defined his
position on the new conditions created by the Cuban Revolution. On that
occasion, he instructed the Argentine delegation to call the attention of the
United States to the underdevelopment of the Latin American region at the
same time that it condemned the Communist threat. In Frondizi's view,
poverty and subversion went hand in hand, and so the fight against Communism went together with the fight against underdevelopment – a formula
that would be popularized by John Kennedy with the Alliance for Progress.
Frondizi appeared to it to ask for economic aid from the United States and to
justify an attitude of independence concerning the U.S. administration's
conflict with Fidel Castro.

In March 1961 Argentina offered its good offices to facilitate an understanding between the United States and Cuba. The offer was rejected, but
the opposition used it to accuse the government of protecting a Communist country. A month later, Frondizi gave new pretexts to his critics when
he signed a friendship treaty with Brazil. The open neutrality of Jânio
Quadros, the Brazilian president, on U.S.–Soviet rivalry and his sympathies towards Cuba jolted the relative calm that prevailed in the military

establishment. For the military the only acceptable posture was one of outright opposition to Fidel Castro. Given its suspicions concerning the ideological inclinations of Frondizi and his collaborators, the military greeted any official position that fell short of firm condemnation of the Cuban Revolution with alarm and outrage. Thus, after Frondizi held a secret interview with Ernesto 'Che' Guevara at the presidential residence in the middle of August, in a new attempt at mediation between Cuba and the United States, he was forced to remove his foreign minister and sign a joint declaration with the armed forces which ratified the condemnation of the communist experiment in Cuba.

The second and final chapter of the conflict between the military establishment and the government over the Cuban question took place at the conference of the Organization of American States (OAS) in January 1962. This meeting was sponsored by the United States, which wanted to apply sanctions against Cuba and expel it from the inter-American system. During the days preceding it the Inter-American Defense Board met in Washington for the same purpose, and the Argentine military delegate voted in favour of the motion to break relations with Fidel Castro's government. However, at the OAS conference, held in Punta del Este, the Argentine foreign minister, together with those of Brazil, Mexico, Chile, Bolivia and Ecuador, decided to abstain on the motion which, with fourteen countries voting, ordered the expulsion of Cuba from the OAS.

The refusal to side with the United States met with unanimous military disapproval. The chiefs of the three armed branches demanded that the president immediately break off relations with Cuba and put an end to the ambiguities in foreign policy. For several days Frondizi and the high command met round the clock, while unrest brewed in the garrisons. Finally, his arguments exhausted, the president had to yield to military pressure and sign the decree ordering the end of relations.

The outcome of the Cuban crisis was the prologue to another, more definitive crisis. In March 1962 elections had to be held in which control of the Chamber of Deputies and of several provincial governments was at stake. Frondizi looked to these for a victory that would permit him to shake loose the military supervision that had ruled his exercise of power, and to this end he made the most daring decision of his four years in government: he authorized the *peronistas* to vote. The risks were obvious. In the congressional elections of 1960 the banned *peronistas* had cast 2,176,864 blank ballots (24.6 per cent), followed by the UCRP with 2,109,948 (23.8 per cent). The official party, the UCRI, took third place with 1,813,455 votes (20.5 per cent). In order to change this picture, Frondizi had to surpass the UCRP vote and become the real alternative to the feared return of *peronismo*. Exploiting the comprehensible anxiety provoked by *peronista* propaganda, Frondizi hoped to transform the election into a plebiscite over who would emerge as the guarantor of peace and progress. Several pilot elections at the provincial level in December 1961 seemed to lend credibility to his hopes. Recovering the territory lost in the congressional elections of 1960, the official party grew at the cost of the UCRP, while the *peronistas*, competing outside their urban bastions, did not appear to be a force to be feared. On 18 March, however, the victory that would have retrospectively justified so many humiliations ended in defeat.

After seven years of political proscription, *peronismo* returned as the leading electoral force, with 32 per cent of the votes. The number of votes received by the various groups in which the *peronistas* participated — since the Partido Justicialista was still illegal — totaled 2,530,238; the UCRI received 2,422,516 votes, and the UCRP 1,802,483. Of the fourteen provincial elections, nine were won by the *peronistas*, including the most important district, the province of Buenos Aires, where the union leader Andrés Framini won the post of governor.

On 19 March the military obliged the president to annul by decree the elections in the districts where the *peronistas* had won. But this was not to be the only price of his lost electoral wager. In rejecting the election results, he apparently violated his constitutional oath to respect the law; his civilian and military enemies needed no other pretext to provoke his overthrow. Thus began ten days during which public opinion hung on secret negotiations in which the military and politicians laboured to find a formula to resolve the crisis. The time invested in this effort clearly illustrates the reluctance of important sectors of the armed forces to regard the democratic experience initiated in 1958 as finished. Finally, the high command prevailed, and on 29 March Frondizi was removed from the presidency.

Thus, in the midst of general indifference, a bold and innovative attempt to confront the problems of post-Perón Argentina came to an end. For four turbulent years, Frondizi tried to reincorporate the *peronista* masses into political life and inaugurate a new phase of import substitution with a view towards promoting economic development. His proposals did not gain the consensus necessary to secure a consolidation of democracy at the same time.

The economic programme was not well received, even in the business community. Although he promised the Argentine bourgeoisie much more than they had been offered in the immediate past, it was too ambiguous an experiment to be believed in. Very few politicians of the Right could discern the project hidden beneath Frondizi's rhetoric. The country was never closer to creating a modern conservative party, but it was a lost opportunity. In truth, the tortuous roads by which Frondizi chose to formulate his programme did nothing to facilitate it. The initiatives he launched from office began a process of great change. The industrialization effort modernized the country's economy and society. To complement foreign investment, the government had to generate additional savings in order to finance the construction of infrastructure and industrial subsidies. The alternative used by Perón – extracting savings from the agricultural sector – was no longer feasible. On the contrary, this sector had to be fortified by a policy of high prices. As a consequence, the government turned to wage reduction. This lowering of salaries was effective in two ways: in the public sector, spending decreased, leaving room for increases in investment; in the private sector, it permitted an expansion of profits. The belief was that greater profits, larger investment and more rapid growth in productivity would make it possible to restore wage levels later. In macro-economic terms this meant a translation of resources from consumption to investment. The ratio of investment to the GDP grew thus from 17.5 to 21.7 in 1961.

Foreign investment tended to concentrate in new areas, where it was guaranteed special protection, but very little was channelled into the modernization of existing sectors. A type of dualist industrial economy was being created in which a modern capital-intensive sector, with a strong presence of foreign companies, advanced technologies and high wages, began to coexist with a traditional sector, predominantly financed with national capital, which had obsolete equipment, was more labour intensive and paid lower wages.

Frondizi's policies encouraged import substitution and the development of the internal market. It was a paradox that the project of import substitution, conceived during the Second World War as an expression of nationalist sentiment, should end by increasing the influence of foreign capital in the economy. The modernization of the productive structure was a necessity, but it was carried out in an unbalanced manner. Limited to the internal market, it did not permit businesses to take advantage of economies of scale, as a greater emphasis on exports would have done. The new structure continued to depend on resources provided by traditional agricultural exports to obtain its critical supplies and capital goods – precisely the dependency that Frondizi's strategy was attempting to eradicate.

THE PRESIDENCY OF JOSÉ MARÍA GUIDO, 1962–3

The overthrow of Frondizi presented the military with the dilemma of how to fill the presidency. A military dictatorship was a solution favoured by only a few factions, and the international context was far from propitious for authoritarian experiments, as the failed intervention of President Kennedy's ambassador on behalf of Frondizi had demonstrated. The dilemma was finally resolved by the naming of the head of the Senate, Dr José María Guido, as president of the country in accordance with the legal provisions governing a vacancy in the office of head of state.

Once this institutional question was resolved, the new minister of the interior, Rodolfo Martínez, a key figure of the military faction opposed to a dictatorial solution, began to unfold a new political plan. In general terms, Martínez's plan resumed Frondizi's policy of very gradually reintegrating the *peronistas* into political life. But for this plan to be realized it was necessary for the legalistic faction of the military to prevail not only within the army but also within the navy and air force. This was the source of the first of a series of military crises that plagued Guido's administration. Within one month of Frondizi's overthrow, the powerful Campo de Mayo military base declared itself in opposition to the Martínez plan.

The navy also exerted its influence in defending the ideals of 1955. Under these circumstances, the minister of the interior resigned, and Guido was forced to sign decrees that annulled all the elections held in March, dissolved Congress and extended federal control also over those provinces where the *peronistas* had not won in the elections. Thus, the search for a political solution which would have included the *peronista* masses – even in a subordinate position – was abandoned.

Guido took charge of the economy in an extremely uncertain climate. In the months preceding the March elections, a flight of capital had been stimulated by signs of crisis in Frondizi's economic programme. The weaknesses of the 1960–1 recovery were becoming evident as the increases in economic activity and public and private investment came to an end, provoking a trade deficit at the end of 1961. The rise in imports stimulated by the great leap forward in industrialization was not matched by the volume of agricultural exports. In addition, the country had to face the large long- and short-term foreign debt contracted in previous years to finance the new investments. The deterioration of foreign currency reserves, aggravated by speculative manoeuvres, further complicated public finances. When the government found itself forced to resort to credit from the Central Bank to finance its running expenses, exceeding the limits agreed upon with the IMF, the international financial institution declared that Argentina had violated its commitments.

To cope with the inglorious finale of the *desarrollista* adventure, President Guido named Federico Pinedo as minister of economy. After twenty-two years, this founding father of liberal-conservatism took up the reins of the economy once more – an eloquent reminder of the permanence of that traditional Argentina against which Frondizi had tried to project his modernization program. Pinedo lasted only a few weeks in office, but this was long enough for him to do the job for which he had been summoned: he devalued the peso from 80 to 120 to the dollar. His replacement was A. Alsogaray, who returned to administer a new agreement with the IMF that incorporated extremely restrictive fiscal and monetary policies. Alsogaray's goal was nothing less than to balance the budget and purge the economy of the 'excess demand' incurred during the last years of Frondizi's term.

The severe monetary restriction provoked a sharp decline in activity. The GDP fell 4 per cent between 1962 and 1963 while business closures and unemployment increased. The crisis of liquidity meant that all payments – in the private as well as the public sectors – began to be postponed and that business checks and vouchers issued by the government circulated as substitutes for paper money. During this period the economy operated under the broadest free-market conditions known since 1930. Nevertheless, the shock therapy, in spite of the sharp recession, did not prevent inflation from accelerating until it reached an annual rate of 20 to 30 per cent. The positive note in this gloomy picture was the excellent crop of 1962, which made possible an improvement in the trade balance and a restocking of the country's foreign currency reserves. The economy, however, continued to be ruled by the uncertainty created by open dissidence among the military chiefs concerning the country's political future.

The outcome of the conflict of April 1962 did not solve the struggle for power within the military high command. In August, those who favoured the dictatorial solution staged another challenge, under the leadership of General Federico Toranzo Montero, the brother of former president Frondizi's most intransigent critic. The object of the uprising was the resignation of the secretary of war on the excuse that the internal promotion regulations of the army had been violated. With the secretary's resignation the search for a replacement was undertaken in a manner that clearly revealed the state of anarchy in the military. A genuine electoral process was set in motion which the country could follow in the press and in which the generals behaved like political bosses. When the ballots were counted and the fire power behind each vote evaluated, the election favoured the army's legalistic faction. President Guido named one of its members secretary of war, but his authority was ignored by the officers who had been defeated. Determined not to retreat, these men, still under Toranzo Montero's leadership, proposed their own candidate and deployed their troops in central Buenos Aires. The legalistic faction also entered the fray, and once again the country stood on the verge of armed confrontation. The military resources of the legalists were superior to those of Toranzo Montero's followers, but the president intervened to prevent open conflict. As in April, the most resolutely anti-*peronista* sectors emerged with a political victory despite the relative balance between the two sides.

Deprived of its military victory, the legalist faction was quick to react. Its spokesmen demanded the return of the constitution, the complete repudiation of dictatorship and the holding of regular elections. When they insisted on a changing of the guard, conflict once again broke out. The army base at Campo de Mayo assumed the leadership of the rebellion under the direction of General Juan Carlos Onganía, making appeals to public opinion over two radio stations in an effort to project the image of a democratic army: 'We're willing to fight for the people's right to vote.'

This time the military factions entered into combat. The legalists called themselves the 'blues' (*los azules*), while their adversaries were known as the 'reds' (*los colorados*). The *colorados* were always on the defensive, and posed no real challenge to the *azules*, who had not only the greater fire power but also the support of the air force, which threatened to bomb the concentrations of *colorado* troops, undermining their fighting spirit. The navy, although it sympathized with the *colorados*, stayed out of the fray. On 23 September 1962, General Onganía's troops obtained the surrender of their adversaries and proceeded to impose the peace of the victor over them. They took the principal army leaders prisoner and carried out a true purge, which put an end to the careers of 140 senior officers.

The victory of the *azul* faction in the army brought Dr Martínez back as minister of the interior, and he renewed the quest for a political formula that would permit the armed forces to return to their bases. The original decision to facilitate the incorporation of the *peronista* masses into institutional life was retained, as was the refusal to allow *peronista* leaders to occupy positions of power. To resolve the dilemma implicit in this dual objective an effort was made to form a broad political front, to which the *peronista* masses would bring their voting power whilst leadership would remain in the hands of other forces. This replay of the experience of 1958 seemed to elicit a favourable response from Perón: faced with the alternative of a military dictatorship, *peronismo* reconciled itself to accepting a slow and gradual return to the institutional system, meanwhile lending its support to the political formula sponsored by the dominant sector of the armed forces. The exiled leader accepted this compromise, entrusting the political moderate Dr Raúl Matera with the local leadership of the movement and removing Andrés Framini, the union leader who, after his frustrated attempt to become governor of Buenos Aires in 1962, had been adopting ever more intransigent positions and moving more towards the forces of the Left.

Under these conditions, the minister of the interior began to reassemble the scattered pieces of the complex political puzzle. Several small parties entered the competition for the coveted candidacy for president of the future electoral front. But Perón and Frondizi refused to give up their efforts to control the political outcome, and they manoeuvred to frustrate the aspirations of those who sought to become the saviours and heirs of the proscribed forces. At the same time, the minister of the interior extended official recognition to a neo-*peronista* party, the Unión Popúlar, which offered to channel the votes of Perón's followers.

This bold move by the minister of the interior provoked understandable unease in the anti-Perón camp, which tried to pressure President Guido into revoking his decision. In an effort to disarm this attempt, the organizers of the political front publicly announced their condemnation of the regime deposed in 1955. At the same time, they prepared another equally bold initiative that, in the end, would be the ruin of their plans. In March 1963 Dr Miguel Angel Zavala Ortiz, a fervently anti-*peronista* leader of the UCRP, refused an offer made by the minister of the interior to occupy second place on a presidential ticket that would be headed by General Onganía and have the backing of all the parties. His rejection and the indignation caused within the anti-*peronista* camp forced Martínez's resignation. Under pressure from his friends, among whom were numerous partisans of General Aramburu, Onganía had to deny that he was a candidate for the proposed alliance.

The divisions within the high command of the army encouraged a further military rebellion, this time centred in the navy, to be staged on 2 April in protest against the electoral policy of the government. After several days of bloody conflict, the army *azules,* with the help of the air force, forced the rebels to surrender. The defeat of the navy, where *colorado* sympathizers were in the majority, signalled its political decline; thirteen years would pass before it would recover its position in the military establishment. In the short term, the acute danger of institutional disintegration convinced the military leaders to abandon their political plans.

The government's change of direction surprised Perón, who was again allied with Frondizi and ready to play by the rules of the game established for the next elections, scheduled for 7 July. The government showed itself to be insensitive to these manifestations of goodwill. After a year of marches and countermarches, in which there had been five ministers of the interior, the new minister in charge of the government's political conduct put an end to ambiguity. Appointed in May 1963, General Osiris Villegas began by excluding the Unión Popular from the electoral race for executive posts, and he subsequently banned all those suspected of representing orthodox *peronismo* or being allied with it.

The endless number of legal obstacles and impediments that confronted the *peronista* front intensified the conflict within its ranks, which existed as a result of the difficulties encountered in trying to agree on a candidate for president. When Perón and Frondizi agreed to support Vicente Solano Lima, a conservative populist, the coalition fell apart. An important sector of the UCRI threw its support behind the candidacy of Oscar Alende despite Frondizi's effort to prevent it. Nor could Perón prevent the Christian Democrats from backing their own candidate, Raúl Matera. When, on the eve of the poll, the confusion provoked by these disagreements was deepened by the imposition of new legal obstacles, Perón and Frondizi called on their followers to cast blank ballots. Remaining in the race were Dr. Arturo Illia, a little known but respected provincial politician, for the UCRP; Alende for the dissident faction of the UCRI; and General Aramburu, the head of the Revolución Libertadora, sponsored by a new political group, the Unión del Pueblo Argentino, in the hope of attracting the anti-*peronista* vote. The effects of this strategy were counter-productive. Important sectors of the *peronista* electorate preferred not to express their protest with a blank ballot but to support the alternatives to Aramburu. The blank ballots totalled 19.2 per cent of the vote, which signified a retreat from the 24.3 per cent cast in 1957. Both sectors of Radicalism benefited from *peronista* support, but the winner, unexpectedly, was Illia, with 2,500,000 votes, followed by Alende, with 1,500,000, followed closely by the blank ballots, which in turn exceeded the 1,350,000 votes cast for General Aramburu.

THE PRESIDENCY OF ARTURO ILLIA, 1963–6

In 1963 Argentina embarked on a new constitutional experience in a climate of relative political relaxation epitomized by the personality of the president-elect. His parsimonious, provincial style seemed well suited to the mood of Argentine society, which, tired out by so much conflict, reacted to Illia without illusions, in sharp contrast to the fervour which had accompanied Frondizi's victory in 1958. Illia understood that the government's first task was to offer Argentina's citizens a moderate policy that would allow them to reconcile their differences. Where Frondizi had tried to innovate, Illia chose the security of the tried and true: respect for the law and periodic elections.

Illia and his party had traversed the changing landscape of post-war Argentina without themselves undergoing any great transformation. Perhaps the greatest change was in their attitude towards *peronismo*. Since 1946, the Radical Party had channelled the feelings of rejection that the movement led by Perón had awakened in the middle and upper classes. The anti-*peronista* reaction expressed resistance not only to the authoritarian tendency of Perón's regime, but also to the social changes that took place under his auspices. Anti-*peronismo* was identified, therefore, with a spirit of social restoration. However, the transformations that had taken place in the country were profound and irreversible. Argentina could not simply return to the past. *Peronismo* had modified the old order, but that order had also been corroded by, for example, industrial development, the modernization of labour relations and the expansion of mass culture. That this new reality was destined to endure was a painful discovery to those who wanted to turn the clock backwards. First Frondizi's attitude and later that of the military *azules* underscored this forced recognition of *peronismo*. The new Illia government, elected thanks to the proscription of the *peronistas,* also promised to make them legal again soon.

However, the Radical Party remained faithful to its traditions in its conception of economic policy. The party's platform since the middle of the 1940s – nationalism, income distribution, state interventionism – dictated some of the government's early measures. During the electoral campaign, the candidates of Radicalism had promised above all to revise

Frondizi's oil policy because it was detrimental to national sovereignty. Illia nullified the contracts signed by the international oil companies. The measure required the payment of important indemnifications, interrupted the oil industry's growth and earned the government the early antipathy of the business community and foreign investors.

The sharp recession of 1962–3 had caused GDP per capita to fall to its lowest level in ten years. The installed capacity of the manufacturing industry – sharply increased by the earlier wave of investment – was operating at about 50 per cent, while unemployment reached 9 per cent of the active population in Greater Buenos Aires and was even higher in the interior of the country. The Radical administration considered that its first objective was to reactivate production. The strategy chosen was to stimulate consumption through expansionist monetary, fiscal and wage policies. Here also the contrast with Frondizi's policies was evident. In 1963 the economy was at a low point in the economic cycle, comparable to that in 1959. Yet whereas in 1960–1 it was investment, financed with foreign resources, that impelled recovery, in 1964–5 the expansion was based on encouraging private consumption. Under the Radical government banking credit to the private sector was increased, which permitted improved financing of the sale of durable consumer goods; the Treasury proceeded to diminish the balance of unpaid debts to public employees and state suppliers and cleared the backlog of federal transfers to the provinces; salaries were also raised and a variable minimum wage law was passed.

The GDP grew 8 per cent in 1964 and 1965 – with annual increments in industry of 15 per cent and unemployment reduced by half – but growth still did not reach pre-recession levels. Moreover, the rapid expansion aroused fears that problems could develop in the balance of payments, not only because of higher demand for imports but also because of the need to confront the external debt obligations assumed during Frondizi's years in office. It was estimated at the end of 1963 public and private external debt service would cost U.S. $1,000 million during 1964 and 1965.

The initial fears about the balance of payments were subsequently reduced by the very good performance of exports, the Illia administration marking a turning point in the behaviour of the external sector. Exports grew from the previous plateau of U.S. $1,100 million that had prevailed since the 1950s to nearly $1,600 million, the level achieved nearly eighteen years before. The continuing rise in prices contributed to this (leading to an improvement of 12 per cent in the exchange rate between 1963 and 1966), but above all it was due to the increase in the volume of production. After remaining stagnant from 1953 to 1963, agricultural production increased by more than 50 per cent between 1963 and 1966. The traditional bottleneck in the Argentine economy – stagnation in agricultural exports – was therefore removed.

The early economic achievements of the government did not earn it greater acceptance among the population. Elected by less than a third of the voters, and lacking roots in the labour movement and in business organizations, the Radicals needed the collaboration of other forces to broaden their bases of support. However, they soon made it clear that they had no intention of sharing the government with other parties. Their rejection of a strategy of alliances provided poor preparation for that moment when the tactical truce that had accompanied their installation in office gave way to a level of conflict more in accordance with the country's recent past.

As for the Radicals' relations with the military, the situation could not have been more paradoxical. The defeat of the *colorado* military faction, with whom the Radicals were associated, had opened the way for elections and made possible Illia's unexpected victory. The marriage of convenience forged between the new government and the leaders of the blue army was, then, fraught with tension. The Radicals were too weak to impose a return of their own military allies and provoke a change in the chain of command of the armed forces. They had, therefore, to resign themselves to accepting the status quo, in which the figure of General Onganía, commander-in-chief of the army, was a key element. For their part, the military commanders had to adjust to the existence of a civilian administration for which they harboured no sympathy whatsoever. And they saw Illia's cautious response to the resurgence of union opposition as clear evidence of a lack of political authority.

Organized labour's opposition to Illia went back to the period before his election as president. In January 1963, the unions managed to reorganize the CGT and approved a campaign to force a return to constitutional order through a series of strikes. When at the eleventh hour the officers who surrounded President Guido decided to veto the participation of the Unión Popular, the CGT called off the scheduled mobilization and instructed its members to boycott the election and condemn its results, and thus Illia's presidency, as illegitimate. The government's positive moves on economic and social matters did not redeem it in the eyes of the unions. In spite of the passage of a minimum wage law – contrary to the wishes of business organizations – the CGT decided to carry out its original plan of action in

May 1964, alleging conditions of poverty which did not accord with the general indication of economic performance.

For several weeks the country watched a wave of occupations of factories which, in their scrupulous planning, resembled a military operation. This formidable demonstration of union power provoked alarm in business circles, but the peaceful nature of the plant occupations revealed their objective to be less a confrontation with business than a weakening of the government. Illia chose to ignore the challenge and did not call in troops, but his isolation was exposed to public view, and demands for a policy of law and order began to increase.

The mobilization of mid-1964 marked the entrance on the political stage of a new style of labour action. The unions were simultaneously agencies for wage negotiation and enterprises which provided their members with a broad network of social services, and as a result an extensive bureaucratic apparatus had been constructed. At the same time, union leaders had become accepted as elements of power in post-*peronista* Argentina. Between 1956 and 1959, when unionism was weak and marginal, it had launched an active protest of the working masses against the state. It now began to adopt a different strategy. Instead of stimulating mass action, it preferred to rely on general strikes, in which the intervention of the rank and file was eliminated in advance and priority was given to organizational efficiency. This strategy of strikes and negotiation went together with a search for allies among those discontented with the government. The person who best embodied this new style was Augusto Vandor, head of the metal-workers' union, a frequent go-between among businessmen, military officers and politicians; Vandor epitomized the leadership of the 62 Organizations.

A no less significant evolution was also taking place within the armed forces. At the risk of dividing the military establishment through involvement in political and sectarian conflicts, the leaders of the *azules* decided to bow to constitutional authority and return to the barracks. The consequent resumption of their institutional mission was intended to permit the armed forces to re-establish patterns of authority and improve the professionalism of their officers. In August 1964, in a speech given at West Point, General Onganía revealed a project to place the military above politics.[6] He said that the armed forces, 'the armed branch of the

---

[6] *La Nación*, 7 August 1964; quoted in M. Cavarozzi, *Autoritarismo y democracia, 1955–1983* (Buenos Aires, 1983), p. 100.

Constitution', could not be substituted for the popular will. He also pointed out, however, that their functions were 'to guarantee the sovereignty and territorial integrity of the nation, preserve the moral and spiritual values of western and Christian civilization, [and] ensure public order and internal peace'. In order to fulfil these functions, he added, it was necessary to reinforce the military as a corporation, as well as the economic and social development of the country.

In this broad vision of the role of the armed forces, their loyalty to the civil powers remained highly conditional. In the same speech, Onganía stressed that '[military] compliance refers ultimately to the Constitution and its laws, never to the men or the political parties who may temporarily hold public power'. Thus, due obedience could lapse 'if, taking shelter behind exotic ideologies, an excess of authority [was] produced' or if the exercise of the vast array of functions pertaining to the armed forces was hindered. The prevention and elimination of internal subversion occupied a central place in the new doctrine. In transforming economic development and the efficient running of the government into conditions necessary for national security, Onganía placed such objectives within the legitimate realm of military jurisdiction, completely erasing the line of demarcation between the military and the civilian. The scheme to place the armed forces above politics effectively eliminated politics itself.

The choice of West Point as the place to introduce General Onganía as the new crusader for the doctrine of national security was no coincidence. The United States was carrying on an active campaign to convert the armies of Latin America into its allies in the struggle against the internal enemy – Communist subversion. Popular mobilization and the crisis of authority in the Goulart administration brought the armed forces to power in Brazil in 1964 in the name of national security. In Argentina, President Illia continued to administer a legal government sharply aware of the fact that it was under close military surveillance. At the beginning of 1965, the military intervention of the United States in the Dominican Republic put the 'entente' between the Radical government and the armed forces to the test. Illia was trapped between the pressure of public opinion, which was hostile to the United States, and the demands of the armed forces, which favoured the intervention. His response was ambiguous: he proposed the creation of an inter-American military force which would re-establish order in Santo Domingo, but he refused to allow Argentine troops to be part of it. The president's refusal to follow the advice of the military chiefs aroused their bitter resentment.

Nor did Illia win the goodwill of the military by restoring legal status to the *peronista* movement, which enjoyed a freedom of action unknown until then. This greater tolerance was also intended to exploit the contradictions which were being created within the movement by Perón from his exile in Spain. Since the defeat of 1955, sharply distinct forces had grown up within *peronismo*. In the provinces least touched by modernization, it managed to preserve its multi-class profile under leaders from the conservative tradition who cultivated *peronista* rhetoric in order to retain Perón's political clientele while prudently submitting to the post-Perón order. Forced to act under new conditions, these local leaders chose to distance themselves from Perón's erratic tactics so as not to risk losing their laboriously reconstructed positions.

In the more modern and urban areas of the country, *peronismo* had lost its support outside the working class and the popular sectors but continued to exercise considerable influence in the union movement, since this was the only structure that had survived the political collapse of 1955. In the first phase, *peronista* unionism followed the instructions of the exiled leader with more discipline than the neo-*peronista* forces of the interior. With time, however, the labour leaders adopted the conservative logic of union institutions which were able to prosper only if they had the goodwill of the centres of national power. It became increasingly difficult for them to follow the strategies of Perón, who, proscribed from political life, had as his dominant objective the destabilization of the forms of government being laboriously erected by his enemies. In the end, then, the former president found himself at odds with the more conformist aspirations of the union leaders. While they sought a political order that would make room for them and allow them to consolidate, Perón waged a tireless war of attrition from exile.

After ten years of precarious existence on the margins of legality, the *peronista* movement began to consider the idea of emancipating itself from the political tutelage of Perón. Many union leaders concluded that disciplined obedience to Perón was preventing them from full inclusion in the prevailing power system. This rupture was not without difficulties. The faithfulness of the *peronista* masses to their absent leader was just as vigorous as ever; furthermore, they harboured the secret illusion of Perón's imminent return to the country, an illusion he encouraged in repeated messages from exile. The myth of Perón's return weakened the authority of the local leaders and conspired against their efforts to institutionalize the movement within the existing rules of the game. In order to remove this obstacle it was necessary to demonstrate that Perón's return was impossible.

At the end of 1964, the *peronista* unions led by Vandor organized the so-called Operation Return. Perón left Madrid by air on 2 December, but when he landed in Rio de Janeiro the Brazilian government, following instructions from Argentine authorities, forced him to go back. The reasons for Perón's participation in this dubious adventure have never been made clear. What is certain is that his prestige in the eyes of his loyal followers was not affected; the responsibility for failure fell squarely on the shoulders of the union leaders and the Radical government.

The calling of congressional elections for March 1965 postponed the resolution of the dispute over power among the *peronistas,* who decided to close ranks behind their candidates. The results yielded 3,400,000 votes for the different *peronista* groups and 2,600,000 votes for the government party. Since only half the seats of the Chamber of Deputies were at stake, the effects of the electoral defeat were attenuated; even so, the government lost its absolute majority and henceforth had to seek the support of other minority parties. Even more seriously the Radicals were further diminished in the eyes of conservatives and the military. Their latest failure to contain the electoral force of the *peronistas* and the government's performance in other areas did little to reduce the party's social and political isolation.

In the middle of 1965, the administration was obliged to admit that inflation, which was now approaching 30 per cent, had once again become a problem. The early expansionist policies now gave way to an anti-inflationary program, which began by reducing aid by the Central Bank to the banking system, especially in credit to the public sector. Efforts to reduce the fiscal deficit ran into difficulties, the government's electoral reverses making their efforts felt when the government failed to get Congress to pass a set of tax laws aimed at reforming public finances. In income policy the results were even worse: pressure from public and private wage-earners produced increases in excess of official guidelines. Finally, at the end of 1965 economic activity began to decline.

The economic policy of the Radical government did not earn the approval of the centres of economic power – especially in so far as this policy relied on a variety of controls and forms of state intervention to limit speculation and sectoral pressures. Accusations of *dirigismo económico, ineficiencia administrativa* and *demogogia fiscal* unified the principal corporations in industry, agriculture and finance in their attack on the government, an attack which was sharpened further still by the president's preferential treatment of small and medium-sized businesses.

In November 1965 an unforeseen confrontation between Onganía and the secretary of war led the former to resign his commission. The government, however, was in no position to alter the military balance of power: the new commander-in-chief, General Pascual Pistarini, came from that sector which regarded Onganía as its natural political leader. Furthermore, Onganía's star burned even more brightly when he left the army, attracting the sympathies of the constantly broadening band of those who were unhappy with the Radical administration.

Nevertheless, the political balance appeared to be most unstable within the *peronista* movement. Months after Perón's failed attempt to return to Argentina, Vandor and his friends believed the moment had arrived to do away with obedience to a person who came between them and the political order in which they sought acceptance. A party congress orchestrated by the unions approved a plan that aimed to substitute the voluble political will of the exiled leader with a structure more representative of the interests of local union chiefs.

His leadership challenged, Perón sent his third and current wife, María Estela Martínez, to Argentina on a mission to nip the rebellion in the bud. Isabel (the nickname by which she was known) began to gather followers among Vandor's rivals. The CGT itself went through a conflict of loyalties and split in two. However, Vandor managed to retain control of the bulk of the union machine as well as the support of the neo-*Peronista* politicians of the interior.

At the beginning of 1966 election for a new governor of the province of Mendoza was due to be held, providing an occasion on which to measure the balance of power between the supreme leader and the local *peronista* caudillos since Perón and his rivals nominated different candidates. A Radical–Conservative alliance prevailed in the elections, but of greater interest was the fact that the obscure candidate backed by Perón won more votes than the candidate backed by Vandor and the other rebels. This outcome was a severe blow to those within and without *peronismo* who were confident of the political decline of the exiled leader. The dissident faction was rapidly losing adherents. Everything pointed to the probability that *peronismo*, now united behind its leader, was on its way to a sure victory in the next elections scheduled for March 1967. It was clear to many that the political order that had arisen from Perón's overthrow would survive only if regular elections were suppressed. The possibility of a coup d'état began to be openly discussed in the media.

At the same time, the cultural and technical modernization of the country begun by Frondizi, paralleled by the economic changes brought about by the investment of foreign capital in industry, had begun to recast Argentina's social landscape. A new stratum composed of professionals, business managers and academics was gaining visibility. In this emerging sector, the values of liberal democracy that had galvanized the resistance to the *peronista* regime enjoyed little popularity. The mobilizing myths were now efficiency and economic dynamism. The new sensibility was expressed in the demand for 'structural change'. Under its auspices institutes were created to diffuse the methods of U.S. 'business schools' throughout the local executive population; weekly magazines reproducing the format of *Time* and *Newsweek* were published, generously supported by the advertising of large national and foreign corporations; a profusion of propaganda encouraged new aspirations and patterns of consumption.

In spite of its vagueness, the slogan of structural change was clear on one point: the biggest obstacle to Argentina's integration into the modern world was the archaism of its political parties. Illia, with his moderate style, was drawn by the caricaturists as a quiet figure with a dove of peace sitting on his head; at the end he had become a symbol of ineffectiveness and decadence.

The discrediting of the government was so intense and effective that public opinion rallied behind the increasingly explicit calls for a coup d'état. At a time when the Radical administration was being subjected to biting criticism, this campaign of psychological action aimed to create a new legitimacy through the exaltation of the armed forces, whose virtues of efficiency and professionalism – deemed absent in the politicians – were praised. Onganía emerged as the natural leader of this ideology of authoritarian modernization, which also found adherents in the labour movement. Many union leaders optimistically watched the rise of a military elite that shared their resentment towards the so-called *partidocracia*. Moreover, the suppression of the electoral system, which Perón was always in a position to influence, would remove some of the obstacles to their attempts to emancipate themselves from the caudillo's political tutelage.

The fate of the Radical government had been sealed for quite some time before the military uprising of 26 June 1966. On 29 May, General Pistarini, at an official ceremony in the presence of the president, delivered a defiant speech in which he expressed the dominant themes of the anti-government propaganda. Contrary to the expectations of the conspirators, who were waiting for an act of authority so they could declare their rebellion, Illia did nothing. Under a foolish pretext, Pistarini then arrested one of the few constitutionalist officers and ignored the orders of the secretary of war to release him. The president's response was to dismiss the commander-in-chief, finally provoking a decisive crisis. On 26 June, the army took over the radio, television and telephone systems and gave Illia six hours to resign. When the time was up, a police detachment expelled him from the presidential palace and sent him home. The search for a constitutional order begun in 1955 had come to a lame end.

On 28 June, the commanders of the three military branches formed a revolutionary junta, the first decisions of which were to dismiss the president and the vice-president, the members of the Supreme Court, the governors and the elected incumbents. Congress and the provincial legislatures were dissolved, all political parties banned and their assets transferred to the state. A proclamation, known as the Acta de la Revolución Argentina, informed the people that they would have a representative government again only after enlightened rule by the armed forces – for as long as was necessary – had dismantled the anachronistic structures and values that stood in the way of national greatness. The junta held power for twenty-four hours and then, predictably, named Onganía president of the new authoritarian government.

THE *REVOLUCIÓN ARGENTINA*, 1966–73

Onganía took over the presidency in 1966 with full powers. The coup d'état had already swept the political parties from the stage. The so-called Statute of the Argentine Revolution went a step further and excluded the armed forces from the responsibilities of government. This concentration of power was the natural corollary of the consensus that surrounded Illia's overthrow: to dismantle the system of *partidocracia*, and preserve the unity of the military, disconnecting it from public policy.

The direction of the new authoritarian regime remained, therefore, dependent on the ideological tastes of Onganía. Lacking personal appeal or rhetorical talent, he quickly surrounded himself with the pomp appropriate to a remote and self-sufficient power. From the heights of this unexpected absolutism, he informed the country of the key ingredients of his preferences. These were scarcely adapted to the image of champion of modernity carefully cultivated by his publicity agents. They were, in essence, those of a devout soldier, imprisoned by the narrowest of Catholic phobias in matters of sex, communism and art. An admirer of Franco's

Spain, Onganía saw in it an example to be imitated in order to restore morals and order to a people he considered licentious and undisciplined.

As had happened before with the rise to power of General Uriburu in 1930, the nationalist colonels in 1943 and, less emphatically, General Lonardi in 1955, the purest expressions of anti-liberal thought re-appeared. The country again witnessed the exaltation of corporatist schemes of government, and the state adopted a paternalistic style, extravagant with prohibitions and good advice in its feverish campaign of moral and ideological vigilance.

The first target of this crusade was the university. In July the public universities were deprived of their autonomy and were placed under the control of the Ministry of the Interior on the grounds that it was necessary to end Marxist infiltration and student unrest. In 1946, a month after Perón's electoral victory, a similar measure had been inflicted upon the Argentine universities. As had happened then, a considerable number of professors resigned to avoid becoming victims of the purge, many of them choosing to go into exile in Europe, the United States and other parts of Latin America.

The search for a new order was then aimed at public services. First came the Port of Buenos Aires. In October the prerogatives enjoyed by the union were abolished in order to place the docks in a competitive position with the rest of the world. In December it was the turn of the railroads, which Frondizi had already tried to modernize, at the cost of prolonged strikes. As in the port, the methods of rationalization ran up against worker protests; in both cases, however, an imposing military presence minimized union resistance. The northern province of Tucumán was a permanent centre of conflict and unrest due to the bankruptcy of the sugar mills, several of which were closed by the government under a somewhat improvised program to do away with the sugar monoculture of the region.

This series of forceful measures seemed to exhaust the repertory of responses of the new administration. It was generally thought that Onganía had stepped into office with a broad plan of action already prepared. However, during the first six months, outside of directing a number of coercive operations, he did nothing but announce grand policy objectives in which it was impossible to perceive any clear innovative economic programme. He had entrusted the Ministry of Economy to a newly rich and militantly Catholic entrepreneur, who failed to make any progress towards the declared objective of putting an end to the inflation-ary, nationalist and expansive policies of the immediate past. The difficulties that had plagued Illia's government intensified. The year 1966 ended with no growth in the national product, a decline in the level of investment, a squeeze in the balance of payments and an inflation rate that refused to decline. The government was slowly discredited among the large national and foreign firms that had applauded its installation. The major unions which had supported the new military regime soon faced the reality of a situation quite different from what they had imagined. On 1 December 1966, the CGT initiated a plan of agitation that would culminate in a national strike.

Thus the Argentine Revolution found itself on the defensive at the end of 1966. Onganía had alienated those who had supported him and was under pressure on the military front. In December came a turning point in the fate of the regime. The appointment of General Julio Alsogaray as commander-in-chief of the army marked the end of the days in which the positions of power were occupied by persons close to the president. Alsogaray was a critic of the nationalist Catholic current led by Onganía and, through his brother, the former minister of economy, Alvaro Alsogaray, he was closely linked to the economic establishment. At the same time, Onganía appointed Adalbert Krieger Vasena to the Ministry of Economy. A minister during Aramburu's presidency and member of the boards of directors of important national and foreign companies closely connected with international financial institutions, Krieger Vasena enjoyed great prestige and was reputedly a liberal economist with pragmatic tendencies.

On political matters, however, Onganía was not prepared to compromise. His new minister of the interior shared his predecessor's view that the political reconstruction of Argentina must be sought through channels other than those of liberal, democratic constitutionalism. The attempt to substitute political pluralism with a community organized around a strong state continued to provoke irritation in liberal circles of the Right. These people knew that the electoral game condemned them to choose among political options all of which were unsatisfactory; lacking sufficient electoral power, they saluted the decision to replace politics with administration but they distrusted Onganía's corporatist nonsense. The president announced that the Argentine Revolution would unfold in three stages: the economic phase, destined to achieve stability and the modernization of the country; the social phase, which would allow for the distribution of the profits reaped during the initial stage; and finally the political phase, with which the revolution would culminate, by transferring power to authentically representative organizations. This grandiose plan, which would take at least ten years to carry out, clarified the role Onganía had reserved for Krieger Vasena and his team of liberal economists: to bring about the economic reorganization of the country so they could then be discarded when the social phase began. The new order pursued by Onganía was as alien to the kind of democracy desired by big business as it was to that sought by the masses. A critic of partyocracy, the president was also critical of capitalism, which was guilty, in his eyes, of a social egotism equally detrimental to the spiritual integration of the nation.

While Onganía was operating on the political and cultural plane with schemes that had become extinct thirty years before, Krieger Vasena launched a programme that differed significantly from earlier stabilization policies. He began by abandoning the 'crawling peg' with a devaluation of the peso of the order of 40 per cent, in a move to extinguish once and for all any speculation on future devaluations. But the real innovation was that this was the first attempt at fully compensated devaluation. Thus, taxes were levied on traditional exports at the same time that import duties were reduced. This meant that the *net* prices of exports and imports changed very little. The inflationary impact of the devaluation was thus minimized and, in the case of export taxes, the government availed itself of much-needed resources for public accounts.

Another central component of the stabilization programme was the establishment of an obligatory income policy. Wages, after being re-adjusted to average 1966 levels, were frozen for two years. Agreements were signed with the five hundred most important companies to ensure that prices would reflect increases only in basic costs. In exchange for the suspension of collective bargaining the unions merely received the promise that real wages would remain constant, while the incentives to get the companies to agree to the price controls were preferential access to bank credit and to government purchasing contracts. Coming from a minister with a background like Krieger Vasena's, the income policy was a complete innovation; it reflected the belief that the markets of goods and wages in a closed economy like Argentina's were far from competitive – a more realistic view than that of other traditional programmes with liberal roots.

The attack on the fiscal deficit was accomplished by improving tax collection, raising charges for public services and reducing public employment and losses in state enterprises. This helped the public sector to play a major role in the rapid expansion of investment, which nearly reached the levels of the boom of 1960–1, this time financed basically by internal savings. Rejecting the opinion of orthodox monetarists, Krieger Vasena opted for an expansive monetary policy to avoid the risks of recession. Banking credit to the private sector grew significantly, in part because the severe fiscal policy permitted a reduction in loans to the state by the Central Bank.

Furthermore, Krieger Vasena succeeded in winning the confidence of the economic community by eliminating exchange controls, renewing contracts with the foreign oil companies and signing a new agreement with the IMF. Conceived as a global economic adjustment to address the needs of the most dynamic and concentrated groups, the programme required other sectoral interests to contribute. Rural producers ceded part of the extraordinary profits derived from the devaluation in the form of taxes on exports; industry had to compete with cheaper imported goods; the unions were deprived of collective bargaining; state enterprises and public administration had to go through a process of rationalization.

The launching of this programme in March 1967 coincided with a great defeat for the unions. The Plan of Action they announced had elicited a severe response from the government. By way of warning, the bank accounts of several unions were frozen; the juridical recognition which was indispensable for them to function was withdrawn from others, and the regime threatened to dissolve the CGT. On 6 March the workers' confederation decided to cancel its protest. A few days later it received the coup de grace when Krieger Vasena suspended collective negotiations, reserving the ability to fix wages to the state for two years.

The collapse of the tactic of strike first, negotiate later, by which the unions had acted until then, provoked a serious crisis of leadership. The majority of the labour leaders chose to take a step backwards, taking refuge in prudent passivity. A smaller but still significant group approached the government in the hope of receiving the small favours that Onganía occasionally handed out to compensate for the oppressiveness of his policies. The president's ambiguous relationship with the liberal economists who surrounded Krieger Vasena awakened, in certain leaders, hopes of re-creating the old nationalist alliance between the armed forces and the unions. The labour movement entered into a long period of political retreat. Thus, the government could boast that in 1967 the man-days lost to strikes were only 242,953 as against 1,664,800 in 1966.

In the meantime, Krieger Vasena's economic programme was bearing fruit. Towards the end of 1968, the annual inflation rate had fallen from

30 per cent to less than 10 per cent, and the economy was beginning to achieve sustained growth. Although the economic reactivation of 1967 and 1968 was fuelled primarily by state investment, especially in public works, the entrance of short-term foreign capital strengthened net reserves of foreign currency and compensated for the unsatisfactory performance of the trade balance. In both 1967 and 1968 the growth of agricultural production did not prevent the net value of exports from falling below the 1963 level due to the deterioration in the terms of trade which had begun in 1964 and would continue until 1972. Moreover, other problems that would deepen over time were coming to light as the strategy of import substitution, based on an internal market protected by tariff barriers, was reaching its limit.

The economic successes of these two years, however, did not broaden the popularity of the military regime. Krieger Vasena's policy, backed by the most powerful factions in the business community, entailed heavy costs for many sectors. The complaints with which rural producers had greeted the export taxes became more shrill when there was an attempt to institute a tax on land in order to stimulate productivity and combat fiscal evasion. Small and medium-sized companies saw their access to cheap credit closed and the tariff protection they had enjoyed in the immediate past eliminated, and they accused the minister of trying to weaken them to the end of concentrating and de-nationalizing the economy. Although wage losses were not very large, the unions were unhappy with the freezing of their power to exert pressure. This accumulation of tension in a variety of sectors nourished growing discontent.

The suppression of the political system had allowed Onganía to protect the state from the play of pressures that had in the past paralysed more than one government. But, inevitably, a dangerous rift was opening up between the forces of civilian society and a state power that was becoming increasingly remote and authoritarian. In an attempt to isolate himself from the exigencies of the economic groups, Onganía undertook little innovation. But while previous presidents had also tried this to safeguard their policies, he made a philosophy of government out of what for others had only been a defensive attitude. Thus, his disdain and arrogance made interest groups feel that all he expected from them was unquestioning adherence to the official line.

Onganía's autocratic style also affected his relations with the military establishment. Repeating on every occasion that presented itself that 'the armed forces neither govern nor co-govern', he was deaf to anxieties in the military hierarchy about the way the revolution was going. In August 1968 this conflictive coexistence finally reached a crisis, and Onganía fired the commanders-in-chief of all three military branches. Stepping down, General Alsogaray explicitly criticized the 'absolutist and personal conception of authority' held by the president, at the same time denouncing the government's 'unclear orientation in political matters'. His successor as head of the army, General Alejandro Lanusse, shared these points of view, and as a result Onganía became progressively more isolated from his comrades at arms.

The fateful year of 1969 began with promising signs for the economy. The level of activity continued to rise, the year closing with an exceptional increase in GDP of 8.9 per cent; the annual inflation rate was about 7 per cent in May; while in the month before the launching of Krieger Vasena's programme net reserves of foreign currency were U.S. $176 million, in April they were $694 million. These successes were the product of the social and political truce imposed by the government. The question was whether these achievements could become permanent.

In spite of the success of the anti-inflation policy, exchange rates had fallen to levels below the devaluation of March 1967. To compensate for inflation, Krieger Vasena kept reducing export taxes, but without being able to avoid a deterioration in the relative prices of agricultural products. Real income, frozen at 1966 levels, also declined. These incipient difficulties, however, did not alter the regime's smugness about the healthy performance of the economy and the solid order imposed on society. The sporadic conflicts that flared up tended to die out rapidly, and it seemed as if political life had been reduced to a domestic quarrel in which Onganía opposed his liberal critics of the Right about the future of the revolution. Nevertheless, there was evidence of the high potential for protest that lay beneath the surface of this authoritarian 'peace'.

In March 1968 a congress was convened to elect officers to the CGT, which had been leaderless since the resignation of those responsible for the great defeat of March 1967. A new, highly radicalized leadership emerged with the backing of the unions most affected by the government's policies. The traditional, more moderate wing of the union movement, represented by Augusto Vandor, then decided to call another congress and create an alternative confederation. The militant CGT issued calls to battle that initially had some response but then lost power, in part due to repression but above all because of defections to Vandor's side. More important in the long run were the series of conflicts at the plant level that began to break out in the industrial zones of the interior, where a new generation of union leaders was beginning to appear at the head of workers' committees imbued with leftist ideology.

In March 1969, in protest against the university authorities, students in the city of Corrientes took to the streets, and on the 15th one of them was killed by the police. The protest extended to the rest of the universities, particularly in Rosario, where another student died and the city was the scene of a vast popular uprising. The governor of Córdoba added a new stimulus to the protest by withholding some fringe benefits enjoyed by the workers of his province, the second most highly industrialized in the country. On 15 May there were sharp confrontations with the police and on the next day a general strike was declared. A few days later came the event which would be called 'el cordobazo': on 29 and 30 May, workers and students occupied the centre of the city. Overwhelmed by the angry crowd and attacked by snipers, the police retreated. With the city in their hands for several hours, the mob turned to burning and sacking government offices and the property of foreign firms. The rebellion was quelled only when the city was occupied by troops.

The events of May provoked astonishment and alarm. The violence in the streets, which amounted to popular insurrection, were expressions of protest that had few antecedents in recent history. It was true that since 1955 political struggle had not taken place only within the legal framework, but the political and labour leaders had always managed to avoid being overwhelmed by their supporters. In fact, they appealed to mass mobilization only as a tactic of compromise. In 1966 Onganía closed off the legal and extra-legal mechanisms within which this political game had been played. The result was the rapid loss of authority by the leaders of the popular movement. The parties fell into a state of paralysis, the labour leaders had to retreat and Perón himself became little more than a political corpse when he lost the electoral stage from which he had managed to undermine both civil and military governments.

In this way, Onganía paved the way for the acts of spontaneous rebellion that were to come. In spite of the repressive measures, the events of May had set an example. Popular uprisings in the cities of the interior now proliferated, wildcat strikes multiplied in open defiance of national union leadership and student unrest took over the universities. Finally, urban guerrilla warfare made its appearance.

The extent and nature of this emerging opposition alarmed the ranks of the Argentine Revolution and opened up a debate about what path to take. General Aramburu, who had remained on the sidelines of the government, began to advocate a retreat negotiated on the basis of the rehabilitation of the political parties. It would be incumbent on them to accomplish the double task of channelling the protest and placing their votes at the service of a presidential candidate acceptable to the armed forces. The proposal did not gain favour: the return of the political class which had so recently been guilty of the crisis of governance was hardly an attractive option. New reverses would be necessary before the idea would finally be approved by the military establishment.

Under the psychological impact of the wave of protest, solidarity initially prevailed within the military, the officer corps closing ranks behind Onganía. The president took advantage of this situation to remove Krieger Vasena, install a *tecnico* with no political background as minister of economy and breathe new life into his corporatist project. In this context, there was a sudden worsening of the economic situation. Uncertainty over the stability of the peso following Krieger Vasena's resignation gave way to a massive flight of capital. Both the economic expansion and the prevailing speculative climate led to a heavy increase in imports. In sum, the reduction of foreign currency reserves was so sudden that the new authorities were forced to impose a more restrictive monetary policy. The recent favourable expectations had turned, by the end of 1969, to a generalized scepticism. Prices began to rise again, affecting the fixed rate of exchange, which the Ministry of Economy obstinately insisted on maintaining as a symbol of continuity. Weakness in the balance of payments together with inflationary tensions created irresistible pressure for a new devaluation.

The optimistic outlook of members of the economic establishment also came to an end with Krieger Vasena's resignation. Their discontent increased proportionately as Onganía announced the imminent arrival of the social phase of the revolution in an effort to contain the proliferation of conflicts. A promise to restore collective bargaining and a law granting labour leaders control of the vast resources of social union funds were gestures in this direction. But the labour leaders were in no condition to dampen popular activism. Even the police were not able to secure the tottering authoritarian order. The armed forces were increasingly obliged to resort to repression, and this led them to press for greater say in policy. But Onganía defended his autocratic prerogatives, and when in June 1970 he refused to share the responsibilities of leadership, the junta decided to depose him.

The Argentina that Onganía left behind was not the same one he had found. His regime had proposed to eradicate political conflict forever, but in the end exacerbated it severely. In his search for a new order, Onganía had eroded the very bases of the modus vivendi within which, at the price of a high level of institutional volatility, the Argentine people had previously resolved their differences. The shattering of this fragile and almost underground system of political coexistence freed forces animated by a violence hitherto unknown. Born in the heart of the middle class, the armed resistance movement left the military and politicians facing a formidable challenge. The attempt to exorcise this simultaneously bewildering and threatening presence would inflict on Argentina its deepest and most lasting wounds.

The guerrilla groups were evolving along the classical model of full-time clandestine militants common in Latin America at this time and similar to those witnessed in Argentina in 1959 and 1964. With the passage of time, they managed to create true organizations of the masses, whose members participated in armed violence to differing extents. It was the broad acceptance the guerrillas achieved among middle-class youth that lent the Argentine experience its most distinctive feature. The two most important guerrilla groups were the Ejército Revolucionario del Pueblo (ERP) of Trotskyist leanings, and the *peronista* Montoneros, so called in memory of the irregular armies of gauchos who fought in the North against Spanish troops during the wars of independence. While the Trotskyist guerrillas saw their acts as an extension of the social struggle, the armed branch of the *peronista* youth wanted to intervene in the political conflicts, including those of the *peronista* movement itself. Its objective was to neutralize any chance of a political resolution of the military crisis, to punish every manifestation of collaboration; thus, the Montoneros took responsibility for kidnapping and later assassinating General Aramburu and for murdering prominent union leaders, among them Vandor.

After Onganía was ousted, the first act of the junta was to reorganize the structure of military power. To avoid a repetition of recent experience, the chiefs of the three branches required the president to consult them on all important decisions. General Rodolfo Levingston, an almost unknown officer who the commanders believed to be above all factional military disputes, was appointed as head of state and entrusted with the task of constructing an efficient, stable and democratic political system.

At least this was the belief of General Lanusse, the army commander who was the real architect of the change of direction and who decisively influenced the composition of the new cabinet, the majority of which was associated with the so-called liberal current within the armed forces. The Ministry of Economy was assigned to a former colleague of Krieger Vasena, Carlos Moyano Llerena. In the emergency, Moyano resorted to measures similar to those taken in March 1967: he devalued the peso from 350 to 400 to the dollar, enabling the government to appropriate funds by imposing new taxes on exports; he lowered import tariffs and called for voluntary price agreements. However, this formula failed to repeat its earlier success, because the political context had changed radically. The devaluation was interpreted as a signal of future changes in parity of the currency, and the acceleration of the inflation rate to more than 20 per cent in 1970 generated heavy pressure on wages. The government was no longer in any condition to turn a deaf ear to the demands of the unions; in September it had to concede a general raise of 7 per cent and promise another 6 per cent at the beginning of 1971. The previous administration's policy of monetary contraction became untenable in the face of rising prices and salaries, so that the money supply had to expand at the same rate as the rise in prices in the second half of 1970. From January 1971 the dollar was also adjusted in small monthly increments. At this point, the eclipse of the policy of stabilization was total.

The result was that the new direction of the military regime was also put in jeopardy. Levingston seemed unwilling to settle for the mission entrusted to him and took upon himself a more elevated role: that of preparing a 'new model for Argentina' based on a more 'hierarchical and orderly' democracy than that associated with the return of the old parties. For this it would be necessary to 'deepen the revolution', an enigmatic slogan the extent of which was revealed in October 1970, when Levingston reorganized the cabinet and prepared to leave his mark on the already convulsed history of the Argentine Revolution.

He named as minister of economy Aldo Ferrer, an economist with ideas diametrically opposed to those of his predecessors, linked to the ideology of the UN Economic Commission for Latin America (ECLA) and favourable to the fortification of state and national industry. The nationalist rhetoric that coloured Ferrer's term appealed to the sentiments of the middle sectors of the Argentine bourgeoisie and the officer corps, which had been alienated by Krieger Vasena's policies favouring big business and foreign capital. The new direction involved a return to protectionism with a rise in import duties, restrictions on foreign investment and the enactment of a law which obliged state enterprises to give priority in their purchases to local supplies. In the short run, Ferrer, besieged by a wave of sectoral demands, prudently limited himself to administrating inflationary pressures through a gradual indexing of the economy.

Prudence, however, was not a characteristic of Levingston's political conduct. After getting rid of the ministers imposed on him by the junta, he sought the support of political figures who had been deprived of nearly all popular following during the vicissitudes of recent times. With their help and the use of nationalist and populist slogans, he attempted to create a new political movement, and this awoke the traditional parties from their lethargy. In November 1970, *peronistas*, Radicals and other minority groups gave birth to the 'Hora del Pueblo', a coalition designed to force the holding of elections. The years spent under military rule had brought the former rivals together in the common demand for a return to democracy. This was particularly striking because since 1955 one side or the other had participated in military coups, hoping either to win influence in the government (the *peronistas* in 1966) or to be its electoral heirs (the Radicals in the Revolución Libertadora).

The reappearance of the parties dealt a rude blow to Levingston's ambitions. His nationalist and populist line, while it antagonized conservative circles, made little impact on those to whom it was directed. Both the unions and the middle class preferred to align themselves with the new opposition than to associate themselves with a president who was growing increasingly isolated. The power structure erected by the military commanders had slipped out of their hands, but they vacillated in the face of their failure. Eventually, Levingston's audacious indiscretions facilitated matters for them. In February 1971 he appointed to the unsettled province of Córdoba a governor whose outlook was close to the fascist conservatism of the 1930s and who began his term with a defiant speech in which he announced exceptionally punitive measures. The response was a new popular uprising, no less violent and widespread than the one of 1969. This second '*cordobazo*' precipitated a national crisis, and on 22 March the junta removed Levingston and assumed the reins of power again.

Thus began the last phase of the military regime, directed at the reestablishment of the democratic institutions. Lacking the cohesion and the capacity for repression necessary to restore the original objectives of 1966, the armed forces began a search for a political solution that would enable them to control the wave of popular protest and return to their barracks. General Lanusse was appointed president and immediately unfolded the new strategy, legalizing the parties and calling for a broad agreement between the military and the political forces to draw up the rules of institutional transition.

The novelty of this initiative was that it included *peronismo*. For the first time since 1955, the armed forces were ready to accept *peronismo*, admitting that any political solution that excluded Perón was illusory and short-sighted. 'Perón is a reality, whether we like it or not', Lanusse recognized publicly,[7] putting an end to one of the most costly taboos of the Argentine military. Perhaps no other officer could have dared to say it. As a young lieutenant, Lanusse had been imprisoned under Perón's first presidency. Moreover, his credentials as a representative of the liberal wing of the army were impeccable, and his family ties linked him to the economic establishment. This background and the prestige he enjoyed among his colleagues, thanks to a style quite distinct from the gruff arrogance of Onganía and Levingston, made him a trustworthy leader for the daring political manoeuvre that lay before him.

What brought the military to negotiate with Perón was not its traditional reluctance to come to terms with the role of the working class in national politics but the threat posed by the middle-class youth movement. The youth radicalized at the end of the 1960s in the struggle against the military regime had adopted *peronismo* as a way of identifying themselves with the people. In a historical twist, the sons of those who most firmly opposed Perón turned their backs on their parents to embrace the very cause they had fought against. Under the spell of the ideas of Che Guevara and Franz Fanon and the theology of liberation, the protagonists of this political patricide transformed Perón and *peronismo* into the militant embodiment of a national socialism. Lanusse's idea was that, once included in the political system, Perón would withdraw ideological support for the revolutionary movement that was invoking his name. A curious paradox of history became apparent: he who once had been identified with one-half of the country came to be everything to everyone. Perón was now called upon to apply his remarkable skills to the rescue of a drifting polity. In 1972 the very governability of the country was at stake.

Lanusse's strategy was close to that which inspired the conservative elite in the first decade of the century, when it resolved to guarantee free, secret elections in order to allow the participation of the Radical Party. Then, too, it was judged less dangerous to incorporate the Radicals into the

---

[7] *Clarín*, 28 July 1972; quoted in L. de Riz, *Retorno y derrumbe, el último gobierno peronista* (Buenos Aires, 1987), p. 46.

system than to leave them out and exposed to revolutionary temptations. However, the conservative elite lost control of the process it launched and the Radicals, led by Yrigoyen, instead of occupying the subordinate position reserved for them, ended up by taking over the government. As time passed, this historical parallel would become much more direct than Lanusse was initially willing to admit.

Lanusse's proposal was aimed at ensuring the participation of *peronismo* under controlled conditions. The *peronistas* would be able to run for any elective office except the presidency. Furthermore, Perón was to disavow publicly the Peronist guerrillas. This proposal, negotiated in secret by agents sent by Lanusse to talk with Perón in Madrid, was part of a broader agreement in which all the major political forces were invited to give their support to a common presidential candidate acceptable to the armed forces. Lanusse received a favourable response from the *peronista* politicians and even the union leaders, for whom a return to democracy promised positions of greater influence. The unknown factor was the attitude Perón himself would take after years of sabotaging the political arrangements painstakingly engineered by those who had overthrown and banned him.

Beyond the historical reparation the negotiation itself implied, Perón was offered the cancellation of all the penalties that had been pending against him since 1955 and something else that was particularly symbolic. In September 1971, the military delivered to him the embalmed body of Evita, which fifteen years earlier had been transported secretly to Europe and buried in an Italian cemetery under another name. Nevertheless, Perón side-stepped the commitments being asked of him. Determined to exploit the initiative given to him by the military crisis, he followed an ambiguous course, leaving open all the possibilities the situation offered. Furthermore, even he, like so many others, could not be absolutely certain about the final outcome.

In October 1971 a military uprising was led by officers sympathetic to Onganía and Levingston, who accused Lanusse of betraying the goals of the revolution and of handing the country over to the old politicians. The rebellion was easily put down, but it changed the conditions of negotiation. Lanusse was so identified with the election that if it failed it was not certain whether he could maintain his leadership of the armed forces. Perón took advantage of this to continue encouraging the guerrillas and to reduce his concessions to a minimum; he made things more tense by forcing the elections to be held on his own terms rather than on terms that were supposedly being imposed on him. In the process he also took into account the widespread repudiation that surrounded the military domination and encouraged the increasingly bold actions of the guerrillas to be viewed with a certain benevolence. The repressive measures, both brutal and ineffective, that were employed against the guerrilla involvement contributed to the military's loss of face, both at home and abroad.

The military government found itself obliged simply to follow the dynamic of the process which it itself had unleashed. Less dramatic circumstances had led to the coup d'état of 1966. This time, however, nothing was done to interrupt the elections scheduled for March 1973. Fear of an explosive fusion between popular discontent and the guerrilla movement strengthened the decision to institutionalize the country. As had occurred every time the prospect of an election was reopened, Perón became a pole of attraction, and he easily manipulated his renewed popularity to build up a network of alliances. Thus, without ceasing to praise the guerrillas, he began to move in two other directions. First, towards the Radicals, with whom he forged a pact of mutual guarantees in which he declared himself respectful of the rights of minority parties at the same time as he demanded that his old enemies promise to hold elections with no vetoes or proscriptions. Second, he began to approach interest groups through Frondizi, whom he included in a political-electoral alliance which proposed nothing that could alarm the landowners and businessmen.

Time worked against Lanusse, who was unable to display the promised fruits of his strategy before his comrades. The Radical Party was not willing to play the role assigned to it. Although it did not oppose official policy so as not to provoke a coup d'état, neither did it wish to support the plans of those who had defeated it in 1966. Lanusse's situation became even more complicated in the middle of 1972, when Perón, in Madrid, revealed the hitherto secret contacts with his emissaries. The furor this produced in official circles could be calmed only when Lanusse publicly announced that he was withdrawing his candidacy for president. This decision was followed by another, obviously directed at Perón, whereby a time limit was set for all candidates to establish residence in the country. Although protesting, the exiled caudillo carefully avoided challenging the outer limits of the now restless military government's tolerance. When the deadline arrived in November 1972, Perón returned to Argentina after an absence of seventeen years, and remained for several weeks. 'I have no hatred or rancour. It is not a time for revenge. I return as a pacifier of spirits'[8] were his words to the Argentine people, who welcomed him with a mixture of amazement and disbelief.

During his stay Perón sealed his reconciliation with the leader of the Radicals, Ricardo Balbín, and lay the cornerstone of the electoral front that would unite the *peronistas*, the Partido Conservador Popular, the followers of Frondizi, the Partido Popular Cristiano and some Socialists. Back in Madrid he named Hector Cámpora, a minor politician known for his dogged fidelity to the populist leader and his recent close links with militant *peronista* youth, as the front's presidential candidate – a decision which provoked visible resentment among union leaders and the moderate politicians in the movement, who felt unjustly passed over. Cámpora, furthermore, came under the electoral restrictions imposed by the government, and many suspected that Perón wanted his candidate to be disqualified, in a new twist of his changing political tactics. Lanusse decided not to respond to this last-minute challenge by Perón. On 11 March 1973, the *peronista* coalition obtained 49 per cent of the votes, the Radicals 21 per cent, the parties of the Right 15 per cent and a leftist front 7 per cent. After the ostentatious failure of Lanusse's strategy, the military abandoned the government, taking as their consolation a vision of the old caudillo facing the titanic task that they had not been able to accomplish: that of constructing a political order capable of maintaining control over the expectations and passions unleashed by nearly two decades of frustration and discord.

THE RETURN AND FALL OF PERÓN 1973–6

Once the votes had been counted and Cámpora's government installed, the political situation rapidly evolved towards an institutional crisis. Encouraged by the backing received from Perón, radical elements accompanied the new president into office and began to practice the politics of mass mobilization. Under Cámpora's complacent gaze, worker revolts in defiance of the union leadership occurred on a daily basis, and many public buildings were occupied by bands of *peronista* youth. The objective that unified this militant offensive was to regain both the government and the movement for the new generation of socialist *peronismo*. Under these conditions, the conflicts that had hitherto been latent within the conglomeration of forces which had supported the return of *peronismo* to power now broke out into the open.

---

[8] Quoted in L. de Riz, *Retorno y derrumbe*, p. 63.

The union chiefs – who had been ignored in the operation that led to the military's defeat – manifested their alarm over a political process that shunned traditional values. This preoccupation was already bothering Perón as well and the members of the intimate circle that accompanied him in exile, notably José López Rega, his secretary, a former chief of police and *aficionado* of the occult sciences. Scarcely forty-nine days after having been sworn in as president, Cámpora was forced to resign, and new elections placed Perón himself in the presidency, with his wife, Isabel, as vice-president. The balloting, held in September 1973, gave the victory to the Perón–Perón ticket with 62 per cent of the votes cast. The magnitude of the electoral triumph was a clear indication that many of his former enemies had decided to vote for the old caudillo in the hope that he would now impose control on his young followers. Two days after the elections, even before the celebrations were over, Perón received an ominous warning when the secretary-general of the CGT, José Rucci, one of his most loyal adherents, was assassinated by the guerrillas.

The tactical shift that would alienate Perón from his young admirers of the Left had been announced on 20 June, the day he returned to live permanently in Argentina. Nearly 2 million people were waiting for him at Ezeiza Airport, most of them under the banners of the revolutionary tendencies of *peronismo*. What should have been a great popular celebration turned into a pitched battle, with many deaths and injuries, when armed bands of the Right and the Left confronted one another. The aeroplane in which Perón was flying was diverted to another airport.

That night, Perón gave a speech revealing the political project with which he was returning.[9] He began with a call for demobilization: 'We have a revolution to make, but for it to be valid it must be a peaceful reconstruction. We are in no condition to keep destroying in the face of a destiny pregnant with ambushes and dangers. It is necessary to return to what in its time was our maxim: from work to home and from home to work'. His new vision of the political community was reflected in this announcement: '*Justicialismo* was never sectarian or exclusive and today it calls upon all Argentines without distinction so that all of us, with solidarity, will join together in the task of national reconstruction'. Later, this summons was more explicit, when he replaced the slogan 'Nothing is better for a *peronista* than another *peronista*', which had divided the country during his first two presidencies, with a new one, 'Nothing is better for an

---

[9] *La Nación*, 21 June 1974; quoted in L. de Riz, *Retorno y derrumbe*, p. 90.

Argentine than another Argentine'. His final words were dedicated to dashing the hopes for a doctrinaire renewal which he himself had stimulated during his last years in exile. 'We are *justicialistas*. We fly a flag that is as distant from one of the dominant imperialisms as from the other. . . . There are no new labels that qualify our doctrine. Those who naïvely think they can corner our movement or take away the power that the people have reconquered are mistaken'.

With this message, Perón validated the bold decision that Lanusse had made two years earlier. To the bewilderment of the young *peronistas*, Perón now set about reversing the shift to the left that marked the struggle against the military regime and that Cámpora erroneously converted into government policy. After the electoral triumph, the ERP ratified its subversive strategy, but the Montoneros suspended their activities, indicating that their future conduct would depend on the new government keeping to its revolutionary promises. Thus, the head of the Montoneros, Mario Firmenich, when asked whether they were abandoning the use of force, answered:

By no means; political power comes out of the mouth of the rifle. If we have come up to this point, it is because we had rifles and we used them. If we abandoned them we would suffer a setback in our political position. In war there are moments of confrontation, such as those which we have gone through, and there are moments of truce, in which preparations are made for the next confrontation. [10]

The change observed in Perón's attitude confronted the young *peronistas* with an agonizing alternative between breaking with him and being excluded from the popular coalition united around his leadership.

The dissidence of the young did not exhaust the questions raised by *peronismo*'s return to power. If Perón now seemed able to change the policies that he had advocated from the opposition, could the same flexibility be expected from a movement that had remained formidable over the previous eighteen years and hardly felt committed to an institutional system in which its participation could at any time be curtailed? How could Perón impress the need for political coexistence on those who had been led into an undisguised sectarianism by constant proscriptions? How could he convince those who had seen the relentless diminution of their share of income that it was prudent to make the demands of labour compatible with the stability of the economy? Finally, how could Perón

[10] *El Descamisado*, 11 September 1973; quoted in Guido Di Tella, *Perón–Perón 1973–1976* (Buenos Aires, 1983), p. 55.

wrest a commitment to peace from those whose violence he had previously endorsed?

The old caudillo's call for conciliation had a more favourable reception among his enemies than among his followers. In Perón's message the former saw a promise for political order in an Argentina shaken by conflict and violence; the latter, by contrast, wanted the electoral triumph to herald their historical vindication. When he came into power in 1946, Perón had faced a similar challenge. But then there had been an energetic and ambitious caudillo in the center of the populist coalition; the Perón who now returned to tame the hopes and passions unleashed by his return was a man of seventy-eight years, in poor health.

During the remaining ten months of his life, Perón invested the still vigorous powers of his charisma in channelling the diffuse and virulent aspirations of his followers and in reconstructing the battered political system he had inherited. The two instruments of his institutional project were the political agreement between the major parties represented in Congress (*peronistas* and Radicals) and the Social Pact between business and the unions. His goal was an 'integrated democracy' in which the old organic model of the organized community was expanded to place the interest groups and the political parties on an equal footing. The attitude towards the armed forces was, in turn, another expression of the new times. During Cámpora's brief administration, the command of the army was exercised by General Jorge Carcagno, who strongly advocated the unity of the armed forces with the people in a pathetic attempt to accommodate himself to the complex situation created by the *peronista* victory. When he became president, Perón ordered changes in the military hierarchy. An apolitical commander-in-chief was appointed to replace Carcagno, who by his overtures to the government had alienated himself from the sentiments dominant among his comrades. With this gesture, Perón meant to underline the professional and non-political role he had reserved for the armed forces during his third presidential term.

Cámpora's original cabinet was purged of its leftist elements, who were replaced by trusted veterans. The two most important figures who survived the purge were López Rega, in the Ministry of Social Welfare, and José Gelbard, in the Ministry of Economy. President of the Confederación General Económica (CGE), the association representing the national bourgeoisie, Gelbard was linked to Perón from the years of his second presidency. His economic programme was mildly nationalist and redistributionist, with a strong accent on state intervention in the economy. The key component was an incomes policy based on a tripartite agreement among the government, business and the unions, with which Gelbard tried to contain the inflationary pressures that dominated the last years of the military regime. In 1971 and 1972, the rise in price levels was 39.2 and 64.2 per cent, respectively, moving up in the first five months of 1973 to an annual rate of 100 per cent.

Together with rising inflation, Gelbard also faced a growing economy. After the peak reached in the year of the *cordobazo* – 8.5 per cent in 1969 – the rate of economic growth continued at 5.4 per cent in 1970, 4.8 per cent in 1971, descending to 3.2 per cent in 1972 and rising again to 5.1 per cent in the first quarter of 1973. This growth had begun in 1964; during the ten years since then, the economy had been growing at an average annual rate of 4 per cent. However, this remarkable performance, which was fuelled by sustained growth in exports and the maturation of investments since the Frondizi era, was clouded by the persistence of conflict and the instability of prices. The new administration, therefore, was concerned about a gloomy future that current economic indicators did not reflect.

The political movement galvanized by nostalgia for Perón's earlier presidencies naturally exhibited a dominant preoccupation with the standard of living of the workers. The decline in real wages in 1972 reflected a real fall in the contribution of wage-earners to national income: from the 46.5 per cent it had reached in 1952 it had tumbled to less than 38 per cent in June 1973. The memory of one of Frondizi's first decisions after being elected with the *peronista* vote – a general salary increase of 60 per cent – encouraged optimistic forecasts by many union leaders, including Minister of Labour Ricardo Otero, a member of the metal-workers' union. The increase granted under the Social Pact, however, was only 20 per cent, and it was accompanied by the suspension of collective bargaining for two years as well as a price freeze.

The signing of the price and wage agreement did not meet with much resistance in the business community, many members of which had anticipated it and already increased their prices. Moreover, the general moderation of the measures facilitated acceptance by those who feared more demagogic policies. In order to obtain the consent of the unions, Perón had to explore all his political authority. The unions grudgingly gave up the freedom to negotiate – a permanent demand under the military regime – since their weak political position within the *peronista* movement left them no alternative. However, by signing the Social Pact, the union leaders reverted to *peronista* orthodoxy, from which they had been alienated so many times in the past. This allowed them to regain Perón's approval; with his backing they led the offensive against the radicalized youth and got from Congress a law that further suppressed internal union democracy and protected their positions from the anti-bureaucratic rebellion that had been under way since the *cordobazo*.

The change in expectations provoked by the Social Pact was impressive. While in the first five months of 1973 the cost of living had risen by about 37 per cent, from July to December it rose by only 4 per cent. Furthermore, with exports 65 per cent higher than those of the previous year and imports that had increased in value about 36 per cent, the trade balance by the end of 1973 was 30 per cent higher than in 1972. But it was in the external sector that the first negative signs appeared to cast a shadow over this optimistic picture. By December the effects of the oil crisis reached the Argentine economy, provoking a sharp increase in the price of imports. Given the freeze on prices, the higher cost of imported goods began to erode business profit margins; some companies interrupted or cut down production, and all joined the clamour against the rigid price policy. Gelbard tried to sanction a resolution authorizing companies to pass on higher costs in the form of higher prices, but Perón forbade this at the demand of the unions, which threatened to withdraw from the Social Pact.

The unions' refusal to approve a rise in prices without a simultaneous rise in wages was fully understandable. While the signing of the Social Pact had frozen their institutional power, labour mobilization had been given new vigour by the electoral triumph. After the *peronista* government took office, conflict at the plant level multiplied, fuelled by disputes over working conditions, disciplinary regulations, dismissals, etc.; the rank and file were in a general state of rebellion. Harassed by the flourishing leftist elements that viewed the Social Pact as a betrayal, the union chiefs blocked Gelbard's proposal, which favoured business. The emergency solution was to resort to the foreign currency reserves built up by the excellent external balance in order to subsidize the purchase of critical supplies with a preferential exchange rate.

However, confidence in the income policy now began to collapse, as was demonstrated by the proliferation of the black market. In addition to the pressure exerted by business for greater price flexibility, at a plant level workers' delegates obtained, through the device of job reclassification or increased bonuses for productivity, hidden salary increases. Meanwhile, an obvious incongruity was becoming apparent between the rigid price policy and the permissive monetary policy adopted to manage a fiscal deficit that exceeded 6 per cent of the GNP.

At the beginning of 1974 the need to revise the price and wage agreements became imperative, and in February Gelbard convened the CGE and the CGT. After several weeks, the parties had to admit that compromise was impossible and Perón was obliged to intercede between them. The arbitration handed down on 28 March established a salary increase 5 to 6 per cent greater than the deterioration in real wages and authorized the companies to raise prices by an amount to be decided by the government. Although the leaders of the CGT were hoping for a greater increase, the decision was interpreted as favourable to the workers. When price levels were announced in April, profit margins were fixed at less than the level demanded by business, which began to launch a systematic and generalized violation of the Social Pact. Between April and May the cost of living rose 7.7 per cent, whereas in January it had increased only 2.8 per cent. The resumption of the income struggle soon converted zero inflation into a thing of the past.

Perón's last public appearance, a month before his death, was also the most dramatic. On 12 June he stepped onto the scene of his past triumphs, the balcony of the Casa Rosada, and threatened to resign before a crowd hastily assembled in an effort to regain the political initiative over a society that in recent weeks had slipped from his command.

On 1 May, the traditional Labour Day celebrations had culminated spectacularly in a confrontation between the radical youth and Perón. Harassed by criticism and chanting that interrupted his speech, Perón accused the youth of being 'mercenaries paid by foreigners' and called for the expulsion of the 'infiltrators' of the *peronista* movement. The rupture had been brewing since the beginning of the year, when the initial exhortations for moderation were followed by a drastic offensive against those positions still held by the radical *peronista* wing. The removal of the governor of the province of Buenos Aires after armed action by the ERP at a military base, the overthrow by force of the governor of Córdoba – both left-wing politicians – an assault on the offices of the *peronista* youth and the suppression of their publications formed part of a campaign that left no doubts about the incompatibility of the two currents that had converged with the return of *peronismo* to power: that which headed the wave of popular mobilization and aimed at the breakdown of the political order in the name of revolutionary populism and that which, based on the party and the unions, corresponded to the traditional ideals of Perón.

Against the background of this confrontation, labour conflict continued with redoubled intensity. The period between March and June registered the highest average number of strikes per month in the three years of *peronista* government. The outcome of the conflict was ensured in large part by a change in attitude on the part of business. The decision of 28 March weakened its already reluctant willingness to compromise on the incomes policy. Wage demands were now accepted only to be translated immediately into higher prices without government authorization. Alarmed by the situation, the CGT leaders went to Perón at the beginning of June to ask for some official reaction that would ease the pressure they were under. On 12 June Perón tried to fill the vacuum that surrounded his government project with his own political authority. But he did not have time to harvest the fruits of this final effort, since he died on 1 July.

Perón had been clearly aware that even the impressive electoral majority of 62 per cent obtained in 1973 was insufficient to keep him in power. A *peronista* government resting solely on its own bases could rapidly become vulnerable to pressures from the opposition, which, although politically defeated, had the powerful backing of big business and the military hierarchy. In order to avoid the predictable risks of political isolation, Perón had sought to build a network of agreements, such as the Social Pact and the convergence with the Radical Party in Congress. With his death, Perón's goals of political reconciliation and social collaboration, which had already suffered appreciable reverses, were abandoned by his successors. Inspired more by sectarianism than by the politics of conciliation, Isabel Perón and her entourage and the union leaders – the two influential groups in the new power structure – dedicated themselves to dismantling the agreements they had inherited. The hour of *peronismo*, they announced, had arrived.

The first step in this direction was taken against Gelbard, who, once the brief armistice that followed Perón's death was over, submitted his resignation in October. With his departure, the links that tied the CGE to the government were weakened. A similar fate befell the inter-party accords. After taking over the presidency, Perón's wife reorganized the cabinet, replacing representatives of the parties who had formed the electoral front with members of her intimate circle. She also brought an end to the special relations with the Radical Party, which was no longer consulted about major government decisions. While this operation of political homogenization was taking place, the violence entered a new phase. At the end of 1974 the Montoneros announced that they were going underground to continue their struggle, now against the government of Isabel Perón. At the same time there emerged a right-wing terrorist group known as the Triple A (Alianza Argentina Anticomunista) armed and commanded by López Rega, the president's minister of social welfare and her private secretary.

Within a few months, the political scene was reduced to the arcane palace manoeuvrings of the presidential entourage and the macabre routines of the practitioners of violence. Worker protest, in turn, declined, partly because of the ruling climate of insecurity and partly because the repression was eliminating, step by step, the bastions of the leftist union opposition. Eventually, the palace clique clustered around Isabel Perón and the union leaders were left face to face. The last contest that led to the downfall of *peronismo* was played out around the aspirations of these two rival sectors.

In spite of the encouraging picture painted by Gelbard when he left office – a 7 per cent growth in GDP in 1974 and a decline in unemployment from 6 per cent in April 1973 to 2.5 per cent in November 1974 – the immediate economic prospects looked dismal. In July the European Economic Community had prohibited the importation of Argentine meat, sharply affecting the volume and value of exports. Meanwhile, the prices of imports continued to rise. Fearful of the effects it might have on real wages and inflationary trends, Gelbard had not readjusted the exchange rate and thereby stimulated a current of speculative importing. The surplus of U.S. $704 million accumulated in 1973 reverted to a deficit of $216 million in the second half of 1974. The first task of the new minister of economy, Alfredo Gómez Morales, was to adjust an economy that was 'overheated' – nearly full employment, a growing money supply and a rising inflation rate – to the unfavourable situation in the external sector.

A central figure in the adoption of the successful stabilization programme of 1952, Gómez Morales had occupied the presidency of the Central Bank during Gelbard's administration, a job he abandoned after disagreement over the permissive fiscal policy. He first attempted to change course through greater control over public spending, reduction of monetary expansion and selective price increases. While necessary, the adjustments were too moderate and did not include the exchange rate, which continued to rise in real terms, with a consequent loss of foreign funds. In March 1975 there was another devaluation, which reduced but did not eliminate the overvaluation of the currency. Consonant with Gómez Morales' gradualist focus, salaries were also increased. This hesitant shift of economic policy collided, in addition, with an unexpected obstacle: the new minister did not belong to the president's intimate circle. Thus, throughout the 241 days of his incumbency, he waited in vain for official endorsement to adopt stricter measures while he contemplated the deterioration of the economic situation.

In this climate of drift, collective bargaining sessions were held as scheduled in February. Very soon, however, discussion of the new wage contracts was stalled by the absence of guidelines for negotiation from the government. The unions had been anxiously waiting for the opening of direct bargaining with the companies so they could rehabilitate their battered leadership after nearly two years of incomes policy. But the president, under the powerful influence of López Rega, paid no attention to their concerns, busy as she was preparing a drastic realignment of the government's political and social bases.

In essence, this policy entailed gaining the confidence of the armed forces and the economic establishment through the suppression of subversion by using the terrorist bands of the Triple A, which would avoid the direct involvement of the military; the eradication of the Left in its last refuge, the university; a return to foreign capital investment and a market economy, with a reduction in wages and the re-establishment of industrial discipline; and finally, the removal of the union movement from the structure of power. In the name of these ambitious goals the military was asked to abandon its political neutrality, which had been maintained since General Carcagno's resignation. This seemed to be achieved when, in May, the new commander-in-chief of the army, General Alberto Numa Laplane, advocated tactical support to the government. Isabel and López Rega then believed that their bold shift to the right, combined with the manipulation of *peronista* symbols, was ready to be launched.

When the day fixed for concluding the wage negotiations – 31 May – arrived without any official effort to facilitate new contracts, worker protest escaped union control in the form of street demonstrations and occupations of factories. On that very day Gómez Morales' resignation was accepted and Celestino Rodrigo, a conspicuous member of the presidential entourage, replaced him. Rodrigo announced a programme of measures that entailed an increase of the order of 100 per cent in the exchange rate and the cost of public services, at the same time recommending an increase of 40 per cent as a guideline in salary negotiations. A readjustment of relative prices was predictable, after a period of repressed inflation and currency overvaluation.

However, both the magnitude of the readjustment and the timing of the announcement seemed to indicate that the president wanted to create an untenable situation for the union leaders relative to the rank and file, thus clipping their political influence. Suddenly, they found themselves struggling not only for a wage increase but also for their own political survival. During the two succeeding weeks they mobilized to obtain the annulment of the restrictions on free wage negotiation. Thus, after a series of stormy meetings, facing businessmen who finally set aside all resistance, they negotiated wage increases amounting on average to 160 per cent.

Isabel Perón's response was equally forceful. On 24 June she nullified the agreements reached between the companies and the unions and offered a wage increase of 50 per cent to be followed by two more increases of 15 per cent in August and October. The union leaders found themselves faced with a dilemma they had desperately tried to avoid: either to continue the confrontation, with the risk of precipitating the fall of the government, or to accept the official offer, resigning themselves to political defeat and the collapse of their prestige before the rank and file. The spontaneous reaction of the workers to the president's announcement paralysed the country. For one week no one went to work. The CGT had no alternative but to ratify this fait accompli and call for a general strike of forty-eight hours on 7 July. This decision, unprecedented in the history of *peronismo,* brought an aggressive crowd before the Casa Rosada to demand the resignations of the president's entourage and the approval of the wage agreements. Contrary to expectations in official circles, the military stayed out of the conflict. Left to their fate, López Rega and Rodrigo tendered their resignations, and Isabel had to retrace her steps and accede to the labour demands. The political crisis concluded with the victory of the union leaders, who, although they renewed their support for Perón's wife, had effectively frustrated the political operation through which she sought to dislodge them from power.

After this dramatic episode, the *peronista* administration was never able to restore its credibility. It survived eight more months, during which the threat of a military coup dogged its every step and deepened the political crisis. After López Rega's resignation, the president temporarily withdrew from her duties on leave of absence, and a coalition of union men and old *peronista* politicians took over the government under the leadership of the president of the Senate, Italo Luder. General Numa Laplane was also forced to resign by the military high command; the new commander-in-chief, General Jorge Videla, again distanced the armed forces from the government, although their involvement in anti-subversive operations became more direct under Luder's instructions.

The immediate consequence of the measures taken by Rodrigo and the union counter-offensive was a violent acceleration in the inflation rate. In the months of June, July and August consumer prices rose 102 per cent, closer to a monthly rate of 7 to 10 per cent than to the 2 to 3 per cent that had been the average over the past thirty years. For the post of minister of economy, the unions proposed Antonio Cafiero, whose policy consisted of a gradual indexing of prices, salaries and the exchange rate. This tactic had the virtue of avoiding major serious distortions in relative prices, but it also implied an admission that it was impossible to reduce inflationary pressures. In all events, it permitted a reversal of the unfavourable trends in the external sector, assisted by the devalued currency that had been inherited and some short-term financing obtained from the IMF and other public and private organisms. The effects would be felt above all during the first quarter of 1976 when the balance of trade would show its first surplus in fifteen months.

Unable to check the high and fluctuating inflation rate, Cafiero had to live with one of its predictable consequences, the dizzying expansion of financial speculation. In the face of the depreciation of the value of goods and salaries, people found it more profitable to engage in feverish manipulation of the differences between the official dollar and the black market dollar, between posted interest rates and the rate of inflation. The voracious speculation attracted capital from the whole economy, from large corporations down to small savers. Under the impact of the acceleration of prices, the economy began a rapid slide from the 'overheated' situation in April, with strong pressures on the side of demand and a low rate of unemployment, to a situation close to recession in July and August. In Buenos Aires unemployment rose from 2.3 per cent to 6 per cent and in Córdoba it reached 7 per cent. The reduction in industrial production was 5.6 per cent in the third quarter of the year and 8.9 per cent in the last quarter. The declining economic situation did not, however, attenuate the level of labour conflicts; instead, the new situation prolonged them and made their resolution more difficult to achieve.

In this context, there was increased activity by the guerrillas, who kidnapped and assassinated plant managers in order to force acceptance of worker demands. These actions unleashed equally violent reprisals from paramilitary groups against union activists. The factories thus became one more site for the wave of violence that provided a tragic backdrop for the critical economic situation. In the second half of 1975 the guerrillas decided to step up their operations; in addition to kidnappings, assassinations and bombings, the Montoneros and the ERP launched more ambitious actions against military targets. The pressure of the security forces, however, obliged them to revert to more rudimentary terrorism, which increased their already irreversible isolation from the movements of popular protest. Dazed by the daily acts of violence, vast sectors of the population began to contemplate the possibility of military intervention. But the military commanders did not seem anxious to act, apparently allowing the crisis to deepen so that their final move would have the broadest support.

The coalition of unionists and politicians that sustained Luder in the presidency failed to fulfil the expectations of stability that they had encouraged. The exaggerated demands of the unions made coexistence with the moderate politicians difficult while at the same time causing alarm in traditional circles. A new business organization, Asamblea Permanente de Asociaciónes Gremiales (APEGE), led by big agrarian and industrial capital, took over the place left vacant by the CGE to assume an openly rebellious stance against the government. In January 1976 Isabel returned to the presidential palace and reorganized the cabinet, getting rid of the ministers linked to the alliance of union leaders and politicians and surrounding herself with figures who were outside the *peronista* movement. Some of them were survivors of the López Rega clique, others were unknown functionaries, but all were ready to follow this lone woman, heir to the ideals of a movement in whose history she had not taken part, a movement whose natural leaders she hated and whose followers inspired only her distrust. The initial reaction of those who had been ousted was indignation; they went so far as to discuss the possibility of filing suit against the president, under charges of misuse of public funds. Very soon, however, they yielded to the inevitable, realizing that her downfall, foreshadowed by an aborted military uprising in December, was imminent.

During these troubled days, the Radical Party tried to regain the role as principal opposition party that had been denied it in the past three years as *peronismo* became both the government and its opposition. Marginalized from the conflicts in which the movement created by Perón was being torn apart, the Radicals had till then centred their discourse on the defence of the institutional order, an attitude that led them to unaccustomed extremes in their tolerance for the conduct of the veteran populist leader and his followers. They now proposed the erection of a government without Isabel. Their call went unheeded. Already looking ahead to the period that would begin after the inevitable coup d'état, the unionists and *peronista* politicians decided to close ranks behind Perón's wife. She, in turn, dedicated her last days to launching a series of economic measures that she imagined were responsive to the needs of the military hierarchy and big business.

During the first days of March a new minister of economy tried to address the economic calamity with another abrupt change in relative prices. The exchange rate and the prices of public services were raised by between 90 and 100 per cent while salaries were increased by 20 per cent. Like Rodrigo's earlier measure, this new readjustment explicitly included a decline in real wages. A wave of strikes began to paralyse the principal centres in heated protest against the economic measures. When everything looked as if it were leading to a confrontation similar to that of June 1975, the military overthrew the government – without opposition.

THE PROCESS OF NATIONAL REORGANIZATION, 1976–83

For a country with a long history of military interventions, the coup d'état of 1976 held no surprises. Accustomed to reading the warning signs, the majority of Argentines saw it as the inevitable outcome of the ongoing political crisis. The armed forces had patiently waited for the deepening of the crisis in order to legitimize their intervention. When they decided to act, many people shared their sombre assessment of the state of the country:

All constitutional measures having been exhausted, all possibilities of rectification through institutional means having been exceeded, and with the irrefutable demonstration of the impossibility of restoring the government process by natural means, a situation resulted which oppressed the nation and compromised its future. . . . Faced with a tremendous power vacuum, capable of overwhelming us with dissolution and anarchy, with the lack of capacity for dialogue that the national government has demonstrated, with the lack of an overall strategy . . . to confront subversion, with the lack of a solution to the basic problems of the nation, the result of which has been a permanent increase of all extremist movements, with the total absence of ethical and moral example by the leaders of the state, with the manifest irresponsibility in managing the economy . . . the armed forces, in the fulfilment of a permanent obligation, have assumed the leadership of the state.[11]

---

[11] Quoted in C. Floria and C. García Belsunce, *Historia política de la Argentina contemporánea* (Madrid, 1988), p. 238.

The commanders-in-chief of the three armed services installed themselves as the supreme power and named General Jorge Videla, the army chief, as president. However, the privileges accorded to the army as the oldest and traditionally pre-eminent branch ended there. Governmental administration was divided equally between the army, the navy and the air force. This institutional innovation owed much to the strong leadership of Admiral Emilio Massera, who managed to regain for the navy the positions lost during the intra-military confrontations of 1962. In initiating a 'process of national reorganization' it was predictable that the military regime would put a policy of repression into practice, but the scale and nature of the violence to which it resorted were unprecedented. The initial measures followed a familiar pattern: the prohibition of political activities, censorship of the press, the arrest of labour leaders and intervention in the unions. To this was added the death penalty, administrated in a form which was different from anything ever known before.

First, there were the victims. Although the goal of the military was to do away with subversion, the repressive measures were not limited to the guerrillas. Videla himself said that 'a terrorist is not only one who carries a bomb or a pistol, but also one who spreads ideas contrary to Western Christian civilization'. Thus, the enemy included all kinds of dissidents; together with the guerrillas and those who aided them by giving them food and refuge, politicians, union members and intellectuals fell within the orbit of repression. For the military, the Communist threat it had intermittently denounced over the past twenty years had finally taken bodily form and dared, furthermore, to defy it with arms.

Second, there was the method of violence. Councils of war were created and given the power to inflict death sentences for a great variety of crimes. But it was not primarily through them that the summary justice of the military operated. The repressive infrastructure was based, rather, on officially authorized but clandestine detention centres and in special units of the three military branches and the police, the mission of which was to kidnap, interrogate, torture and, in the majority of cases, kill. This infrastructure was highly decentralized; the real authority was invested in the regional commanders, who in their own territory were the supreme power and reported only to their immediate superiors. This decentralization and autonomy granted the shock forces enormous impunity. This mechanism had several advantages: it was a difficult network to infiltrate, it was immune to the influence of well-connected relatives of the victims and it allowed the government to deny any responsibility for the violation of human rights.

Between 1976 and 1979 a wave of terror swept the country. The activities of the repressive apparatus were basically secret, making it difficult to establish the number of victims. They were part of a group for which Argentina became tragically famous: *los desaparecidos* (the missing ones), those about whom nothing was ever heard again. At first, the violence was not entirely one-sided. In the nine months that followed the coup d'état, the guerrillas carried out acts of terrorism against military targets. The response of the armed forces was explosive and crushing. Hundreds of guerrillas were killed in the streets while they mounted a desperate resistance. But the main cause of the defeat of the guerrillas were the kidnappings and their consequences. Over time, the majority of those kidnapped had their spirits broken. Driven by the physical pain of torture, without hope for the future of a struggle that was only suffering defeats, the victims ended by informing on their comrades and thus increasing the number of victims. Many innocent people met the same fate, trapped in the vast net of counter-insurgency operations.

The policy of extermination launched by the armed forces fed on the culture of violence that flourished in Argentina after the *cordobazo* of 1969. Public opinion had been subjected to an intense propaganda campaign aimed at making the use of violence acceptable. First came the rebellion of the youth, who in the name of revolution postulated the need to resort to arms. Then the terrorist bands of the Right took the same course, with the result that the military regime's repression was imposed on a country where the cult of violence was already deeply rooted. All the moral obstacles were removed when Argentina became submerged in what the military itself called the 'dirty war'.

The resort to violence initially relied on a certain tolerance on the part of politicians and intellectuals. When the armed utopia of the youth movement materialized in the early 1970s, many saw it as an understandable reaction to military authoritarianism. During the dramatic years of the *peronista* return to power, violence became an everyday occurrence to which public opinion resigned itself. Now, the moral collapse of a defenceless society opened the doors to a repression that was implacable, clandestine and indifferent to basic human rights. The panic of those who had encouraged the guerrilla movement was silenced by the attitude of the majority of Argentines, who, tired and afraid, opted to ignore the bloody experience that they knew was taking place behind their backs.

This atmosphere of collective debility enabled the military regime to mount its ideological crusade, couched in a language rich in medical imagery. For the new rulers, civil society was seriously ill. The disease that afflicted the country came from below and had to be met by decisive surgery from above. There was, however, something new in the message. The ideologues of the Catholic Right, who ten years earlier had accompanied General Onganía in his advocacy of a corporatist system, had no influence whatsoever in 1976, when the ideas of liberal-conservatism enjoyed a dominant position within the military regime.

Traditionally, the military had been in conflict with this ideology prevalent in the economic establishment. Although the armed forces shared its disdain for political parties and universal suffrage, they never fully accepted the liberal critique of nationalist and interventionist state policies, of the inward-looking model of industrialization or of the excesses of labour legislation. As a result of the lessons of the recent *peronista* experience, the liberals were able to show that the policies and practices they were criticizing had created the conditions for social subversion. To preserve national security meant not only to destroy the guerrilla movement but also to eradicate the model of development that was its breeding ground. Thus, the liberals managed to impose their ideological stamp – although the high-ranking military chiefs did not renounce their own obsessions and set limits and conditions. The man who personified the ideals of liberal-conservativism was the minister of economy, José Martínez de Hoz, member of a traditional landowning family and president of the largest private steel company, who had held the same office during Guido's precarious presidency in 1962.

The critical state of the external sector was at the top of the new minister's agenda. Available reserves of foreign currency were practically exhausted. Thanks to his access to international financial sources, Martínez de Hoz was able to run the risk of stopping payments. In August a stand-by agreement was signed with the IMF which supplied U.S. $300 million and facilitated a loan of $1,000 million by a pool of banks led by Chase Manhattan. Inflation next claimed the minister's attention. The anti-inflationary policy, of orthodox inspiration, was helped by a number of decisions made by the previous administration. A short time before the coup, there was a final shock to relative prices as a result of adjustments in the cost of public services and the exchange rate to levels above the growth in wages. Martínez de Hoz took advantage of this to freeze wages, at the same time eliminating existing price controls. As a consequence, real wages fell sharply. Five months later, when the purchasing power of wages was less than 40 per cent of what it had been in 1972, nominal remuneration was periodically adjusted to inflation. The fiscal deficit was, in turn, reduced by half, to about 8.4 per cent of the GDP during the last part of 1976, by means of a real increase in collections and a fall in the wages of public employees. After an initial spurt in prices when controls were lifted, the inflation rate stood at 4.3 per cent in July. This success was offset by a decline in economic activity due to lower demand deriving from the decrease in real wages. But the reduction in labour costs provoked expansion in investment and exports. All in all, the government believed that it had found a quick solution to the crisis. The drop in real wages was not considered a negative factor but rather the inevitable price of reorganizing the economy.

This formula, which combined growth with a regressive redistribution of income, had already been used at the beginning of the 1960s. Martínez de Hoz thought the moment had come to launch his more ambitious outward-looking project. This strategy tried to break the pattern of the past fifty years, during which Argentine industry had been protected by high tariff barriers. In the official view, this model of semi-autarchic development had created the conditions for state intervention and, by discouraging competition, was the cause of Argentine industry's lack of efficiency. The first measure in the new direction was a plan to reduce ad valorem rates on imports over a five-year period.

The government's optimism did not last long. Inflation failed to come down further. On the contrary, in early 1977 prices rose at between 7 and 10 per cent each month and exposed the new economic behaviour induced by the inflationary acceleration of 1975. Since then it had become a general practice amongst entrepreneurs to make rapid adjustments in their prices in response to changes in the economic environment. Contracts were short term, salaries were revised every three months and the absence of price controls allowed companies to react quickly to variations in public sector charges, the exchange rate or salaries. The economy became increasingly indexed, fortifying the extraordinary resilience of the inflation rate.

The persistent rise in prices began to unsettle the military junta, which had made the taming of inflation one of its immediate objectives. In April 1977 Martínez de Hoz asked business for a 120-day truce, but this was carried out with so little conviction that its effects were negligible. In the middle of the year, the economic team made its own diagnosis: inflation was a monetary phenomenon, and failure to curb it was due to the fact that the money supply had not been strictly controlled. Consequently, the new attempt to control inflation lay in a restrictive monetary policy, implemented within the framework of a major financial reform.

The reform changed the system imposed by the previous *peronista* administration and fixed the capacity of banks to grant loans in direct relation to the deposits they could attract from the public. This led to the liberation of interest rates to facilitate competition. However, the military opposed eliminating the Central Bank guarantee on deposits. Thus, a dangerous hybrid system developed in which uncontrolled interest rates and guaranteed deposits coexisted, making competition for funds among financial entities very easy and risk-free. This led to over-expansion of the financial system, which became populated with speculators and fortune-seekers.

Interest rates increased substantially in real terms and prejudiced the economic reactivation begun at the end of 1976. Nevertheless, after two years of contraction, 1977 ended with a positive growth rate of 4.9 per cent. There was also a trade surplus of U.S. $1,500 million, and the fiscal deficit continued to decline (3.3 per cent of the GNP). But the annual rise in consumer prices reached the extraordinary rate of 180 per cent.

The successes promised by the restrictive monetary policy were slow to materialize, and the armed forces were not willing to face the social and political consequences of a prolonged recession. In contrast to the case in Chile, the military junta had vetoed resorting to unemployment.

In March 1978, against the backdrop of a monthly inflation rate of 11.1 per cent and the lowest level of activity since 1973, Martínez de Hoz again changed his policy. Inflation was now conceived as an expression of the expectations of economic agents who, in a climate of uncertainty, adopted defensive measures. He thus decided to defer the increases in public charges and the exchange rate in relation to past inflation. In December 1978 this decision became formal policy through a program that determined future increases in the exchange rate and public charges and fixed guidelines for the increase in the volume of internal credit. In January 1979 the increases forecast for these economic variables were established at much lower levels than the indexes of inflation registered at the end of 1978.

While this daring economic experiment was being launched, Argentina was moving towards a serious conflict with Chile. A year earlier the military junta had rejected the verdict of the arbitration entrusted to Great Britain in a long dispute with Chile over the control of the Beagle Channel in the extreme south of Argentina. By December 1978 bilateral talks with Pinochet's government had reached an impasse. The Argentine armed forces were ready to take action. Only the last-minute intervention of the Vatican averted the imminent war. The principal economic consequence of this incident was the refurbishing of the armed forces. In 1979, 1980 and 1981 military spending reached unprecedented levels and was largely responsible for the deterioration of fiscal deficit and the increase in foreign debt because of arms purchases abroad.

In 1979 repression was eased. Its objectives had been reached. The guerrilla movement had been destroyed; those who escaped with their lives secretly left the country. A majority of leftist intellectuals were also forced into exile. The oppressive atmosphere of the first years of military rule was relaxed. General Roberto Viola, who replaced Videla as army commander-in-chief after the latter had been confirmed as president for another three years in the middle of 1978, presented a less sullen and authoritarian image than his predecessor.

The first signs, albeit weak, of a liberalization of the regime put the hard-line sectors of the army on guard. At the end of 1979 General Luciano Menéndez tried to stage a rebellion from Córdoba, calling for the re-establishment of the total prohibition on political activity and the silencing of the increasingly loud demands for an official explanation of missing persons. The attempt failed, but it was a revealing symptom of the conflicts that were brewing in the military corporation. In contrast to Menéndez's attitude, Admiral Massera, who was responsible for one of the bloodiest chapters of the repression before stepping down from the leadership of the navy in 1978, began to dissociate himself publicly from the dirty war.

The upper class and the economic establishment which had backed Videla did not conceal their disgruntlement over Argentina's international isolation. In spite of the self-assigned mission of the military junta – the defence of Western values at the dawn of a third world war – they had garnered little sympathy. Relations with the United States were extremely tense, owing to the conflict between the methods being used by the military junta to carry out its mission and the human rights policy of President Carter. The good relations with the international financial community were, perhaps, the only positive aspect in a very unfriendly climate. Hostility towards the military regime was symbolically manifested when a little known but tenacious human rights militant, Adolfo Pérez Esquivel, won the Nobel Peace Prize in 1980.

The program of de-indexing launched by Martínez de Hoz in December 1978 was based on a daring gamble. Given the decreasing rate of devaluation, the economic authorities hoped that the growth rate of internal prices would eventually coincide with the sum of the predetermined rate of devaluation and the international inflation rate. This exchange rate policy was supported by the surge in exports provoked by a sharp increase in agricultural production. Income from exports went from U.S. $3,000–4,000 million in 1976–7 to $6,000–8,000 million in 1979–80. These increases reflected a certain lag in the exchange rate, which was the key tool of the programme. The immediate consequence of this policy was the anger of rural producers and the resignation of some members of the economic team who were linked to this sector.

In an effort to accelerate the convergence of the inflation rate with the official exchange rate policy, the level of exposure of the economy to international competition was increased. Convinced that if the industrial firms did not discipline themselves, there would be no success in the battle against inflation, Martínez de Hoz intensified the reduction of tariffs. This would allow price increases to be fixed by competition with imported goods, while simultaneously helping to eliminate inefficient enterprises. This challenge to a highly protected structure opened a new focus of conflict, this time with the industrial sector.

The anti-inflationary programme turned out to be more problematic than expected. During the first eight months of the regime, the growth rate of domestic prices was nearly double the guideline for the devaluation rate. Following this, inflation tended to decelerate, from 175 per cent in 1978 to 160 per cent in 1979 to 100 per cent in 1980. However, the lag in exchange rate required to decelerate inflation generated a growing deficit on the current account; in turn, higher domestic interest rates were needed to close the gap with the external sector. In a context of repressed inflation, higher interest rates became impossible for the productive sectors, and the growing unpaid debts of business pushed the financial system into crisis.

Reviewing the sequence followed by Martínez de Hoz's experiment, it can be seen that the decline of inflation was achieved at the cost of an enormous devaluation of the peso: between 40 and 50 per cent more than the average of the previous thirty years. The trade surplus of U.S. $2,000 million in 1978 turned into a deficit – a modest one in 1979 and a not so modest $2,500 million in 1980. Through the 1970s, the trade balance had been a surplus, except in 1975. But while the 1975 deficit was produced by strong increases in domestic activity, the deficits of 1979 and 1980 occurred in a context of recession, where the increase in spending on imports – induced by the exchange rate lag and the lowering of tariffs – was oriented towards goods that competed with local production.

Martínez de Hoz endeavoured to cover imbalances in the current account by encouraging the entry of foreign capital. As a result, the deregulation of the financial system undertaken in 1977, the progressive lifting of restrictions on obtaining foreign credit and the domestic policy of expensive money led to a growing process of a foreign debt. This process acquired a new impulse after December 1978, when the peso was progressively revalued by making the real interest rate negative in local money and thus stimulating an intense demand for foreign capital. Net foreign debt went from U.S. $6,459 million at the end of 1978 to $19,478 million in 1980, tripling in only two years.

As the external sector began to deteriorate and the Banco Central lost the reserves it had accumulated, doubts arose about the economic authorities' promise to maintain the predetermined devaluation rate. This uncertainty, in turn, drove up the cost of money, and by the end of 1979 interest rates had become strongly positive. Businesses entered into a crisis of liquidity, harassed by more expensive credit and declining sales. Many went bankrupt, immobilizing the active portfolios of the banks. In March 1980 there was a financial panic when the Banco de Intercambio Regional, the most important private bank, could not meet its obligations and was closed, along with twenty-seven others which successively declared bankruptcy, by the Central Bank, which had to inject an enormous quantity of liquid funds in order to pay off the closed banks' depositors.

Public confidence in the official exchange rate policy was severely affected. Many took advantage of what seemed to be the last months of a free financial market to get their capital out of the country. By this time, the bleeding of reserves could not be stopped. The economic authorities sought to compensate for the outflow of capital by forcing public enterprises to incur foreign debt. The pressure on the exchange rate market continued to rise; in February 1981, Martínez de Hoz abandoned the guideline policy, deciding on a devaluation of 10 per cent, which was, however, insignificant in the face of a lag of about 50 per cent. The economic experiment begun in December 1978 had come to an end.

This disheartening picture formed the backdrop to the presidential succession. In accordance with the political timetable fixed by the military junta, the new president had to take over from Videla in March 1981. The natural candidate was General Roberto Viola, commander-in-chief of the army, but his candidacy awoke significant resistance in the navy and important sectors of the army, which feared that he would attempt a process of political liberalization. After several months of negotiation, Viola's appointment was finally made official in October 1980, but over the six months before he took office there was a notable increase in concern over the already uncertain course of the economy. The 10 per cent devaluation decreed by Martínez de Hoz was not enough to quiet speculation over future devaluations, particularly because Viola's economic advisers were known critics of the policy in force. In addition, the hard-liners in the armed forces, led by General Leopoldo Galtieri and Admiral Jorge Anaya, the commanders-in-chief of the army and the navy, respectively, distrusted the political opening the new president was attempting.

The project of Videla's successor recalled General Lanusse's attempt in 1971, but circumstances were not equally favourable. Ten years earlier, Lanusse was able to justify a return to open politics to his colleagues by invoking the need to contain a strong social opposition. Now, the protest against the military regime lacked the destabilizing potential it had then. For Viola's critics in the military establishment the step he was ready to take was hasty. The ominous memory of the final outcome of Lanusse's attempt condemned any pretence at repeating a similar project. Outside the conservative groups, the military leaders of 1976 had not developed a significant political following. *Peronismo* and Radicalism continued to be the most popular political forces. A rapprochement with them would lead to free elections and a return to the rule of law. From the perspective of the military hard-liners, this meant shelving the goals of the coup of 1975 in favour of the same politicians they had dislodged from power.

Hence, General Viola took office in March 1981 representing one sector of the armed forces but under the watchful eye of the other. Nine months later he was removed and his open policy brought to a close. During this brief interregnum, critics of Martínez de Hoz's policy joined the cabinet and made official contacts with the unions and political parties. In July 1981 the so-called Multipartidaria was created which, like the Hora del Pueblo in 1971, was a coalition of parties whose majority sectors were *peronista* and Radical. Its objectives were the same as ever: to negotiate a political transition and prevent the uncontrolled growth of a radicalized opposition. The cautious advances of General Viola and the moderate proposals of the Multipartidaria ran in the same direction. Neither wanted to antagonize the rigid sectors of the military junta, which were issuing repeated warnings against a populist detour and were discouraging any hope of rapid institutionalization. Their prudence was in vain.

The crisis of credibility that accompanied Viola's brief presidency did not assist management of the critical economic situation that had been inherited. Viola's minister of economy began in April with a devaluation of 30 per cent in order to tackle the collapse of Martínez de Hoz's exchange rate policy. But he could not cool the markets, and in July he had to announce another devaluation of 30 per cent. The real exchange rate was fortified, although at the price of accentuating the recession and the decline in real wages. Later, Viola had to introduce restrictions in the exchange markets in order to block the flight of capital. In turn, the devaluations further complicated the situation of companies that had borrowed short-term credit from abroad. The government then offered them guarantees and subsidies that tended to stimulate the renewal of the debts, with the goal of averting pressures on the exhausted reserves of foreign currency. At the cost of significant fiscal weakening, the transfer of private debt to the public sector thus began.

In December 1981 the leadership of the military regime was entrusted to General Galtieri, who combined three posts: president, member of the junta and commander-in-chief of the army. Under his direction, the Argentine military reverted to the regime's original stance, re-establishing authoritarian control over political life. The rise of the new strong man owed a great deal to the change in the international context. The arrival of Ronald Reagan in the White House put an end to the regime's isolation. Galtieri had travelled twice to the United States during 1981 and gained the sympathies of the Republican administration, which was quick to set aside Carter's human rights policy. The future Argentine president repaid these attentions, offering to lend military support to the U.S. counter-insurgency operations in Central America. Argentine experts in intelligence and anti-subversive operations were sent to El Salvador, Guatemala and Honduras. The lessons learned during the years of the dirty war were also used to train former Somoza supporters in actions against the Nicaraguan government.

With the backing of his hosts in Washington, whom this tall, uncouth and rough-spoken man had amused with imitations of General Patton, Galtieri reintroduced the liberal economists into the Ministry of Economy. They were led by Roberto Alemán, who had been minister in 1961 and was highly respected in financial circles for his orthodoxy. Alemán tried to reproduce the liberal political economy of the first years of the regime, endeavouring to control inflation by reducing the role of the state. Although public spending did decrease, this was not due to a reform of the

state – which was never undertaken – but because government employees' salaries and the cost of public services were frozen. Both measures
helped to slow down inflation in the short run. Alemán also lifted the
controls on the exchange market imposed by his predecessor and allowed
the peso to float freely. This implied a devaluation of about 30 per cent,
which, added to the successive devaluations since April 1981, improved
the trade balance. The goal was to generate a strong surplus with which to
confront foreign payments, since access to international financial markets
was closed.

Galtieri's minister of economy tried to assuage the financial community's anxiety about Argentina's growing crisis of payments. But the
uncertainty did not disappear. The exchange rate began to move in an
erratic pattern, and Alemán had to back away from his policy of a free-
floating exchange in a retreat that was also clearly related to developments
on the political scene. The return of economic orthodoxy had caused
widespread discontent, which took a more militant form than in the
recent past. This growing protest seemed to conspire against the idea
largely shared among military leaders of reducing their isolation and
preparing for the political succession of the regime. Although not all
senior officers admitted it openly, they were aware that they were passing
through one of those familiar moments in Argentine history when pressure
for an institutional solution was irreversible. Admiral Massera was already
engaged in the creation of his own party and had made contact with some
peronista sectors. Against this backdrop, Galtieri launched a daring operation to shore up the battered legitimacy of the regime and keep it in
power: the occupation of the Islas Malvinas (Falkland Islands), which had
been a British possession since 1833.

The issue of the Falklands had always been present on the military's
international policy agenda. In December 1976 Argentina had persuaded
the UN Assembly to urge Great Britain, for the third time, to open talks on
the de-colonization of the islands. The British chose to continue their
procrastinating tactics for the next four years, while frustration and irritation mounted in Buenos Aires. The Argentine navy began to prepare a plan
of invasion. At the end of 1981 London decided to reduce its presence in the
South Atlantic, and the Argentine government made a new effort to unlock
the negotiations. When General Galtieri took office, after the failure of
diplomatic overtures, he gave permission to Admiral Anaya, who had
played a key role in his rise to power, to begin operations. On 2 April 1982
the first Argentine sailors disembarked on the Falkland Islands.

General Galtieri's political expectations were immediately satisfied. Widespread nationalistic fervour swept the country, and the regime was provided with much-needed popular backing. The Plaza de Mayo, which four days earlier had been the scene of a labour mobilization that had been violently repressed by police, was now filled with an enthusiastic crowd cheering the military. Confident that once its prestige was restored the military would be less reluctant to leave office, the political parties also lent their support. In the end, however, this patriotic wave carried the armed forces beyond their original plans. The invasion had been conceived to exert pressure on Britain. It was expected that, in light of the Argentine government's decision, the international community would oblige the British prime minister, Margaret Thatcher, to enter into negotiations; as soon as these began, the Argentine troops, after a short stay on the islands, would return to their bases. But the triumphant tone of the official propaganda caused the military junta to lose control over events. Moreover, Mrs Thatcher was unwilling to compromise. The United States, upon whose neutrality the Argentine military had been counting, remained loyal to its traditional ally. Argentina found itself at war with a major power. By 4 June 1982, the Falklands were again in British hands.

The political aftermath of the defeat in the South Atlantic war precipitated the disintegration of the Argentine military regime, just as the defeat by the Turks in the war for Cyprus had put an end to the government of the Greek Colonels in 1974. The military survived in power for one more long year, during which the conflicts which divided it rose shamelessly to the surface. The military junta was dissolved with the departure of the navy and the air force. The army remained in charge of the government and appointed General Reynaldo Bignone to the presidency with the mission of transferring power as quickly as possible. While the three services settled their accounts in public, accusing each other of responsibility for the military defeat, the administration had to confront the immediate economic problems.

With the reserves of the Banco Central virtually exhausted, exchange controls were imposed and external payments were suspended. The external debt now exceeded U.S. $35 billion, half of which fell due at the end of 1982. Until 1981 it had been possible to make the scheduled repayments by taking new short-term loans. Now, however, Argentina's credibility in international financial circles was destroyed. Bignone also found that he could not negotiate freely with creditors, since some elements of the military were trying to maintain a state of financial hostility. A middle line was established, and negotiations began with the IMF and the commercial banks in an attempt to settle the past due amounts and postpone new payments.

In January 1983 a new stand-by agreement was approved with the IMF, whereby the government promised to correct an economic crisis characterized by a fiscal deficit of 14 per cent of the GNP, an annual inflation rate of 310 per cent and a deficit in the balance of payments of U.S. $6,700 million. The economic programme agreed on reflected the traditional view of the IMF that the external deficit was attributable to excess internal spending. However, while Argentina's external imbalances had in the past been expressed by a deficit in the balance of trade, the trade account now had a surplus, and the imbalance was provoked by the payment of interest on the external debt and by the rise in international interest rates. The stand-by agreement with the IMF and the subsequent negotiation of the debt with commercial banks allowed the amassing of the $3,700 million needed to take care of the external situation in the short term.

In parallel developments, the administration embarked on a financial reform designed to aid the private sector. The existing internal debt was extended obligatorily for five years at low interest rates fixed by the Central Bank, which also provided the funds. The basic idea in this respect was to reactivate the stagnant economy through a liquidation of the private sector's debt, which had reached dangerous levels due to high interest rates and the enormous devaluation of the peso – 800 per cent over the increase in prices in the past eighteen months. Equally serious was the debt contracted by the government in local markets. The intention of the government was to unleash a once-and-for-all jump in prices that would reduce public and private debt in real terms through a permanent transfer of resources from depositors to debtors; consequently, prices rose at a new monthly level of between 15 and 20 per cent. The administration also continued to be generous with the external debt of the private sector, taking new steps to transfer the majority of external obligations to the public sector. Camouflaged by the collapse of the military regime, this shock of heterodox measures for the business community's benefit provoked strong public discontent. Bignone had to reorganize the Ministry of Economy, naming as its new head Jorge Whebe, who had already occupied the position during the last part of Lanusse's presidency in 1973. This symbolic choice was a clear sign that the military was about to withdraw.

The economic situation it left behind was hardly healthy. Between 1976 and 1982 the global GDP showed a negative cumulative annual rate of 0.2

per cent. During four of the seven years of military administration, GDP decreased in absolute terms (1976, 1978, 1981, 1982). The level of global activity in 1982 was 1.3 per cent lower than that in 1975, when the long period of growth that began in 1964 was interrupted. The fall was even more acute in industry and trade: manufacturing output was 20 per cent lower than that in 1975, while trade activity was 16.4 per cent lower. The negative growth of the economy was associated with a decline in internal demand, as well as with the substitution of domestic production by imports. This went along with a decline in industry, which fell to 22.3 per cent of the GDP in 1982 from 27.8 per cent in 1975. During the same period the number of industrial workers fell 35 per cent.

The only positive development had been in exports, although an increase of 8.1 per cent between 1976 and 1982 did not offset the flooding of imports into local markets. A paradoxical effect of the liberal policies was the growth of public investment over total investment. The uncertainty dominant during these years turned state investment projects into a hedge against stagnation, attracting private businessmen to public contracts.

One predictable result of these policies was a contraction in the real income of wage-earners; this can be estimated at between 30 and 50 per cent in the period from 1976 to 1982, accelerating a regressive redistribution of income. Thus, the 5 per cent of the population who received the highest incomes saw their share of the total income grow from 17.2 per cent in 1974 to 22.2 per cent in 1982. To this concentration of income must be added the flight of capital, which converted a significant number of upper-middle-class investors into holders of thousands of millions of dollars in foreign financial centres. At the end of 1982 the external debt was U.S. $43,600 million. In contrast to the situation in other indebted nations, the growth of the external debt was not accompanied by growth of the GDP but was generated to sustain a policy that led to de-industrialization and stagnation.

The other legacy of the military was the sequel to the policy of repression. During the final phase of its period in power, the military had made a fruitless effort to obtain assurances from the parties that they would not be punished for the violation of human rights. The armed forces therefore had to transfer power without having reached any agreement on how to deal with its profoundly divisive heritage. This was a conspicuous difference between the Argentine situation and the processes under way in Brazil and Uruguay, where the military was in a position to influence the dynamics of the political transition. Elections were scheduled for October 1983, the parties competing in distancing themselves from the military regime. Of the two most important forces – the *peronistas* and the Radicals – it was the latter, contrary to expectations, which succeeded best in this regard.

Since 1946 the *peronistas* had come first every time the population was able to express its political preferences freely through elections. The Radical Party faced this challenge with an internal reorganization, from which the new leadership of Raúl Alfonsín emerged. In order to confront the revival of the old populist rhetoric of the *peronistas*, Alfonsín formulated an original platform. He defined the electoral competition in terms of democracy versus authoritarianism and announced that his party was best equipped to reconstruct a democratic system in Argentina. In this manner, he won over the voters who wanted to leave a long decade of political violence behind them. *Peronismo* was unable to present itself as a credible representative of this collective aspiration, which was much more moderate than the one that had handed it victory in 1973. Furthermore, during the campaign Alfonsín made an explicit and convincing connection between the *peronistas* and the military by warning of the existence of a 'union–military pact' and alleging that the high command of the armed forces had decided to support a future *peronista* government, in exchange for which the *peronista* union leaders would promote a pardon for the military's violation of human rights.

The results of the elections of 30 October 1983 gave the Radicals 7,725,873 votes (50 per cent) and the *peronistas* 5,994,406 (39 per cent). The contrast with the percentages from 1973, when the Radicals won 26 per cent and the *peronistas* 65 per cent, could not have been greater. In addition to those traditionally loyal to Radicalism, the triumphant coalition gained the support of the Centre–Right electorate, the votes of small groups of leftists and a significant percentage of *peronista* adherents; it also received a majority of the female and youth vote. In the context of a grave economic crisis and with the wounds of repression still open, a new democratic experiment began in Argentina.

THE ALFONSÍN PRESIDENCY AND THE TRANSITION TO DEMOCRACY, 1983–9

Once surprise over the outcome of the election had dissipated, Raúl Alfonsín's assumption of the presidency was received, both in Argentina and abroad, with widespread relief and hope. The new government emerged out of the ruins of two experiences that, marked by violence and crisis, had profoundly affected the collective consciousness: the return and fall of the *peronista* government and the collapse of the military dictatorship. Indeed, the democratic experiment that was initiated at the end of 1983 was invested with a desire for a new beginning after forty years of political instability and economic failure.

However, the same conditions that had made this seem possible also raised difficult challenges. First, the authoritarian regime left power without establishing a political pact. While in Brazil and Uruguay the military explicitly or implicitly entered into an agreement with civilians on the return to constitutionality, in Argentina their rapid loss of power prevented the armed forces from fixing the terms under which they abandoned control of the state. The democratic leaders were, as a result, free of commitments but, at the same time, weighed down by a grave responsibility in deciding how to manage the unresolved military question. The memory of recent human rights violations complicated the future even more.

Second, the first *peronista* electoral defeat in free elections had unexpected consequences. The outcome could be interpreted as the end of one political era and the beginning of another; this was the dominant perception among the Radicals, in spite of the important number of votes given to the Partido Justicialista. The Radicals thought that the *peronista* defeat, as well as the crisis that broke out among its rank and file, forecast the disintegration of this formerly powerful political force. Confident of this interpretation, they prepared to form a new political movement, centralized around the leadership of Alfonsín and enlarged by the collapse of *peronismo*. This vision encouraged attitudes that made it very difficult to arrive at agreements with the *peronistas* on crucial questions about the democratic transition. The 1983 electoral defeat was an unexpected and damaging shock indeed to the *peronistas*, who were accustomed to thinking of themselves as the natural governing party. The electoral results added fuel to the continuing internal crisis experienced by the party since Perón's death. Afraid of losing their identity in the political offensive launched by the new government, the *peronistas* accentuated their role as the party of the opposition. This strategy kept them united but, at the same time, it led them to act according to the logic of adversarial politics, which did not facilitate the search for accord. As a result, the two principal political forces entered the post-authoritarian period in open competition.

The consequences of the political polarization between Radicals and *peronistas* were magnified by the distribution of institutional power that resulted from the 1983 elections. The Radical Party won the presidency but was deprived of a clear majority in Congress. The Radicals achieved a slight majority in the Chamber of Deputies: 129 seats out of a total of 254. The Partido Justicialista won 111 seats, thus maintaining an important position from which to assert pressure that was supplemented by their strength in the Senate, where they won 21 out of 46 seats while the Radicals held 18. (The remaining 7 were distributed among provincial parties.)

Despite the magnitude of the problems he inherited, Alfonsín, galvanized by the success, domestically and internationally, of his democratizing crusade, approached the tasks of government in a daring and decisive manner. His first measures were dictated by the message of justice that had captured the imagination of so many Argentines during the campaign. Three days after assuming office, the government dictated two decrees. The first ordered the arrest and criminal prosecution of the members of the three military juntas that had governed the country between 1976 and 1983. The second ordered the criminal prosecution of the surviving guerrilla leaders.

With respect to the military institutions, Alfonsín's strategy had two objectives: the punishment of military officers who had committed human rights violations and the incorporation of the armed forces into the new democratic order. For this reason, a legal process was undertaken that should have resulted in the military passing judgement on itself. A successful self-purification, Alfonsín was convinced, would permit the punishment of those with primary responsibility for the repression without antagonizing the military institution as a whole. He therefore sent to Congress a project amending the Code of Military Justice that gave the Supreme Council of the Armed Forces initial jurisdiction over military personnel. With the aim of obtaining a prompt judgement, this measure established that if, after six months from the beginning of the legal process, the military tribunal had not handed down a decision, the case would be judged by civilian courts. The amendment also limited the number of military personnel incriminated. During the electoral campaign Alfonsín had distinguished three groups of personnel with differing levels of responsibility: those who had given orders of repression, those who had committed excesses in carrying out orders and those who had done no more than carry out orders. The weight of punishment would fall on the first two groups, while the third would be pardoned for having acting according to the norms of military discipline.

While Alfonsín unfolded his strategy, the human rights organizations exerted pressure for the formation of a congressional commission to investigate the disappearance of individuals. This was an initiative loaded with risk for the government's objectives. Alfonsín instead created the Comisión Nacional de Desaparecidos (CONADEP), composed of independent figures whose only mission was to receive and verify accusations within a period of six months. However, during its period of activity, CONADEP served to sensitize public consciousness, which, after both forced and voluntary ignorance, was awakening to the extent of the military repression through testimonies given by relatives of the victims, the discovery of clandestine torture centres and cemeteries where unidentified persons were buried.

Congressional consideration of the amendment to the Code of Military Justice upset the delicate balance on which Alfonsín's strategy rested. Following a proposal by a *peronista* senator, Congress modified the concept of due obedience, excluding from its benefits those who had committed aberrant or atrocious acts. This new version frustrated the government's intention to limit the number of accused, given that a majority of the cases to be judged could fall into this vague category. The success of the official policy came to depend more than ever on the collaboration of the military tribunals: if these failed to complete the mission assigned them by Alfonsín, the entire strategy would be endangered because the cases would pass to the civilian courts and these, jealous of their recovered independence in the new democratic climate, would be unlikely to collaborate with the government.

At the end of September 1984, with the proscribed period of its jurisdiction ended, the Supreme Council of the Armed Forces issued a declaration supporting the procedures used in the war against subversion. On 22 April 1985 the public trial of senior military officers therefore began. After three and a half months of great tension, General Videla and Admiral Massera were, by unanimous decision, condemned to life sentences, while General Viola was sentenced to seventeen years in prison, Admiral Armando Lambruschini to nine years, and Brigadier Osvaldo Agosti to four and a half years. The members of the third military junta were released for lack of sufficient evidence but General Galtieri, as well as Admiral Anaya and Brigadier Basilio Lami Doza, had to stand trial by courts martial for the defeat in the Malvinas War. The sentences against Videla and Massera were received with satisfaction by democratic sectors, although they would have preferred stiffer sentences for the other military leaders. In contrast, in circles associated with the military, the sentences were judged to be a political manoeuvre to erode the prestige of the armed forces. For some, the violation of human rights had not been sufficiently castigated; for others, the officers who had been punished were men who, in defeating subversion, had saved the nation.

Alfonsín's policy towards the trade unions encountered similar difficulties. Together with the military, the unions had been the preferred targets of Radical Party propaganda in the 1983 campaign. The old Radicals who returned to the government with Alfonsín had not forgotten the hostility of the *peronista* trade unions towards President Illia between 1964 and 1966. This memory and the more recent suspicion of a union–military pact led the new government to give priority to a change in union leadership. As it had been necessary for political leaders to revalidate their legitimacy in the 1983 elections, so now came the turn of the union leaders. At the beginning of 1984 Alfonsín sent Congress a proposed law for organizing union elections which, due to a lack of political competition, many leaders won year after year.

The government's draft law proposed a very liberal structure for the selection of candidates and voter qualification with the objective of facilitating the rise of new leaders. It also charged the Ministry of Labour with supervising the elections. This placed union leaders on a war footing since they had always enjoyed unrestricted control over the political life of their organizations. The undisguised official offensive had the effect of unifying the *peronista* movement. The same union leaders who had, until then, been seen as responsible for the electoral defeat now mobilized the support of *peronista* congressmen. In spite of having been approved by the Chamber of Deputies, the law was defeated by the vote in the Senate.

Following the failure of the initiative, Alfonsín's labour minister had to resign; his successor managed to achieve union democratization but, to do so, he had to make compromises with union leaders. A new law, with more restrictive conditions and less government intervention, was approved by Congress after an agreement was reached between Radicals and *peronistas*. The union elections, which took place at the end of 1984, did not, however, produce many surprises. The government's hope for a renovation of the union leadership was to a large degree disappointed. This failed attempt was early evidence of the limits placed on the new government's aspirations by the distribution of institutional power.

The resolution of the controversy with Chile over the small islands in the Beagle Channel was more successful. After the near confrontation of 1978, both countries agreed to submit the matter to arbitration by the pope. In 1983 the military government and the political parties decided jointly that a response to the arbitration award would be made by the incoming elected government. In January 1984 Argentina and Chile signed a Declaration of Peace and Friendship in Rome, which gave Chile possession of the islands in dispute. Despite the reaction of nationalist sectors, Alfonsín strongly endorsed the award and set 25 November 1984 as the date for a national referendum to decide on the issue. The intent of this popular consultation, the first in Argentina, was to put pressure on Congress, where the *peronista* opposition threatened to use its power to deny ratification of the treaty. In a large turn-out, more than 80 per cent voted to accept the terms of the treaty, which was later ratified by Congress, although by a small majority. Not much progress was made on the other central issue of foreign policy, the dealings with Great Britain on the Islas Malvinas (Falkland Islands). Mrs Thatcher was unwilling to discuss sovereignty over the islands or to dismantle new defence installations, and Alfonsín could not resort to step-by-step diplomacy because of the military intransigency of the *peronistas* and the military.

In the management of the economy, Alfonsín initially underestimated the magnitude of the crisis. First, the new government inherited an economy which in 1983 had a GDP equal to that of 1974. Second, the Argentine economy was characterized by the highest inflation in the world; by 1983 the consumer price index had registered annual increases of three digits during nine consecutive years. Third, Alfonsín inherited a public sector with deficit of the order of 14 per cent of GDP in 1983. Finally, the new government took over a highly indebted economy. Service payments to foreign creditors rose from 2.2 per cent of GDP in 1980 to 9.9 per cent in the first year of the constitutional government. The total foreign debt of U.S. $45 billion required interest payments of $5.4 billion in 1984, or $3 billion less than the trade balance.

The new government lacked a proper diagnosis of the economy. It had only the analytical tools and the economic policies the Radicals had successfully implemented twenty years before. On the one hand, it was thought that economic stagnation could be attacked by a Keynesian redistributionist strategy while maintaining a high level of public spending; on the other hand, there was the view that inflation could be defeated by implementing a gradualist incomes policy, without substantially reducing the fiscal deficit. Finally, it was assumed that the establishment of a democratic regime would in itself open the way to a favourable renegotiation of the foreign debt. The initial economic policy barely lasted eight months, and its results were clearly discouraging for a government that expected simultaneously to reactivate the economy, increase real wages and slow down inflation. In fact, real wages grew by more than 35 per cent compared with the previous year, mainly as a consequence of an acceleration in the revaluation of the domestic currency. But other indicators quickly showed how brittle the government's programme was: the GDP growth rate slowed down; the annual inflation rate went from 626 per cent during the last quarter of 1983 to 1,080 per cent during the third quarter of 1984.

In June 1985, after a brief and failed attempt to stop inflation with the traditional instruments of demand management, Alfonsín's government launched a heterodox anti-inflationary plan – the so-called Austral Plan – that contained the basic requirement for a shock stabilization: an instantaneous shift towards fiscal–monetary balance, a rigid incomes policy (the freezing of wages, prices, the exchange rate and public utility rates) and monetary reform.

The fiscal–monetary balance was to be achieved by means of a dramatic increase in public sector resources through higher taxes on foreign trade, a tax reform and, particularly, a higher real tax collection rate due to the effect of falling inflation. The new fiscal deficit estimated for the second semester of 1985 would not exceed 2.5 per cent of GDP (including servicing of the foreign debt) and would be financed with foreign credit. The freeze – decided after careful adjustment in the exchange rate and public utility rates that accelerated inflation before the shock – was to meet the essential goal of breaking inflationary inertia and establishing a visible mechanism for the coordination of the many micro-economic decisions that would otherwise have tended to reproduce inflation. Finally, the monetary reform was aimed at avoiding the large transfers of wealth from debtors to creditors that could have resulted from the sudden drop in the inflation rate. The reform included a change in the currency (from the Argentine peso to the austral) and the establishment of a scale for converting from the old currency to the new one to honour the real terms of those contracts – agreed to before but cancelled after the reform – while preserving distributional neutrality.

Even though some sectors refused to accept the plan – particularly the trade unions, which staged a general strike – the general public placed their trust in it, as was shown by the renewal of bank deposits, the falling exchange rate of the U.S. dollar on the black market and acceptance of the price freeze, although there were no major bureaucratic controls. Within ninety days after the launching of the Austral Plan, most of the population felt that inflation had been beaten and that the country was finally facing a period of economic stability. In July wholesale prices had already dropped below their nominal terms, something that had not occurred since November 1973; consumer prices, which had increased 30.5 per cent in June, rose only 6.2 per cent in July, 3.1 per cent in August and 2 per cent in September. The demand for money, which had touched a historic low in the days before the stabilization plan's announcement, began to rise after a brief initial period during which firms reduced their inventory; production and private investment picked up, the purchasing power of wages was improved by the sudden drop in inflation and, finally, the imbalance in public accounts was significantly improved. Consequently, at the end of 1985, President Alfonsín's government seemed to have gained control over the economic situation. With these credits under its belt, the Radical Party passed its first electoral test. In November's partial elections for the Chamber of Deputies, Alfonsín's party received 43 per cent of the vote, while the *peronistas*, fragmented by internal conflicts, managed to capture only 34 per cent.

Galvanized by his domestic successes and by the recognition he received when travelling abroad, where he was hailed as the embodiment of the new Argentine democracy, Alfonsín attempted to govern on his own terms. This implied a relative marginalization of the Radical Party, which, although proven as a vote-winning machine, did not offer Alfonsín the skilled cadre needed to run the administration. The presidential cabinet was progressively staffed with professionals and independents more attuned to the modernizing spirit that marked the government. These new faces, best exemplified by the economic team led by Juan V. Sourrouille, were not always welcomed by veteran party members. But the UCR that took over in 1983, having doubled its historical following and overwhelmed by the new experience, was far from being able to create a well-defined party identity. Many Radicals claimed to know where they came from but few were certain as to where they were heading. In fact, 'alfonsinismo', as the new style of political action was called, developed mainly as a consequence of the exercise of power. Confined to a supporting role, the Radical Party followed Alfonsín's initiatives, although sometimes with little conviction and after manifesting its resistance.

Alfonsín's inclination to govern autonomously could not fail to upset the sensibilities of sectors and institutions accustomed to exercising informal leverage over public policies. The Church, for example, reacted with undisguised displeasure over the policies of a president who, confident of his democratic legitimacy, encouraged the most diverse expressions of pluralism and cultural modernization without consulting its opinion. The ecclesiastical hierarchy, perhaps the most conservative in South America, was uneasy with the re-establishment of freedom of expression and innovations in education. In 1986 the proposed divorce law put the Church on a war footing, which led to a call for a popular mobilization against congressional approval. The response was slight. The question of divorce did not divide the country or awaken great passions. When Congress finally passed the law, Argentina ceased sharing with Ireland the anachronistic status of being the only countries without legal divorce, thereby granting delayed sanction to a reform that public opinion had accepted long before. The Church never abandoned its attitude of mistrust towards the government of Alfonsín.

The Austral Plan permitted Alfonsín a bridge to the business community. For the first time, the government of a party suspicious of business could forge a modus vivendi with a corporate sector that had traditionally reciprocated its prejudices. This was a development laden with implications. For many years the prevalent conviction among the largest companies had been that in order to achieve the stability and predictability necessary for managing the economy it was convenient to suppress the arenas of policy negotiation characteristic of democratic life. This had led them to support military governments and restrictions on the activity of political parties and trade unions. Such a conviction was severely shaken by the manifest failure of the recent military regime; now businessmen appeared more disposed to reconcile themselves to the new democratic order. Alfonsín's conversion to a more austere and rigorous economic policy facilitated this process, which, although never translated into manifest sympathy for the government, at least contributed to neutralizing the traditional animosity of the world of big business. At the same time, the favourable attitude of the United States towards the Argentine democratic transition contributed to this process.

By 1986, only three sectors were explicitly excluded from the consensus that surrounded Alfonsín. First were important groups within the armed forces, resentful over what they understood to be a campaign of slander towards the military orchestrated from within governing circles and over financial belt-tightening after a reduction by half of defence spending, which in 1983 represented 4 per cent of GDP. Next were the trade union leaders, particularly those of the CGT, which since 1984 had chosen open confrontation with the government by means of repeated general strikes. Finally, the Partido Peronista, which, in the midst of an internal crisis it could not overcome, contested Alfonsín's policies with populist and nationalist slogans that were its trademark in Argentine political life.

The central role played by the president in a situation of crisis and economic emergency such as gripped Argentina was a normal and predictable phenomenon. But those in the circles that surrounded Alfonsín went beyond this and succumbed to the temptation, always present in the national political culture, to claim a hegemonic position. There was talk about a 'Third Historical Movement' that, resuscitating the broad popular coalitions which had been raised first around Yrigoyen and later Perón, would now be articulated around the leadership of Alfonsín. There were grand schemes to found a 'Second Republic', such as moving the capital of the country to the South and reforming the constitution, ostensibly with the intention of effecting Alfonsín's re-election as president for a second term.

Consumed by a vision of a Radical hegemony over Argentine political life and convinced that *peronismo* was incapable of overcoming the crisis that followed its 1983 defeat, the Alfonsín team did not correctly evaluate the gradual change in leadership that had begun to take place among the followers of Perón. In the 1985 elections, those who had given birth to what was called the *peronista* Renovation made important advances. In provinces like Buenos Aires and Córdoba they broke with the party leadership and presented their own tickets. Their relative triumphs in the midst of the party's debacle opened a new stage in its development. The construction of a democratic *peronismo* was the banner of the new current. In contrast with the pejorative tone used by Perón when speaking of politics and '*partidocracia*', the new figures, such as Antonio Cafiero, Manuel de la Sota and Carlos Grosso, spoke in very positive terms of democracy and political parties. The institutionalist message, while an effect of the new political spirit motivated by Alfonsín, also pointed towards a questioning of the Radical democratic monopoly. The aim of the 'Renovators' was to distance themselves from Alfonsín and his policies. They tended to characterize the Austral Plan as a continuation of the economic policies of the military government: it reflected submission to the IMF and the interests of creditor banks, while being ineffective in reactivating the economy.

The Austral Plan did not open the new economic era promised by the government in 1985. Hyperinflation was avoided, but various structural and institutional factors – seasonal scarcity of foodstuffs, the continuation of indexation in labour contracts and an increase in the price of private personal services, all omitted from the freeze – combined to complicate a reduction in inflation. As a result, consumer prices rose at 3.8 per cent per month in the third quarter of 1985, at 2.5 per cent in the final quarter and 3.1 per cent in the first quarter of 1986. This level of inflation created obvious difficulties, and early in 1986 it was necessary to end the freeze on prices and wages. This shift towards a short-term policy of greater flexibility occurred, however, within the context of diminished attention to securing stability. The government was harried by the unions, the *peronista* opposition and some industrial sectors which insisted that the country had entered a deep recession. Although the facts did not support this claim, it weakened the will of the ruling party. Seeking respite from pressure, the government relaxed restrictions on the terms of agreements between companies and unions. Day by day it became more evident that this was conducive not to strengthening the programme of stability but to reviving the traditional distributive conflicts of the Argentine economy.

Contrary to the initial policies of the minister of economy, during 1986 wages rose by a monthly rate of 5 per cent whilst public prices increased by 3.9 per cent and the official exchange rate by 3.5 per cent. As a consequence of this disparity, the economic programme became imbalanced. At the same time, monetary policy followed an expansionist course in an effort to palliate, through credit, constant demands for greater support for production and employment. The instrumental success of the Austral Plan was not paralleled at an ideological level: the notion of stability rapidly retreated in the face of the more attractive slogans encouraging growth and reactivation.

This weakness was mirrored in the unstable character of fiscal adjustments. As time passed the emergency measures applied to decrease public expenditure and increase revenues were abandoned without being replaced by new policies of comparable strength. The fiscal deficit, which stood at 14 per cent of GDP in 1983, fell to 12 per cent in 1984, the first year of the Alfonsín administration. As a result of the Austral Plan it was further reduced to 6 per cent in 1985 and 4.3 per cent in 1986. This was achieved on the expenditure side through adjustment of items more vulnerable to administrative manipulation: pensions, public sector wages and small public works. In contrast, by virtue of protection through specific legislation, tax subsidies for private companies, large public works and holders of state contracts were not affected and suffered only slightly from the fiscal adjustments. Neither the provinces nor the state-owned companies supported the economic effort of the central government. The provinces, which were permanently seeking larger transfers from the federal administration, actually managed to avoid the cuts that had to be borne by other sectors of the state. The state-owned companies had to reduce investments, but were at least able for some time to defend a privileged position within the wage structure of the public sector.

Initial advances on the revenue side were also stalled. Giving priority to the success of their policy of shock, the government directed its attention to those resources that were transitory by definition (windfall tax on high incomes and companies) or were a one-off result of the decrease in inflation (reduced losses incurred between the formal date of tax payments and their actual receipt by the state) or were exceptionally blessed by the temporary high agricultural prices on the world market.

The fragility and unevenness of the fiscal adjustment showed clearly the difficulty of imposing a stabilization plan when only a few, even within the ruling party, had the fight against inflation as their priority. With most of the provinces in the hands of the opposition, with only partial control of the legislature and with a public administration in which indifference prevailed, the day-to-day operation of the Austral Plan suffered from obstructionism and compromise. The external environment was also unfavourable to the plan. Throughout 1985, 1986, and 1987 international cereal prices fell sharply. In 1987 they were 35 per cent lower than in 1984, resulting in a major loss of export revenue. Moreover, while the government upheld an exchange rate designed to control inflation in 1985 and 1986, the fall in dollar prices was followed by a reduction in the revenue of agricultural production for the internal market. In order to compensate for this, export taxes were lowered with a predictably adverse effect on public finances.

The reduction in international prices of agricultural products – which during the first four years of the Alfonsín administration produced a fall in the terms of trade of 40 per cent – dramatized the effects of another burden that hampered the stabilization program: the external debt. In 1983 the external debt was 77.3 per cent of GDP and remained around this level during subsequent years. If all the interest due had been paid, the transfers of resources abroad would have been, on average, 6.5 per cent of GDP. The government was able to reduce the transfers of resources through negotiations with the creditors to half of this amount, but the interest that was not paid increased the total debt from U.S. $45.9 billion in 1983 to $56.8 billion in 1987. Not only was the external debt a constraint on growth; it also had a domestic dimension. Because the debt was nationalized during 1981–3, most external indebtedness was in the public sector. As a result, the responsibility for its servicing fell mainly on the government, which had to purchase the private trade surplus to meet these obligations. Thus, the interest payments added 5.1 per cent of GDP between 1984 and 1987 to the fiscal deficit, creating more obstacles for the stabilization plan.

The Austral Plan was already a falling star at the beginning of 1987, when the country entered a crucial electoral year, with half the lower house and all the provincial governments to be renewed in September. In February, the government introduced a new wage and price freeze in a desperate attempt to break a potentially inflationary spiral. The economic authorities were afraid of an acceleration in prices as a consequence of a generalized push by most interest groups at a time when the ruling party would give in to pressures. The freeze was intended to hold the line until September, after which a more serious stabilization programme would be implemented.

The approaching elections dictated another official initiative that added a new source of instability to the management of the economy. Alfonsín appointed Carlos Alderete, a trade union leader, as minister of labour. This was the culmination of negotiations begun between government officials and an important group of trade unions. By this step, the former were looking to weaken the CGT, obtain a labour truce and deprive the Partido Justicialista of union support in the coming elections. The initial motivation of the union leaders was their discontent with the CGT's policy of confrontation, which had been an obstacle to changing the system of labour relations. After three years of democracy, labour legislation was the same as it had been under the previous military government. This impeded collective bargaining, the re-election of union leaders by their organizations and the independent management of the considerable resources of the union's social and health programmes. Moreover, the politicians of the *peronista* Renovation, with the aim of capturing independent voters, had opted for conducting an electoral campaign without the irritating presence of the unionists. Resentful of their marginalization, they sought to draw closer to the government in order to dispute power within the *peronista* movement subsequently.

In the short run, the government objective of diminishing labour conflict was achieved, but at a high price. To a large degree, the conflicts were transferred inside the government. The daily confrontation between the minister of economy and the minister of labour complicated the adoption of policies and forced Alfonsín into a position of permanent arbitration. At the same time, the government postponed the project to decentralize collective bargaining and regulate the right to strike. In its place, the new labour minister managed to gain congressional approval of free collective bargaining and a legal framework similar to that put into place under the last *peronista* government in 1974, which operated under the direct influence of the trade unions.

At the beginning of 1987 the military also dramatically reappeared on the scene. Once the leaders of the military juntas had been condemned in 1985, the civil courts had proceeded with other trials. Every time an officer was summoned to appear before the courts, progressively less disguised expressions of unrest emerged from within the military. Despite the growing official concern, Alfonsín did not act, because he had little support from the *peronista* opposition and faced resistance by some sectors of his own party. Finally on 5 December 1986 he submitted to Congress the so-called *Punto Final* law whereby, following enactment, a sixty-day term was fixed for the filing of legal actions; once the term expired, there would be no further chance to initiate claims against military personnel. Congress passed the bill swiftly, though not easily: *peronistas* chose not to take part in the Chamber of Deputy sessions, and Alfonsín had to employ all of his influence to persuade his own people to vote favourably. The law was enacted on 24 December, but the official initiative backfired. Judges decided to interrupt their annual vacation period, which normally took place in January, and stood by to accept all the cases presented in the sixty days set by the law. On 23 February 1987, when the period was to end, legal action had been taken against more than three hundred top-ranking officers.

A period of high tension ensued. On 16 April in Córdoba a military officer due in court on charges of human rights violations became a fugitive from justice and took refuge in a local regiment. At the Campo de Mayo garrison in Buenos Aires, Lieutenant Colonel Aldo Rico rallied a hundred officers, who pressed the government for a 'political solution' to the trials and the removal of the army's high command for having subordinated the interests of the institution to Alfonsín's political convenience. The president issued the order to end the revolt; no military unit obeyed. As massive civilian protest erupted and a crowd estimated at 400,000 gathered in the Plaza de Mayo, Alfonsín went to the rebel stronghold and convinced the rebels to lay down their arms. On 13 May, bowing to the rebels' demands and after replacing the army high commander, the government submitted to Congress a bill that clearly specified the scope of due obedience in order to protect the middle levels of the armed forces, but now in much broader terms than Alfonsín originally intended and the Congress had later stipulated. On 4 June the official party once again had to enact a law against the solid opposition of the *peronista* deputies.

The Due Obedience Law fulfilled one of the objectives included in the government's agenda since the very beginning: to limit the sentences for human rights violations to a small number of top-ranking officers. However, the circumstances surrounding its approval led it to be perceived as a capitulation, thus weakening Alfonsín's credibility weeks before the September 1987 elections. At the same time, inflation again accelerated as a result of the government's policies. The February freeze did not last more than three months; inflation reached 13.7 per cent, the highest since 1985, one month before the elections. Although official efforts to prevent the economy from spiralling into hyperinflation had hitherto been quite successful, this was too modest a conquest for a society that had been promised much more four years before.

The government, as well as the opposition, converted the September elections into a referendum. Thanks to the Renovators, *peronismo* managed to recover legitimacy as a democratic alternative, depriving the Radicals of one of their principal banners. The *peronistas* won 41 per cent, compared with 34 per cent in 1985, whilst the Radical vote declined from 43 to 37 per cent. The outcome was even more adverse for the governing party at the gubernatorial level. The Partido Justicialista not only kept the provinces it had won in 1985 but also added five of the seven provinces that had been in the hands of the Radicals, thus controlling seventeen of twenty-two provinces. Within this overall picture, the defeat of the Radical candidate in Buenos Aires Province was particularly important, since the two candidates, Antonio Cafiero and Juan Manuel Casella, were potential candidates for the presidency in 1989. The electoral results had special significance for the *peronista* Renovators, which later took Cafiero to the presidency of the party; they won without the explicit support of the trade unions.

The fact that the elections were broadly seen as a plebiscite compounded the effects of defeat on the government's legitimacy. In a parliamentary system Alfonsín would have been obliged to resign, but under the constitution the president still had two years of his term to serve. This anomalous position was eased somewhat by an improvement in relations between Alfonsín and Cafiero and by the fact that the opposition's strengthened representation allowed it to drop its confrontational approach in favour of negotiating on behalf of its constituency. In this light, Congress regained its importance – hitherto diminished by the executive's use of decree laws – and long-delayed legislation, such as the National Defence Law and the statute to regulate financial relations between the republic and the provinces, was finally approved. Discussions over reform of the constitution were also renewed with a view to establishing a semi-parliamentary system. However, this process of increased collaboration and the attendant notion of co-government were short-lived and always restricted by enduring suspicion on both sides. In the second half of 1988 Radicals and *peronistas* began to select their presidential candidates for the elections of 1989, and the logic of political competition reopened traditional hostilities.

At Alfonsín's direct injunction, the Radical Party nominated the governor of Córdoba, Eduardo Angeloz, whose efficient administration had enabled him to survive the recent electoral defeats suffered by the governing party. Alfonsín's decision cut short the internal debate engendered by this set-back, and the official candidate was grudgingly accepted by militants who would have preferred an ideologically less moderate figure. After the experience of 1987 political realism demanded a search for votes in the centre of the political spectrum, and this became even more imperative once the *peronistas* elected their presidential candidate.

In July 1988 the supporters of *peronismo* were able for the first time in their history to elect their presidential slate. As a consequence the heterogeneity latent in the *peronista* revival was brought out into the open. The victory of Carlos Menem, with 53 per cent of the votes against 47 per cent for Cafiero, represented a distinctive current within the new *peronismo*. As governor of La Rioja, a small and underdeveloped northern province which he ruled as if it were his personal fiefdom, Menem incarnated the antipolitical traditions of *peronismo*. Cafiero was much more closely associated with republican institutions and the party system. Menem's victory owed much to the support of the poorest sectors of society and trade union leaders who reacted to the brusque treatment they had received at the hands of Cafiero in 1987.

The election campaigns of Menem and Angeloz presented Argentines with two clearly contrasting visions of the country's problems and the means by which they should be solved. The *justicialista* candidate toured the cities and countryside making promises of large wage increases and a moratorium on the external debt, but above all he called for confidence in his own person. Angeloz's message, by contrast, placed more emphasis on an austere and efficient state and an economy more open to world trade. Both sought to distance themselves from Alfonsín, whose prestige was now badly eroded. Menem did this directly, attacking the president as responsible for the economic crisis; Angeloz was more moderate, accusing Alfonsín of demonstrating a lack of will in confronting the crisis.

In the meantime Alfonsín himself had to preside over a government that had little time left to serve and yet was being subjected to rising pressure. In December 1988 there was a further military revolt led by Colonel Mohamed Seneildin, who returned to the country from Panama, where he had been training General Noriega's forces, to direct an insurrection with the objective of restoring political legitimacy to the war against subversion. The uprising did not last long, but it highlighted another conflict wracking the military. The rebels, largely members of elite units, accused the high command of corruption and lack of martial spirit, which they held responsible for the army's growing problems since the Malvinas War. A month later an unexpected and rapidly suppressed attack on a barracks by a small left-wing group reawakened memories of the recent past that were exploited by the armed forces to justify their previous actions and cast aspersions on the weak pacifism of the Alfonsín government.

The Alfonsín government was also confronted by growing economic difficulties as inflation and fiscal disequilibrium continued despite the October 1987 renewal of wage and price freezes and accompanying emergency taxes. In an effort to regain the initiative, and out of frustration at the failure of the Austral Plan, the government introduced a new programme of economic reforms aimed at correcting structural weaknesses in the public sector and progressively opening the economy to international trade. These measures were an attempt to strike at the causes of inflation from a position much closer to that of economic liberalism than had been the case in 1983–4. A policy of deregulation was introduced for public services in order to eliminate the legal obstacles to private investment in them; 40 per cent of the state airline and the public telephone system was put up for sale; the system of industrial support was reformed with a limited reduction in public subsidy to the private sector; the domestic price of petrol was brought towards the international level and encouragement given to private investment in the oil industry; progress was made in deregulating certain basic industries – paper, steel, petrochemicals – that had traditionally been protected by high tariffs; and a start was made in the progressive diminution of quantitative restrictions on imports.

These policies were introduced not by a strong government, such as that which had launched the Austral Plan in 1986, but by one weakened by recent electoral defeat, and the reform programme yielded uneven results. The policy of privatization, which had to be approved by Congress, did not come to fruition because of *peronista* obstructionism and because many Radicals were in two minds about it, whilst others saw it as a surrender of the party's programme. The measures for commercial and industrial deregulation and reductions in public subsidies were strongly resisted by private firms and had to be moderated as a result. The reform policies were intended to correct structural faults in the economy that encouraged inflation, but there was little to suggest that they could in themselves guarantee short-term stability. The first part of 1988 saw a test of the imbalance between the policy of stabilization and that of reform. Under the argument that it was necessary to halt Treasury financing of public corporations, the government began to increase public sector prices sharply. At the same time wage negotiations were freed and controls on private prices relaxed, further accelerating inflation, which reached a monthly rate of 25 per cent by July, its highest level since 1985.

In these circumstances and in the face of widespread public scepticism, the government felt obliged to make a final effort to avoid the hyper-inflationary crisis which had hovered over it since 1984. In August 1988 the Plan Primavera was introduced with the aim of controlling the economy until the presidential poll of May 1989. But the Alfonsín administration now lacked the political resources upon which it had been able to rely in the past. A wage and price freeze was no longer possible, since Congress had approved the free collective bargaining long demanded by the unions. Moreover, fiscal adjustments could not be carried out through new taxes, since it was unlikely that the congressional opposition would consent to them. Export taxes were similarly excluded because Alfonsín had promised the rural sector that, following the Plan Austral, they would not be reimposed. Finally, support from the international financial community was constrained by the fact that in April, as a result of a fall in reserves, the government had ceased paying interest on the external debt and had silently introduced a moratorium.

As the presidential campaign got under way Menem's populist campaign engendered disquiet amongst business sectors, and this in turn prompted co-operation among the government, the Unión Industrial and the Cámara Argentina de Comercio in an agreement to sustain free collective bargaining whilst maintaining controlled prices. However, rural interests were not included in this concordat. One of the main means for improving public finances was the development of an exchange rate mechanism that effectively imposed an export tax, which, it had formally been agreed, would not be levied. The state thereby appropriated the higher international prices currently prevailing for agricultural produce as a result of the U.S. drought, and these funds were used to finance the fiscal deficit. This produced an open conflict with the Sociedad Rural. Externally the IMF refused to support Alfonsín's anti-inflationary programme, but the World Bank, acting in accord with the U.S. Treasury, broke ranks and released an important set of credits to assist the country's reserves. With this combination of domestic and foreign backing, the plan achieved some initial success; the monthly inflation rate fell from 27.6 per cent in August to 6.8 per cent in December. Nevertheless, behind this apparently favourable result there was a growing disequilibrium caused by a programme that was designed to reduce price increases by relying on periodic adjustments below those of past inflation with consequent lags in the exchange rate and public prices. But the Plan Primavera faced a still greater threat from the uncertainty surrounding the election campaign, which kept alive the dangers of a run on the austral. The government kept interest rates high, while clinging to the hope (in the event, unfulfilled) that Angeloz would at least keep pace with the *peronista* candidate, whose platform frightened the business community. At the end of January 1989 the World Bank notified the government informally that it would not release a significant portion of the credit it had promised on the grounds that the conditions for payment had not been met. This was indeed the case, but the decision also reflected an unexpected result of the inauguration of the Bush administration: the replacement in the Treasury Department of those officials who had been favourably disposed towards the Plan Primavera by others who opposed it. A little later the creditor banks renewed their pressure for payment of overdue interest, and the IMF confirmed its refusal to offer support. These decisions were carefully leaked to the press and immediately unleashed the feared run on the austral.

An important sector of financiers, including local branches of the creditor banks, began to sell off their holdings of australes and buy dollars from the Central Bank. On 6 February, with reserves almost exhausted, the government was forced to halt its sale of dollars. This confirmed the worst fears of the populace, provoking a rise of 45 per cent in the price of the dollar on the free market in just six days. At the same time, the Central Bank was shown to be powerless to stop the loss of reserves, because the grain exporters were now able to take their revenge and refused to release hard currency. This weakness was further emphasized when, despite a series of devaluations, the exporters continued their refusal to come to the government's aid. As a result, savers became convinced that a major external blockade was being imposed, and in March there was a massive withdrawal of dollar deposits from the banks.

The political foundation of the Plan Primavera also disintegrated. The Unión Industrial and the Cámara de Comercio distanced themselves from both the government and the failure of its economic programme in an effort to gain a more favourable position for what now seemed an inevitable *peronista* election victory. At the end of March the minister of economy and his team resigned. The Alfonsín administration slid from a state of impotence to one of complete prostration whilst the country finally entered full hyperinflation.

The crisis in the exchange rate, which increased the price of the dollar by 100 per cent between February and April, affected consumer prices, deepened the fiscal deficit, severely destabilized the banking system and drove the population back to a range of defensive reactions. Confronted by the threat of the dissolution of their capital, businessmen resorted to pre-emptive price increases and reduced supply; workers demanded advances on their wages up to three times per month; exporters continued to withhold goods despite the record exchange rates; generalized speculation was fuelled by the retention of taxes and failure to pay public bills.

It was in this context that, on 14 May, the electorate voted for the Partido Justicialista's presidential candidate. Menem received 49 per cent of the vote, while Angeloz obtained 37 per cent. But it was no time for celebration. At the end of May food riots broke out, reflecting growing social unrest. In mid-June and after a failed attempt to gain Menem's support for a joint economic action, Alfonsín announced that he would resign in order to shorten his mandate due to end in December 1989. On 8 July, as Argentines learned that the inflation rate of the previous month had been 114 per cent, Alfonsín transferred power to Menem. For the first time in sixty years an elected president was succeeded by one who had also been democratically elected. This remarkable achievement of the democratic transition was clouded, however, by the general atmosphere of crisis.

The distribution of institutional power resulting from the elections gave Menem more favourable leverage than Alfonsín had had in 1983; *peronistas* had a majority in the lower house, the Senate was under full *peronista* control and seventeen of twenty-two governors were *peronistas*. Sensing the unavoidable weight of extra-institutional power, however, Menem made a bold decision that took everyone by surprise: he made overtures to the economic establishment and, with the enthusiasm of the newly converted, gave full support to a programme of fiscal austerity, privatization and economic liberalization. Later, yielding to the demands of the military, he granted a presidential pardon to high-ranking officers accused of human rights abuses and those who had been involved in the rebellions against Alfonsín. With his new allies in the business community, with backing from the armed forces and confident of his charisma, Menem led *peronismo*, reeling from the political U-turn, into a new experience in governing a conflictive society.

The first stage of the democratization process initiated in 1983 having been completed, the balance remained uncertain. Institutions had managed to survive the challenges posed by a serious economic crisis. Hyperinflation had not prevented the transfer of power in 1989 from one democratically elected president to another. Thus, it had been possible to dissociate the legitimacy of democratic institutions from the negative evaluation of their economic and social performance. However, though a catastrophic outcome had been averted, the reality was that many of the hopes raised by the new political cycle had been disappointed.

Throughout the period after 1983, the stagnant condition of the Argentine economy persisted: between 1984 and 1988 GDP increased at an annual rate of only 0.3 per cent. The unemployment rate, which in October 1983 was 3.9 per cent, by the end of 1988 had reached 6.2 per cent. Nor was the process of deindustrialization begun during the previous military administration reversed. The level of industrial employment, which in 1983 was 69 per cent of that of 1970, at the end of 1988 was 59 per cent. As for industrial wages, the last quarter of 1988 found them at the same level as they had been in 1983. All of these indicators worsened drastically when hyperinflation broke out in 1989.

The political parties and their leaders paid a high price in popularity and credibility for the economy's deterioration. In fact, Menem's ascent to power was due in large part to his ability to portray himself as a popular leader far removed from the discredited political class. The open involvement of the major economic corporations in the polity was still another sign of the current weakness of the traditional seats of the representative system: Congress, the parties and the presidency. Furthermore, the successive amnesties granted, under military pressure, to officers on trial for human rights violations revealed that force endured as a means of attaining political objectives.

Neither Argentina's economic decline nor its tendencies towards political praetorianism appeared to have changed during the years of the restoration of democracy. As the 1990s began, the search for an alternative to the economic and political order born in 1946 continued amid the recurrent but failed attempts to change it.

BIBLIOGRAPHICAL ESSAYS

I. FROM INDEPENDENCE TO NATIONAL ORGANIZATION

The bibliography of nineteenth-century Argentina can be approached through Joseph R. Barager, 'The Historiography of the Río de la Plata Area since 1930', *Hispanic American Historical Review*, 39 (1959), 588–642, and James R. Scobie, *Argentina. A City and a Nation* (New York, 1964), 248–74. A more specialist work is Julio O. Chiappini, *Bibliografía sobre Rosas* (Rosario, 1973).

Public documents are reproduced in a number of collections. The formal policy reviews of the executive are given in H. Mabragaña, *Los mensajes, 1810 1910*, 6 vols. (Buenos Aires, 1910); for the governors of Buenos Aires a better version is provided by Archivo Histórico de la Provincia de Buenos Aires, *Mensajes de los gobernadores de la provincia de Buenos Aires 1822–1849*, 2 vols. (La Plata, 1976). Basic legislative, constitutional and inter-provincial texts are to be found in Emilio Ravignani (ed.), *Asambleas constituyentes argentinas*, 6 vols. (Buenos Aires, 1937–9). The main documentation concerning Rosas is that of Adolfo Saldías (ed.), *Papeles de Rosas*, 2 vols. (La Plata, 1904–7), which can be supplemented by two convenient compilations of his thought and policy, Andrés M. Carretero, *El pensamiento político de Juan M. de Rosas* (Buenos Aires, 1970), and Arturo Enrique Sampay, *Las ideas políticas de Juan Manuel de Rosas* (Buenos Aires, 1972), and by a further collection of his correspondence, Juan Carlos Nicolau (ed.), *Correspondencia inédita entre Juan Manuel de Rosas y Manuel José García* (Tandil, 1989). Aspects of the opposition to Rosas are documented in Gregorio F. Rodríguez (ed.), *Contribución histórica y documental*, 3 vols. (Buenos Aires, 1921–2), and Archivo Histórico de la Provincia de Buenos Aires, *La campaña libertadora del general Lavalle (1838–1842)* (La Plata, 1944). Amidst other and smaller collections the monumental writings of Argentina's three most eminent figures of politics and letters stand out, beginning with Juan B. Alberdi, *Obras completas*, 8 vols. (Buenos Aires, 1876–86) and *Escritos póstumos*, 16 vols. (Buenos Aires, 1895–1901). Bartolomé Mitre, *Archivo del General Mitre: Documentos y correspondencia*, 28 vols. (Buenos Aires, 1911–14), can be supplemented by *Correspondencia literaria, histórica y política del General Bartolomé Mitre*, 3 vols. (Buenos Aires, 1912) and *Correspondencia Mitre–Elizalde* (*Documentos para la historia argentina*, 26, Buenos Aires, 1960). Domingo F. Sarmiento, *Obras completas*, 52 vols. (Santiago, 1887–1902), is an indispensable source for Argentine history, together with *Sarmiento-Mitre: Correspondencia, 1846–1868* (Buenos Aires, 1911), *Facundo* (La Plata, 1938), and *Epistolario entre Sarmineto y Posse, 1845–1888*, 2 vols. (Buenos Aires, 1946–7).

The subject is rich in narrative sources, and the following is no more than a brief selection. Sir Woodbine Parish, *Buenos Ayres and the Provinces of the Río de la Plata*, 2nd ed. (London, 1852), a work first published in 1938, is an objective and scholarly account by the former British chargé d'affaires. William MacCann, *Two Thousand Miles' Ride through the Argentine Provinces*, 2 vols. (London, 1853), brings the economy and the people of the pampas to life. One of the first approaches to quantification is provided by Victor Martin de Moussy, *Description géographique et statistique de la Conféderation Argentine*, 3 vols. (Paris, 1860–4). Thomas Joseph Hutchinson, *Buenos Ayres and Argentine Gleanings* (London, 1865), is a less accurate account, by the British consul at Rosario, but takes the story to 1862–3. Wilfred Latham, *The States of the River Plate*, 2nd ed. (London, 1868), is an amplified version of a book first published in 1866 and written from the author's 'home in the campo', a large sheep farm.

General histories are headed by the Academia Nacional de la Historia, *Historia de la nación argentina*, 2nd ed., 10 vols. (Buenos Aires, 1939–50), with it sequel, *Historia argentina contemporánea, 1862–1930* (Buenos Aires, 1965). These are composite works, uneven in quality. Tulio Halperín Donghi, *Argentina: De la revolución de independencia a la confederación rosista* (Buenos Aires, 1972), is analytically superior, as is his masterly essay introducing *Proyecto y construcción de una nación* (*Argentina 1846–1880*) (Caracas, 1980), a selection of texts from major writers of Argentina's age of nation-building. Haydée Gorostegui de Torres, *Argentina: La organización nacional* (Buenos Aires, 1972), gives a balanced account of the period 1852–74.

Study of the economy can begin with Jonathan C. Brown, *A Socioeco-*

nomic History of Argentina, 1776–1860 (Cambridge, Eng., 1979), which combines synthesis, original research and a sense of chronology. Miron Burgin, *The Economic Aspects of Argentine Federalism 1820–1852* (Cambridge, Mass., 1946), is still unsurpassed for data and interpretation. Tulio Halperín Donghi, *Guerra y finanzas en los orígenes del estado argentino (1791–1850)* (Buenos Aires, 1982), studies the role of the state as a participant as well as a policy-maker in the economy. Juan Carlos Nicolau, *Rosas y García (1829–35): La economía bonaerense* (Buenos Aires, 1980), concentrates on financial and fiscal policy, while his *La reforma económico-financiera en la Provincia de Buenos Aires (1821–1825): Liberalismo y economía* (Buenos Aires, 1988) includes new research on merchants and artisans, liberal economic policy, and the origins of emphiteusis. The basic institutional account of landowning is Miguel A. Cárcano, *Evolución histórica del régimen de la tierra pública, 1810–1916,* 3rd ed. (Buenos Aires, 1972), first published in 1917. Further details on land acquisition and concentration are provided by Jacinto Oddone, *La burguesía terrateniente argentina,* 3rd ed. (Buenos Aires, 1956), but for more accurate data, see Andrés M. Carretero, 'Contribución al conocimiento de la propiedad rural en la provincia de Buenos Aires para 1830', *Boletín del Instituto de Historia Argentina 'Doctor Emilio Ravignani',* 2nd series, 13/22–23 (1970), 246–92, and *La propiedad de la tierra en la época de Rosas* (Buenos Aires, 1972). Cattle-raising can be studied in Horacio C. E. Giberti, *Historia económica de la ganadería argentina* (Buenos Aires, 1961), and the processing plants in Alfredo J. Montoya, *Historia de los saladeros argentinos* (Buenos Aires, 1956), and *La ganadería y la industria de salazón de carnes en el período 1810–1862* (Buenos Aires, 1971). Aspects of early industrial developments are covered in José M. Mariluz Urquijo, *Estado e industria 1810–1862* (Buenos Aires, 1969), a collection of texts; Juan Carlos Nicolau, *Antecedentes para la historia de la industria argentina* (Buenos Aires, 1968), and *Industria argentina y aduana, 1835–1854* (Buenos Aires, 1975); and Clifton Kroeber, *The Growth of the Shipping Industry in the Río de la Plata Region, 1794–1860* (Madison, 1957). Foreign trade and its participants are studied in a useful article and two important books: Juan Carlos Nicolau, 'Movimiento marítimo exterior del puerto de Buenos Aires (1810–1854)', *Nuestra Historia,* 12 (1973), 351–61; H. S. Ferns, *Britain and Argentina in the Nineteenth Century* (Oxford, 1960); Vera Bliss Reber, *British Merchant Houses in Buenos Aires, 1810–1880* (Cambridge, Mass., 1979). For the wool cycle and the economy in transition, see José Carlos Chiaramonte, *Nacionalismo y liberalismo económicos en la Argentina, 1860–1880* (Buenos Aires, 1971),

Hilda Sábato, 'Wool Trade and Commercial Networks in Buenos Aires, 1840s to 1880s', *Journal of Latin American Studies*, 15, 1 (1983), 49–81, and the now classic H. Gibson, *The History and Present State of the Sheepbreeding Industry in the Argentine Republic* (Buenos Aires, 1893). Finally, see Hilda Sábato, *Agrarian Capitalism and the World Market. Buenos Aires in the Pastoral Age, 1840–1890* (Albuquerque, N. Mex., 1990).

Society in its demographic aspect is well described by Ernesto J. A. Maeder, *Evolución demográfica argentina de 1810 a 1869* (Buenos Aires, 1969), while for a shorter period population change is measured by Susana R. Frías, César A. García Belsunce, et al., *Buenos Aires: Su gente, 1800–1830* (Buenos Aires, 1976), based on censuses of the city of Buenos Aires. These should be supplemented by George Reid Andrews, *The Afro-Argentines of Buenos Aires, 1800–1900* (Madison, 1980). On immigration, see Juan Antonio Oddone, *La emigración europea al Río de la Plata* (Montevideo, 1966). New research on the life and labour of the Irish is provided by Juan Carlos Korol and Hilda Sábato, *Como fue la inmigración irlandesa en la Argentina* (Buenos Aires, 1981). The most powerful social group is studied by María Sáenz Quesado, *Los estancieros* (Buenos Aires, 1980). Gauchos, peons and vagrants are placed in their historical context by Gastón Gori, *Vagos y mal entretenidos*, 2nd ed. (Santa Fe, 1965), Ricardo Rodríguez Molas, *Historia social del gaucho*, 2nd ed. (Buenos Aires, 1982), and Richard W. Slatta, *Gauchos and the Vanishing Frontier* (Lincoln, Nebr., 1983). Mark D. Szuchman, *Order, Family, and Community in Buenos Aires 1810–1860* (Stanford, 1988), uses family history in a search for the responses of the masses to political leadership. On Indian society, Raúl Mandrini, 'La sociedad indígena de las pampas en el siglo XIX', in Mirta Lischetti (ed.), *Antropología* (Buenos Aires, 1985), is the surest guide. Rubén H. Zorrilla, *Extracción social de los caudillos 1810–1870* (Buenos Aires, 1972), discusses the social base of *caudillismo*.

Political history can be divided into three periods, comprising Rivadavia, Rosas and national organization. On the first, Ricardo Piccirilli, *Rivadavia y su tiempo*, 2nd ed., 3 vols. (Buenos Aires, 1960), is a work of scholarship, and Sergio Bagú, *El plan económico del grupo Rivadaviano 1811–1827* (Rosario, 1966), a cogent interpretation with documents. The enormous bibliography on Rosas is a hindrance rather than a help to understanding. Adolfo Saldías, *Historia de la Confederación Argentina: Rosas y su época*, 9 vols. (Buenos Aires, 1958), a work first published in 1881–87 from official Rosas sources, is a useful chronicle of events. Roberto

Etchepareborda, *Rosas: controvertida historiografía* (Buenos Aires, 1972), is a modern survey of the 'problems'. Enrique M. Barba, *Cómo llegó Rosas al poder* (Buenos Aires, 1972), explains the conquest of power. Among the *rosista* historians, Carlos Ibarguren, *Juan Manuel de Rosas, su vida, su drama, su tiempo* (Buenos Aires, 1961), first published in 1930, provides a well-documented political biography; and Julio Irazusta, *Vida política de Juan Manuel de Rosas, a través de su correspondencia*, 2nd ed., 8 vols. (Buenos Aires, 1970), supplies much detail and documentation. Ernesto H. Celesia, *Rosas, aportes para su historia*, 2nd ed., 2 vols. (Buenos Aires, 1968), is hostile but well researched. Benito Díaz, *Juzgados de paz de campaña de la provincia de Buenos Aires (1821–1854)* (La Plata, 1959), studies a vital agency of the regime. On the foreign blockades and other forms of intervention, see John F. Cady, *Foreign Intervention in the Río de la Plata 1838–50* (Philadelphia, 1929), and Nestor S. Colli, *La política francesa en el Río de la Plata: Rosas y el bloqueo de 1838–1840* (Buenos Aires, 1963), as well as the work by Ferns already cited. The international context of the fall of Rosas is explored by the *rosista* historian José María Rosa, *La caída de Rosas: El Imperio de Brasil y la Confederación Argentina (1843–1851)*, 2nd ed. (Buenos Aires, 1968). For a modern history of Rosas, his power base and his policy, see John Lynch, *Argentine Dictator: Juan Manuel de Rosas 1829–1852* (Oxford, 1981). The period contained a history of reform as well as reaction, expertly studied in its legislation by David Bushnell, *Reform and Reaction in the Platine Provinces 1810–1852* (Gainesville, Fla., 1983). And in the Littoral alternative forms of political control developed, investigated by José Carlos Chiaramonte, 'Finanzas públicas de las provincias del Litoral, 1821–1841', *Anuario del IEHS* 1 (Tandil, 1986), 159–98, and 'Legalidad constitucional o caudillismo: El problema del orden social en el surgimiento de los estados autónomos del Litoral argentino en la primera mitad del siglo XIX', *Desarrollo Económico*, 26, 102 (1986), 175–96.

In the period of national organization the transitional figure is Urquiza: see Beatriz Bosch, *Urquiza y su tiempo* (Buenos Aires, 1971). Older accounts of the decade after Rosas are now superseded by James R. Scobie, *La lucha por la consolidación de la nacionalidad argentina, 1852–1862* (Buenos Aires, 1964). The great constitutional statesmen have attracted a number of biographies, of which Jorge M. Mayer, *Alberdi y su tiempo* (Buenos Aires, 1963), is outstanding. Sarmiento receives scholarly attention from Ricardo Rojas, *El profeta de la pampa: Vida de Sarmiento* (Buenos

Aires, 1945); Paul Verdevoye, *Domingo Faustino Sarmiento. Educateur et publiciste entre 1839 et 1852* (Paris, 1963); and José S. Campobassi, *Sarmiento y su época,* 2 vols. (Buenos Aires, 1975).

On the Paraguayan War, Pelham Horton Box, *The Origins of the Paraguayan War* (Urbana, Ill., 1929), is still worth reading, but should be supplemented by Efraím Cardozo, *Vísperas de la guerra del Paraguay* (Buenos Aires, 1954), and *El Imperio del Brasil y el Río de la Plata* (Buenos Aires, 1962). The same author's *Hace cien años,* 8 vols. (Asunción, 1967–72), is a useful chronicle of events based on contemporary Paraguayan newspapers. Ramón J. Cárcano, *Guerra del Paraguay,* 3 vols. (Buenos Aires, 1938–40), still has value as a work of reference. For a history of the war in English see Charles Kolinski, *Independence or Death. The Story of the Paraguayan War* (Gainesville, Fla., 1965).

2. THE GROWTH OF THE ARGENTINE ECONOMY, c. 1870–1914

The best and most complete bibliographical study of the economic history of Argentina in the period 1870–1914 is Tulio Halperín Donghi, 'Argentina,' in Roberto Cortés Conde and Stanley J. Stein (eds.), *Latin America: A Guide to Economic History 1830–1930* (Berkeley and Los Angeles, 1977). Among the general works which appeared after the Second World War, Ricardo M. Ortiz, *Historia económica de la Argentina, 1850–1930,* 2 vols. (Buenos Aires, 1955), was, for many years, the most widely read work on the economic history of Argentina. During the 1960s two works in this field were to have a significant influence: Aldo Ferrer, *La Economía argentina: Las etapas de su desarrollo y problemas actuales* (Buenos Aires, 1964), which, like Celso Furtado's study of Brazil, examines the structure of the economy from the colonial period to the present and is strongly influenced by the literature on development from ECLA/CEPAL; and Guido Di Tella and Manuel Zymelman, *Las etapas del desarrollo económico argentino* (Buenos Aires, 1967), originally conceived as a thesis under the supervision of W. W. Rostow, which accepts the rapid growth of the period 1880–1914 and seeks to explain why it was not sustained after 1914. See also the essays in D. C. M. Platt and G. Di Tella (eds.), *The Political Economy of Argentina, 1880–1946* (London, 1986), including David Rock, 'The Argentine Economy, 1880–1914: Some Salient Features'.

The first chapter of Carlos F. Díaz Alejandro's important work, *Essays on the Economic History of the Argentine Republic* (New Haven, Conn., 1970), considers the period prior to 1930. Díaz Alejandro moves away from previous interpretations of the period and stresses that Argentina, like Canada and the United States, deserves to be seen within the framework of the staple theory of economic growth (on which see Melville H. Watkins, 'A Staple Theory of Economic Growth', *Canadian Journal of Economic and Political Science*, 29/2 (1963)). Vicente Vásquez Presedo, *El caso argentino* (Buenos Aires, 1971), also sees the Argentine case as being unique and different from that of other underdeveloped countries and closer to that of recently settled Anglo-Saxon countries. See also John Fogarty, Ezequiel Gallo and Hector Diéguez (eds.), *Argentina y Australia* (Buenos Aires, 1979); Tim Duncan and John Fogarty, *Australia and Argentina: On Parallel Paths* (Melbourne, 1984); D. C. M. Platt and G. Di Tella (eds.), *Argentina, Australia and Canada: Studies in Comparative Development, 1870–1965* (New York, 1985). The first two chapters of Roberto Cortés Conde, *El progreso argentino 1880–1914* (Buenos Aires, 1979) consider the territorial formation and regional structure of Argentina from the colonial period until the nineteenth century, while the central chapters discuss the development of the land and labour markets during the period 1880–1910.

Other general works that deserve mention are Roque Gondra, *Historia económica de la República Argentina* (Buenos Aires, 1943), which was an obligatory text in teaching for many years, as was Federico Pinedo, *Siglo y medio de economía argentina* (Mexico, 1961). See also Academia Nacional de la Historia, *Historia argentina contemporánea 1862–1930*, vol. 3 *Historia económica* (Buenos Aires, 1965). Among older but nevertheless indispensable works are two studies by Juan Alvarez, *Estudios sobre las guerras civiles argentinas* (Buenos Aires, 1914) and *Temas de historia económica argentina* (Buenos Aires, 1929), as well as Ernesto Tornquist's *The Economic Development of the Argentine Republic in the Last Fifty Years* (Buenos Aires, 1919) and M. G. and E. T. Mulhall, *Handbook of the River Plate*, 1863, 1875, 1883, 1892 (reprint, Buenos Aires, and London, 1982).

On demographic change, and especially internal and international migration, Zulma L. Recchini de Lattes and Alfredo E. Lattes, *Migraciones en la Argentina* (Buenos Aires, 1969) and *La población de Argentina* (Buenos Aires, 1975) are indispensable. See also this volume, bibliographical essay 3.

For many years, the most widely accepted work on the rural sector was

Horacio C. E. Giberti, *Historia económica de la ganadería argentina* (Buenos Aires, 1954), based principally on the excellent essays of the 1908 Census; it became a classic in its field. Another well-known book is James Scobie, *Revolution on the Pampas: a Social History of Argentine Wheat* (Austin, Tex., 1964). Recent works include Ezequiel Gallo, 'Agricultural Colonization and Society in Argentina. The Province of Santa Fe, 1870–95', unpublished D. Phil. thesis, Oxford, 1970; Sp. trans. *La Pampa Gringa* (Buenos Aires, 1983); Alfredo R. Pucciarelli, *El capitalismo agrario pampeano, 1880–1930* (Buenos Aires, 1986); Carl E. Solberg, *The Prairies and the Pampas: Agrarian Policy in Canada and Argentina, 1880–1930* (Stanford, 1987), and Hilda Sábato, *Agrarian Capitalism and the World Market. Buenos Aires in the Pastoral Age, 1840–1890* (Albuquerque, N.Mex., 1990). See also Alfredo J. Montoya, *Historia de los saladeros argentinos* (Buenos Aires, 1956); Fernando Enrique Barba, 'El desarrollo agropecuario de la provincia de Buenos Aires (1880–1930)', *Investigaciones y Ensayos*, 17 (July–December 1974), 210–310; Roberto Cortés Conde, 'Patrones de asentamiento y explotación agropecuaria en los nuevos territorios argentinos (1890–1910)', and Ezequiel Gallo, 'Ocupación de tierras y colonización agrícola en Santa Fe', both in Alvaro Jara (ed.), *Tierras nuevas* (Mexico City, 1969); Roberto Cortés Conde, 'Tierras, agricultura y ganadería', and Colin Lewis, 'La consolidación de la frontera argentina a fines de la década del setenta. Los indios, Roca y los ferrocarriles', both in Gustavo Ferrari and Ezequiel Gallo (eds.), *La Argentina del ochenta al centenario* (Buenos Aires, 1980); and M. Sáenz Quesada, *Los estancieros* (Buenos Aires, 1980). A number of older works are worthy of special mention because of their permanent value: Miguel Angel Cárcano, *Evolución histórica del régimen de la tierra pública 1810–1916*, 3rd ed. (Buenos Aires, 1917); Jacinto Oddone, *La burguesía terrateniente argentina* (Buenos Aires, 1930); Mark Jefferson, *Peopling the Argentine Pampas* (New York, 1926); Carl C. Taylor, *Rural Life in Argentina* (Baton Rouge, La., 1948); Simon G. Hanson, *Argentine Meat and the British Market: Chapters in the History of the Argentine Meat Industry* (Stanford, 1938). Estanislao Zeballo, *Descripción amena de la República Argentina* (Buenos Aires, 1888) and the studies carried out by the División de Economía Rural del Ministerio de Agricultura (1900) are indispensable.

On foreign trade and foreign investment, John H. Williams, *Argentine International Trade under Inconvertible Paper Money, 1880–1900* (Cambridge, Mass., 1920; repr. New York, 1969), has still not been surpassed; because of its wealth of information on balance of payments, prices, wages, and so on it has, in fact, come to be considered the best economic history of the period. See also Vásquez-Presedo, *El caso argentino*, chapter 2; H. S. Ferns, *Britain and Argentina in the Nineteenth Century* (Oxford, 1960); A. G. Ford, *The Gold Standard 1880–1914: Britain and Argentina* (Oxford, 1962), and an older work, Harold J. Peters, *The Foreign Debt of the Argentine Republic* (Baltimore, 1934). Héctor L. Diéguez, 'Crescimiento e inestabilidad del valor y el volumen físico de las exportaciones argentinas en el período 1864–1963', *Desarrollo Económico* 12,46 (1972), is an article which transcribes information from the important recompilation of statistical evidence on Argentina's foreign trade presented in Roberto Cortés Conde, Tulio Halperín Donghi and H. Gorostegui de Torres, *El comercio exterior argentino – exportaciones 1863–1963* (mimeo, Instituto Torcuato Di Tella, Buenos Aires, n.d.), which corrects many previous statistical errors and deficiencies. Also important are D. C. M. Platt, *Finance, Trade and Politics in British Foreign Policy 1815–1914* (Oxford, 1971), and *Latin America and British Trade, 1806–1914* (London, 1972); A. G. Ford, 'British Investment in Argentina and Long Swings 1880–1914', *Journal of Economic History*, 31/3 (1971), reprinted in Roderick Floud (ed.), *Essays in Quantitative Economic History* (Oxford, 1974), and 'British Investment and Argentine Economic Development, 1880–1914' in David Rock (ed.), *Argentina in the Twentieth Century* (London, 1975).

The works of Williams and Ford are mainly studies of the working of the gold standard in Argentina. The work of Williams goes up to the end of the century while that of Ford considers two separate periods, the first from 1880 to 1885 which he classifies as a failure of the system, and the second from 1900 to 1910, which he terms a success. See also Ferns, *Britain and Argentina*, and David Joslin, *A Century of Banking in Latin America* (London, 1963). See also Rafael Olarra Jiménez, *El dinero y las estructuras monetarias* (Buenos Aires, 1967), and his more recent 'Las reformas monetarias 1880–1910', together with Charles Jones, 'Los bancos británicos', in Ferrari and Gallo (eds.), *La Argentina del ochenta al centenario*. Among older works, see Emilio Hansen's classic study, *La moneda argentina* (Buenos Aires, 1916), and José A. Terry, *Cuestiones monetarias* (Buenos Aires, 1899), and *Finanzas* (Buenos Aires, 1918).

The bibliography on transport is, of course, dominated by the railways. The most complete recent work is Eduardo A. Zalduendo, *Libras y rieles* (Buenos Aires, 1975) which also examines British investment in the railways of Brazil, Canada and India. Also important is Winthrop R. Wright, *British-Owned Railways in Argentina: Their Effect on Economic Nationalism*

1854–1948 (Austin, Texas, 1972). See too Colin Lewis, 'Problems of Railway Development in Argentina 1857–1890', *Inter-American Economic Affairs*, 22/2 (1962) and *British Railways in Argentina 1857–1914* (London, 1983); Paul Goodwin, 'The Central Argentine Railway and the Economic Development of Argentina 1854–1881', *Hispanic American Historical Review*, 57/4 (1977); and the most recent study by Eduardo A. Zalduendo, 'Aspectos económicos del sistema de transporte en la Argentina (1880–1914)', in Ferrari and Gallo (eds.), *La Argentina del ochenta al centenario*. Among older works, which are nevertheless indispensable for various reasons, Raúl Scalabrini Ortiz, *Historia de los ferrocarriles argentinos* (Buenos Aires, 1957), an anti-British view, and A. E. Bunge's well-documented *Ferrocarriles argentinos* (Buenos Aires, 1917), which, as the author points out, is also a contribution to the study of national wealth, deserve mention.

On industry, Adolfo Dorfman's study, published originally as *La evolución industrial argentina* (Buenos Aires, 1942) and later as *Historia de la industria argentina* (Buenos Aires, 1970), remains important. Among more recent works, see Vásquez Presedo, *El caso argentino*, and 'Evolución industrial 1880–1910', in Ferrari and Gallo (eds.), *La Argentina del ochenta al centenario;* Ezequiel Gallo, 'Agrarian Expansion and Industrial Development in Argentina', in Raymond Carr (ed.), *Latin American Affairs. St Antony's Papers, no. 22* (Oxford, 1970); Lucio Geller, 'El crecimiento industrial argentino hasta 1914 y la teoría del bien primario exportado', in Marcos Giménez Zapiola (ed.), *El régimen oligárquico. Materiales para el estudio de la realidad argentina hasta 1930* (Buenos Aires, 1975), 156–200.

3. SOCIETY AND POLITICS, 1880–1916

There are a number of general works on the political process in Argentina between 1870 and 1914: Academia Nacional de la Historia, *Historia argentina contemporánea 1862–1930*, vols. I and II (Buenos Aires, 1964 and 1966); Ricardo Levillier (ed.), *Historia argentina*, vol. IV (Buenos Aires, 1968); E. Gallo and R. Cortés Conde, *La república conservadora* (Buenos Aires, 1972); N. Botana, *El orden conservador. La política argentina entre 1880 y 1916* (Buenos Aires, 1977); G. Ferrari and E. Gallo (eds.), *La Argentina del ochenta al centenario* (Buenos Aires, 1980); and David Rock, *Argentina 1516–1982. From Spanish Colonization to the Falklands War* (Berkeley, Calif., 1985). Still useful are the classic studies by L. H. Sommariva, *Historia de las intervenciones federales en las provincias*, 2 vols. (Buenos Aires, 1929), José N. Matienzo, *El gobierno representativo federal en la República Argentina* (Madrid, 1917), and Rodolfo Rivarola, *Del régimen federativo al unitario* (Buenos Aires, 1908). Also worth consulting is the documentary compilation by Isidoro Ruiz Moreno (ed.), *La federalización de Buenos Aires* (Buenos Aires, 1980).

Some biographies contain useful information on the period. See, for example, two studies by Agustín Rivero Astengo, *Juárez Celman. Estudio histórico y documental de una época argentina* (Buenos Aires, 1940), and *Pellegrini, 1846–1906*, 2 vols. (Buenos Aires, 1941); R. Sáenz Hayes, *Miguel Cané y su tiempo, 1851–1905* (Buenos Aires, 1955); José Arce, *Roca 1843–1914. Su vida y su obra* (Buenos Aires, 1960); F. Luna, *Soy Roca* (Buenos Aires, 1989); A. W. Bunkley, *The Life of Sarmiento* (Princeton, N.J., 1952); J. Campobassi, *Mitre y su época* (Buenos Aires, 1980); and D. F. Weinstein, *Juan B. Justo y su época* (Buenos Aires, 1978). Also worth consulting are Leandro Alem, *Mensaje y destino* 8 vols. (Buenos Aires, 1955), and Hipólito Yrigoyen, *Pueblo y gobierno*, 12 vols. (Buenos Aires, 1956). Among the most useful memoirs or autobiographies of active politicians are Paul Groussac, *Los que pasaban* (Buenos Aires, 1919); Ezequiel Ramos Mejía, *Mis memorias* (Buenos Aires, 1936); Ramón J. Cárcano, *Mis primeros ochenta años* (Buenos Aires, 1944); Nicolás Repetto, *Mi paso por la política, de Roca a Irigoyen* (Buenos Aires, 1956); Carlos Ibarguren, *La historia que he vivido* (Buenos Aires, 1955); and Enrique Dickman, *Recuerdos de un militante socialista* (Buenos Aires, 1949).

Not much, until recently, has been written on the history of ideas. The theme is given summary treatment in José L. Romero, *Las ideas políticas en la Argentina* (Mexico City, 1956); Eng. trans. *The History of Argentine Political Thought* (Stanford, 1963). Extremely valuable is T. Halperín Donghi, *Proyecto y construcción de una nación (Argentina 1846–1880)* (Caracas, 1980). This work should be read in conjunction with other studies by the same author: 'Un nuevo clima de ideas' in Ferrari and Gallo (eds.), *La Argentina del ochenta al centenario*, and '¿Para qué la inmigración? Ideología y política migratoria y aceleración del proceso modernizador: El caso argentino (1810–1914)', *Jahrbuch für Geschichte von Staat, Wirtschaft und Gesellschaft Lateinamerikas*, 13 (1976). The following are also worth consulting: H. Biaggini, *¿Cómo fue la generación del ochenta?* (Buenos Aires, 1980); M. Monserrat, 'La mentalidad evolucionista: una ideología del progreso' in Ferrari and Gallo (eds.), *La Argentina del ochenta al centenario;* J. C. Chiaramonte, *Nacionalismo y liberalismo económico en la Argentina* (Buenos Aires, 1971), and T. Duncan, 'La prensa política: Sud-América, 1884–1942', in Ferrari and Gallo (eds.), *La Argentina del ochenta al centenario.* Two important recent contributions have been made by Natalio Botana, *La tradición republicana. Alberdi, Sarmiento y las ideas políticas de su tiempo* (Buenos Aires, 1984), and *La libertad política y su historia* (Buenos Aires, 1991). See also T. Halperín Donghi, *José Hernández y sus mundos* (Buenos Aires, 1985), and Carlos Escudé, *El fracaso del proyecto argentino. Educación e ideología* (Buenos Aires, 1990). For social catholicism, see N. T. Auzá, *Corrientes sociales de catolicismo argentino* (Buenos Aires, 1984). A recent and very valuable contribution is E. Zimmermann, 'Liberals, Reform and the Social Question' (unpublished D. Phil. thesis, Oxford University, 1991).

There are a few general works on political parties: see Carlos Melo, *Los partidos políticos argentinos* (Córdoba, 1970); Alfredo Galletti, *La política y los partidos* (Buenos Aires, 1961); Dario Cantón, *Elecciones y partidos políticos en la Argentina. Historia, interpretación y balance 1910–1966* (Buenos Aires, 1973); and K. Remmer, *Party Competition in Argentina and Chile. Political Recruitment and Public Policy* (Lincoln, Nebr., 1984). On political practices, see H. Sábato and E. Plati, '¿Quién votaba en Buenos Aires? Práctica y teoría del sufragio, 1850–1880', *Desarrollo Económico*, 30, 119 (1990), and E. Gallo, 'Un quinquenio difícil: Las presidencias de Carlos Pellegrini y Luis Sáenz Peña', in G. Ferrari and E. Gallo, *La Argentina del ochenta al centenario*. The Radical party has received the most attention from historians. Besides the essays in Alem, *Mensaje y destino*, and Yrigoyen, *Pueblo y gobierno*, other important works are Gabriel Del Mazo, *El radicalismo. Ensayo sobre su historia y doctrina* (Buenos Aires, 1957); David Rock, *Politics in Argentina, 1890–1930. The Rise and Fall of Radicalism* (Cambridge, Eng. 1975); and E. Gallo and S. Sigal, 'La formación de los partidos políticos contemporáneos: La Unión Cívica Radical (1890–1916)', *Desarrollo Económico*, 3,1–2 (1963). On the Socialist party, R. J. Walter, *The Socialist Party in Argentina 1890–1930* (Austin, Tex., 1977); D. Cuneo, *Juan B. Justo y las luchas sociales en la Argentina* (Buenos Aires, 1963); J. Oddone, *Historia del socialismo argentino* (Buenos Aires, 1943); and M. Mullaney, 'The Argentine Socialist Party' (unpublished Ph.D. thesis, University of Essex, 1983), are all useful.

Less has been published on the conservative forces in Argentine politics in this period. But see O. Cornblit, 'La opción conservadora en la política argentina', *Desarrollo Económico*, 15,56 (1975), 599–640, and E. Gallo, 'El Roquismo', *Todo es Historia*, 100 (1975). Although not devoted specifically to the topic, useful information may be found in J. M. Dulevich, *Caos social y crisis cívica* (Buenos Aires, 1980). Nothing has been written on the different groups which rallied behind the banner of *mitrismo*, and very little on the provincial factions. On the latter, various regional histories contain information: Juan Alvarez, Ensayo sobre la historia de Santa Fe (Buenos Aires, 1910); H. F. Gómez, *Los últimos sesenta años de democracia y gobierno en la provincia de Corrientes* (Buenos Aires, 1931); A. Díaz de Molina, *La oligarquía argentina. Su filiación y régimen (1840–1898)* (Buenos Aires, 1973); and Carlos Páez de la Torre, 'Tucumán, vida política y cotidiana, 1904–1913', *Todo es Historia,* 27 (1973). There are also a number of valuable unpublished doctoral theses: Donald Peck, 'Argentine Politics and the Province of Mendoza, 1890–1914' (University of Oxford, 1977); A. Liebscher, 'Commercial Expansion and Political Change in Santa Fe Province, 1897–1916' (Indiana University, 1975); Donna Guy, 'Politics and the Sugar Industry in Tucumán, Argentina, 1870–1900' (Indiana University, 1973), and G. Heaps-Nelson, 'Argentine Provincial Politics in an Era of Expanding Political Participation. Buenos Aires and Mendoza, 1906–1918' (University of Florida, 1975).

The armed rebellions of this period have attracted considerable attention. On the revolution of 1874, there is A. Terzaga, 'La revolución del 74. Una estrella que sube', *Todo es Historia,* 59 (1974). For the events of 1880, see B. Galíndez, *Historia política Argentina. La revolución de 1880* (Buenos Aires, 1945); S. Ratto de Sambucetti, *Avellaneda y la nación versus la provincia de Buenos Aires (1873–1880)* (Buenos Aires, 1975); E. M. Sanucci, *La renovación presidencial de 1880* (Buenos Aires, 1959); and N. Botana, '1880. La federalización de Buenos Aires', in G. Ferrari and E. Gallo (eds.), *La Argentina del ochenta al centenario.* Much has been published on the revolution of 1890: J. Balestra, *El noventa. Una evolución política argentina* (Buenos Aires, 1971); H. Zorraquín Becú, *La revolución del noventa. Su sentido político* (Buenos Aires, 1960); L. V. Sommi, *La revolución del 90* (Buenos Aires, 1957); and a special edition of the *Revista de Historia* (1957) on 'La crisis del 90'. On the provincial revolts of 1893, see R. Etchepareborda, *Tres revoluciones. 1890–1893–1905* (Buenos Aires, 1968), and E. Gallo, *Farmers in Revolt. The Revolution of 1893 in the Province of Santa Fe* (London, 1976). Etchepareborda's work also analyses the aborted radical uprising of 1905. See also C. Martinez, *Alsina y Alem. Porteñismo y milicias* (Buenos Aires, 1990), and M. J. Wilde, 'Las milicias santafecinas', *Revista Histórica,* 10 (1982).

On international relations, see H. S. Ferns, *Britain and Argentina in the Nineteenth Century* (Oxford, 1960); T. McGann, *Argentina, the United States and the Inter-American System. 1880–1914* (Cambridge, Mass., 1967); G. Ferrari, 'Argentina y sus vecinos' in Ferrari and Gallo (eds.), *La Argentina del ochenta al centenario;* and Joseph S. Tulchin, *Argentina and the United Staes. A Conflicted Relationship* (Boston, 1990). An important subject which has attracted little attention is that of relations with Italy and Spain, the home countries of the vast majority of immigrants.

For the social history of the period, fundamental are the three excellent national censuses of 1869, 1895 and 1914, and the two agricultural censuses (1888 and 1908). There are also two good provincial census reports (Buenos Aires, 1881 and Santa Fe, 1887), and three municipal censuses for the city of Buenos Aires (1887, 1904 and 1909). Much information on the social life of Argentina can be found in descriptions and studies published by foreign writers. The list is a long one, but the following deserve mention: *Handbook of the River Plate* by M. G. and E. T. Mulhall, 1863, 1875, 1883 and 1892 (reprint, Buenos Aires and London, 1982); E. Daireaux, *Vida y costumbres en el Plata,* 2 vols. (Buenos Aires, 1888); Jules Huret, *En Argentine: de Buenos Ayres au Gran Chaco* (Paris, 1914); A. N. Schüster, *Argentinien: Land, Volk, Wirtschaftsleben und Kolonisation,* 2 vols. (Munich, 1913); and P. de Giovanni, *Sotto il sole de Maggio. Note e impressione de la Argentina* (Castielo, 1900). Of considerable use is the volume published by Lloyd's, *Twentieth Century Impressions of Argentina. Its History, People, Commerce, Industries and Resources* (London, 1911).

A topic which has received particular attention from historians is demographic growth, especially in relation to immigration. Useful studies are J. A. Alsina, *La inmigración en el primer siglo de la independencia* (Buenos Aires, 1910); Zulma L. Recchini de Lattes and Alfredo E. Lattes, *La población de Argentina* (Buenos Aires, 1975); N. Sánchez-Albornoz, *La población de América Latina desde los tiempos pre-colombinos al año 2000* (Madrid, 1973); G. Beyhaut, 'Los inmigrantes en el sistema institucional argentino', in Torcuato di Tella et al., *Argentina, sociedad de masas* (Buenos Aires, 1965); and E. Maeder, 'Población e inmigración en la Argentina entre 1880 y 1910', in Ferrari and Gallo (eds.), *La Argentina del ochenta al centenario.* See also Carl Solberg, *Immigration and Nationalism in Argentina and Chile 1890–1914* (Austin, Tex., 1970). On European immigration to rural areas, see J. C. Korol and H. Sábato, *Como fue la inmigración irlandesa en Argentina* (Buenos Aires, 1981), and Ezequiel Gallo, *La pampa gringa* (Buenos Aires, 1983).

Much research has been carried out recently on specific groups of immigrants. See, for instance, the articles in F. Korn (ed.), *Los italianos en la Argentina* (Buenos Aires, 1983); F. J. Devoto and G. Ronzoli (eds.), *L'Italia nella societá argentina* (Rome, 1988); and N. Sánchez Albornoz (ed.), *Españoles hacia América. La emigración en masa* (1880–1930) (Madrid, 1988). See also O. Weyne, *El último puerto. Del Rhin al Volga y del Volga al Plata* (Buenos Aires, 1986).

On urban growth, see Z. Recchini de Lattes, 'El proceso de urbanización en la Argentina: Distribución, crecimiento y algunas características de la población urbana', *Desarrollo Económico*, 13,48 (1973), and *La población de Buenos Aires* (Buenos Aires, 1971); P. H. Randle, *La ciudad pampeana* (Buenos Aires, 1977); J. Scobie, *Buenos Aires. From plaza to suburb, 1870–1910* (New York, 1974); Guy Bourdé, *Urbanisation et immigration en Amérique Latine, Buenos Aires, XIX et XX siècles* (Paris, 1974); and F. Korn, *Buenos Aires 1895: una ciudad moderna* (Buenos Aires, 1981). For the development of some of the interior cities, see J. Scobie, *Secondary cities of Argentina. The social history of Corrientes, Salta, and Mendoza, 1850–1910* (Stanford, 1988).

On social structure, see G. Germani, *Estructura social de la Argentina* (Buenos Aires, 1955); S. Bagú, *Evolución histórica de la estratificación social en la Argentina* (Buenos Aires, 1961); F. Korn, et al., *Buenos Aires. Los huéspedes del '20* (Buenos Aires, 1974); and the unpublished Ph.D. thesis by R. Sautu, 'Social stratification and economic development in Argentina (1914–1955)' (London, 1968). Also useful are G. Germani, 'La movilidad social en la Argentina' in S. M. Lipset and R. Bendix (eds.), *Movilidad social en la sociedad industrial* (Buenos Aires, 1963); D. Cuneo, *Comportamiento y crisis de la clase empresaria* (Buenos Aires, 1967); and O. Cornblit, 'Sindicatos obreros y asociaciones empresarias' in Ferrari and Gallo (eds.), *La Argentina del ochenta al centenario*. For relations between the agrarian and industrial sectors, see E. Gallo, 'Agrarian Expansion and Industrial Development in Argentina, 1880–1930' in R. Carr (ed.), *Latin American Affairs. St Antony's Papers, no. 22* (Oxford, 1970). For the interior provinces, see the unpublished Ph.D. theses by Donald Peck and Donna Guy cited above. Also valuable are E. Gallo, 'The Cereal Boom and Changes in the Social and Political Structure of Santa Fe, Argentina 1870–95', in K. Duncan and I. Rutledge (eds.), *Land and Labour in Latin America* (Cambridge, 1977); J. Balán, 'Una cuestión regional en la Argentina: Burguesías provinciales y el mercado nacional en el desarrollo exportador', *Desarrollo Económico*, 18,69 (1978); H. Sábato, *Agrarian Capitalism and the World Market. Buenos Aires in the Pastoral Age, 1840–1890* (Albuquerque, N.Mex., 1990), and H. F. Castillo and J. S. Tulchin, 'Developpement capitaliste et structures sociales des régions en Argentine (1880–1930)', *Annales: Economies, Sociétés, Civilizations* 6 (1968).

On living conditions, the classic studies are A. Bunge, *Riqueza y rentas en la Argentina* (Buenos Aires, 1915) and *Los problemas económicos del presente* (Buenos Aires, 1919), and J. Bialet Masset, *Informe sobre el estado de las clases obreras en el interior de la Argentina* (Buenos Aires, 1904). An important mordern work is R. Cortés Conde, *El progreso argentino 1880–1914* (Buenos Aires, 1979). See also J. Panettieri, *Los trabajadores* (Buenos Aires, 1968). One of the few studies on housing is O. Yujdnovsky, 'Políticas de vivienda en la ciudad de Buenos Aires', *Desarrollo Económico* 14,54 (1974), 327–71. But see now F. Korn and L. de la Torre, 'Housing in Buenos Aires. 1887–1914' in D. C. M. Platt (ed.), *Social Welfare 1850–1950, Australia, Argentina and Canada Compared* (London, 1989). See also in the same volume C. Escudé, 'Health in Buenos Aires in the Second Half of the Nineteenth Century'. Worth consulting are some of the articles included in L. L. Johnson (ed.), *The Problem of Order in Changing Societies. Essays in Crime and Policing in Argentina and Uruguay, 1750–1919* (Albuquerque, 1990). On education, see J. C. Tedesco, *Educación y sociedad en la Argentina (1880–1900)* (Buenos Aires, 1970), and Francis Korn and L. de la Torre, 'Constituir la Unión Nacional', in Ferrari and Gallo (eds.), *La Argentina del ochenta al centenario.*

On the labour movement the literature is more abundant. Of the studies published by those who participated actively in union organization, the most useful are S. Marotta, *El movimiento sindical argentino*, 3 vols. (Buenos Aires, 1960), and D. Abad de Santillán, *La FORA. Ideología y trayectoria* (Buenos Aires, 1971). Modern studies include M. Casaretto, *Historia del movimiento obrero argentino* (Buenos Aires, 1947); Hobart A. Spalding, Jr., *La clase trabajadora argentina. Documentos para su historia (1890–1912)* (Buenos Aires, 1970); and I. Oved, *El anarquismo en los sindicatos argentinos a comienzos de siglo* (Tel Aviv, 1975).

Recent comparative work with Australia and Canada provides valuable information and insights into social and political developments in Argentina. See T. Duncan and J. Fogarty, *Australia and Argentina: On Parallel Paths* (Melbourne, 1984); C. Solberg, *The Prairies and the Pampas: Agrarian Policy in Canada and Argentina 1880–1930* (Stanford, 1987); and the articles contained in J. Fogarty, E. Gallo and H. Diéguez (eds.), *Argentina y Australia* (Buenos Aires, 1979); K. Boulding et al., *Argentina and Australia. Essays in Comparative Economic Development* (Victoria, 1985); D. C. M. Platt and G. Di Tella (eds.), *Argentina, Australia and Canada. Studies in Comparative Development, 1870–1965* (London, 1985); and D. C. M. Platt (ed.), *Social Welfare, 1850–1950,* cited above.

4. ARGENTINA IN 1914: THE PAMPAS, THE INTERIOR, BUENOS AIRES

A major statistical source for the study of Argentina on the eve of the first world war is Ernesto Tornquist, *The Economic Development of the Argentine Republic in the Last Fifty Years* (Buenos Aires, 1919). For the war period itself students should also consult Tornquist's quarterly publication, *Business Conditions in Argentina* (Buenos Aires, 1913–22). A second compound source of information is the writings of Alejandro E. Bunge. See his *Ferrocarriles argentinos* (Buenos Aires, 1917) and *Los problemas económicos del presente* (1919; Buenos Aires, 1979). Both are encyclopaedic collections of facts and figures. Slightly later came Bunge's *La economía argentina*, 4 vols. (Buenos Aires, 1928–30), a work containing many of the author's press writings from past years and articles from a major journal he edited, the *Revista de Economía Argentina*. Other important publications are the national census of 1914, *Tercer Censo Nacional* (Buenos Aires, 1915–17) which is far more than a mere population count, and Alberto B. Martínez and Maurice Lewandowski, *The Argentine in the Twentieth Century* (London, 1911). For population, see also *Recensement général de la ville de Buenos Aires* (Buenos Aires, 1910).

The most outstanding contemporary study of Argentina from abroad in this period is the publication by Lloyd's Bank to celebrate the centennial anniversay of 1910: Reginald Lloyd (ed.), *Twentieth Century Impressions of Argentina. Its History, People, Commerce, Industries and Resources* (London, 1911). Pierre Denis, *The Argentine Republic. Its Development and Progress*, translated by Joseph McCabe (London, 1922), is a useful geographical survey by a Frenchman, though much inferior to its predecessor from the 1860s by Martin de Moussy. There are insights into manners and customs in W. H. Koebel, *Argentina: Past and Present* (London, 1914). John Foster Fraser, *The Amazing Argentine* (London, 1914), has virtues, though it is often very negative and a little graceless. The view from Spain can be found in Adolfo Posada, *La República Argentina* (Madrid, 1912), and a little later in the many writings of José Ortega y Gasset. Other major works of a similar type are James Bryce, *South America: Observations and Impressions* (London, 1912); Georges Clemenceau, *South America Today: A Study of Conditions Social, Political and Commercial in Argentina, Uruguay and Brazil* (London, 1911); John A. Hammerton, *The Real Argentine: Notes and Impressions of a Year in the Argentine and Uruguay* (New York, 1915); Jules Huret, *En Argentine: de Buenos Ayres au Gran Chaco* (Paris, 1914); Adolf N.

Schüster, *Argentinien: Land, Volk, Wirtschaftsleben und Kolonisation*, 2 vols. (Munich, 1913); Mark C. Jefferson, *Peopling the Argentine Pampas* (New York, 1926). An almost indispensable source for historians of this period is the Argentine press, especially the two great *porteño* dailies, *La Prensa* and *La Nación*.

Several major issues of this period are surveyed in Guido Di Tella and D. C. M. Platt (eds.), *The Political Economy of Argentina, 1880–1946* (London, 1986). Essays in this volume include studies by Platt on the financing of the city of Buenos Aires, by Joseph S. Tulchin on rural Argentina, and by Tulio Halperín on symptoms of decline in the export economy. Since the completion of this essay scholars have started to examine the social history of Argentina more deeply. Research has begun on such areas as social policy, the history of women and rural social structures. See, for example, Diego Armus (ed.), *Mundo urbano y cultura popular. Estudios de historia argentina* (Buenos Aires, 1990), which contains essays on housing, ethnic communities, artisans, and female and child labour.

The full history of land tenure patterns on the pampas remains to be written. An outstanding contribution is James R. Scobie, *Revolution on the Pampas. A Social History of Argentine Wheat, 1860–1910* (Austin, Tex., 1964).

Most studies of the regions beyond the pampas are partial and fragmentary. The one exception is James R. Scobie, *Secondary Cities of Argentina. The Social History of Corrientes, Salta, and Mendoza, 1850–1910*, completed and edited by Samuel L. Baily (Stanford, Calif., 1988). See also Jorge Balán, 'Urbanización regional y producción agraria en Argentina: Un análisis comparativo', *Estudios CEDES*, 2/2 (1979); Marcos Giménez Zapiola, 'El interior argentino y el "desarrollo hacia afuera": El caso de Tucumán', in M. Giménez Zapiola (ed.), *El régimen oligárquico. Materiales para el estudio de la realidad argentina hasta 1930* (Buenos Aires, 1975), 72–115; Donna J. Guy, 'Politics and the Sugar Industry in Tucumán, Argentina, 1870–1900' (unpublished Ph.D. thesis, Indiana University, 1973) and 'The Rural Working Class in Nineteenth Century Argentina: Forced Plantation Labor in Tucumán', *Latin American Research Review*, 13/1 (1979), 135–45; Donald M. Peck, 'Argentine Politics and the Province of Mendoza, 1890–1914' (unpublished D.Phil. thesis, Oxford, 1977); Juan Carlos Agulla, *Eclipse of an Aristocracy. An Investigation of the Ruling Elites of Córdoba*, translated by Betty Crowse (University, Alabama, 1976); Alejandro E. Bunge, *Las industrias del norte argentino* (Buenos Aires, 1922);

Juan Antonio Solari, *Trabajadores del norte argentino* (Buenos Aires, 1937); Osvaldo Bayer, *Los vengadores de la Patagonia trágica*, 2 vols. (Buenos Aires, 1972); and Carl E. Solberg, *Oil and Nationalism in Argentina* (Stanford, Calif., 1979), for further comments on conditions in Patagonia. Ian Rutledge, 'The Sugar Economy of Argentina, 1930–1943', in K. Duncan and I. Rutledge (eds.), *Land and Labour in Latin America* (Cambridge, Eng., 1976) also contains information on the history of Salta and Jujuy before 1930.

On the history of Buenos Aires in this period the following are useful: James R. Scobie, *Buenos Aires. From Plaza to Suburb 1870–1910* (New York, 1974); Francis Korn et al., *Buenos Aires. Los huéspedes del '20* (Buenos Aires, 1974); Oscar Yujnovsky, 'Políticas de vivienda en la ciudad de Buenos Aires', *Desarrollo Económico*, 14,54 (1974), 327–71; Hobart A. Spalding, Jr, *La clase trabajadora argentina. Documentos para su historia (1890–1916)* (Buenos Aires, 1970) and *Organized Labor in Latin America. Historical Case-studies of Workers in Dependent Societies* (New York, 1977); José Panettieri, *Los trabajadores* (Buenos Aires, 1968); Roberto Cortés Conde, *El progreso argentino 1880–1910* (Buenos Aires, 1979), chapter on urban wages; Nicolás J. Labanca, *Recuerdos de la comisaría 3a* (Buenos Aires, 1969), a policeman's memoir. For studies of the elites and the middle classes, see Jorge Federico Sábato, 'Notas sobre la formación de la clase dominante en la Argentina moderna (1880–1914)', mimeo, CISEA (Buenos Aires, 1979), and David Rock, *Politics in Argentina, 1890–1930: The Rise and Fall of Radicalism* (Cambridge, Eng., 1975).

5. FROM THE FIRST WORLD WAR TO 1930

On the economy between 1914 and 1930 there are several useful traditional sources: Harold J. Peters, *The Foreign Debt of the Argentine Republic* (Baltimore, 1934); Vernon L. Phelps, *The International Economic Position of Argentina* (Philadelphia, 1938); Ricardo M. Ortiz, *Historia económica de la Argentina, 1850–1930*, 2 vols. (Buenos Aires, 1955), especially vol. 2. Among several more recent studies the most outstanding are Carlos F. Díaz Alejandro, *Essays on the Economic History of the Argentine Republic* (New Haven, Conn., 1970) and Guido Di Tella and Manuel Zymelman, *Las etapas del desarrollo económico argentino* (Buenos Aires, 1967). On industrial growth, see Javier Villanueva, 'El origen de la industrialización argentina', *Desarrollo Económico*, 12,47 (1972), 451–76, and Eduardo F. Jorge, *Industria y concentración económica* (Buenos Aires, 1971).

For international economic relations, see Jorge Fodor and Arturo O'Connell, 'La Argentina y la economía atlántica en la primera mitad del siglo veinte', *Desarrollo Económico*, 13,49 (1973), 1–67; Joseph S. Tulchin, *The Aftermath of War. World War I and U.S. Policy towards Latin America* (New York, 1971) and 'The Argentine Economy during the First World War', *Review of the River Plate* (19 June – 10 July 1970); Pedro Skupch, 'El deterioro y fin de la hegemonía británica sobre la economía argentina 1914–47', in L. Marta Panaia, Ricardo Lesser and Pedro Skupch (eds.), *Estudios sobre los orígenes del peronismo*, vol. 2 (Buenos Aires, 1973); and Roger Gravil, 'Anglo–US Trade Rivalry in Argentina and the D'Abernon Mission of 1929', in D. Rock (ed.), *Argentina in the Twentieth Century* (London, 1975). Also Harold F. Peterson, *Argentina and the United States, 1810–1960* (New York, 1964).

For complete electoral data for the period 1916–30, see Dario Cantón, *Materiales para el estudio de la sociología política en la Argentina*, 2 vols. (Buenos Aires, 1969). On Yrigoyen's first government (1916–22), see David Rock, *Politics in Argentina, 1890–1930: The Rise and Fall of Radicalism* (Cambridge, Eng., 1975). See also Peter H. Smith, *Argentina and the Failure of Democracy: Conflict among Political Elites* (Madison, Wisc., 1974), *Politics and Beef in Argentina. Patterns of Conflict and Change* (New York, 1969) and 'Los radicales argentinos en la defensa de los intereses ganaderos', *Desarrollo Económico*, 7,25 (1967), 795–829; Richard J. Walter, *Student politics in Argentina. The University Reform and its Effects, 1918–1964* (New York, 1968) and *The Socialist Party in Argentina 1890–1930* (Austin, Tex., 1977); Paul B. Goodwin, *Los ferrocarriles británicos y la U.C.R., 1916–1930* (Buenos Aires, 1974); Osvaldo Bayer, *Los vengadores de la Patagonia trágica*, 2 vols. (Buenos Aires, 1972). Among more traditional accounts the most useful are Roberto Etchepareborda, *Hipólito Yrigoyen. Pueblo y gobierno*, 10 vols. (Buenos Aires, 1951); Gabriel Del Mazo, *El radicalismo. Ensayo sobre su historia y doctrina* (Buenos Aires, 1957); and Manuel Gálvez, *Vida de Hipólito Yrigoyen* (Buenos Aires, 1959). On the Alvear administration (1922–8) the field is more limited, but see Rock, *Politics in Argentina;* Smith, *Argentina and the Failure of Democracy;* and Raúl A. Molina, *Presidencia de Marcelo T. de Alvear* (Buenos Aires, 1965).

An important study of provincial politics is Richard J. Walter, *The Province of Buenos Aires and Argentine Politics, 1912–1943* (Cambridge, Eng., 1985). The standard study of the authoritarian groups is Marysa Navarro Gerassi, *Los nacionalistas* (Buenos Aires, 1969). A more recent work is Sandra McGee Deutsch, *Counterrevolution in Argentina, 1900–1932. The Argentine Patriotic League* (Lincoln, Nebr., 1986).

For the meat issue, see Smith, *Politics and Beef;* also Simon G. Hanson, *Argentine Meat and the British Market. Chapters in the History of the Argentine Meat Industry* (Stanford, 1938), and Oscar B. Colman, 'Luchas interburguesas en el agro-argentino: La crísis de la carne en el "20" ', *Estudios* (Buenos Aires, 1973). The tariff issue has attracted much attention. Of recent literature the best is Díaz Alejandro, *Essays;* Laura Randall, *An Economic History of Argentina in the Twentieth Century* (New York, 1978), 120–6; and Carl E. Solberg, 'Tariffs and Politics in Argentina, 1916–1930', *Hispanic American Historical Review* 53/2 (1973), pp. 260–84. See also Carl E. Solberg, 'Agrarian Unrest and Agrarian Policy in Argentina, 1912–30', *Journal of Inter-American Studies and World Affairs,* 13 (1971), 15–55. On oil, see above all Carl E. Solberg, *Oil and Nationalism in Argentina* (Stanford, Calif., 1979); also Arturo Frondizi, *Petróleo y política. Contribución al estudio de la historia económica argentina y las relaciones entre el imperialismo y la vida política nacional* (Buenos Aires, 1955), and Marcos Kaplan, 'Política del petróleo en la primera presidencia de Hipólito Yrigoyen, 1916–22', *Desarrollo Económico* 12,45 (1972), 3–24.

The army and the revolution of 1930 are best approached through Robert A. Potash, *The Army and Politics in Argentina, 1928–1945. Yrigoyen to Perón* (Stanford, 1969) and José Maria Sarobe, *Memorias sobre la revolución de 6 de septiembre de 1930* (Buenos Aires, 1957).

6. ARGENTINA, 1930–1946

Still among the best and liveliest introductions to Argentina in the period between the revolution of 1930 and the rise of Perón (1943–6) are three English-language books published in the early 1940s: John W. White, *Argentina, the Life Story of a Nation* (New York, 1942), which aptly captures the puzzled response among North Americans to the apparently hostile attitudes of Argentines during the late 1930s until 1942; Ysabel Rennie, *The Argentine Republic* (New York, 1945), which remains one of the best general introductions to Argentine history and offers an excellent analysis of the years 1943–5; and Felix Weil, *Argentine Riddle* (New York, 1944). Weil, a member of one of the 'Big Four' grain-exporting families, argued for the type of future association between Argentina and the United States that Pinedo and the liberals had aspired to in 1940, in which the United States would take charge of industrializing Argentina. If the book contains this thread of wishful thinking, it also shows an extremely well informed knowledge of Argentine society and the issues facing the country at this critical juncture. Other highly informative accounts by American and British observers are: Robert J. Alexander, *The Perón Era* (New York, 1951); COI (Congress of Industrial Organizations), Committee on Latin American Affairs, *The Argentine Regime. Facts and Recommendations to the United Nations* (New York, 1946); CTAL (Confederación de Trabajadores de América Latina), *White and Blue Book. In Defense of the Argentine People and against the Fascist Regime Oppressing it* (Mexico City, February, 1946); Ray Josephs, *Argentine Diary. The Inside Story of the Coming of Fascism* (New York, 1944); Nicholas John Spykman, *America's Strategy in World Politics. The United States and the Balance of Power* (New York, 1942); Sumner Welles, *Where Are We Heading?* (New York, 1946). A more recent general introduction, containing several excellent essays, is Mark Falcoff and Ronald H. Dolkart (eds.), *Prologue to Perón: Argentina in Depression and War* (Berkeley, 1975). See also David Rock, *Argentina, 1516–1982* (Berkeley, 1985), chap. 6, and for a reinterpretation of the 1940s, Carlos H. Waisman, *The Reversal of Development in Argentina: Post-war Counterrevolutionary Policies and Their Structural Consequences* (Princeton, N.J., 1987).

No single book deals exclusively or quite fully with economic issues in this period. The best introductions are Aldo Ferrer, *La economía argentina: Las etapas de su desarrollo y problemas actuales* (Buenos Aires, 1964); Guido Di Tella and Manuel Zymelman, *Las etapas del desarrollo económico argentino* (Buenos Aires, 1967); Carlos F. Díaz Alejandro, *Essays on the Economic History of the Argentine Republic* (New Haven, Conn., 1970); and Laura Randall, *An Economic History of Argentina in the Twentieth Century* (New York, 1978). For an account of the Argentine economy by an informed contemporary, see Alejandro E. Bunge, *Una nueva Argentina* (Buenos Aires, 1940). For statistical data, see United Nations, ECLA/CEPAL, *El desarrollo económico de la Argentina*, 4 vols. (Mexico City, 1959). On farming, see Carl C. Taylor, *Rural Life in Argentina* (Baton Rouge, La., 1948); Darrell F. Fienup, Russell H. Brannon and Frank A. Fender, *The Agricultural Development of Argentina: A Policy and Development Perspective* (New York, 1969); and Jaime Fuchs, *Argentina: Su desarrollo capitalista* (Buenos Aires, 1965). On industry, see George Wythe, *Industry in Latin America* (New York, 1945); Adolfo Dorfman, *Historia de la industria argentina* (Buenos Aires, 1970); Thomas C. Cochran and Rubén Reina, *Espíritu de empresa en la Argentina* (Buenos Aires, 1965), which examines the career of Torcuato Di Tella, the industrialist;

and Miguel Murmis and Juan Carlos Portantiero, 'Crecimiento industrial y alianza de clases en la Argentina (1930–1940)', in Miguel Murmis and Juan Carlos Portantiero (eds.), *Estudios sobre los orígenes del peronismo*, vol. 1 (Buenos Aires, 1971). An important recent addition to this literature is Paul H. Lewis, *The Crisis of Argentine Capitalism* (Chapel Hill, 1990). The best available studies of population and migration stem from the Centro de Estudios de Población in Buenos Aires, headed by Alfredo E. Lattes; for an introduction, see Zulma Recchini de Lattes and Alfredo E. Lattes, *La población de Argentina* (Buenos Aires, 1975). Foreign investment, foreign debt and many trade issues are discussed in Harold J. Peters, *The Foreign Debt of the Argentine Republic* (Baltimore, 1934); Vernon L. Phelps, *The International Economic Position of Argentina* (Philadelphia, 1938); and Roger Gravil, *The Anglo–Argentine Connection, 1900–1939* (Boulder, Colo., 1985).

The two best general introductions to Argentine politics after 1930 are Robert A. Potash, *The Army and Politics in Argentina, 1928–1945: Yrigoyen to Perón* (Stanford, Calif., 1969), and Alain Rouquié, *Poder militar y sociedad política en la Argentina*, 2 vols. (Buenos Aires, 1982). See also Alberto Ciria, *Parties and Power in Modern Argentina* (Albany, N.Y., 1974). For additional information on the 1930 revolution, see David Rock, *Politics in Argentina, 1890–1930: The Rise and Fall of Radicalism* (Cambridge, Eng., 1975); and Peter H. Smith, 'The Breakdown of Democracy in Argentina, 1916–1930', in Juan J. Linz and Alfred Stepan (eds.), *The Breakdown of Democratic Regimes in Latin America* (Baltimore, 1978), pp. 3–25. For economic policy issues under Justo, see Peter H. Smith, *Politics and Beef in Argentina: Patterns of Conflict and Change* (New York, 1969); Daniel Drosdoff, *El gobierno de las vacas, 1933–1956: Tratado Roca–Runciman* (Buenos Aires, 1972); Pedro Skupch, 'El deterioro y fin de la hegemonía británica sobre la economía argentina, 1914–1947', in L. Marta Panaia et al. (eds.), *Estudios sobre los orígines del peronismo*, vol. 2 (Buenos Aires, 1973); and Gravil, *The Anglo–Argentine Connection*.

Studies of the political parties during this period are almost nonexistent. But see A. Ciria, *Parties and Power*, and Peter G. Snow, *El radicalismo argentino* (Buenos Aires, 1972). A pioneering study in regional politics is Richard J. Walter, *The Province of Buenos Aires and Argentine Politics, 1912–1943* (Cambridge, Eng., 1985). On trade unions, see Hiroschi Matsushita, *Movimiento obrero argentino: Sus proyecciones en la historia del peronismo* (Buenos Aires, 1983); Louise Doyon, 'Organized Labor and Perón: A Study in the Conflictual Dynamics of the Peronist Movement' (unpublished Ph.D. dissertation, University of Toronto, 1978); David Tamarin, *The Argentine Labor Movement, 1930–1945* (Albuquerque, N.Mex., 1985); Joel Horowitz, *Argentine Unions, the State and the Rise of Perón, 1930–1945* (Berkeley, 1990); and, above all, Juan Carlos Torre, *La vieja guardia sindical y Perón: sobre los orígenes del peronismo* (Buenos Aires, 1990). See also the chapter on Argentina in Charles W. Bergquist, *Labor in Latin America; Comparative Essays on Chile, Argentina, Venezuela and Colombia* (Stanford, Calif., 1986). The best known contemporary account is José Peter, *Crónicas proletarias* (Buenos Aires, 1968). Tamarin's work not only deals most informatively with the unions, but provides an excellent account of the workers' role in the events of October 1945. A second outstanding piece is Daniel James, 'October 17th and 18th, 1945: Mass Protest, Peronism and the Argentine Working Class', *Journal of Social History*, 2 (Spring 1988), 441–61. On the Fuerza de Orientación Radical de la Juventud (FORJA), see Mark Falcoff, 'Argentine Nationalism on the Eve of Perón: The Force of Radical Orientation of Young Argentina and Its Rivals, 1935–45' (unpublished Ph.D. dissertation, Princeton University, 1970) and 'Raul Scalabrini Ortiz: The Making of an Argentine National-ist', *Hispanic American Historical Review*, 52, no. 1 (Feb. 1972), 74–101; and Arturo Jauretche, *FORJA y la década infame* (Buenos Aires, 1962). For the *nacionalistas*, see Marysa Navarro Gerassi, *Los nacionalistas* (Buenos Aires, 1969); Enrique Zuleta Alvarez, *El nacionalismo argentino*, 2 vols. (Buenos Aires, 1975); and María Inés Barbero and Fernando Devoto, *Los nacionalistas, 1910–1932* (Buenos Aires, 1983). Federico Ibarguren, *Los orígenes del nacionalismo argentino, 1927–1937* (Buenos Aires, 1969), pro-vides a fascinating glimpse into the *nacionalista* mentality. Other impor-tant studies or contemporary accounts of the Nationalist Right, which commanded so much influence during this period, are Mario Amadeo, *Hoy, Ayer, Mañana* (Buenos Aires, 1956); Paul Everett Brown, 'Ideological Origins of Modern Argentine Nationalism' (unpublished Ph.D. dis-sertation, Claremont Graduate School, 1975); Cristián Buchrucker, *Nacionalismo y peronismo. La Argentina en la crisis ideológica mundial (1927–1955)* (Buenos Aires, 1987); Juan E. Carulla, *Al filo de medio siglo* (Paraná, 1951); Alicia S. García and Ricardo Rodríguez Molas, *En autoritismo y los argentinos. La hora de la espada (1924–1946)* (Buenos Aires, 1988); Juan José Hernández Arregui, *La formación de la conciencia nacional*, 2d ed. (Buenos Aires, 1973); Austen A. Ivereigh, 'Nationalist Catholic thought in Argentina, 1930–1946. Monseñor Gustavo Franceschi and *Criterio* in the Search for a Post-liberal Order' (unpublished M.A. thesis, University of Oxford, 1990); Leopoldo Lugones, *La patria fuerte* (Buenos Aires, 1930) and *La grande Argentina* (Buenos Aires, 1930); Sandra McGee Deutsch, *Counterrevolution in Argentina, 1900–1932: The Argentine Patriotic League* (Lincoln, Nebr., 1986); Marcelo Sánchez Sorondo, *La revolución que anunciamos* (Buenos Aires, 1945); Oscar A. Troncoso, *Los nacionalistas argentinos. Antecedentes y trayectoria* (Buenos Aires, 1957). For *nacionalismo* in the army, see Robert A. Potash (comp.), *Perón y el G.O.U.: Los documentos de una logia secreta* (Buenos Aires, 1984). For an introduction to nationalist historical revisionism, see Rodolfo Irazusta and Julio Irazusta, *La Argentina y el imperialismo británico: Los eslabones de una cadena, 1806–1933* (Buenos Aires, 1934).

The past few years have seen the appearance of several high-quality works on the British–Argentine–U.S. triangle in both its economic and political aspects. The most recent is Guido Di Tella and D. Cameron Watt, *Argentina between the Great Powers, 1939–46* (Pittsburgh, 1989). But see also Jorge Fodor and Arturo O'Connell, 'La Argentina y la economía atlántica en la primera mitad del siglo veinte', *Desarrollo Económico*, 13,49 (1973), 1–67; Michael J. Francis, *The Limits of Hegemony: United States Relations with Argentina and Chile during World War II* (Notre Dame, Ind., 1977); Mario Rapoport, *Gran Bretaña, Estados Unidos y las clases dirigentes argentinas, 1940–45* (Buenos Aires, 1981); Carlos Escudé, *Gran Bretaña, Estados Unidos y la declinación argentina, 1942–1949* (Buenos Aires, 1983); R. A. Humphreys, *Latin America and the Second World War*, 2 vols. (London, 1981–2); and C. A. MacDonald, 'The Politics of Intervention: The United States and Argentina, 1941–1946', *Journal of Latin American Studies*, 12, pt. 2 (November 1980), 365–96. For wartime British attitudes towards Argentina, see Sir David Kelly, *The Ruling Few, or The Human Background to Diplomacy* (London, 1953), and for the official line from the United States, Cordell Hull, *The Memoirs*, 2 vols. (New York, 1948). David Green, *The Containment of Latin America: A History of the Myths and Realities of the Good Neighbor Policy* (Chicago, 1971), sheds much light on the attitudes and behaviour of U.S. policy-makers. See also Bryce Wood, *The Dismantling of the Good Neighbor Policy* (Austin, Tex., 1985). A facsimile of the Pinedo Plan appears in *Desarrollo Económico*, 19,75 (1979), 403–26.

On the rise of Perón, the most outstanding works are Potash, *Army and Politics*, and Samuel L. Baily, *Labor, Nationalism, and Politics in Argentina* (New Brunswick, N.J., 1967). See also Félix Luna, *El '45* (Buenos Aires, 1971); Paul W. Lewis, 'Was Perón a Fascist? An Inquiry into the Nature of Fascism', *The Journal of Politics*, 42(1980), 242–56; Rodolfo Puiggrós, *El peronismo: Sus causas* (Buenos Aires, 1971); Doyon, 'Organised Labour', Matsushita, *Movimiento obrero*, Horowitz, *Argentine Unions*, Torre, *La vieja guardia sindical*, Tamarin, *Argentine Labor Movement*, all cited above; Eldon Kenworthy, 'The Formation of the Peronist Coalition' (unpublished Ph.D. dissertation, Yale University, 1970); and Enrique Díaz Araujo, *La conspiración del '43* (Buenos Aires, 1971). For personal details on Perón, see Joseph A. Page, *Perón: A Biography* (New York, 1983). The best accounts of Braden's role in 1945–6 are MacDonald, 'The Politics of Intervention', and Green, *Containment of Latin America*. The 1946 election has been studied intensively in Manuel Mora y Araujo and Ignacio Llorente (eds.), *El voto peronista: Ensayos de sociología electoral argentina* (Buenos Aires, 1980). Of particular note are essays by Peter H. Smith and Gino Germani. For statistics on the election, see Dario Cantón, *Materiales para el estudio de la sociología política en la Argentina*, 2 vols. (Buenos Aires, 1969). A valuable primary source on the 1943–6 period is Juan Perón, *El pueblo quiere saber de qué se trata* (Buenos Aires, 1944).

7. ARGENTINA SINCE 1946

Economy

G. Di Tella and M. Zymelman, *Las etapas del desarrollo económico argentino* (Buenos Aires, 1967), is a general work inspired by W. W. Rostow's stages of growth theory. Aldo Ferrer, *The Argentine Economy* (Berkeley, 1967), first published in Spanish in 1964, is a less factual, much more interpretive account that reflects views on development and dependency typical of the late 1950s and early 1960s. Ferrer's *Crisis y alternativas de la política económica* (Buenos Aires, 1977) brings the analysis up to the late 1970s. Carlos Díaz Alejandro, *Essays on the Economic History of the Argentine Republic* (New Haven,, Conn., 1970), is a collection of excellent economic analyses of different aspects of Argentine history that has been very influential. Laura Randall, *An Economic History of Argentina in the Twentieth Century* (New York, 1978), tries to interpret Argentina's development as a succession of rather clear-cut economic models; some historians have found it unconvincing. R. Mallon and J. V. Sourruoille, *Economic Policy in a Conflict Society: The Argentine Case* (Cambridge, Mass., 1975), explores economic problems, particularly in the mid-1960s, without excluding political variables. D. Rock, *Argentina, 1516–1987: From Spanish Colonization to*

Alfonsín (Berkeley, 1988), is a comprehensive history that reveals great economic insight; it is the best introduction to the history of Argentina in this period. Gary Wynia, *Argentina in the Post-War Era: Politics and Economic Policy Making in a Divided Society* (Albuquerque, N. Mex., 1978), concentrates on decision making in the period from 1946 to 1976. Two general essays discuss the main issues in the economic history of the period: G. Di Tella, 'Controversias económicas en la Argentina, 1930–1970', in J. Fogarty, E. Gallo and H. Diéguez (eds.), *Argentina y Australia* (Buenos Aires, 1979), pp. 165–84; and C. Díaz Alejandro, 'No Less Than One Hundred Years of Argentine Economic History Plus Some Comparisons', in G. Ranis, R. L. West, M. W. Leiserson and C. Taft Morris (eds.), *Comparative Development Perspectives: Essays in Honor of Lloyd G. Reynolds* (Boulder, Colo., 1984), pp. 328–58. One of the best and most comprehensive collections of essays on the economic history of post-war Argentina is G. Di Tella and R. Dornbusch (eds.), *The Political Economy of Argentina, 1946–1983* (London, 1989), which analyses the economic policies of every government from Perón's first presidency to the military administrations of the period 1976–83. J. C. de Pablo, *La economía que yo hice* (Buenos Aires, 1980), presents a series of interviews with officials in charge of economic affairs since the 1940s and contains much useful historical information.

Beginning in 1949 the influence of the UN Economic Commission for Latin America (ECLA) under the intellectual leadership of R. Prebisch was widely felt in both political and professional fields. The 1949 ECLA Survey reflected the post-war spirit in its deep scepticism of the role of foreign trade and its stress on import substitution industrialization and in the internal market. See also ECLA, *Economic Development of Latin America and Its Principal Problems* (New York, 1949). The questioning of the ECLA model in the 1960s is reflected in Mario Brodershon (ed.), *Estrategias de industrialización para América Latina* (Buenos Aires, 1967); the contribution by David Félix, 'Más allá de la sustitución de importaciones, un dilema latinoamericano', is a good example of the new perspective. See also Félix's 'The Dilemma of Import Substitution: Argentina', in G. Papanek (ed.), *Development Policy: Theory and Practice* (Cambridge, Mass., 1968), pp. 55–91. M. Diamand, *Doctrinas económicas, desarrollo e independencia económica* (Buenos Aires, 1973), presents an original analysis of the structural imbalance found in the Argentine productive sectors. In the 1970s and 1980s the focus of interest shifted to the causes of Argentine stagnation and decline. A good example of the changing emphasis is the work of J. J. Llach and P. Gerchunoff on the 1964–74 growth experience: 'Capitalismo industrial, desarrollo asociado y distribucíon del ingreso entre los dos gobiernos peronistas', *Desarrollo Económico*, 15,57 (1975), 3–54, and the subsequent debate in *Desarrollo Económico*, 16,60 (1976), 612–39. The weak economic performance of Argentina and the need for institutional reforms are explored in D. Cavallo and Y. Mundlak, 'Agriculture and Economic Growth: The Case of Argentina', *Research Report 36* (Washington, D.C., 1982); D. Cavallo, *Volver a crecer* (Buenos Aires, 1984); J. J. Llach, *Reconstrucción o estancamiento* (Buenos Aires, 1987); Secretaría de Planificación, *Lineamientos para una estrategia de crecimiento* (Buenos Aires, 1985); and C. A. Rodríguez, 'Estabilización versus cambio estructural: La experiencia argentina', Centro de Estudios Macroeconómicos de Argentina, Documento de Trabajo 62 (1988).

On inflation and stabilization policies in the 1950s and 1960s, see A. Ferrer (ed.), *Los planes de estabilización en Argentina* (Buenos Aires, 1967), with contributions from the editor, M. Brodershon, and E. Eshag and R. Thorp; Eshag and Thorp's article, 'Economic and Social Consequences of Orthodox Policies in Argentina in the Post-War Years', was originally published in *Bulletin of the Oxford Institute of Economics and Statistics* (February 1965), 3–44. See also C. Díaz Alejandro, *Exchange Rate Devaluation in a Semiindustrialized Country: The Experience of Argentina, 1955–1961* (Cambridge, Mass., 1965). Against the conventional wisdom of the time, Díaz Alejandro demonstrated that exchange devaluations may have recessive consequences in a country with an export-oriented agriculture and an inward-oriented industry. This idea had a far-reaching impact. For the period from 1966 to 1973, J. C. de Pablo, 'Relative Prices, Income Distribution and Stabilization Plans, 1967–1970', *Journal of Development Economics*, 1(1974), 50–78, is an important article; an expanded version is *Política anti-inflacionaria en Argentina, 1967–1970* (Buenos Aires, 1972). On the same period, see G. Maynard and W. van Ryckeshen, 'Stabilization Policy in an Inflationary Economy', in Papanek (ed.), *Development Policy*, pp. 207–35. G. Di Tella, *Argentina under Perón, 1973–1976* (London, 1983), studies the problems of stabilizing the economy under a labour-based government; see also A. Canitrot, 'La experiencia populista de redistribución de ingresos', *Desarrollo Económico*, 15,59 (1975), 331–51, which underlines the inherent contradictions of the populist model. The stabilization efforts of the military regime between 1976 and 1982 produced very interesting analyses from different perspectives: A. Canitrot, 'Teoría y práctica del liberalismo: Política antiinflacionaria y apertura económica en la Argentina', *Desarrollo Económico*, 21,82 (1981), 131–89; J. L. Machinea, 'The Use of Exchange Rates as an Anti-inflationary Instrument in a Stabilization–Liberalization Attempt' (unpublished Ph. D. dissertation, University of Minnesota, 1983); R. B. Fernández and C. A. Rodríguez (eds.), *Inflación y estabilidad* (Buenos Aires, 1982); and J. Schvarser, *Martínez de Hoz, la lógica política de la política económica* (Buenos Aires, 1983). For conceptual approaches to the theory of inflation, see J. Olivera, 'On Structural Inflation and Latin American Structuralism', *Oxford Economic Papers*, 16 (November 1964), 321–32; idem, 'On Structural Stagflation', *Journal of Development Economics*, 6/4 (1979), 549–55; and A. Canavese, 'The Structuralist Explanation in the Theory of Inflation', *World Development*, 10 (July 1982), 523–9. The monetarist approach is well argued in Fernández and Rodríguez (eds.), *Inflación y estabilidad*. J. J. Llach, 'La megainflación argentina', in N. Botana and P. Waldman (eds.), *El impacto de la inflación* (Buenos Aires, 1988), pp. 75–98, presents an institutional approach. The role of inertial factors in inflation is underlined in R. Frenkel, 'Salarios e inflación: Resultados de investigaciones recientes en Argentina, Brasil, Colombia, Costa Rica y Chile', *Desarrollo Económico*, 26,100 (1986), 387–414, an approach which inspired the Austral Plan launched by the Alfonsín administration in 1985. For the latter experience, see the essays in M. Bruno, G. Di Tella and R. Dornbusch (eds.), *Inflation Stabilization: The Experience of Israel, Argentina, Brazil, Bolivia and Mexico* (Cambridge, Mass., 1988); D. Heyman, *Tres ensayos sobre inflación y políticas de estabilización* (Buenos Aires, 1986); P. Gerchunoff and C. Bozzalla, 'Posibilidades y límites de un programa de estabilización heterodoxo', in J. Villanueva (ed.), *Empleo, inflación y comercio internacional* (Buenos Aires, 1988), pp. 61–105; R. Dornbusch and M. Simonsen, *Inflation Stabilization with Income Policy Support* (Cambridge, Mass., 1986); and R. Frenkel and J. M. Fanelli, *Políticas de estabilización hiperinflación en Argentina* (Buenos Aires, 1990). The account of J. L. Machinea (president of the Central Bank at the time), 'Stabilization under Alfonsín's Government', Centro de Estudios de Estado y Sociedad (CEDES), Documento de Trabajo 42 (1990), must be consulted.

On the evolution of Argentine industry, see A. Dorfman, *Cincuenta años de industrialización argentina, 1930–1980* (Buenos Aires, 1983); J. Katz and B. Kosacoff, *El sector manufacturero argentino: Maduración, retroceso y prospectiva* (Buenos Aires, 1989); and B. Kosacoff and D. Aspiazu, *La industria argentina, desarrollo y cambios estructurales* (Buenos Aires, 1989). On the controversial issue of industrial policies a number of works deserve mention: H. H. Schwartz, 'The Argentine Experience with Industrial Credit and Protection Incentives, 1943–1958' (unpublished Ph.D. dissertation, Yale University, 1967), is a pioneer work. See also O. Altimir, H. Santamaría and J. V. Sourrouille, 'Los instrumentos de la promoción industrial en la postguerra', *Desarrollo Económico*, 7,24 (1967), 709–34; J. Berlinski and D. Schydlowsky, 'Incentives for Industrialization in Argentina', in B. Balassa (ed.), *Development Strategies in Semi-industrialized Countries* (Baltimore, 1982), pp. 83–121; J. Berlinski, 'La protección efectiva de actividades seleccionadas de la industria argentina', Instituto Di Tella, CIE, Documento de Trabajo 119 (1985); D. Artana, 'Incentivos fiscales a la inversión industrial', Instituto Di Tella, CIE, Documento de Trabajo 151 (1987); J. Schvarser, 'Promoción industrial Argentina', Centro de Investigaciones Sociales sobre Estado y Administración (CISEA), Documento de Trabajo 90 (1987); S. Teitel and F. Thomi, 'From Import Substitution to Exports: The Recent Experience of Argentina and Brasil', *Economic Development and Cultural Change* (April 1986), 455–90; and J. Nogues, 'Economía política del proteccionismo y la liberalización en Argentina', *Desarrollo Económico*, 28,110 (1988), 159–82.

On agriculture, see C. Díaz Alejandro, 'An Interpretation of Argentine Economic Growth since 1930', *Journal of Development Studies*, pt. 1 (1966), 14–41, pt. 2 (1967), 155–77, a good example of a negative view of Perón's agricultural policies; J. Fodor gives a different account in 'Perón's Policies for Agricultural Exports, 1946–1948: Dogmatism or Common Sense?' in D. Rock (ed.), *Argentina in the Twentieth Century* (London, 1975), pp. 135–61. For many years, works in this field focussed on the alleged lack of price elasticity of agricultural production. L. Reca made a substantial contribution, emphasizing the role of prices, which had previously been underrated, in 'The Price and Production Duality within Argentine Agriculture' (unpublished Ph.D. dissertation, University of Chicago, 1967), and further works such as 'Determinantes de la oferta agropecuaria en la Argentina', *Instituto de Investigaciones Económicas de la CGE, Estudios sobre la economía argentina*, 5 (1969), pp. 57–65. Later, E. S. de Obschatko and M. Piñeiro, *Agricultura pampeana: Cambio tecnológico y sector privado* (Buenos Aires, 1986), drew attention to the great technological transformation which took place in agriculture from the 1970s and led to a great increase in production and productivity.

On the labour market and wages, the following works are recommended: J. J. Llach and C. Sánchez, 'Los determinantes del salario en Argentina', *Estudios*, 7,29 (1984), 1–47; H. Dieguez and P. Gerchunoff, 'Dinámica del mercado laboral urbano en Argentina, 1976–1982', *Desarrollo Económico*, 24,93 (1984), 3–40; A. Marshall, *El mercado del trabajo en el capitalismo periférico* (Santiago de Chile, 1978); L. Beccaria and G. Yoguel, 'Apuntes sobre la evolución del empleo industrial en 1973–1984', *Desarrollo Económico*, 28,102 (1988), 589–606; R. Frenkel, 'Salarios industriales e inflación, 1976–1982', *Desarrollo Económico*, 24,95 (1984), 387–414; and J. L. Llach, *Políticas de ingresos en la década del noventa: Un retorno a la economía política* (Buenos Aires, 1990). The reports produced by Proyecto Argentina PNUD and International Labor Organization entitled *Employment, Human Resources and Wages* and published by the Ministry of Labour between 1984 and 1989 are indispensable.

Little attention was given to the public sector until the mid-1980s; Secretaría de Hacienda, *Política para el cambio estructural en el sector público* (1989), brings together the presidential messages to Congress on the occasion of the passage of the 1986–9 budget laws; particularly useful is the 1989 message, which traces the evolution of the role of the public sector in Argentina since 1930. On the fiscal crisis three works deserve mention: P. Gerchunoff and M. Vicens, *Gasto público, recursos públicos y financiamiento de una economía en crisis: El caso de Argentina* (Buenos Aires, 1989); R. Carciofi, *La desarticulación del Pacto Fiscal: Una interpretación sobre la evolución del sector público argentino en las últimas dos décadas* (Buenos Aires, 1989); and A. Porto, *Federalismo fiscal* (Buenos Aires, 1990). For a different point of view, see Fundación de Investigaciones Económicas Latinoamericanas (FIEL), *El fracaso del estatismo: Una propuesta para la reforma del sector público argentino* (Buenos Aires, 1987).

For the external debt and its repercussions, see E. A. Zalduendo, *La deuda externa* (Buenos Aires, 1988); E. Feldman and J. Sommer, *Crisis financiera y endeudamiento externo en la Argentina* (Buenos Aires, 1986); R. Frenkel, J. M. Fanelli and J. Sommer, 'El proceso del endeudamiento externo argentino', CEDES, Documento de Trabajo 2 (1988); R. Bouzas and S. Keifman, 'Las negociaciones financieras externas de Argentina en el período 1982–1987', in R. Bouzas (ed.), *Entre la heterodoxia y el ajuste* (Buenos Aires, 1988), pp. 27–84; A. García and S. Junco, 'Historia de la renegociación de la deuda externa argentina', *Boletín Informativo Techint*, 245 (1987), 29–58; and J. C. de Pablo and R. Dornbusch, *Deuda externa e inestabilidad macroeconómica en Argentina* (Buenos Aires, 1988).

Politics and society

There are few general works on political and social development over the entire period from 1946 to 1989. The best account available in English is D. Rock, *Argentina, 1516–1987* (Berkeley, 1988). See also C. Floria and C. García Belsunce, *Historia política de la Argentina contemporánea, 1880–1983* (Madrid, 1988); J. E. Corradi, *The Fitful Republic: Economy, Society and Politics in Argentina* (Boulder, Colo., 1985); G. Wynia, *Argentina: Illusions and Reality* (New York, 1986); and a well-documented chronicle, E. Crawley, *A House Divided: Argentina, 1880–1980* (London, 1985). Although their main subject is the role of the military in politics, R. Potash, *The Army and Politics in Argentina, 1945–1962* (Stanford, Calif., 1980), and A. Rouquié, *Pouvoir militaire et société politique en Republique Argentine* (Paris, 1978), provide general insights for the years up to the 1970s. T. Halperín Donghi, *Argentina, la democracia de masas* (Buenos Aires, 1983), is another valuable contribution. See also M. Peralta Ramos, *Acumulación de capital y crisis políticas en Argentina, 1930–1974* (Mexico City, 1978). In a more interpretive vein, several essays deserve mention: G. O'Donnell, 'State and Alliances in Argentina, 1956–1976', *Journal of Development Studies,* 15 (1978), 3–33 and 'El juego imposible: Competición y coaliciones entre partidos políticos en la Argentina, 1955–1966', which is included in his *Modernization and Bureaucratic Authoritarianism: Studies in South American Politics* (Berkeley, 1973), pp. 180–213; M. Mora y Araujo, 'El ciclo político argentino', *Desarrollo Económico,* 22,86 (1982), 203–30 and 'El estatismo y los problemas políticos desarrollo argentino', in C. Floria (ed.), *Argentina política* (Buenos Aires, 1983), pp. 31–64; and J. C. Portantiero, 'La crisis de un régimen: Una visión retrospectiva', in J. Nun and J. C. Portantiero (eds.), *Ensayos sobre la transición democrática argentina* (Buenos Aires, 1987), pp. 57–80.

On Argentina's social structure, the works of G. Germani, *Estructura social de la Argentina* (Buenos Aires, 1955) and *Política y sociedad en una época de transición* (Buenos Aires, 1965), are of seminal importance. See also ECLA, *Economic Development and Income Distribution in Argentina* (New York, 1969); J. L. Imaz, *Those Who Rule* (Albany, N.Y., 1970); O. Altimir, 'Estimaciones de la distribución del ingreso en Argentina, 1953–1980', *Desarrollo Económico,* 25,100 (1985), 521–66; H. Palomino, 'Cambios ocupacionales y sociales en Argentina, 1947–1985', CISEA, Documento de Trabajo 88 (1987), p. 213; J. Nun, 'Cambios en la estructura social de la Argentina', in Nun and Portantiero (eds.), *La transición democrática argentina*, pp. 117–37; S. Torrado, 'La estructura social de la Argentina, 1945–1983', Centro de Estudios Urbanos, Documentos de Trabajo 14 and 15 (1988); Instituto Nacional de Estadísticas y Censos, *La pobreza en Argentina* (Buenos Aires, 1984); idem, *La pobreza en el conurbano bonaerense* (Buenos Aires, 1989). A good bibliography can be found in S. Bagú, *Argentina, 1875–1975: Población, economía y sociedad – Estudio temático y bibliográfico* (Mexico City, 1978).

On the military, in addition to the books by Potash and Rouquié already mentioned, see G. O'Donnell, 'Modernization and Military Coups: Theory, Practice and the Argentine Case', in A. Lowenthal (ed.), *Armies and Politics in Latin America* (New York, 1976), pp. 197–243; A. Rouquié, 'Hegemonia militar, estado y dominación social', in A. Rouquié (ed.), *Argentina hoy* (Mexico City, 1982); and D. Cantón, *La política de los militares argentinos, 1900–1971* (Buenos Aires, 1971). On the Church, a very neglected subject, see J. M. Ghio, 'The Argentine Church and the Limits of Democracy' in A. Stuart-Gambino and E. Cleary (eds.), *The Latin American Church and the Limits of Politics* (Boulder, Colo., 1991).

On political parties and the Congress, see D. Cantón, *Elecciones y partidos políticos en la Argentina* (Buenos Aires, 1973); P. Snow, *Political Forces in Argentina* (Boston, 1971); L. Schoultz, *The Populist Challenge: Argentine Electoral Behaviour in the Post War Era* (Chapel Hill, 1983); D. James, 'The Peronist Left', *Journal of Latin American Studies* 8/2 (1976), 273–96; M. Acuña, *De Frondizi a Alfonsín: La tradición política del radicalismo*, 2 vols. (Buenos Aires, 1984); M. Cavarozzi, *Peronismo y radicalismo: transiciones y perspectivas* (Buenos Aires, 1988); D. Cantón, *El Parlamento argentino en épocas de cambio* (Buenos Aires, 1966); M. Goretti and M. Panosyan, 'El personal parlamentario frente a un contexto político cambiante', in *Dos ensayos de ciencia política* (Buenos Aires, 1986); L. de Riz et al., *El parlamento hoy* (Buenos Aires, 1986); and idem, 'Régimen de gobierno y gobernabilidad: Parlamentarismo en Argentina', in D. Nohlen and A. Solari (eds.), *Reforma política y consolidación democrática: Europa y América Latina* (Caracas, 1988), pp. 273–85.

On trade unions, see S. Baily, *Labor, Nationalism and Politics in Argentina* (New Brunswick, N.J., 1967); R. Carri, *Sindicatos y poder en Argentina* (Buenos Aires, 1967); M. Cavarozzi, 'Peronismo, sindicatos y política en la Argentina, 1943–1981', in P. González Casanova (ed.), *Historia del movimiento obrero en América Latina* (Mexico City, 1984), pp. 146–99; D. James, *Resistance and Integration: Peronism and the Argentine Working Class, 1946–1976* (Cambridge, Eng., 1988); G. Ducatenzeiler, *Syndicats et* politique en Argentine, 1955–1973 (Montreal, 1981); R. Rotondaro, Realidad y dinámica del sindicalismo (Buenos Aires, 1974); T. Di Tella, El sistema político argentino y la clase obrera (Buenos Aires, 1964); R. Zorrilla, Estructura y dinámica del sindicalismo argentino (Buenos Aires, 1974); S. Senen González, Diez años de sindicalismo, de Perón al proceso (Buenos Aires, 1984); and E. C. Epstein, 'Labor Populism and Hegemonic Crisis in Argentina', in Epstein (ed.), Labor Autonomy and the State in Latin America (Boston, 1989), pp. 13–37.

On entrepreneurs, see J. Freels, El sector industrial en la política nacional (Buenos Aires, 1970); J. Niosi, Los empresarios y el estado argentino (Buenos Aires, 1974); D. Cúneo, Crisis y comportamiento de la clase empresaria (Buenos Aires, 1967); M. L. de Palomino, Tradición y poder: La sociedad rural argentina, 1955–1983 (Buenos Aires, 1988); D. Azpiazu, E. Basualdo and M. Khavisse, El nuevo poder económico en la Argentina de los años 80 (Buenos Aires, 1986); R. Sidicaro, 'Poder y crisis de la gran burguesía agraria argentina', in A. Rouquié (ed.), Argentina hoy, pp. 51–104; and most recently Paul H. Lewis, The Crisis of Argentine Capitalism (Chapel Hill, 1990), and P. Ostiguy, Los capitanes de la industria (Buenos Aires, 1990).

On Argentina's foreign relations, see in particular J. A. Lanus, De Chapultepec al Beagle (Buenos Aires, 1984); J. S. Tulchin, Argentina and the United States: A Conflicted Relationship (Boston, 1990); and C. Escudé, Gran Bretaña, Estados Unidos y la Declinación Argentina, 1942–1949 (Buenos Aires, 1983).

On Perón's first two terms in office between 1946 and 1955, see the perceptive and colorful historical reconstruction by F. Luna, Perón y su tiempo, 3 vols. (Buenos Aires, 1984–6). Profiles of the two major characters of those years can be found in J. Page, Perón: A Biography (New York, 1983), and Nicholas Fraser and Marysa Navarro, Eva Perón (New York, 1980). The sociological approach is represented by J. Kirkpatrick, Leader and Vanguard in Mass Society: A Study of Peronist Argentina (Cambridge, Mass., 1971), and P. Waldman, El peronismo (Buenos Aires, 1981). A suggestive attempt to assess the impact of Perón's policies on subsequent Argentine political development is Carlos H. Waisman, The Reversal of Development in Argentina: Post-War Counterrevolutionary Policies and Their Structural Consequences (Princeton, N.J., 1987). A. Ciria, Política y cultura popular, la Argentina peronista, 1946–1955 (Buenos Aires, 1983), deals well with the workings of peronista ideology in practice. A useful introductory treatment of a neglected topic is offered by W. Little in 'Party and State in Peronist Argentina', Hispanic American Historical Review, 53

(1973), 628–56. L. Doyon, 'Organized Labor and Perón: A Study in the Conflictual Dynamics of the Peronist Movement' (unpublished Ph.D. dissertation, University of Toronto, 1978), is indispensable. Some chapters of Doyon's thesis and other valuable contributions are collected in J. C. Torre (ed.), *La formación del sindicalismo peronista* (Buenos Aires, 1988); see also J. C. Torre, *La vieja guardia sindical y Perón: sobre los orígenes del peronismo* (Buenos Aires, 1990). The relations between Perón and the military are examined in the books already mentioned by R. Potash and A. Rouquié. An informative account of Perón's fall in 1955 is given in J. Godio, *La caída de Perón* (Buenos Aires, 1973).

On Frondizi's government, see Celia Szusterman, 'Developmentalism and Political Change in Argentina, 1958–1962' (unpublished D.Phil. dissertation, Oxford University, 1986); M. Barrera, *Information and Ideology: A Case Study of Arturo Frondizi* (Beverly Hills, Calif., 1973); D. Rodríguez Lamas, *La presidencia de Frondizi* (Buenos Aires, 1984); N. Babini's memoirs, *Frondizi: De la oposición al gobierno* (Buenos Aires, 1984); and E. Kvaternik, *Crisis sin salvataje* (Buenos Aires, 1987). On Illia's presidency, see E. Kvaternik, *El péndulo cívico militar: La caída de Illia* (Buenos Aires, 1990). On both presidencies, C. Smulovitz, 'Opposition and Government in Argentina: The Frondizi and Illia Years' (unpublished Ph.D. dissertation, Pennsylvania State University, 1990), deserves mention.

The period of military rule between 1966 and 1972 is the subject of a major work by G. O'Donnell, *El estado burocrático autoritario* (Buenos Aires, 1981). See also William C. Smith, *Authoritarianism and the Crisis of the Argentine Political Economy* (Stanford, Calif., 1989); N. Botana, R. Braun and C. Floria, *El régimen militar, 1966–1972* (Buenos Aires, 1973); F. Delich, *Crisis y protesta social: Córdoba, mayo de 1969* (Buenos Aires, 1970); and R. Perina, *Onganía, Levingston, Lanusse: Los militares en la política argentina* (Buenos Aires, 1983). The memoirs of General Onganía's secretary, Roberto Roth, *Los años de Onganía* (Buenos Aires, 1980), and those of General Agustín Lanusse, *Mi testimonio* (Buenos Aires, 1977), deserve careful reading.

On Perón's return to power in 1973, see G. Di Tella, *Argentina under Perón* and L. de Riz, *Retorno y derrumbe: El último gobierno peronista* (Mexico City, 1981). The collection of essays compiled by F. Turner and J. E. Miguenz, *Juan Perón and the Reshaping of Argentina* (Pittsburgh, 1983), contains good analyses of the period. See also M. Mora y Araujo, 'Las bases estructurales del peronismo' and 'Peronismo y desarrollo', in M. Mora y

Araujo and I. Lorente (eds.), *El voto peronista: Ensayos de sociología electoral argentina* (Buenos Aires, 1980), pp. 397–440. The role of trade unions is studied in J. C. Torre, *Los sindicatos en el gobierno, 1973–1976* (Buenos Aires, 1983). A very illuminating study of Perón's political discourse and its relation to the youth movement is S. Sigal and E. Veron, *Perón o muerte* (Buenos Aires, 1986).

On the military regime of 1976–83 see, for a general view, P. Waldman and E. Garzón Valdez (eds.), *El poder militar en Argentina, 1976–1983* (Frankfurt, 1982); M. Peralta Ramos and C. Waisman (eds.), *From Military Rule to Liberal Democracy in Argentina* (Boulder, Colo., 1987); and Smith, *Authoritarianism,* pp. 224–66. A. Fontana, 'Policy Making by a Military Corporation: Argentina, 1976–1983' (unpublished Ph.D. dissertation, University of Texas, 1987), deserves mention. On the guerrilla movement the best study available is R. Gillespie, *Soldiers of Perón: Argentina's Montoneros* (Oxford, 1982). For documents and reports on the human rights issue, see Comisión Nacional sobre la Desaparición de Personas, *Nunca más* (Buenos Aires, 1984; Engl. trans., 1986); and Organization of American States, Inter-American Commission on Human Rights, *Report on the Situation of Human Rights in Argentina* (Washington, D.C., 1980). C. Escudé, 'Argentina: The Costs of Contradiction', in A. F. Lowenthal (ed.), *Exporting Democracy: The United States and Latin America* (Baltimore, 1991), sheds light on the contradictions of President Carter's human rights policy. The Malvinas War has been extensively documented; O. Cardozo, R. Kirshbaum and E. Van de Kooy, *Malvinas: La trama secreta* (Buenos Aires, 1983), and M. Hastings and S. Jenkins, *The Battle for the Falklands* (New York, 1983), present both sides of the conflict.

Although a global assessment of Alfonsín's presidency is still lacking, several works deserve mention: M. Mora y Araujo, 'The Nature of the Alfonsín Coalition', and M. Cavarozzi, 'Peronism and Radicalism: Argentina's Transition in Perspective', in P. Drake, and E. Silva (eds.), *Elections and Democratization in Latin America* (San Diego, Calif., 1986), pp. 143–88; E. Catterberg, *Los Argentinos frente a la política* (Buenos Aires, 1989); N. Botana et al., *La Argentina electoral* (Buenos Aires, 1985); Nun and Portantiero (eds.), *La transición democrática argentina;* N. Botana and A. M. Mustapic, 'La reforma constitucional frente al régimen político argentino', Instituto Di Tella, Documento de Trabajo 101 (1988); M. Cavarozzi and M. Grossi, 'De la reinvención democrática al reflujo político y la hiperinflación', *Consejo Latinoamericano de Ciencias Sociales,* GTPP 12 (1989); J. C. Torre, "Economia ed política nella transizione argentina: Da

Alfonsín a Menem', in G. Urbani and F. Ricciu (eds.), *Dalle armi alle urne: economia, società e politica nell'America Latina degli anni novanta* (Bologna, 1991); L. de Riz, M. Cavarozzi and J. Feldman, 'El contexto y los dilemas de la concertación en la Argentina actual', in M. dos Santos (ed.), *Concertación político-social y democratización* (Buenos Aires, 1987), pp. 189–224; C. H. Acuña and L. Golbert, 'Empresarios y política', *Boletín Informativo Techint*, 263 (1990), 33–52; R. Gaudio and A. Thompson, *Sindicalismo peronista y gobierno radical* (Buenos Aires, 1990); A Fontana, 'La política militar en un contexto de transición: Argentina, 1987–1989', CEDES, Documento de Trabajo 34 (1989); R. Fraga, *La cuestión militar argentina, 1987–1989* (Buenos Aires, 1989).

INDEX

Printed in the United States
134367LV00003B/20/A

ARGENTINA SINCE INDEPENDENCE

The following titles drawn from
The Cambridge History of Latin America edited by Leslie Bethell
are available in hardcover and paperback:

Colonial Spanish America

Colonial Brazil

The Independence of Latin America

Spanish America after Independence, *c.* 1820 – *c.* 1870

Brazil: Empire and Republic, 1822–1930

Latin America: Economy and Society, 1870–1930

Mexico since Independence

Central America since Independence

Cuba: A Short History

Chile since Independence

Argentina since Independence